RETHINKING THE
NATURE OF WAR

Have globalisation, virulent ethnic differences, and globally operating insurgents fundamentally changed the nature of war in the last few decades?

Interpretations of war as driven by politics and state rationale, formulated most importantly by the nineteenth-century practitioner Carl von Clausewitz, have received strong criticism. Political explanations have been said to fall short in explaining conflicts in the Balkans, Africa, Asia and the attacks of September 11 2001 in the United States. This book aims to re-evaluate these criticisms by not only carefully scrutinising Clausewitz's arguments and their applicability, but also by a careful reading of the criticism itself. In doing so, the contributions on this book present empirical evidence on the basis of several case studies, addressing various aspects of modern war, such as the actors, conduct and purposes of war. The book concludes that while the debate on the nature of war has far from run its course, the interpretation of war as postulated by Clausewitz is not as inapplicable as some have claimed. Furthermore, the label a war receives, such as civil war, does not necessarily say much about the way this war is fought. Civil wars are not always irregular or unconventional wars. Changes in the conduct of war have unmistakably occurred but change should not overshadow the important continuities that exist in the nature of war and warfare.

Isabelle Duyvesteyn is a lecturer at the History of International Relations Department, Utrecht University, The Netherlands.

Jan Angstrom is a researcher at the Department of War Studies, Swedish National Defence College.

CASS CONTEMPORARY SECURITY STUDIES SERIES

RETHINKING THE NATURE OF WAR

Edited by

Isabelle Duyvesteyn

and

Jan Angstrom

FRANK CASS
London and New York

First published 2005
by Frank Cass
2 Park Square, Milton Park, Abingdon, Oxon OX14 4RN

Simultaneously published in the USA and Canada
by Frank Cass
270 Madison Avenue, New York, NY 10016

Transferred to Digital Printing 2006

Frank Cass is an imprint of the Taylor & Francis Group

© 2005 Selection and editorial matter Isabelle Duyvesteyn and
Jan Angstrom, individual chapters the contributors.
With the exception of Chapter 5
© British International Studies Association, published by
Cambridge University Press. Reprinted with permission.

Typeset in Times by Steven Gardiner Ltd, Cambridge
Printed and bound in Great Britain by
TJI Digital, Padstow, Cornwall

British Library Cataloguing in Publication Data
A catalogue record for this book is available from the British Library

Library of Congress Cataloging in Publication Data
A catalog record for this book has been requested

ISBN 0–415–35461–7 (hbk)
ISBN 0–415–35462–5 (pbk)

TO THE LYCEUM,
WHICH TAUGHT US WELL

CONTENTS

PREFACE AND ACKNOWLEDGEMENTS

This book is the product of two panel discussions during the British International Studies Association Conference, which was held in December 2002 at the London School of Economics and Political Science. The title of the panel sessions was 'The Military Theory of Low Intensity Conflict'. The editors of the book were the chief organisers of the sessions and had invited several experts to contribute in the form of a discussion paper. Several other contributions have been added, based on material presented in other settings.

The book provides a new contribution to the debate about the nature of war that has been conducted since the early 1990s. This debate centres on the question whether the nature of war has fundamentally changed during the past decade and a half. The book not only brings together several of the most important contributors to the debate but seeks to move the debate on. Important fundamental principles underlying the claims made in the 'new war' debate are questioned and an opportunity provided for some proponents of the new war thesis to respond to this criticism. Since the new war debate has widely denounced the applicability of the ideas of Carl von Clausewitz, considered by many to be the founding father of the discipline of strategic studies, his writings are carefully scrutinised in the book. Several contributions try to swing the debate back in the direction of Clausewitz and point to important aspects that indicate his continued relevance for understanding the nature of war.

Acknowledgements

The editors, Isabelle Duyvesteyn and Jan Angstrom, would like to thank the participants at the BISA conference sessions, the editorial board at the Department of War Studies, the Swedish National Defence College (which at one stage reviewed the chapters), and the anonymous reviewers at Frank Cass for their helpful comments on earlier drafts of the chapters. Several, but not all, of the chapters were published by the Swedish National Defence College in the volume *The Nature of Modern War: Clausewitz and his Critics Revisited* (2003) for the benefit of the staff college curriculum. Several of the contributions that were included in that publication have been further developed and revised for the present book.

The editors would also like to express their gratitude to Andrew Humphrys, senior book editor at Frank Cass/Taylor and Francis for his encouragement. They are also grateful to the Swedish National Defence College for much appreciated assistance in realising the publication of this book. Cambridge University Press has kindly granted permission to reprint in this book the chapter by Colin McInnes.

A special word of thanks is extended to all the contributors in the present volume; without them and their stimulating and thought-provoking ideas there would be no book.

Finally we are grateful to our families, and the new generation that came along during the preparation of the book, for being there – even when sometimes we were not.

Isabelle Duyvesteyn
Jan Angstrom
May 2004

NOTES ON CONTRIBUTORS

Jan Angstrom, Researcher at the Swedish National Defence College and research student in the Department of War Studies, King's College, London. He previously taught political science at Mid Sweden University. He has published articles on low-intensity conflict in several journals, among others, *Civil Wars, Security Studies* and *Studies in Conflict and Terrorism*.

Bob de Graaff, Senior lecturer in the History of International Relations Department, University of Utrecht. Dr de Graaff was a member of the research team of the Netherlands Institute for War Documentation that published J. C. H. Blom and P. Romijn (eds), *Srebrenica. Een 'veilig' gebied. Reconstructie, achtergronden, gevolgen en analyses van de val van een Safe Area* (Amsterdam: 2002). An English-language version of this work can be found on the Internet at <www.screbrenica.nl>

Isabelle Duyvesteyn, Lecturer in the History of International Relations Department at the Institute of History at Utrecht University, The Netherlands. She completed her PhD at the Department of War Studies at King's College in London. Her research focused on the nature of war in the developing world. Previously she has worked at the Royal Military Academy in the Netherlands and the Netherlands Institute for International Relations. Her work has been published in several journals, among others *Civil Wars, Security Studies* and *Studies in Conflict and Terrorism*.

Kersti Larsdotter, Research Assistant in Military Theory at the Swedish National Defence College. She is the co-editor of *Essär inom krigsvetenskap* [*Essays in War Studies*] (Stockholm: Försvarshögskolan, 2002). She has published 'Taktik och stridsteknik i lågintensiva konflikter: En fallstudie av Operation Anaconda', [Tactics and Combat Technique in Low Intensity Conflicts: A Case Study of Operation Anaconda] in Arne Baudin *et al.* (eds), *En ny medeltid? En introduktion till militärteori i lågintensiva konflikter*, [*The New Middle Ages? An Introduction to Military Theory in Low Intensity Conflicts*] (Stockholm: Försvarshögskolan, 2002).

Mary Kaldor, Professor at the Centre for the Study of Global Governance, London School of Economics and Jean Monnet Reader in Contemporary European Studies at the Sussex European Institute of the University of Sussex. Her publications include *New and Old Wars: Organized Violence in a Global Era* (Cambridge: Polity, 1999) and, with Basker Vashee, *Restructuring the Global Military Sector, Volume I New Wars* (London: Pinter, 1997).

Stathis Kalyvas, Arnold Wolfers Professor of Political Science, Director, Program on Order, Conflict, and Violence at Yale University. His research focuses on violence and civil wars. He is in the process of completing a book on 'The Logic of Violence in Civil War'.

John Mackinlay left the British Army in 1991 to become a research academic at Brown University, Rhode Island, followed by teaching appointments at the George Marshall European Centre for Security Studies in Garmisch, Germany, the UK Joint Services Staff College, and King's College, London, where he currently researches and teaches War Studies. Dr Mackinlay's recent books include *Globalisation and Insurgency* (Oxford University Press, 2002) as well as the co-edited *Regional Peacekeepers: The Paradox of Russian Peacekeeping* (United Nations University Press, 2003).

Colin McInnes, Professor in the Department of International Politics, University of Wales, Aberystwyth. His most recent book is *Spectator Sport War: The West and Contemporary Conflict* (Lynne Rienner, 2002).

Paul B. Rich, Centre of International Studies, University of Cambridge. He has published extensively on African politics from many perspectives, including five books on African politics and British colonial policy. He has edited five books on warfare in Africa, including *Warlords in International Relations* (St Martin's Press, 1999) and *The Counter-Insurgent State: Guerrilla Warfare and State Building in the Twentieth Century* (St. Martin's Press, 1997). Paul Rich is the editor of the academic journal *Small Wars & Insurgencies* (Frank Cass).

Mike L. R. Smith is Reader in War Studies, King's College, University of London. He has previously worked as Senior Lecturer at the Royal Naval College and the Joint Services Command and Staff College, UK. Between 1992 and 1995 he was Lecturer in the Department of History at the National University of Singapore. He is author of *Fighting for Ireland? The Military Strategy of the Irish Republican Movement* (1995), *Reinventing Realism: Australian Foreign and Defence Policy at the Millennium* (2000) and co-editor of *The Changing Face of Military Power* (2002).

1

INTRODUCTION

Debating the nature of modern war

Jan Angstrom

> This is another type of war, new in its intensity, ancient in its
> origins – war by guerrillas, subversives, insurgents, assassins.
> War by ambush instead of combat; by infiltration instead of
> aggression; seeking victory by eroding and exhausting instead of
> engaging him.
>
> John F. Kennedy[1]

What is the nature of modern war? Currently, there are several different
arguments suggesting that modern war displays inherently new characteristics, implying that a major change in the nature of war has occurred. Some,
most notably Mary Kaldor, argue that war in the last decade has changed
into something completely *new*.[2] The globalisation of the economy, she
argues, in combination with the pursuit of exclusionary identity politics,
have eradicated the differences between war and peace, crime and war, and
between war and systematic abuse of human rights in a growing number of
internal conflicts. As the introductory quote from President John F.
Kennedy indicates, it is not the first time that non-state warfare has been
perceived to be 'new'. Others assert that the new features in modern war –
precision-guided munitions, network-centric warfare – are signs of an
allegedly ongoing 'revolution in military affairs', which implies 'a major
change in the nature of warfare'.[3] Still others maintain that by increasingly
relying upon 'smart' bombs and air power, war has become virtual – a postmodern spectator sport for the West.[4] Finally, in the wake of the terrorist
attacks in New York and Washington on September 11 2001, some have put
forward the notion that President George W. Bush's war on terrorism has
changed the nature of war in so far as it redefines our notions of victory and
defeat in war.[5]

To what extent are modern wars 'new'? Has the nature of war changed or
do modern wars display features commonly found in all wars – past and
present? What does it mean to say that war has changed from being an inter-
state to a primarily intrastate phenomenon, at least over the past 50 years?[6]

Are the forms (*Formen*) of war new but its essence (*Wesen*) the same, to use Clausewitz's differentiation of the phenomenon war?[7] Or have Clausewitzian notions of war and warfare been rendered obsolete by events during the past decades? Philip Wilkinson, for example, comments that warfare 'based upon the European Westphalian state model and Clausewitzian approach to military operations has been thoroughly challenged and found wanting' when applied to modern low-intensity conflicts.[8] Does it matter, as Azar Gat points out, that Clausewitz's understanding of the nature of war was formed during an era long gone and 'reflected the earth-shattering collapse of the warfare of the *ancien régime* when confronted by the revolutionary and Napoleonic art of war', rather than the post Cold War world?[9] Or is Colin Gray correct in his assessment that 'Clausewitz still rules, OK'?[10] Mike Smith even claims that 'What we call low intensity conflict can be fully understood – can only be understood – within Clausewitzian parameters, which embrace the entire spectrum of war. War is war, regardless of what tactics are used'.[11] Do the 'wars by other means', for example peace-support operations or the conflicts in which the operations take place, represent something unprecedented?[12] How should we understand and conceptualise modern war? Is it still rational – as Clausewitz held – or are the wars in the developing world irrational and chaotic?

The aim of this book is to contribute to the debate on the nature of modern war and modern warfare, in particular conflicts in the developing world. In analysing modern warfare, other studies have overlooked the levels of strategy in these conflicts. The different chapters produce empirical evidence from, among others, cases in Africa, the Balkans, Algeria, Lebanon, Vietnam, Afghanistan, the United States, as well as theoretical discussions. In doing so, they – albeit from differing perspectives – take issue with the notion of 'new' wars. Although far from agreeing among themselves, the chapters collectively provide a challenge to our common understanding of the nature of modern war and modern warfare.

It is important to stress that the book does not attempt to explain the outbreak of large-scale violence.[13] Instead, the puzzle at hand is how we should understand and conceptualise modern war, especially with respect to war in the developing world. It is also important to stress that we have not tried to impose a unified conceptual framework upon the contributions. Although terminological unity may be important, so too is conceptual precision.

There are several arguments suggesting that a study such as this is important – and late in coming. First, so-called low-intensity conflict (or whatever we choose to call wars that seem to evade the traditional understanding of war as interstate and conventional) has been the predominant form of armed conflict in the international system since at least the late 1950s. Quantitative studies suggest that during the 1990s, over 90 per cent of the armed conflicts took place within states rather than between states.[14] Hence, there is a high degree of correlation – not perfect, though – between 'modern war' and 'low-intensity conflict' or 'non-state' war. The fact that the overwhelming majority of wars are not interstate wars means that it is of utmost importance to understand the nature of these conflicts. There are no reasons, moreover, to believe that low-intensity conflicts will become less of a problem in the future. Basil Liddell Hart's gloomy prediction over 40 years ago still rings true today:

> Campaigns of this kind [guerrilla warfare] are more likely to continue because it is the only kind of war that fits the conditions of the modern age, while being at the same time suited to take advantage of social discontent, racial ferment, and nationalist fervors.[15]

Second, the military theory of low-intensity conflicts deserves more scholarly attention also because of the fact that an understanding of the nature of war is often just a tacit assumption in analyses of the causes of modern wars. Analyses of the causes of modern war will improve if we understand the nature of war better. Hence, further study of the nature of modern wars is needed if we are to be better able to explain them.

Third, understanding the nature of a conflict has obvious policy implications for intervening forces. As Clausewitz stated:

> The first, the supreme, the most far-reaching act of judgment that the statesman and commander have to make is to establish by that test the kind of war on which they are embarking; neither mistaking it for, nor trying to turn it into, something that is alien to its nature.[16]

Underestimating the importance of, or ignoring, a correct analysis could lead to failed interventions – as, Manwaring and others have pointed out, happened in Vietnam.[17] The point, in short, is that force commanders and/or political decision-makers must understand the nature of the war in which they are intervening, or considering intervening in, to avoid making mistakes that ultimately could cost lives and unnecessarily prolong the conflict.

Finally, while humanitarian intervention as a military undertaking has given rise to numerous publications on the what, when and how of this type of military action, very little attention has been devoted to the strategies and tactics that have been prevalent in the armed conflicts these humanitarian interventions have tried to ameliorate.[18] Hence, while understandably focusing on the immediate policy concerns, the more fundamental questions of a strategic nature that underpin the analysis of the policy issues have been ignored. This book seeks to fill this gap by focusing on a classical question in military theory: what is the nature of war?

The aim of this introductory chapter is to introduce the general puzzle, that is, the nature of modern war and its main discursive battle-lines, as well as introduce each chapter in the general scheme of the volume. The next section reviews the debate on the nature of modern war. It seeks to show how what are in fact three current parallel debates on the nature of war relate to the writings of Carl von Clausewitz. The point of such an exercise is that relating Clausewitz's ideas, usually regarded as one of the great theorists of war, to the current debate can illuminate the extent to which military theory is at odds with a debate largely dominated by scholars of international relations. One should, however, keep in mind that the aim of the book is not necessarily to evaluate whether or not Clausewitz's analysis is still valid.

Debating the nature of war

At the moment there are at least three debates raging on the nature of modern war. All three discuss, to a large extent independently of one another, whether or not there is something inherently *new* in modern war. The first deals with non-state warfare and some of its participants claim that these conflicts are new. I will explore this debate in more detail than the others since this book is more directly concerned with evaluating these claims. The second debate deals with the so-called revolution in military affairs (RMA) and contends that the way future (and some current) wars will be fought is 'new'. The third debate deals with so-called 'postmodern' war.[19] The argument put forward by the proponents of this line of thought is that war has become 'virtual'. This section will first outline the broad character-istics of these discussions and then show how they relate to the writings of Clausewitz.

In a discussion on the nature of war it seems appropriate to begin with recapitulating some of Carl von Clausewitz's ideas on war. In his masterpiece *On War*, 'not simply the greatest but the only truly great book on war', Clausewitz asserted that war is a rational and political phenomenon.[20] By suggesting that 'war is a continuation of politics by other means', he meant to show that war is instrumental in nature and should therefore be under-stood as a rational phenomenon.[21] At 'the heart of the matter', he argued, 'war is a violent duel: two forces of will, standing opposed to each other, each trying to overpower the other. '*War is thus an act of force to compel our enemy to do our will*'.[22] The aim of war is thus a peace on terms that are acceptable, or preferable, to the parties, while physical force is the means to this end. That Clausewitz included violence in his understanding is obvious:

> Essentially war is fighting, for fighting is the only effective principle in the manifold activities generally designated as war. Fighting, in turn, is a trial of moral and physical forces through the medium of the latter. [. . .] Still, no matter how it is constituted, the concept of fighting remains unchanged. That is what we mean by war.[23]

4

In Clausewitz's understanding, the violent duel is the essence of war. Even if all wars share this common ground, he acknowledges that wars differ from one another across time and space:

> War is more than a true chameleon that slightly adapts its character-istics to a given case. As a total phenomenon its dominant tendencies always make war a paradoxical trinity – composed of primordial violence, hatred, and enmity, which are to be regarded as blind natural force; of the play of chance and probability within which the creative spirit is free to roam; and of its element of subordination, as an instrument of policy, which makes it subject to reason alone.[24]

Somewhat paradoxically, therefore, while understanding the essence of war as a constant, Clausewitz's reasoning also implies that change is a part of his understanding of the nature of war. The inherent change, the inescapable element of chance, and the ever-present friction are the factors Clausewitz identifies that imply that war cannot be reduced to 'only mathematics'.[25] As an analytical model, Clausewitz suggests that war consists of a trinity made up of the people, the government, and the army.[26] War is comprised of, and balances between, the creative forces (symbolised by the general and his army), rational forces (symbolised by the government), and emotional forces (symbolised by the people). Hence, in Clausewitz's understanding of war, the armed forces are separable from the people (who do not take an active part in the fighting) and from the government, which leads the war. This analysis was clearly influenced by the political and military context in which Clausewitz lived.

His trinity has, however, received extensive criticism. John Keegan and Martin van Creveld, for example, have questioned to what extent Clausewitz's analysis is meaningful, since distinctions between government, people, and army might be difficult to uphold in modern war with weak states (and its dominant form, that is, non-state warfare) and different warrior cultures.[27] It is important to recognise that this criticism is levelled at the second tier of Clausewitz's trinity, that is, the operationalisation of the forces, rather than the forces themselves. Van Creveld argues:

> It follows that, where there are no states, the threefold division into government, army, and people does not exist in the same form. Nor would it be correct to say that, in such societies, war is made by governments using armies for making war at the expense of, or on the behalf of, their people.[28]

The Clausewitzian notion that there is an eternal nature of war while its manifestations vary throughout time and space has been influential. What one should be wary about, however, is that seeking out the common denominator

5

in all wars might lead us to something trivial. How insightful and precise can statements be that treat all wars throughout history? It is perhaps better to analyse and distinguish between types of war.

There is a possible tension in Clausewitz's notion of the nature of war that is aptly captured by Beatrice Heuser. She points out that Clausewitz modified his thinking during his work on *On War*, but because he did not finish revising the entire book due to his early death, there are 'two' Clausewitzes to be found: the 'young idealist' and the 'mature realist'. The tension between the two becomes evident in his statements on the nature of war. On the one hand, 'young' Clausewitz argues that there are no logical limits to the violence. War will strive toward its 'utmost boundaries' as a result of the interaction between two opponents, both aiming to win. The mutual fear of the enemy means that the combative parties will constantly try to outdo one another in an ascending spiral of violence. Thus violence in itself knows no boundaries and will therefore escalate.[29] On the other hand, the 'mature' Clausewitz maintains that war is bound by politics – and is political in its nature.[30]

This means that Clausewitz here suggests that war is not compelled to become total with escalating violence. Many have also noted that Clausewitz took for granted that the state is the primary actor in war – not least because Clausewitz placed primacy on politics over war, and politics are closely linked with the state. Although recognising that other forms of polities wage war, Clausewitz rarely relies upon these cases in arriving at his conclusions on the nature of war. The question then becomes how Clausewitz's ideas relate to the current debates on the nature of war, which concern non-state warfare, RMA, and postmodern war. Has anything changed? How should we understand and conceptualise modern war?

Clausewitz and non-state warfare

The strategic landscape since the end of the Cold War has been an interesting topic for debate. Indeed, endless debates on what to call conflicts that seem to escape the traditional understanding of war as 'organised large-scale violent conflict between the armed forces of two or more states' have raged throughout the 1990s. In these debates, the number of terms has proliferated. Terms such as 'new and old wars', 'the third kind of war', 'uncivil wars', 'intrastate wars', 'resource conflict', variants of 'ethnic war', 'internal war', 'ideological civil wars', 'shadow wars', 'peoples' wars', 'foreign internal defence', 'military operations other than war', 'terrorism', 'indirect wars', 'communal war', 'low-intensity conflicts', 'small wars', 'insurgencies', 'complex emergencies', and many others have been used to describe the conflicts raging in sub-Saharan Africa, the Balkans, and other parts of the developing world.[31]

The debate on how to conceptualise modern war indicates that far from being readily accepted, Clausewitz's ideas on the nature of war have become increasingly challenged. Implicit in many of the contributions to the non-state warfare segment of the debate on the nature of modern war is the tacit assumption that non-state war is different from war between states. The nucleus of this argument is that the nature of war depends to a high degree upon the nature of the actors and their war-conducting institutions. Hence, wars conducted by irregular militias will be fought differently and therefore have a different nature than wars conducted by states and their armies. To develop this argument further, it is necessary to take a closer look at the main theoretical divide in studies of the nature of modern war: between those who adhere to Clausewitz in regarding war as a rational phenomenon, and those who suggest that war has become irrational. I will deal with these two broad perspectives separately.

Rather than understanding war as instrumental, there are those who suggest that non-state warfare is irrational. According to this line of thought, imposing rationality misleads our analyses of these wars. Instead, identity, emotions and psychology are better suited to understand modern war. The most common claim during the 1990s in this regard was that identity – in particular ethnic identity, or the slightly more narrow religious identity – determined the conduct of the wars in, for example, the Balkans. One should be careful in distinguishing those who argue that ethnic identity is the cause of the violence and those who merely suggest that ethnic identity has an impact on the conduct of the wars (once they have started). Among those who deal with the conduct of ethnic war, one strand maintains that modern war is a non-Clausewitzian maelstrom of irrational barbaric violence bordering on chaos between every member of the ethnic groups – in contrast to war as an organised rational phenomenon.[32] The Tofflers, for example, warn about 'a new dark age of tribal hate, planetary desolation, and wars multiplied with wars'.[33] Moreover, Donald Snow argues:

> In a sense, what has emerged is a kind of 'new–old' form of war that is both pre-Clausewitzian and possibly post-Clausewitzian. What is most notable about it is the essential divorce of war from politics. In this style, war is not so clearly the continuation of politics by other means, a situation that some, including Keegan, contend is more historically prevalent than the conception of war during the Clausewitzian interlude. In that sense, the new warfare is pre-Clausewitzian, apolitical, and self-justifying. At the same time, the apparent chaos, savagery, and pointlessness of much of the new internal war would shock most pre-Clausewitzians of the period when armed conflict was imbued with notions of warrior ethic and chivalry.[34]

Monty Marshall, moreover, even argues that it is misleading to term this 'war', as ethnic violence is not organised.[35] Flirting with the same ideas, Kalevi Holsti argues that:

Attrition, terror, psychology, and actions against civilians highlight 'combat'. Rather than highly organized armed forces based on a strict command hierarchy, wars are fought by loosely knit groups of regulars, irregulars, cells, and not infrequently by locally-based warlords under little or no central authority.[36]

Snow also suggests that some internal wars after the Cold War are 'new'. He suggests that the 'new internal wars' demonstrate differences from classic insurgent warfare in so far as they have an 'absence of clear military objectives', the fighting forces are irregulars, which display an 'absence of even an appearance of military order and discipline', resulting in a 'level of ferocity and even atrocity that is routinely committed in these conflicts'.[37] Moreover, Snow points out that in the classic insurgencies the parties to the conflict partly shared the same centre of gravity: the legitimacy of the target population. This had a moderating effect on the warfare, which in the new internal wars is not present. Snow contends:

> Ethnic conflict, civil disintegration, and interference with humanitarian relief efforts all make up the complex of actions that defies neat classification in traditional politico-military terms. They are the kinds of acts that one associates with the failed states and that give the new internal war its distinctively politically chaotic and military atrocious character. As one looked aghast at the genocide in Rwanda or the random atrocities against civilians in Sarajevo, one could not avoid observing that this was not warfare as we had known it. The new internal war simply does not conform to standard definitions of war.[38]

Pursuing a similar idea, Lee Harris argues that we should not understand the terrorist attacks of September 11 2001 as a first instrumental stage in a war against the US. Instead, as the attacks were directed against the symbols of US power, the attack could be understood as a demonstration that al-Qaeda's version of Islamic fundamentalism has God on its side and is directed primarily to the Muslim population worldwide.[39] Similarly, martyrdom is difficult to understand in purely rationalistic terms, as martyrdom is an end in itself, at least in the modern Shia interpretation of Islam.

Harris' notion of how to understand terrorism is closely linked with Jerrold Post's argument on the 'psycho-logic' of terrorism. Post suggests that we cannot understand terrorism as an 'intentional choice selected from a range of perceived alternatives', as rationalism implies. Instead, he argues that terrorists become terrorists to commit terrorist acts.[40] It is the psychological set-up that predisposes some to be drawn towards extreme groups and extreme rhetoric. Once on the 'inside', individuals are controlled by strong group dynamics as well as the continuous reinforcement of the terrorist identity. In other words, a terrorist must continue to commit terrorist acts to reinforce his/her identity. This understanding of terrorism draws upon a logic that is not compatible with rationalist accounts of terrorism or modern warfare.

The common denominator of many of the advocates of the 'barbaric violence' thesis is the conviction that identity is primordial. Pursuing a closely related argument, Samuel Huntington even suggested a coming clash of civilisations, where Huntington's civilisations were primarily based upon the world religions.[41] The novelty of this thesis is that the politically relevant identity is moved 'up' at a supranational level rather than 'down' to a sub-national level. Another common denominator is that most of the advocates of this thesis draw upon evidence from so-called 'failed' or 'collapsed' states.[42]

Finally, Martin van Creveld, also criticising Clausewitz's understanding of war as a rational phenomenon, argues that it is 'preposterous [. . .] to think that, just because some people wield power, they act like calculating machines that are unswayed by passions. In fact, they are no more rational than the rest of us.'[43] Van Creveld suggests that the trinitarian war model simply does not apply in the greater part of today's armed conflicts. Instead, 'what we are dealing with here is neither low-intensity nor some bastard offspring of war. Rather, it is WARRE in the elemental, Hobbesian sense of the word, by far the most important form of armed conflict in our time.'[44] Non-trinitarian war, as van Creveld terms it, is determined by the psychological set-up of men (*men*, not mankind). He argues that:

> In any war, the readiness to suffer and die, as well as to kill, represents the single most important factor. Take it away, and even the most numerous, best organized, best trained, best equipped army in the world will turn out to be a brittle instrument. This applies to all wars regardless of time, place, and circumstance. It also applies regardless of the degree of technological sophistication involved, whether it is with the aid of sticks or tanks that the actual fighting is done.[45]

The 'readiness', van Creveld holds, should not be understood as a means but an end itself. In this reasoning, his argument is closely related to Post's idea of terrorism's psycho-logic. However, van Creveld grounds his logic in men being compelled to play and war is the most interesting game as it contains the highest stake of all – life.[46] War should therefore be understood as an end, rather than as a means.

The notion that war is irrational has received continuous and extensive criticism, however. Gérard Prunier has pointed out that the Hutu militia in Rwanda had a five times higher kill rate than the Nazis in the concentration camps. This certainly implies a high degree of organisation.[47] Martin Shaw advances a closely related argument in interpreting genocide as a form of war,

not the least due to high degree of organisation as well as what he sees as
intrinsic to war: mass killing. He argues;

> To organize a force that can carry out slaughter requires extensive
> preparation. It takes organization and ideas for warriors to overcome
> pervasive taboos against killing. It takes discipline to make soldiers
> aggressive against people they don't know, to inflict force in a way
> that achieves intended results and to overcome powerful instincts
> of self-preservation and fear. If all human killing requires social
> relations and beliefs to make it possible, the kind of mass killing
> involved in war requires peculiarly developed, conscious social
> organization and justification.[48]

Similarly, as evidence of the war in Bosnia slowly emerges, it seems certain
that even the bloody escapades of the irregulars there were orchestrated and
organised. Jan Willem Honig and Norbert Both, for example, point out that
the Bosnian-Serb army, when entering Srebrenica, 'were acting on the basis of
a carefully prepared plan', which included separating refugees (mainly women
and children) and those who would be eliminated (mainly men), and acquiring
fuel and means of transportation for the refugees and the Dutch UN soldiers
(in order to remove the witnesses as well as carry out the massacres).[49] Hence,
although the violence may, at first hand, seem indiscriminate – especially from
the distant TV couches of the Western world, it is not. It follows a rationale.
James Gow, too, has recently argued that Serbian behaviour during the
Yugoslav wars was far from haphazard or irrational. Instead, it consisted
of a conscious, well-planned strategy of deception, while only gradually
implementing its war aims, to 'limit the chances of the Serbian project being
seen for what it was and crossing the threshold that might warrant international action'.[50] John Mueller also observes that neither the Bosnian nor
the Rwandan wars were Hobbesian 'wars of all against all'. Instead, they were
primarily fought between something that resembled the armed forces in
conventional wars.[51] The act of selecting a few who carried out the violence
in itself indicates a degree of organisation. Another line of criticism is that
irregulars may actually serve the same state-building purposes as did regular
(and sometimes mercenary) troops in seventeenth-century Europe.[52] This
implies a certain degree of rationality.

The above-mentioned criticism of modern war as irrational leads us to
those who, following Clausewitz, understand the nature of war as rational.
Even among this disparate group, though, there are those who claim that wars
are 'new'.

Most significantly, there is one school of thought – the 'globalists' – that
maintains that modern wars follow a different rationale than Clausewitz
suggested.[53] Its principal advocate, Mary Kaldor, suggests that these wars
are completely new. The unique combination of the parties' emphasis on

identity politics, their mode of warfare, and their globalised war economies, she argues, have created a new form of war, with the war in Bosnia as the archetypical case.[54] By stressing ethnic identity as one of the variables in characterising the 'new' wars, Kaldor's argument is seemingly linked with the irrational-violence thesis. However, Kaldor is not suggesting that ethnicity *per se* is the prime motivator for war. Instead, it is the clash of cosmopolitan and particularist ideologies that fuels the war. In contrast to the second perspective, she also adds the special mode of warfare, specifically its inclination to target the civilian population, as a criterion to separate 'new' wars from 'old'. Arguably, however, ethnic identity has been prevalent before, so too have irregular forces and irregular conduct of wars. Therefore, Kaldor also adds globalisation to the equation. The global trade links that are used to support the armed movements fighting in these wars are the key characteristic of the new wars.

There are also other advocates of an economic rationale in war.[55] Here, the argument is that economic incentives determine the conduct of the war. In contrast to Clausewitz's rationality in terms of politics, this argument suggests that 'war may be a continuation of *economics* by other means'.[56] This does not necessarily mean that the wars are caused by economic shortcomings but rather that the conduct, and continuation, of the war is determined by economic incentives. It suggests that personal enrichment is the prime incentive to join and carry out military operations in some parts of the developing world.

This notion that military undertakings are the results of economic incentives is not new. Analyses of wars during the Middle Ages usually attribute some explanatory power to economic incentives. There are also those who attribute the economic rationale in modern war to the claim that modern war in the developing world is unorganised. Kalevi Holsti argues:

> The new mediaevalism is demonstrated most dramatically in the nature of armed conflict in these states. War has become de-institutionalized in the sense of central control, rules, regulations, etiquette, and armaments. Armies are rag-tag groups frequently made up of teenagers paid in drugs, or not paid at all. In the absence of authority and discipline, but quite in keeping with the interests of the warlords, 'soldiers' discover opportunities for private enterprises of their own.[57]

However, the globalisation thesis can also be criticised. Not all conflicts in the developing world that do not fit in the traditional understanding of war are marked by ethnic differences or 'identity politics'. One very notable example has been the war in Somalia, an ethnically homogenous state. Furthermore, trade links have always existed between rebel movements and the outside world. These movements need to sustain their combat actions by means of trade. It can be argued that these have changed in quality and quantity because the world has changed and not because of their own making. Furthermore, it can be questioned to what extent economic resources determine the violence. Why, if economics are that important, is fighting often fierce around symbols of national power such as the capital or the presidential palaces?

Kaldor's assumption that modern wars are different in their nature than wars in history, has received yet further criticism. It could be argued that contemporary wars in the developing world have more features in common with regular conventional warfare than irregular combat. This school of thought emphasises the continuities of war rather than the changes and implies that we should understand modern war in the developing world as conventional. Students of warfare on the European continent, for example, have observed that prominent features of today's wars in the developing world, such as famine as an instrument of war, plunder, living off the land, and avoiding direct confrontations were also visible in Europe, most notable during the Thirty Years War.[58] Stathis Kalyvas, too, has argued that the 'new war thesis' exaggerates the criminal elements in modern warfare.[59] Antony Beevor, moreover, demonstrates that warfare directed at civilians (from both sides) also was a major part of the operations at the Eastern Front during the Second World War.[60] Finally, Errol Henderson and David Singer maintain that the already existent categories of war are able to incorporate the 'novel' wars.[61]

There are, however, problems with this interpretation too. For example, very local practices of combat seem to be alien to European notions of conventional war. One only has to think of the practices of disguise and extreme acts of cruelty – even cannibalism – that have been notable features of recent wars in West and Central Africa.

Another strand of thinking within the rationalistic camp suggests that we should understand modern war in the developing world as similar to insurgency.[62] During the 1960s and 1970s, the political as well as the scholarly agenda on non-state war was dominated by the notion of 'war of national liberation' from colonial rule as well as 'revolutionary war', 'insurgency', and eventually 'counter-insurgency'. Following primarily the writings of Mao Tse-tung, Giap and, to a lesser extent, Castro and Che Guevara, war was depicted as a struggle between insurgents aiming to overthrow the presiding government and the government's forces. Mao himself, however, did not distance himself from Clausewitz. Instead, he once expressed his admiration for Clausewitz to then West German Chancellor Helmut Schmidt:

> Marx, Engels and Lenin have interpreted his [Clausewitz's] famous dictum as though war were nothing special, but merely the continuation of politics with other means. I [Mao], by contrast, prefer to read Clausewitz's tenet as a lesson for the military, i.e., even in war, the political leadership has to have primacy.[63]

Mao emphasised that guerrilla warfare 'must not be considered as an independent form of warfare' but rather as 'one step in the total war, one aspect of the revolutionary struggle'.[64] Thus, Mao recognised, in accord with Clausewitz, that war was political. Heuser points out that Mao's most significant development of Clausewitz's ideas was his insistence upon mixing – rather than separating as Clausewitz advocated – guerrillas and regular forces.[65] It was precisely the combination and interaction between the guerrillas and regular forces that was the foundation of Mao's famous three-stage analysis of guerrilla warfare. By using primarily indirect fighting techniques, such as avoiding main confrontations with the enemy and striking with lightning speed at the weak points of the opponent, the insurgents could initially – during the *strategic defence* phase – undermine the legitimacy of the incumbent government. Mao explains guerrilla strategy:

> In guerrilla warfare, select the tactic of seeming to come from the east and attacking from the west; avoid the solid, attack the hollow; attack; withdraw; deliver a lightning blow, seek a lightning decision. When guerrillas engage a stronger enemy, they withdraw when he advances; harass him when he stops; strike him when he is weary; pursue him when he withdraws. In guerrilla strategy, the enemy's rear, flanks, and other vulnerable spots are his vital points, and there he must be harassed, attacked, dispersed, exhausted, and annihilated.[66]

During the second phase – *stalemate* – the insurgent forces should adopt a more conventional strategy and acquire control over rural areas to further consolidate their claim for power. In the final phase – *strategic offensive* – the insurgents should lean more to their regular forces than the guerrillas and conduct a massive conventional offensive to beat the government's forces in the cities. The analogy with revolutionary war is still prevalent in analyses of modern conflicts. Some but by no means all writers on this analogy distance themselves from the revolutionary insurgency model à la Mao and suggest instead that the term 'insurgency' should be interpreted more widely to include other forms of ideologically based movements rather than only the original communist insurgents.[67] In many of the modern armed conflicts in the developing world, however, a political ideology, even apart from that of Mao, is completely missing. The ideological underpinning of state power is not attacked. This crucial difference makes it difficult to fit these wars into this category of warfare. It seems therefore that the insurgency framework of analysis has some shortcomings, making it problematic for understanding modern war.

The criticism suggests that insurgencies (or internal wars) may need qualification. Hence, many have suggested that insurgencies may just as well be ethnic in nature (with the extended ambition of not only seizing power but sometimes demanding secession). One should not confuse this literature with the irrational-hatred thesis, which also stresses ethnic identity. Although this strand had its early advocates during the 1960s and 1970s, the argument came to dominate the scholarly agenda in the early part of the 1990s following the Yugoslav break-up wars and the genocide in Rwanda. This less radical version of the ethnic-war argument suggests that insurgencies are less ideological and more ethnic in character. Rather than being fixed from birth as primordialism maintains, this line of thought follows either an instrumental or a constructivist understanding of ethnicity, in which power-maximising elites or the continuous interaction between ethnic groups continuously recreate ethnic identity. According to this view, ethno-political conflicts are no more mysterious or irrational than other forms of conflict; they just take place between ethnic groups rather than ideological groupings or states. The moderate version of the ethnic-war thesis has been more successful in incorporating ideas from other disciplines, most notably International Relations. During the 1990s, realist- and liberal-inspired analyses of ethnic conflicts became quite commonplace.[68] For this school of thought, Clausewitzian notions on the nature of war are easily incorporated.

Terrorism, too, can also be understood as rational rather than irrational. Martha Crenshaw, for example, suggests that terrorism is the result of strategic rational considerations.[69] For a relatively weak opposition, terrorist actions can have positive effects by undermining the incumbent regime, inspiring others by action, and provoking repressive counter actions (which could further undermine the legitimacy of the government). Moreover, violent terrorism has an agenda-setting effect. However, there are also negative aspects of terrorism. The violence in itself, for example, can turn potential supporters away from the aims of the terrorists. The rational understanding of terrorism is hardly at odds with Clausewitz in so far as it stresses the political aims of the terrorist movement, and violent actions are only the means to this political end. Stretching the understanding of terrorism, Max Taylor and John Horgan argue that aspects of the Bosnian war can only be understood as terrorism. They point out that of 'deaths and injuries sustained by children' in Sarajevo, 20–25 per cent were the result of snipers and 'injury through sniping, unlike shrapnel injury, is not random. It requires a deliberate act of aiming the weapon.' Since children do not have a role in the war, the purpose of these shootings cannot have been anything else than 'producing fear and despondency amongst the population at large', i.e. terrorism.[70]

In summary, in the debate on the nature of non-state warfare there are several who claim that these wars are non-Clausewitzian. There are, however, also those who oppose this view, arguing that Clausewitz's understanding of the nature of war is still applicable. Some even suggest that there is no such thing as guerrilla warfare.[71] One should, perhaps, note that even though the violence seems to be irrational for analysts in the Western world, it is no guarantee that the violence does not follow its own logic. There may of course be instances of irrational violence in these conflicts but this does not mean that the main patterns of warfare do not follow a rationale – even though it may be difficult to detect for Western analysts.

Clausewitz and RMA

In the debate on the so-called 'revolution in military affairs' (RMA), other aspects are claimed to be 'new' in warfare.[72] According to the advocates of RMA, the Gulf War in 1991 signalled a change in the nature of war. While there has been a vivid debate about whether or not the RMA constitutes a revolution or only an evolution, the appeal of the RMA arguments in Western societies is the combination of so-called 'smart' weapons and their possibilities for 'clean' wars. Regardless of its causes, RMA and network-centric warfare has seized a sizeable chunk of current strategic thought.

Most of the analysts view this revolution as driven by the technological development over the last decades. Perhaps significantly, a great deal of the technology is civilian rather than military. Elinor Sloan argues that 'the central tenet of an RMA is that advances in technology must lead to significant changes in how military forces are organised, trained, and equipped for war, thereby reshaping the way in which wars are fought'.[73] Improvements in battle space awareness, in particular, it is argued, will famously be able to lift the 'fog of war', that is, remove Clausewitzian friction and uncertainty from war.[74] Although the belief of ridding war from friction and chance may be quite optimistic, since soldiers and commanders still are men and women who eventually will become exhausted, be afraid, make mistakes, and have different fortunes in war, the notion of the increased possibilities to control a battlefield and strike accurately has taken a strong hold, especially on the US armed forces. Others suggest that even though the RMA is technology-driven, the technology is just an indication of a much wider change. The Tofflers, for example, argue that the character of war depends a great deal upon the nature of the society that pursues the war.[75]

The development of weapons and platforms, which become more and more stealthy, accurate and in sync with each other in their use, suggests, according to the advocates of the RMA, that wars will change their nature. The 'system of systems', as it has been called, will become more effective, thus leading to dominance of quality over quantity. This development seems to earn support from comparing the Gulf War in 1991 and the Iraqi War in 2003. In the most recent war, there have been fewer troops involved on the Coalition side, and despite being outnumbered with respect to number of battle tanks, there are no reports of even a single Coalition tank being destroyed by an Iraqi tank. Bruce Berkowitz concludes:

> Today *the ability to collect, communicate, process, and protect infor-*
> *mation is the most important factor defining military power.* In the past

armor, firepower, and mobility defined military power, but now it often matters less how fast you can move or how much destructive force you can apply. Stealth trumps armor, precision trumps explosive force, and being able to react faster than your opponent trumps speed.[76]

Moreover, the technology can also be used in so-called 'information operations', which brings with it yet another change, as noted by van Creveld:

> In conventional warfare, the fact that an advance has to be made, supplies brought forward, ground occupied, and garrisons left behind tend to work against the attack and in favor of the defense; in so far as traversing territory takes time, the same is true of that factor. In information warfare, both geographical space and time is irrelevant. Attacks scarcely require a base. They do not demand that supplies be gathered first, and can be directed at any point from any other point regardless of distance.[77]

The increased reliance upon accurate weapons and – perhaps in a not so distant future – non-lethal weapons also means that collateral damage could be minimised. By removing deadly violence the RMA proponents certainly have a claim to have changed warfare.

There are, however, several arguments suggesting caution about the RMA. Most obviously, this debate is heavily influenced by the future: future visions of war, future wars, and future technology. We cannot therefore evaluate the claims of a change in the nature of war as they are made by the RMA proponents. Still, it may not be an altogether distant future. In the Iraqi war in 2003, coalition forces, by 10 April, had used 68 per cent precision guided munitions as compared to only 9 per cent in the whole of the Gulf War in 1991.[78] Furthermore, it is questionable to what extent the development in mainly Western armed forces can influence modern war in general. Most of the wars or minor armed conflicts take place in the developing world, where the RMA development is absent. The RMA also presupposes that it is possible to drive up the costs of war without killing the enemy's soldiers. It is not certain that killing is a nonessential part of warfare. Perhaps 'young' Clausewitz was correct: war is essentially fighting, and its violence escalates as both sides try to win, thereby ultimately costing lives.

Clausewitz and postmodern war

Drawing partly upon the debates discussed so far, some have argued that war itself has become *postmodern*.[79] The 'new' features of war, at least according to the proponents of this view, are that war essentially has become a media event – a 'spectator sport' – rather than something that has an impact on the entire society. Because wars take place on the television screens and so few of the society's resources are utilised, wars take place in a societal vacuum. Michael Ignatieff argues:

> War thus becomes virtual, not simply because it appears to take place on screen, but because it enlists societies only in virtual ways. Due to nuclear weapons, it is no longer a struggle for national survival; with the end of conscription, it no longer requires the actual participation of citizens; because of the bypassing of representative institutions, it no longer requires democratic consent; and as a result of the exceptional growth of the modern economy, it no longer draws on the entire economic system. These conditions transform war into something like a spectator sport.[80]

The prime reason for the emergence of the virtual war is the West's reluctance to become militarily involved unless it enjoys overwhelming superiority in military and, especially, technological power. Furthermore, the increasing dependence upon airpower and precision-guided munitions among Western armed forces, means that the West even tries to 'take death out of wars' – not only by reducing its own losses through the predominant use of airpower in their conduct of war but also by minimising collateral damage. In the most recent war in Iraq, for example, even if civilian casualties may exceed military losses we have not witnessed devastating results of the strategic bombing campaign, as occurred during the Second World War, for example. It becomes more and more obvious that the postmodern war thesis draws upon the RMA debate. One of the more scintillating, but perhaps ultimately futile, notions is the development of non-lethal weapons. Surely, the removal of death from wars would represent a change in the nature of war, but the postmodern war advocates also maintain there is a danger that wars would become more, rather than less, frequent as society becomes more and more disconnected from the decisions, conduct and suffering in war.

Among others, Ignatieff bases his analysis upon the way the West conducted its campaign in Kosovo. The notion of postmodern war, therefore, partly relies upon the limited wars in which the West has been involved, in stark contrast to the great war against the Soviet Union, which its military practised and prepared for during the Cold War, and partly upon the new technologies that the RMA debate is concerned with.

Similar criticism as levelled against the RMA understanding of modern war can be levelled against war as postmodern. For example, although taking death out of war may imply a change in its nature, it presupposes that war is costly even if killing is not carried out. There are also other criticisms against the notion of postmodern war. Most importantly, perhaps, there is nothing postmodern about being directly involved in the fighting, as the inhabitants of

Kosovo surely would agree. Hence, even if war may appear for the West to be a spectator sport, the rest of the world is not in such a position.

In summary, the current debates on the nature of modern war and modern warfare are wide-ranging and thought-provoking. They each claim that the nature and forms of war have changed over the last decades. As we have seen, virtually no part of Clausewitz's understanding of the nature of war has been left untouched. It has been suggested that war is frictionless, non-lethal, non-political, and irrational. The aim of this volume is to evaluate the extent to which these claims are correct, especially with regard to modern war in the developing world. Has the nature of war changed?

The plan of the book

The following chapters deal with the puzzles outlined above. In the second chapter, Mike Smith argues that modern low-intensity conflicts are best understood through the lenses provided by Clausewitz. Categories such as 'low-intensity conflict' and 'terrorism', Smith argues, are analytically flawed and do not form proper classes of war of themselves. Instead, by analysing how studies of non-state warfare during the Cold War gradually became detached from the field of security studies, at the time a field obsessed with counting the nuclear arsenals of the super powers, Smith explains how non-state warfare became regarded as something different from war proper.

In the third chapter, propounding a closely related argument but one based on analyses of the wars in Liberia and Somalia in the beginning of the 1990s, Isabelle Duyvesteyn contends that these conflicts demonstrate hitherto unrecognised features common in conventional interstate wars in Europe. Contrary to the dominant expert opinion, armed conflicts in developing states, in particular in cases of state collapse, have more similarities with conventional warfare rather than guerrilla war. Modern warfare in Africa, at least in these two cases, therefore is not 'new'. Conventional wars and warfare in low-intensity conflicts seem not to be as different as we have previously thought.

Taking issue with Smith and Duyvesteyn, Stathis Kalyvas (in the following chapter) describes three different types of civil warfare, roughly corresponding (though not a perfect correlation) to three different types of conflict process. He argues that conventional warfare exists in secessionist conflicts, irregular warfare is intimately linked with rural insurgencies, while 'symmetric non-conventional warfare' (his term) is connected to state collapses. Kalyvas then explores the causal effects of warfare on the intensity and form of violence in continued war. In doing so, he develops theory and hypotheses for further research.

In the next chapter, Colin McInnes traces the conduct of the Afghan War to US methods of warfare during the 1990s. Rather than finding a 'new war', McInnes emphasises the continuity of US-led operations from Somalia to Afghanistan. Specifically, the wars have limited – if any – potential to spread to the US mainland, the opponents are regimes rather than peoples, minimising collateral damage is pivotal, and the society at large is quite indifferent to the wars in so far as they hardly take an active part.

Reaching a closely related result, Kersti Larsdotter stretches the analysis to the Vietnam War. In her analysis of new wars and old warfare, she compares US tactics in Vietnam and Afghanistan to evaluate the impact of the technological development of the last decades. Larsdotter demonstrates that despite claims of 'new' US tactics in Afghanistan, especially the use of special forces in combination with airpower, similar tactics were used by American forces in Vietnam. The conduct of the wars, at the tactical level, therefore indicates that in actual warfare few things are truly original. Her analysis therefore questions the utility of using warfare as an indicator of types of wars.

Bob de Graaff, meanwhile, provides an in-depth analysis of the war in Bosnia – the prime example of Kaldor's 'new wars' thesis. The chapter provides evidence that the Bosnian war was to a high degree controlled by the state. De Graaff argues that high-flying spin doctors in Belgrade acting upon their political master's orders managed to define the conflict to Western media in ethnic terms. Western decision-makers – and analysts, according to de Graaff – were thereby lured into believing that violence in Bosnia was primarily privatised and locally orchestrated, while in reality it was directed from Belgrade. Rather than chaotic violence, the war in Bosnia therefore should be understood as a result of aspirations of groups to form new states.

John Mackinlay offers an analysis of modern insurgencies. He outlines different types of insurgency and argues that the emergence of 'global insurgents' further complicates the situation for analysts and practitioners alike. He suggests that by focusing on the development of 'peace-doing' doctrines, Western armed forces ignored the hard-earned lessons of the counterinsurgency literature. In examining the nature of al-Qaeda, the archetype of global insurgency, Mackinlay finally outlines a counterstrategy for the West.

Paul Rich discusses warlordism and its connections to a global economy. His chapter examines the debate in International Relations theory on globalisation and its relevance for explaining the heightening of sub-state conflict in the post Cold War period. It argues that globalisation provides only a weak rather than a strong explanation for sub-state conflict since its intellectual origins lie in antimilitarist liberal ideas of increasing economic integration at the international level. A rethinking of globalisation is necessary, one which takes account of modern warfare that is termed 'non-trinitarian war' and which marks contrasts with the era of industrialised total warfare of the nineteenth and twentieth centuries. The last part of the chapter warns against any simplistic application of this theory (as in Robert

Kaplan's idea of a 'coming anarchy') and calls for a detailed anthropological study of warlord and ethnic formations in terrains of state breakdown.

In the next chapter, Mary Kaldor responds to the criticism levelled at the 'new war' thesis. Although accepting some of the criticism, she argues that the 'new war thesis' still provides a valid assessment of the war in Bosnia. Finally, in a novel way, she connects the debate on the new aspects of non-state war and the postmodern war thesis (what she terms 'spectacle wars') by arguing that they are both the product of three interrelated processes dominating current world politics: the destructive force of new military technology; the information technological revolution; and globalisation, which are transforming the state.

Finally, Isabelle Duyvesteyn summarises what we have learned and evaluates the various contributions of the book to our understanding of the nature of modern war with respect to still unsolved controversies and an emerging consensus. In returning to the debates on the nature of modern warfare, she structures her discussion on the contributions to the book according to the actors of war, the methods of war, and the purposes of war.

Notes

1 Address to West Point graduates in 1962. Quoted in William P. Yarborough, 'Counterinsurgency: The US Role – Past, Present, and Future', in Richard D. Schultz *et al.* (eds), *Guerrilla Warfare and Counterinsurgency*, Lexington, MA: Lexington Books, 1989, pp. 103–4.
2 Mary Kaldor, *New and Old Wars: Organised Violence in a Global Era*, Cambridge: Polity Press, 1999.
3 Benjamin S. Lambeth, 'The Technology Revolution in Air Warfare', *Survival*, 39, 1 (1997), p. 75, quoted in Elinor C. Sloan, *The Revolution in Military Affairs: Implications for Canada and NATO*, Montreal: McGill's, 2002, p. 3.
4 Michael Ignatieff, *Virtual War: Kosovo and Beyond*, Toronto: Viking Books, 2000.
5 See the contributions in Ken Booth and Tim Dunne (eds), *Worlds in Collision: Terror and the Future of Global Order*, London: Palgrave, 2002.
6 Kalevi J. Holsti, *War, the State, and the State of War*, Cambridge: Cambridge University Press, 1996.
7 Carl von Clausewitz, *On War*, trans. Michael Howard and Peter Paret, London: Everyman's Library, 1993, pp. 99–101. Beatrice Heuser notes that the notion of an eternal essence of war while forms of war differed throughout time and space was commonplace not only in Clausewitz's texts but also other Prussian military thinkers in the early nineteenth century. See Beatrice Heuser, *Reading Clausewitz*, London: Pimlico, 2002, p. 186. For a discussion on a possible transformation of the character of modern war (but one that does not question a change in the nature of war), see the contributions in Zeev Maoz and Azar Gat (eds), *War in a Changing World*, Ann Arbor, MI: University of Michigan Press, 2001.
8 Philip Wilkinson, 'The Changing Nature of War: New Wine in Old Bottles – A New Paradigm or Paradigm Shift?', *The Royal Swedish Academy of War Sciences: Proceedings and Journal*, 207, 1 (2003), p. 29.
9 Azar Gat, *A History of Military Thought: From the Enlightenment to the Cold War*, Oxford: Oxford University Press, 2001, p. 202.

10 Colin Gray, 'Clausewitz rules, OK? The Future is the Past – with GPS', *Review of International Studies*, 25, special issue (December 1999), pp. 161–82.

11 M. L. R. Smith, 'Guerrillas in the Mist: Reassessing Strategy and Low Intensity Warfare', *Review of International Studies*, 29, 1 (2003), p. 37. See also Stephen Biddle, 'Afghanistan and the Future of Warfare', *Foreign Affairs*, 82, 2 (2003), pp. 31–46.

12 John T. Fishel, 'War By Other Means? The Paradigm and its Application to Peace Operations', in John T. Fishel (ed.), *The Savage Wars of Peace: Toward a New Paradigm of Peace Operations*, Boulder, CO: Westview Press, 1998, pp. 3–17.

13 The literature dealing with this puzzle is vast. For introductory but still authoritative texts, see James B. Rule, *Theories of Civil Violence*, Berkeley: University of California Press, 1988; Michael Howard, *The Causes of Wars*, London: Unwin, 1983; Geoffrey Blainey, *The Causes of War*, 3rd edn, New York: Free Press, 1988, and Holsti, *The State, War, and the State of War*.

14 Nils Petter Gleditsch *et al.*, 'Armed Conflict 1946–2001: A New Dataset', *Journal of Peace Research*, 39, 5 (2002). For further quantitative studies, see Meredith Reid Sarkees, Frank Whelon Wayman, and J. David Singer, 'Inter-State, Intra-State, and Extra-State Wars: A Comprehensive Look at Their Distribution over Time, 1816–1997', *International Studies Quarterly*, 47, 1 (2003), pp. 49–70.

15 Basil H. Liddell Hart, 'Foreword' in Mao Tse Tung and Che Guevara, *Guerrilla Warfare*, London: Cassell, 1962, p. xi.

16 Clausewitz, *On War*, p. 100.

17 Max Manwaring, *Internal Wars: Rethinking Problem and Response*, Carlisle, PA: Strategic Studies Institute, 2001, p. 5.

18 One of the few exceptions is Robert E. Harkavy and Stephanie G. Neumann, *Warfare and the Third World*, London: Palgrave, 2001.

19 Note that this take on the debate is different from, for example Bjorn Moller, who argues that van Creveld's 'non-trinitarian war' is synonymous to postmodern war. See Bjorn Moller, 'Faces of War', in Håkan Wiberg and Christian P. Sherrer (eds), *Ethnicity and Intra-State Conflict: Types, Causes, and Peace Strategies*, Aldershot: Ashgate, 1999, pp. 15–34.

20 Bernard Brodie, 'The Continuing Relevance of *On War*', in Clausewitz, *On War*, p. 58.

21 Clausewitz, *On War*, p. 99.

22 Ibid., p. 83 (emphasis in original).

23 Ibid., p. 145.

24 Ibid., p. 101.

25 Ibid., pp. 84–5.

26 Ibid., p. 101.

27 John Keegan, *A History of Warfare*, London: Pimlico, 1993 and Martin van Creveld, *The Transformation of War*, New York: Free Press, 1991. For an alternative interpretation of Clausewitz's trinity, see Edward J. Villacres and Christopher Bassford, 'Reclaiming the Clausewitzian Trinity', *Parameters*, 25, 3 (1995), pp. 9–19.

28 Van Creveld, *The Transformation of War*, p. 50.

29 Clausewitz, *On War*, p. 85.

30 Heuser, *Reading Clausewitz*, especially pp. 24–43 and pp. 186–90.

31 See, for example, Kaldor, *New and Old Wars*; Holsti, *War, the State, and the State of War*; Donald M. Snow, *Uncivil Wars: International Security and the New Internal Conflicts*, Boulder, CO: Lynne Rienner, 1996; Martin van Creveld, *The Transformation of War*, New York: The Free Press, 1991; the special issue on so-called 'small wars' in *The Annals of the American Academy of Political and*

Social Science, 541 (September, 1995); Chaim D. Kaufmann, 'Interventions in Ethnic and Ideological Civil Wars: Why One Can Be Done But the Other Can't', *Security Studies*, 6, 1 (Autumn 1996), pp. 62–103; and Kimberly A. Maynard, *Healing Communities in Conflict: International Assistance in Complex Emergencies*, New York: Columbia University Press, 1999. For an attempt to synthesise the many terms and the debate on internal war in particular, see Jan Angstrom, 'Towards a Typology of Internal Armed Conflict: Synthesising a Decade of Conceptual Turmoil', *Civil Wars*, 4, 3 (2001), pp. 93–116.

32 See, for example, Robert Kaplan, *The Coming Anarchy: Shattering the Dreams of the Post Cold War*, New York: Random House, 2000.

33 Alvin Toffler and Heidi Toffler, *War and Anti-War: Survival at the Dawn of the 21st Century*, London: Little & Brown, 1994, p. 1.

34 Donald M. Snow, *Distant Thunder: Patterns of Conflict in the Developing World*, 2nd edn, London: M. E. Sharpe, 1997, p. 129.

35 Monty Marshall, 'Systems at Risk: Violence, Diffusion, and Disintegration in the Middle East', in David Carment and Patrick James (eds), *Wars in the Midst of Peace: The International Politics of Ethnic Conflict*, Pittsburgh: University of Pittsburgh Press, 1997, pp. 88–9.

36 Holsti, *War, the State, and the State of War*, p. 20.

37 Snow, *Uncivil Wars*, pp. 106–7.

38 Ibid., p. 105.

39 Lee Harris, 'Al Qaeda's Fantasy Ideology', *Policy Review*, No. 114, <http://www.policyreview.org/AUG02/ harris.html>, accessed 19 August 2002.

40 Jerrold M. Post, 'Terrorist Psycho-Logic: Terrorist Behavior as a Product of Psychological Forces', in Walter Reich (ed.), *Origins of Terrorism: Psychologies, Ideologies, Theologies, States of Mind*, Cambridge: Cambridge University Press, 1990, pp. 25–40.

41 Samuel Huntington, *The Clash of Civilizations and the Remaking of World Order*, London: Touchstone, 1996.

42 For differentiation and precision of these terms, see Robert I. Rotberg (ed.), *State Failure and State Weakness in a Time of Terror*, Washington DC: Brookings, 2003.

43 Van Creveld, *The Transformation of War*, p. 157.

44 Ibid., p. 22.

45 Ibid., p. 160.

46 Ibid., pp. 161–87.

47 Gérard Prunier, *The Rwanda Crisis*, London: Hurst & Co., 1998, p. 261.

48 Martin Shaw, *War and Genocide: Organized Killing in Modern Society*, Cambridge: Polity Press, 2003, p. 21.

49 Jan Willem Honig and Norbert Both, *Srebrenica: Record of a War Crime*, London: Penguin, 1996, pp. 29–30.

50 James Gow, *The Serbian Project and its Adversaries: A Strategy of War Crimes*, London: Hurst, 2003, p. 23.

51 John Mueller, 'The Banality of Ethnic War: Yugoslavia and Rwanda', *International Security*, 25, 1 (2001), pp. 42–70.

52 For a study on the effects of paramilitaries on state-building, see the contributions in Diane E. Davis and Anthony W. Pereira (eds), *Irregular Armed Forces and their Role in Politics and State Formation*, Cambridge: Cambridge University Press, 2003.

53 Here, too, one has to be careful in distinguishing between those who argue that economic incentives are the cause of the war and those who merely suggest that economic incentives have an impact on the conduct of war. In this volume, we are mostly concerned with the latter argument.

54 Kaldor, *New and Old Wars*, pp. 6–9.
55 This literature and their arguments are related to, but should not be confused with, Marxist analyses of civil wars. According to the Marxist argument, the conflict is caused by grievances resulting from economic injustice. These grievances also have an impact on the conduct of the war. The globalists, instead, argue that the conduct of the war and the prime motivator to join and continue the war is financial rewards, for example by hi-jacking international aid transports, 'protecting' lucrative mine industries, etc. See David Keen, *The Economic Functions of Civil War*, Adelphi Paper 320 (London: IISS, 1998) and the contributions in Mats Berdal and David M. Malone (eds), *Greed and Grievance: Economic Agendas in Civil Wars*, Boulder, CO: Lynne Rienner, 2000.
56 David Keen, 'Incentives and Disincentives for Violence', in Berdal and Malone (eds), *Greed and Grievance*, p. 27 (emphasis in original).
57 Kalevi J. Holsti, 'The Coming Chaos? Armed Conflict in the World's Periphery', in T. V. Paul and John A. Hall (eds), *International Order and the Future of World Politics*, Cambridge: Cambridge University Press, 1999, p. 304.
58 See for Thirty Years War and early modern period, Herfried Münkler, *Die neuen Kriege* (Rowohlt, 2002). For pre-state war see also van Creveld, *The Transformation of War*.
59 Stathis N. Kalyvas, 'New and Old Civil Wars: A Valid Distinction?', *World Politics*, 54, 1 (2001), pp. 99–118.
60 Antony Beevor, *Stalingrad*, London: Viking, 1998 and Antony Beevor, *Berlin: The Downfall 1945*, New York: Viking, 2002.
61 Errol A. Henderson and J. David Singer, ' "New Wars" and Rumors of "New Wars" ', *International Interactions*, 28, 2 (2002), pp. 165–90.
62 Thomas R. Mockaitis, 'From Counter-Insurgency to Peace Enforcement: New Names for Old Games?', in Erwin A. Schmidl (ed.), *Peace Operations: Between War and Peace*, London: Frank Cass, 2000, pp. 40–57.
63 Quoted in Heuser, *Reading Clausewitz*, p. 141.
64 Mao Tse-tung, *On Guerrilla Warfare*, translation Samuel B. Griffiths, Chicago: University of Illinois Press, 1961, p. 41.
65 Heuser, *Reading Clausewitz*, p. 139.
66 Mao Tse-tung, *On Guerrilla Warfare*, p. 46.
67 See, for example, Kaufmann, 'Interventions in Ethnic and Ideological Civil Wars: Why One Can Be Done But the Other Can't'.
68 See, for example, Barry Posen, 'The Security Dilemma and Ethnic Conflict', in Michael E. Brown (ed.), *Ethnic Conflict and International Security*, Princeton, NJ: Princeton University Press, 1993, pp. 103–24 and Jan Angstrom and Isabelle Duyvesteyn, 'Evaluating Realist Explanations of Internal Conflict: The Case of Liberia', *Security Studies*, 10, 3 (2001), pp. 186–219.
69 Martha Crenshaw, 'The Logic of Terrorism: Terrorist Behavior as a Product of Strategic Choice', in Reich (ed.), *Origins of Terrorism*, pp. 7–24.
70 Max Taylor and John Horgan, 'Future Developments of Political Terrorism in Europe', *Terrorism and Political Violence*, 11, 4 (1999), p. 87.
71 Smith, 'Guerrillas in the Mist', pp. 20–3.
72 For a good review of the 'first round' of this debate, see Stephen Biddle, 'The Past as Prologue: Assessing Theories of Future Warfare', *Security Studies*, 8, 1 (1998), pp. 1–74.
73 Sloan, *The Revolution in Military Affairs*, p. 3.
74 William Owens (with Ed Offley), *Lifting the Fog of War*, New York: Farrar, Straus and Giroux, 2000.
75 Toffler and Toffler, *War and Anti-War*.

76 Bruce Berkowitz, *The New Face of War: How War Will be Fought in the 21st Century*, New York: The Free Press, 2003, p. 21.
77 Martin van Creveld, 'The Transformation of War Revisited', *Small Wars and Insurgencies*, 13, 2 (2002), pp. 10–11.
78 *New York Times*, 10 April 2003.
79 Some of the key texts in this debate are Colin McInnes, *Spectator Sport War: The West and Contemporary Conflict*, Boulder, CO: Lynne Rienner, 2002; Christopher Coker, *Humane Warfare: The New Ethics of Postmodern War*, London: Routledge, 2001; James Der Derian, *Virtuous War: Mapping the Military–Industrial–Media–Entertainment Network*, Boulder, CO: Westview Press, 2001; Michael Ignatieff, *Virtual War: Kosovo and Beyond*, Toronto: Viking Books, 2000; Chris Hables Gray, *Postmodern War: The New Politics of Conflict*, London: Routledge, 1997.
80 Ignatieff, *Virtual War*, p. 191.

References

Angstrom, Jan, 'Towards a Typology of Internal Armed Conflict: Synthesising a Decade of Conceptual Turmoil', *Civil Wars*, 4, 3 (2001), pp. 93–116.
—— and Isabelle Duyvesteyn, 'Evaluating Realist Explanations of Internal Conflict: The Case of Liberia', *Security Studies*, 10, 3 (2001), pp. 187–222.
Beevor, Antony, *Berlin: The Downfall 1945*, New York: Viking, 2002.
—— *Stalingrad*, London: Viking, 1998.
Berdal, Mats and David M. Malone (eds), *Greed and Grievance: Economic Agendas in Civil Wars*, Boulder, CO: Lynne Rienner, 2000.
Berkowitz, Bruce, *The New Face of War: How War Will be Fought in the 21st Century*, New York: The Free Press, 2003.
Biddle, Stephen, 'Afghanistan and the Future of Warfare', *Foreign Affairs*, 82, 2 (2003), pp. 31–46.
—— 'The Past as Prologue: Assessing Theories of Future Warfare', *Security Studies*, 8, 1 (1998), pp. 1–74.
Blainey, Geoffrey, *The Causes of War*, London: Macmillan, 1999.
Booth, Ken and Tim Dunne, 'Worlds in Collision', in Ken Booth and Tim Dunne (eds), *Worlds in Collision: Terror and the Future of Global Order*, London: Palgrave, 2002, pp. 1–23.
Clausewitz, Carl von, *On War*, translated by Michael Howard and Peter Paret, London: Everyman's Library, 1993.
Coker, Christopher, *Humane Warfare: The New Ethics of Postmodern War*, London: Routledge, 2001.
Crenshaw, Martha, 'The Logic of Terrorism: Terrorist Behavior as a Product of Strategic Choice', in Walter Reich (ed.), *Origins of Terrorism: Psychologies, Ideologies, Theologies, States of Mind*, Cambridge: Cambridge University Press, 1990, pp. 7–24.
Creveld, Martin van, 'The Transformation of War Revisited', *Small Wars and Insurgencies*, 13, 2 (2002), pp. 3–15.
—— *The Transformation of War*, New York: The Free Press, 1991.
Davis, Diane E. and Anthony W. Pereira (eds), *Irregular Armed Forces and their Role in Politics and State Formation*, Cambridge: Cambridge University Press, 2003.
Der Derian, James, *Virtuous War: Mapping the Military–Industrial–Media–Entertainment Network*, Boulder, CO: Westview Press, 2001.

Fishel, John T., 'War By Other Means? The Paradigm and its Application to Peace Operations', in John T. Fishel (ed.), *The Savage Wars of Peace: Toward a New Paradigm of Peace Operations*, Boulder, CO: Westview Press, 1998, pp. 3–17.

Gat, Azar, *A History of Military Thought: From the Enlightenment to the Cold War*, Oxford: Oxford University Press, 2001.

Gleditsch, Nils Petter *et al.*, 'Armed Conflict, 1946–2001: A New Dataset', *Journal of Peace Research*, 39, 5 (2002), pp. 615–37.

Gow, James, *The Serbian Project and its Adversaries: A Strategy of War Crimes*, London: Hurst, 2003

Gray, Colin, 'Clausewitz rules, OK? The Future is the Past – with GPS', *Review of International Studies*, 25, special issue (1991), pp. 161–82.

Hables Gray, Chris, *Postmodern War: The New Politics of Conflict*, London: Routledge, 1997.

Harkavy, Robert E. and Stephanie G. Neumann, *Warfare and the Third World*, London: Palgrave, 2001.

Harris, Lee, 'Al Qaeda's Fantasy Ideology', *Policy Review*, No. 114 (2002).

Henderson, Errol A. and J. David Singer, 'New Wars and Rumours of New Wars', *International Interactions*, 28, 2 (2002), pp. 165–90.

Heuser, Beatrice, *Reading Clausewitz*, London: Pimlico, 2002.

Holsti, Kalevi J., 'The Coming Chaos? Armed Conflict in the World's Periphery' in T. V. Paul and John A. Hall (eds), *International Order and the Future of World Politics*, Cambridge: Cambridge University Press, 1999, pp. 283–310.

—— *War, the State, and the State of War*, Cambridge: Cambridge University Press, 1996.

Honig, Jan Willem and Norbert Both, *Srebrenica: Record of a War Crime*, London: Penguin, 1995.

Howard, Michael, *The Causes of Wars*, London: Unwin, 1983.

Huntington, Samuel, *The Clash of Civilizations and the Remaking of World Order*, New York: Simon & Schuster, 1996.

Ignatieff, Michael, *Virtual War: Kosovo and Beyond*, London: Chatto and Windus, 2000.

Kaldor, Mary, *New and Old Wars: Organized Violence in a Global Era*, Cambridge: Polity Press, 1999.

Kalyvas, Stathis N., ' "New" and "Old" Civil Wars. A Valid Distinction?', *World Politics*, 54, 1 (2001), pp. 99–118.

Kaplan, Robert D., *The Coming Anarchy: Shattering the Dreams of the Post Cold War*, New York: Random House, 2000.

Kaufmann, Chaim D., 'Interventions in Ethnic and Ideological Civil Wars: Why One Can Be Done But the Other Can't,' *Security Studies*, 6, 1 (1996), pp. 62–103.

Keegan, John, *History of Warfare*, London: Pimlico, 1993.

Keen, David, 'Incentives and Disincentives for Violence', in Mats Berdal and David Malone (eds), *Greed and Grievance: Economic Agendas in Civil Wars*, Boulder, CO: Lynne Rienner, 2000, pp. 19–41.

—— *The Economic Functions of Civil Wars*, Adelphi Paper No. 320, New York: International Institute of Strategic Studies, 1998.

Liddell Hart, Basil H., 'Foreword' in Mao Tse Tung and Che Guevara, *Guerrilla Warfare*, London: Cassell, 1962.

Mao Tse-tung, *On Guerrilla Warfare*, tr. Samuel Griffiths, New York: Praeger, 1965.

Maoz, Zeev and Azar Gat (eds), *War in a Changing World*, Ann Arbor, MI: University of Michigan Press, 2001.

Manwaring, Max, *Internal Wars: Rethinking Problem and Response*, Carlisle, PA: Strategic Studies Institute, 2001.

Marshall, Monty, 'Systems at Risk: Violence, Diffusion, and Disintegration in the Middle East', in David Carment and Patrick James (eds), *Wars in the Midst of Peace: The International Politics of Ethnic Conflict*, Pittsburgh: University of Pittsburgh Press, 1997, pp. 82–115.

Maynard, Kimberly A., *Healing Communities in Conflict: International Assistance in Complex Emergencies*, New York: Columbia University Press, 1999.

McInnes, Colin, *Spectator-Sport War: The West and Contemporary Conflict*, Boulder, CO: Lynne Rienner, 2002.

Mockaitis, Thomas R., 'From Counter-Insurgency to Peace Enforcement: New Names for Old Games?', in Erwin A. Schmidl (ed.), *Peace Operations: Between War and Peace*, London: Frank Cass, 2000, pp. 40–57.

Møller, Bjørn, 'Faces of War', in Håkan Wiberg and Christian P. Scherrer (eds), *Ethnicity and Intra-State Conflict: Types, Causes and Peace Strategies*, Aldershot: Ashgate, 1999, pp. 15–34.

Mueller, John, 'The Banality of Ethnic War: Yugoslavia and Rwanda', *International Security*, 25, 1 (2001), p. 42–70.

Münkler, Herfried, *Die neuen Kriege*, Rowohlt, 2002.

Owens, William A. (with Ed Offley), *Lifting the Fog of War*, New York: Farrar, Straus and Giroux, 2000.

Posen, Barry, 'The Security Dilemma and Ethnic Conflict', in Michael E. Brown (ed.), *Ethnic Conflict and International Security*, Princeton, NJ: Princeton University Press, 1993, pp. 103–24.

Post, Jerrold M., 'Terrorist Psycho-Logic: Terrorist Behavior as a Product of Psychological Forces', in Walter Reich (ed.), *Origins of Terrorism: Psychologies, Ideologies, Theologies, States of Mind*, Cambridge: Cambridge University Press, 1990, pp. 25–40.

Prunier, Gérard, *The Rwanda Crisis*, London: Hurst, 1998.

Reid Sarkees, Meredith, Frank Whelon Wayman, and J. David Singer, 'Inter-State, Intra-State, and Extra-State Wars: A Comprehensive Look at Their Distribution over Time, 1816–1997', *International Studies Quarterly*, 47, 1 (2003), pp. 49–70.

Rotberg, Robert I. (ed.), *State Failure and State Weakness in a Time of Terror*, Washington DC: Brookings, 2003.

Rule, James B., *Theories of Civil Violence*, Berkeley: University of California Press, 1998.

Shaw, Martin, *War and Genocide: Organized Killing in Modern Society*, Cambridge: Polity Press, 2003.

Sloan, Elinor C., *The Revolution in Military Affairs: Implications for Canada and NATO*, Montreal: McGill's, 2002.

Smith, M. L. R., 'Guerrillas in the Mist: Reassessing Strategy and Low Intensity Warfare', *Review of International Studies*, 29, 1 (2003), pp. 19–37.

Snow, Donald M., *Distant Thunder: Patterns of Conflict in the Developing World*, 2nd edn, London: M. E. Sharpe, 1997.

—— *Uncivil Wars: International Security and the New Internal Conflicts*, Boulder, CO: Lynne Rienner, 1996.

Taylor, Max and John Horgan, 'Future Developments of Political Terrorism in Europe', *Terrorism and Political Violence*, 11, 4 (1999), pp. 83–93.

Toffler, Alvin and Heidi Toffler, *War and Anti-War: Survival at the Dawn of the 21st Century*, London: Little & Brown, 1994.

Wilkinson, Philip, 'The Changing Nature of War: New Wine in Old Bottles – A New Paradigm or Paradigm Shift?', *The Royal Swedish Academy of War Sciences: Proceedings and Journal*, 207, 1 (2003), pp. 25–35.

Villacres, Edward J. and Christopher Bassford, 'Reclaiming the Clausewitzian Trinity', *Parameters*, 25, 3 (1995), pp. 9–19.

Yarborough, William P., 'Counterinsurgency: The US Role – Past, Present, and Future', in Richard D. Schultz *et al.* (eds), *Guerrilla Warfare and Counterinsurgency*, Lexington, MA: Lexington Books, 1998.

2

STRATEGY IN AN AGE OF 'LOW-INTENSITY' WARFARE

Why Clausewitz is still more relevant than his critics

M. L. R. Smith

What are we doing about guerrilla warfare?

John F. Kennedy[1]

. . . the consequences of guerrilla war are a study area in which the assertions of ideologists and advocates serve as substitutes for effective analysis of realities and limitations.

Morris Janowitz[2]

War is more than a true chameleon that slightly adapts its characteristics to the given case.

Carl von Clausewitz[3]

Introduction: a phenomenon in search of a category

Interest in ideas of so-called low-intensity conflict, especially issues connected with 'international terrorism', has surged in the post '9/11' era, raising consciousness of the threats posed by violent non-state actors. In the decade prior to September 11 2001, awareness of low-intensity conflict was somewhat less acute but of growing curiosity in academic circles. An indication of this increasing analytical interest in the immediate post Cold War era generally was the development of the notion of 'new war'.[4] Prompted by the wars of dissolution in the territories of the former Yugoslavia and former Soviet Union during the early 1990s, 'new war', it was posited, bred an assertive identity politics based on ethnicity and religious fundamentalism that possessed the capacity to generate publicity, raise money and purchase arms in order to spread terror and instability.[5]

Despite the pre September 11 prognoses for the growth of the new war,[6] there was, of course, nothing intrinsically new in violent non-state insurgent challenges, either as a phenomenon or as an object of study. Over the years we have become familiar with many terms describing low-intensity conflict. Guerrilla warfare, insurgency and terrorism are well established in the popular lexicon. The number of different terms continued to expand in the immediate post Cold War period with the addition of 'new war' synonyms such as 'complex emergencies', 'intra-state war' and 'ethnic conflict'. Many of these descriptions are often used interchangeably with one another. Of itself this betrays a large element of definitional confusion. Moreover, a number of the apostles of the new war thesis and its variations have set themselves against what they see as the outdated and damaging legacy of Clausewitzian thinking about warfare that had, so it was claimed, left armed forces and their governments ill-prepared to comprehend an ostensibly new age of low-intensity conflict. The concern of this study, therefore, is with exploring the analytical complexities surrounding ideas of low-intensity warfare. The core of the argument is that we need to think more carefully about the way we use descriptions like 'low-intensity conflict', 'terrorism' and 'guerrilla warfare'. It is necessary to ask ourselves whether these terms really do aid our comprehension of the source and direction of the varied non-state threats and challenges at work in the contemporary international system. This analysis concludes that the conceptual lenses provided by Clausewitzian thought, as set out in his major work *On War*, still provides the best way to appreciate – and in fact the only way to properly understand – the nature of war phenomena that we often carelessly subsume under the rubric of low-intensity conflict.

The elusive guerrilla

The profusion of different terms denoting the phenomenon of low-intensity conflict is symptomatic of the difficulty in trying to identify a particular category of war imbued with its own distinct characteristics. The resulting confusion in definitions and the occlusion of different terms and meanings has been noted by analysts in the past.[7] Much of the literature on guerrilla war and low-intensity conflict reveals how definitional confusion and analytical ambiguity befuddles the best of minds. Rarely will works in the field offer a precise definition of guerrilla warfare (or its many variants). More often, it is declared to be a style of warfare that has been around for a very long time, which it is possible to trace from pre-biblical times to the present.[8] The concept of guerrilla war is, in other words, mostly located in a tradition, rather than a definition.[9] The inference being: we cannot define guerrilla warfare properly, but we know what it is when we see it.

To overcome irritating semantic details it is very tempting to assume that the phenomenon one is looking for is empirically obvious. However, if one cannot define and articulate precisely the object of one's inquiry, then plainly the effort to describe the essence of a particular kind of strategic practice is likely to be flawed. The problem is that by locating guerrilla warfare in a tradition, rather than pinning down the idea explicitly as a definition, writers are inviting audiences to accept a series of implicit assumptions that are not always watertight. There are four main examples of these intellectual sleights of hand.

First, implicit in a lot of writing is that guerrilla warfare, low-intensity conflict, terrorism and the like, is about a weaker side confronting a more powerful adversary.[10] The weaker combatant tries to play the situation to its advantage by employing guerrilla or terrorist methods to overcome the superior resources ranged against it. Superficially this seems a reasonable generalisation. But in no war can there ever be exact parity between combatants. One side will always be, or appear to be, physically weaker than the other. All strategies are to a greater degree about maximising strengths and minimising weaknesses.

Second, it is often asserted that guerrilla warfare is all about non-state groups fighting the existing authority of the state. This is a common assumption but easily exposed. In the Vietnam War, often seen as an archetypal guerrilla conflict, a fully-fledged state – North Vietnam – sponsored a guerrilla insurgency against the South Vietnamese state, the main backer of which was the United States. The involvement of non-state organisations is not a prerequisite for guerrilla war/low-intensity conflict to occur.

Third, one cannot assume that guerrilla warfare necessarily denotes, or is an overriding characteristic of, intra-state war.[11] Arguably, only in a minority of cases are civil wars dominated by guerrilla conflict. One only has to think of the American Civil War, the English Civil War, or even the Chinese Civil War, from which much guerrilla theorisation evolved, where pitched battles were either the norm or the most decisive element, in order to defeat this generalisation.

Finally, in contrast to much of the literature on the subject, one cannot say that guerrilla war is all about hit and run tactics. Ambushes, sabotage operations, raids behind enemy lines, the use of special forces, and so on are regular features of what we call 'normal war'.[12]

The central point is that what we call guerrilla operations is a form of fighting – a set of tactics – that can be employed by any belligerent in any type of war.[13] It is a mistake to believe that the use of guerrilla methods connotes a weapon of the weak and the presence of non-state actors operating in conditions of civil war. Yet time and again writers continually allude to examples of conflict throughout history claiming to identify the guerrilla phenomenon but without distinguishing what exactly that phenomenon is. Analysts have pointed to the ambiguities inherent in the concept of low-intensity warfare,[14] but it is necessary to pursue these doubts to the logical conclusion: that if the object one is trying to categorise defies categorisation, then does it actually exist as an empirical reality?

It is the unresolved issues of categorisation that result in continuing confusion surrounding guerrilla war/low-intensity conflict, and which in the past has contributed to distorted understandings of particular conflicts, sometimes with damaging implications for policy-making. The remainder of this analysis will illustrate the sources of the persisting intellectual difficulties in theorising about low-intensity warfare, their consequences for strategy and policy-making, and how they might be addressed in the future through the utilisation of Clausewitzian logic and methodology. Using strategic theory to examine the notion of guerrilla war, this argument will suggest that while the guerrilla method may exist as a tactic within war, it does not constitute a proper category of warfare in itself.

In order to analyse these issues it shall first be elaborated how treating guerrilla war as an exceptional category, detached from other traditional notions of modern war, creates an unconvincing explanatory tool that contains the capacity to misapprehend certain forms of conflict. The analysis will then examine how guerrilla warfare came to be seen as a separate, and often mysteriously complex, form of war and how this has damaged strategic studies as a whole. Finally, this analysis will articulate a case for the inclusion of what we call guerrilla warfare/low-intensity conflict within more basic understandings of war as defined by strategic theory and the Clausewitzian paradigm of war.

The grammar of the guerrilla: the analytical redundancy of low-intensity conflict

This section intends to show how our conceptions of low-intensity conflict ideas are often unstable and superficial. Now, it should be first acknowledged that most analytical separations in the social realm are arbitrary distinctions and can easily be unravelled, or 'deconstructed' as the fashionable academic argot would have it. One does not have to be very clever to deconstruct something. Indeed, there is nothing especially intelligent in doing this. Therefore, to be clear, this argument does not advocate that attempts at categorisation in the social sphere are inherently fruitless and cannot provide useful guidelines for policy and planning purposes. Nor is it the intention to deride those – in the armed forces, for example – who for valid operational reasons have sought to incorporate concepts of low-intensity war fighting into their doctrines and procedures, no matter how artificial they may be in pure intellectual terms. What is suggested here, however, is that the idea of low-intensity warfare is bound by sufficient levels of imprecision that render its usage as a category of warfare unsustainable. This is illustrated below by highlighting three common terms that are used to describe what are often conceived, erroneously as it shall be argued, as guerrilla-type activities.

Low-intensity conflict

On the surface low-intensity conflict appears to be one of the more satisfactory descriptions because it is nebulous enough to capture various

31

forms of violence that do not necessarily fit into the stereotype of non-state actors pursuing hit and run military operations. Thus, the United States Joint Chiefs of Staff defined low-intensity conflict in the following way:

> Political-military confrontation between contending states or groups below conventional war and above the routine, peaceful competition among states. It frequently involves protracted struggles of competing principles and ideologies. Low intensity conflict ranges from subversion to the use of armed forces.[15]

The generality of this term is, of course, its principal analytical weakness. The American writer on military affairs, Harry Summers, criticised the Joint Chiefs' conception of low-intensity warfare. It was, he contended, not a definition, but merely 'a description masquerading as an explanation',[16] being so imprecise to be capable of encompassing almost any level of military campaigning. According to one US Army Major, Mitchell M. Zais, cited by Summers, 'Even the massive commitment of US forces in the Vietnamese war could be characterized as low intensity conflict'.[17]

The vagueness of the term prefaces more awkward questions, such as how does one actually quantify a low-intensity conflict? If one can include the US intervention in South Vietnam as an example, as Zais indicates it could be under the definition of the Joint Chiefs of Staff, then it would be interesting to ask an American combat veteran whether he thought he was involved in a 'low-intensity war'? For example, there is an often-quoted belief that the average US combat soldier in Vietnam was exposed to hostile fire every single day of their tour of duty, which would seem to register a much higher level of intensity than even World Wars I and II. Such comparisons are extremely difficult to verify and, indeed, may actually be complete myths.[18] However, from the many studies of Post Traumatic Stress Disorder conducted after the Vietnam war, we know that from the point of view of the average combatant, any war, regardless of how small it may seem to others, can be an overpowering experience.[19] A study of psychological trauma among Hawaiian veterans of the Vietnam war poignantly makes the case.

> More than one out of every two Native Hawaiian veterans experienced war-related trauma in Vietnam. The war traumas included being under fire on helicopters, cargo and reconnaissance aircraft, patrol boats, navy ships, or cargo and transport trucks; being on frequent or prolonged combat missions in enemy territory (including Cambodia and Laos); and encountering ambushes and firefights. Traumas also included being attacked by sappers, snipers, artillery, or rockets; witnessing death and terrible harm to their own or others' bodies; and performing very hazardous duties as walking point,

radio operators, medics, scouts, tunnel rats, perimeter sentries, long range patrollers, or door gunners.[20]

All this in a 'low-intensity' conflict. The point is simply that how one classifies the intensity of individual wars is highly observer-orientated. One can pose analogous questions to those who were exposed to other supposedly low-intensity conflicts from Northern Ireland to Bosnia.[21] In most cases it is unlikely that those who had involvement in such conflicts would necessarily characterise their experience as 'low-intensity'. Even if one tries to quantify low-intensity warfare by calculating the relative attrition of resources, this still does not get us very far. It is still subjective. The United States' involvement in Vietnam might be considered on one set of calculations to constitute a limited, low-intensity commitment by the Americans themselves, but for much of the Vietnamese population the conflict constituted a massive deluge.[22] So, how does one objectively distinguish between high- and low-intensity war? The answer is: one cannot.

Political violence

In scholarly writings the expression 'political violence' has been in regular usage to denote anything from civil disorder to large-scale insurgencies. But if one reflects upon this term from the vantage point of strategic theory, it is descriptively redundant. All war arises from political circumstances: the continuation of politics by other means. 'Policy', as Carl von Clausewitz stated, 'will permeate all military operations and in so far as their violent nature will admit, it will have a continuous influence on them.'[23] The phrase 'political violence' is therefore a truism. There can be no such thing as apolitical violence. Spontaneous outbreaks of motiveless violence may exist only in certain forms of psychopathology (though since the 1960s, when definitions of mental health came under scrutiny, even this can be challenged). All violence will be carried out with some goal or rationale in mind. It may not be ideologically inspired in a traditional left–right sense but there will always be a reason.[24] To adapt Colin Gray's phrase: all violence is political but some forms of violence are more politicised than others.[25] As a result, the phrase 'political violence' provides no clarity into the use of armed force of any kind, low intensity or otherwise.

To elaborate this point further, there will be those who will insist on misinterpreting the claim that all violence can, in theoretical terms, be seen as politicised (that is, undertaken to attain an objective). Invariably, and without solid foundation, it will be asserted that differentiations can be made between politically orientated violence and, say, 'criminal' violence. The implicit assumption is that the idea of politics relates only to the ordering of government and national affairs, and that any violent activity that falls outside this category cannot be looked upon as politically instrumental. Straight away we can perhaps discern the potential for incoherence in such artificial distinctions. In the first instance, who defines what is criminal may be a deeply political act itself. Seeing politics only in terms of governance contains the possibility of interpreting all violent actions by non-state entities as devoid of political meaning and therefore 'criminal' in nature. Indeed, many states that have confronted insurgent challenges in the past have sought to characterise their opponents as criminal. The British government, for instance, embarked on an explicit policy of 'criminalisation' of the Irish Republican Army (IRA) in the mid 1970s with the intention of highlighting the illegitimacy of its campaign.[26] Now, the activities of the IRA, and similar organisations that employ violence in ostensibly democratic societies, may well rightly be regarded as illegitimate but they are not any *less political* for it.

In order to qualify the violence of non-state actors as political, critics might argue that notions of politics and governance also embrace the desire by sub-state actors to affect the composition of society, as opposed to, say, violence committed in the act of burglary for the purposes of obtaining pecuniary advantage. But, of course, this is an equally defective understanding and leads to further problems. The goals of war and politics need not necessarily be about affecting the conditions of society. Indeed, crude, self-interested economic aggrandisement has been an object of warfare for centuries. Further, certain political theories of a Marxist provenance would no doubt hold that pecuniary crime, and any violence associated with it, is in fact the product of political conditions arising out of material inequality. Hence, trying to insert all kinds of arbitrary caveats about the essence of what violence is leads to confusion. Under the tenets of strategic theory, *all* violence is rationally purposive to achieve certain goals, be it the breaking and entry for the purposes of selfish acquisition through theft of a lone burglar or the waging of war among states with mass armies over contested ideologies.

In stating that all acts of violence are rationally instrumental – implemented for a reason – may give rise to another erroneous assumption. Some might allege that this stands for a relativistic position that views all acts of violence as morally equivalent to each other, no matter what the methods or the goals they serve. This is not so. Whose violence is morally acceptable, and whose should be properly condemned, is a matter of ethical debate and judgement. But this is a separate philosophical issue from trying to deduce the innate characteristics of violent conduct. The strategic approach tries to describe the inherent characteristics of goal-orientated action, including the use of physical force. A moral philosopher, on the other hand, tries to discern whose actions may be considered just or unjust. But trying to dissolve two different disciplinary questions such as these into one is to commit what philosophers of language call a 'category mistake',[27] something which many analysts of low-intensity war do time and again. For the strategic theorist at least (who attempts to evaluate the correlation of ends and means), the attempt to separate out what constitutes rationally purposive violence from irrational or unjust violence is a meaningless intellectual exercise. It is a diversion and is to miss the theoretical point being advanced, namely, that strategy and policy are universal ideas. The understanding that 'policy', to cite a conventional dictionary definition, involves 'a planned line of conduct in the light of which individual decisions are made and coordination achieved' applies to all walks of life.[28] It applies to individuals as much as the collective.

For a final act of clarification we can turn to Clausewitz's phraseology, which is instructive. In stating that 'war is a continuation of political intercourse, carried on with other means',[29] he also asserted that the intrinsic action in war – the deed of violence itself – *is an act of force to compel the enemy to do our will*' (emphasis in original).[30] What 'our will' actually represents is entirely open and is not circumscribed in Clausewitzian theory by capricious divisions into what constitutes political goals and what does not. The aim of war is to fulfil one's objectives. Politics is the act of seeking an objective: 'to do our will'. It does not intrinsically matter what that objective is. Strategy is thus the endeavour to relate means to ends. And in that sense, all violence can be seen as purposive. It is done for a reason. It is rationally instrumental to achieve an end. In its theoretical essence, then, all violence, to some degree can be construed as political in nature.

Terrorism

Most of us associate the word terrorism with a particular form of insurgent activity, usually signifying indiscriminate acts of violence against civilians, and often, if not exclusively, practised by sub-state actors. In fact, from a strategic theory perspective, terrorism is one of the least problematic actions to describe. Simply, terrorism can be defined as the use of violence to create fear for political ends. As a tactic it can be employed by state or non-state actors alike, and is not necessarily indiscriminate in that attacks are often chosen for the political and psychological effect they will engender rather than their actual capacity for physical destruction.[31] This is not to say that the use of terrorist tactics cannot also be hugely destructive, as of course was graphically demonstrated by the loss of 3,000 lives in the September 11 attacks. Likewise, it can be plausibly maintained that the counter-city targeting strategies practised by Allied aerial bombing in World War II, which carried an explicit rationale to shatter enemy morale, would also constitute the terroristic use of violence under this definition.

However, the inclusive and objective understanding of terrorism within strategic analysis has largely been undermined by mixing up terrorism as a perfectly good description of a particular tactic – using violence to instil fear for political ends – with a moral judgement.[32] Again, this is a classic category mistake. Frequently, commentators have sought to use terrorism as a pejorative term to stigmatise an actor whose goals or actions they disagree with. Branding someone a 'terrorist' and the bloodcurdling imagery this may conjure in the popular mind, it is hoped, will act as a weapon of condemnation[33] (regardless of whether or not the political actor concerned is really engaged in a campaign of instilling fear into his target). Similarly, those who do practice terrorism will almost always prefer to be called guerrillas or revolutionaries, because this denotes agents of social reform and justice.[34]

At the same time, more semantic atrocities are committed by others who have employed the term to exert a moral relativism towards all forms of violence by proclaiming the meaningless slogan 'one man's terrorist is another man's freedom fighter'. Logically you can actually be both. For example, there is no doubt that in strategic terms the *Front de Libération Nationale* (FLN) which fought against the French occupation of Algeria between 1954 and 1962 were practitioners of terrorism, and therefore by implication could be described as terrorists. They planted bombs in cafés frequented by *colon* teenagers and explicitly set out to terrorise people, that is, to spread fear among the French settler community and other more moderate nationalist groups.[35] Equally, by any moral calculus (which we must remember is a separate intellectual judgement) few are likely to dispute that the FLN's quest for Algerian independence against the often highly repressive French colonial regime would put them in the category of 'freedom fighters'.

Once a descriptive term becomes wrapped up with judgemental connotations then any hope for an effective meaning has been lost.[36] The conflation of two entirely different intellectual questions – a category mistake – renders the word next to useless as a term of explanation. The consequence has been that the word terrorism has been misused and endlessly disputed, with over a hundred different definitions of terrorism being advanced.[37] The resulting confusion is that terrorism is employed glibly as an abstract noun, often as a rhetorical flourish, as the phrase 'war on terrorism' perhaps amply demonstrates. In strategic terms, terrorism is a tactic in war. You cannot have a war against a tactic. Literally speaking, a war against terrorism has no more intrinsic meaning than a war against war, or a war against poverty in that it defines no specific threat, does not identify a precise enemy and thus defines no realisable ends.[38]

The dangers of de-contextualisation

The reason for expounding upon these three common terms is not only to reveal their shortcomings as descriptive tools, but also, taken together, to indicate how unstable they are – along with the panoply of similar terms – as a basis for analytical inquiry and policy formulation.

Most seriously, the attempt to identify and describe the alleged incidence of low-intensity warfare leads the study of certain wars to become de-contextualised. Trying to connect a diverse range of conflicts and political actors purely on the basis of their tactical similarity provides a poor, even non-existent, foundation upon which to explicate a particular military phenomenon. It is like proclaiming that World War II, the Arab–Israeli Six Day War in 1967 and the Indo–Pakistan War of 1971 were all directly comparable because the belligerents at some stage used tanks and machine guns. The comparison is bland and futile. Yet, linking not necessarily linkable wars as if this was capable of offering insight, is exactly what descriptions of low-intensity conflict in its various guises has, over the years, tried to do.[39] Rather than treat the practitioners of armed force, and the conflicts of which they are a part, as uniquely individual objects of study, they are instead drawn together under the rubric of low-intensity conflict and regarded as in some way analogous. Disparate examples of conflict are thereby disconnected from their historical and political settings by the attempt to make theoretical generalisations primarily on the grounds of their *modus operandi*.[40]

The operational and policy-making implications of this approach can be harmful. The consequence of focusing on tactical modality as the principal defining element of low-intensity conflict, can lead, and has in the past led, to an obsessive concern for developing counter-measures, sometimes to the detriment of comprehending the long-term drivers of a conflict. Such a concern is, of course, understandable, reflecting as it does public policy imperatives to control and eliminate perceived dangers whatever their apparent tactical manifestation, be they 'wars of national liberation' or the current-day scourge of 'international terrorism'. As a rule, the general population is unlikely to be impressed with a convoluted discourse on the nature of 'the problem' and will expect those charged with upholding public safety to afford protection from the clear dangers in the present, whatever the difficulties of turning theory into practice. That said, there is a legitimate intellectual problem to be debated in the academic arena, which is, if the phenomenon one is meant to be countering is itself ambiguous and contestable, then both the thinking and operational methods designed to combat it are likely to be faulty.

It is often very attractive for politicians and military practitioners to assume that general operational solutions can be devised against ethereal notions such as terrorism or low-intensity conflict. The resulting potential for tactical counter-measures to develop into a rigid creed is, therefore, profound. This can be seen, for instance, in the rise of 'counter-insurgency' theory in the United States during the early 1960s. The belief, real enough in many cases, that the Western world was facing a global challenge from communism led policy-makers, particularly in the United States, to equate all forms of anti-Western insurgency with 'guerrilla warfare', resulting in the idea that 'guerrilla warfare' was the problem and that counter-guerrilla (that is, counter-insurgency) doctrine, was the 'solution'. This was yet another category mistake, and was encapsulated in President Kennedy's exhortation contained at the top of this chapter: 'What are we doing about guerrilla warfare?' Semantically speaking, of course, you cannot do anything about 'guerrilla warfare'. The practical effect, though, was as Summers observed:

'Counterinsurgency became not so much the [US] Army's doctrine as the Army's dogma, and stultified military strategic thinking for the next decade' because of the prevailing 'myth' that guerrilla wars 'were something unique in the annals of warfare'.[41]

Summers goes on to argue in another publication that the notion of 'low-intensity conflict' is potentially hazardous for policy-making because it 'obscures the nature of the task and obfuscates what needs to be done'.[42] It possesses the capacity to insulate politicians, military planners and the wider public from the implications of certain military challenges because they are deemed to be low-intensity, therefore of low importance and thus not worth confronting with serious intent.[43] To an extent, such a claim is possibly exaggerated since so-called low-intensity campaigns like Vietnam were, of course, tolerated by both US policy-makers and public at vast cost for many years before they finally got sick of the war from the late 1960s. Still, one does not have to travel with the argument all the way to recognise the validity of Summers' general point, that bracketing a range of politico-military phenomena under the heading of low-intensity conflict is not conducive to understanding the manifold complexity of different conflicts and their implications for policy-making. As a consequence, it is not an effective classification. It is defeated by its very inclusiveness.

The conflict with Clausewitz

The very fact that what we call low-intensity conflict has been seen as a unique form of war gives rise to the subsequent problems in definition and analysis. The principal reason that it is pigeon-holed in this way is because many commentators insist on treating what they conceive as low-intensity warfare as something that resides outside a traditional understanding of war. This is most clearly reflected in the expressions 'unconventional' or 'irregular' warfare. Understandings of conventional war postulate the notion of two more or less equally matched belligerents deploying highly organised armed forces in face-to-face battle, as opposed to the 'unconventional' image of a gaggle of rebels pursuing hit-and-run tactics. In particular, guerrilla combatants, and specifically the conflicts in which they partake, are felt to exist beyond the Clausewitzian paradigm,[44] where war is not regarded as a rational instrument of policy but as the product of primordial urges that are entirely resistant to 'conventional' forms of military coercion.[45] In John Keegan's view, for example, the wars that broke out in the Balkans and Transcaucasia in the 1990s were 'ancient in origin' and would be, he claimed, familiar to anthropologists as examples of 'primitive war'. Such conflicts, which it is asserted have often been characterised by guerrilla fighting and paramilitary methods, 'are fed by passions and rancours that do not yield to rational measures of persuasion or control: they are apolitical to a degree for which Clausewitz made little allowance'.[46]

Indeed, the outbreak of seemingly intractable 'ethnic conflicts' during the early years of the post Cold War era gave a considerable boost to the idea of low-intensity conflict as a singular category of war. Analysts stepped forward to denounce the influence of Clausewitz and all his works for allegedly deluding military establishments the world over into preparing for 'conventional' inter-state wars, thus leaving them ill-equipped to comprehend and deal with the vast array of low-intensity conflicts that were bursting forth in places as far afield as Bosnia and Rwanda.[47] The case against Clausewitz is that he failed to recognise that conflict had moved beyond state-based warfare.[48] So outmoded and perplexing do Clausewitz's writings now appear that some commentators like Bruce Fleming, a professor of English at the US Naval Academy, Annapolis – following the thinking of literary theorist Hayden White[49] – proposes 'that *On War* be taught as poetry, even in the staff colleges'.[50] Equally provocatively, Martin van Creveld has argued: 'If any part of our intellectual baggage deserves to be thrown overboard, surely it is . . . the Clausewitzian definition of war'.[51]

To say that military establishments were unprepared for low-intensity challenges is a simplistic generalisation,[52] but whether they were or not is a different issue from whether any lack of preparation stemmed from the malign influence of Clausewitzian thought. Of course, it is easy to get into obscure theological discussions about what Clausewitz said and meant. Like any other interesting philosopher Clausewitz's writings contain inconsistencies that render them susceptible to deep and thoughtful critique as those like Azar Gat have shown.[53] However, this is different from the often superficial readings of Clausewitz that subscribe to him positions that no careful or fair-minded evaluation can sustain. As scholars like Christopher Bassford have demonstrated, many of the denunciations of Clausewitz in recent years are based on impressionistic and seriously flawed readings of his work.[54] For example, one of the principal advocates of the new war hypothesis and Clausewitz antagonist, Mary Kaldor, in her 1999 book *New and Old War* not only misquotes Clausewitz, but manages to misunderstand one of his most crucial observations about war and politics. In maintaining that war was an instrument of politics Clausewitz argued that if war 'were a complete, untrammelled, absolute manifestation of violence, war would of its own independent will usurp the place of policy the moment policy has brought it into being; it would then drive policy out of office and rule by the laws of its own nature'.[55] In this respect, he contended that war's 'grammar, may indeed be it's own, but not its logic'.[56] That is, war may be fought within its own terms encompassing particular sets of tactics and battles, etc. (the grammar of war) but war can never be waged for its own sake: it thus has no innate logic. War is always governed by the 'logic' of politics. Yet Kaldor maintains, without citation, that the Clausewitzian conception of war 'entails the regulation of certain types of social relationship and has its own particular logic',[57] which is precisely what he was not saying. Claiming that war contains its own self-regulating logic reduces the entire Clausewitzian construct of war (and by implication Kaldor's own thesis about 'old war') to absurdity.

In misrepresenting Clausewitzian thinking on war at such a basic level, writers reveal their own mystification at the notion of low-intensity conflict. Kaldor, for one, goes on to criticise Clausewitzian thinking for being unable to contend with examples of 'new war' as embodied by ethnic conflict.[58] At the same time, she advances the contention that ethnic conflict can be manufactured to serve political ends,[59] which is, of course, specifically what Clausewitzian ideas concerning the instrumental rationality of force suggest in the first place.[60] This leads us to ask how such confusions have arisen and in particular how, and why, so-called examples of low-intensity conflict came to be seen mistakenly as a separate category of war.

The orphaned child of strategy

How the image of guerrilla warfare came to be perceived, and further compartmentalised, as a distinctive concept of war is a story bound up with the rise, and catastrophic fall, of counter-insurgency doctrine in the 1960s. In the aftermath of World War II and coinciding with the era of the de-colonisation of the European empires, an entirely new facet of warfare was believed to be emerging, that of 'revolutionary war', sometimes also referred to as 'wars of national liberation'. Revolutionary war encompassed the idea that guerrilla tactics could be fused with an overt propaganda campaign and employed by sub-state actors to win over the masses through political agitation, while simultaneously eating away at the moral and physical authority of the state through violence, leading to the eventual overthrow of the government.

The victory of the communist forces in China in 1949 led by Mao Tse-tung, who proclaimed victory through a strategy of 'protracted people's war',[61] provided the catalyst that gave rise to the idea of revolutionary war. The outbreak of rural insurgencies in places such as Malaya, French Indochina and Latin America, most notably culminating in Fidel Castro's ascent to power in Cuba in 1959, prompted thinkers in the United States and Europe to consider that they were facing a new and prolific form of war aimed at subverting pro-Western regimes and stoked up by the forces of a global communist conspiracy.[62] It is from the era of so-called revolutionary wars that much of the continuing popular imagery about guerrilla warfare persists, imagining bands of peasants with AK47 rifles, sneaking around in jungles or mountains.

The term 'revolutionary war', then, was an analytical response to the fear of communist insurgency during the 1950s and 1960s and, as intimated above, was to lead to the creation of an opposing body of military thought that came to be known as counter-insurgency. There was, however, a tension between counter-insurgency theory and counter-insurgency doctrine as operationalised by the military. Counter-insurgency military doctrines were logical and consistent within their own terms of reference (in other words, and to employ the correct understanding of Clausewitzian theory, they had their own 'grammar') and often met with considerable tactical success on the ground. But two bitterly contested wars, in Algeria and especially in Vietnam, brought this tension to the fore and devastated the reputation of much counter-insurgency thinking, which was to further isolate the study and comprehension of so-called low-intensity wars.

During the Cold War a number of counter-insurgency methods were developed. The British evolved an *ad hoc* counter-insurgent practice based on their tradition of colonial policing.[63] This tradition emphasised civil and military co-ordination, anti-guerrilla interdiction through intelligence operations and, most importantly, a willingness to negotiate limited political compromises with adversary groups from a position of strength or stalemate. It was an approach that met with some success in Malaya, Kenya, Cyprus, and later in Northern Ireland.[64] However, it was in French and American military thinking that counter-insurgency doctrine reached its most formidable expression.

Following its defeat in Indochina by the Vietminh, the French military establishment set about constructing a counter-revolutionary doctrine to explicitly oppose protracted communist insurgencies. Known as *guerre revolutionaire*, the doctrine advocated that, along with the adoption of more sophisticated anti-guerrilla techniques, the French armed forces, and French society as a whole, had to become ideologically motivated to defend the West from subversion in exactly the same manner as they perceived their communist opponents to be in pursuit of their goals.[65] The effect of this doctrine in the war in Algeria was a human and political catastrophe. Despite its effectiveness in purely military terms, the problem was that *guerre revolutionaire* so radicalised sections of the French military that when the politicians in Paris were believed not to be supporting the war against the supposed communist insurgents of the FLN with the necessary vigour, the armed services felt it their duty to make sure they did.[66] This led to political turmoil in France itself, accompanied by a military coup by French forces in Algeria in May 1958, followed later by violent internal subversion by sections of the armed forces, which ended in national humiliation when President Charles de Gaulle decided to grant Algeria independence.

American counter-insurgency, influenced by aspects of French thinking, sprang from a number of sources encompassing features of containment doctrine and limited-war thinking derived from strategic nuclear deterrence theorisation, which posited that the United States should be prepared to show resolve – and thereby uphold general deterrence between both super-powers – by confronting communist-inspired challenges below the nuclear threshold.[67] United States counter-insurgency doctrine also stressed nation-building intended to stabilise pro-American regimes both economically and politically.[68] While reaping some success through the provision of military and police advisers in Latin America, it was, of course, the *dénouement* in Vietnam that scarred American counter-insurgency efforts after it became apparent that the doctrine could not comprehend effectively the nature of the particular enemy the Americans were facing, nor the regime they were trying to support, nor the consequences for the American domestic polity arising from the failure to win quickly.

In retrospect, there were two major interrelated weaknesses in the idea of revolutionary war that ultimately condemned much counter-insurgency theorising. First, there was a conceptual problem: simply, what did one mean by 'revolutionary'? We conceive revolutions to be about change of a radical and dramatic kind. But what is meant by change and how do we measure it? All wars are about change – fighting either to promote or prevent it. So what is particularly revolutionary about 'revolutionary wars'? What added to the definitional problem was that the term 'revolutionary' could also be applied to the methods of fighting, implying that they were themselves unique, a notion embodied in the title of Regis Debray's seminal 1960s text on armed radicalism, *Revolution in the Revolution*.[69] Drawing promiscuously on theories derived from Maoist 'people's war' and Cuban *focoquismo* strategy[70] gave rise to the belief that political power could be won without the extensive use of military force. The false promise of these novel military techniques inspired a generation of political radicals and insurgent-nationalists to challenge state authority from the late 1950s onwards.[71] Given its slippery nature and the occlusion of various meanings, the term 'revolutionary war' ended up as a somewhat arbitrary and politically loaded idea that, among both defenders and protagonists of the status quo alike, tended to denote only those conflicts that involved non-state challenges to pro-Western regimes.

Second, from a counter-revolutionary war perspective such arbitrary understandings sometimes resulted in the selective application, and thus misapplication, of the notion of 'revolutionary war', with ensuing consequences. The bipolar nature of the Cold War and the fear of communism led to a belief that almost any outbreak of localised violence in the 'Third World' was communist-inspired and an example of revolutionary war to be countered, despite the fact that in Algeria, and even South Vietnam, this was not necessarily so. In the case of the United States, its intervention in Vietnam, according to Colin Gray, bore the hallmarks of 'counterinsurgency faddism' that was naïvely captivated by the 'cult of the guerrilla' and the 'aura of Special Forces'.[72] The resulting preoccupation with military technique caused the weakness and corruption of the South Vietnamese state to be overlooked and the nationalist dimension of the conflict to be misunderstood.

In essence, then, there is nothing revolutionary about revolutionary war. Like other low-intensity conflict terminology it was mainly a politically convenient, rather than a strategically accurate, label with which to append certain wars. The failure by analysts to apprehend the complexities that caused internal instabilities in places like South Vietnam meant that incoherent counter-measures were designed to combat an incoherent idea. Few of the leading lights in the US strategic and policy-making community during the 1960s had much to say about how to fight such wars and, in the words of Herman Kahn, 'what they did contribute was often misleading and irrelevant'.[73] Contemporary critics like Colin Gray charged that the influence of civilian academic strategists, seduced by the power of wielding influence over US military policy, were in part responsible for the misguided application of theories of deterrence, escalation and flexible response to the Vietnam context, with correspondingly disastrous results.[74] In the aftermath of the US withdrawal from Indochina, the feeling grew that dealing with low-intensity conflicts was unbearably problematic. It meant having to comprehend the multitude of complex socio-political and psychological factors that informed regional conflicts and drove actors, be they state or non-state, to employ or sponsor violent insurgencies. It contained a dangerous tendency to politicise both military and scholarly practice. It killed off a generation of the best and the brightest.

In analytical terms, as Richard Betts observed, 'Vietnam poisoned the academic well', causing strategic studies to retreat into a nether world that was largely 'ahistorical and technical'.[75] The scholarly focus in the discipline concentrated around narrow, managerial issues of arms control, deterrence and other bureaucratically enclosed matters of national defence policy. Consequently, post Vietnam, most strategic thinking centred on 'Elaborate debates between rival schools of nuclear deterrence and hair-splitting, abstruse exchanges between analysts over the relative merits of competing nuclear weapons systems to maintain the balance of terror'.[76] The language of strategy became further distanced, abstract, clinical, and victimless. Absorbing this technocratic agenda to the full, many strategic analysts and the wider international relations community gained a collective personality disorder, often becoming humourless, solipsistic and self-referential.[77]

Military establishments too – most notably in the United States – reversed their once enthusiastic interest in counter-insurgency doctrines and revolutionary war in order to get back to planning for a 'normal' war on the Central European front. Both in academia and military circles this tendency was fortified by a perception (mistaken though it was), that the incidence of insurgency was declining.[78] By the early 1970s, with the outbreak of separatist violence in Northern Ireland and Spain and ideologically motivated acts of terrorism by off-shoots of the radical student movements of 1968 in states like Italy and West Germany, the nature of the threat appeared to shift to urban-based guerrilla challenges. Policy and analytical responses to this violence were seen to reside in the areas of policing and public order, rather than having military and strategic relevance. Any residual scholarly interest in such matters was cast off into the sub-grouping of terrorist studies, which was treated as a narrow sect, mainly a British, West European and Israeli pastime, possessing next to no relationship with the wider field of strategic studies.[79]

So it was that the study of insurgency became the orphaned child of strategy. Brought into the world as an object of study by the military and scholarly communities in the 1960s, heralded as something novel and, indeed, 'revolutionary', it was then abandoned by its own dysfunctional parents when it became too burdensome. It was left to wander the academic by-ways as a separate category of study – not that many did study it. From then on it was regarded as a thing apart from the academic mainstream of strategic studies, thought of with wariness and suspicion – or preferably something not to be thought about at all.

The impact of the Cold War: the unconventional convention

Isolating insurgency as a separate form of conflict permitted a number of things to happen during the Cold War, which, while convenient for academic strategists, damaged the discipline and undermined the study of warfare as a whole. There is no better illustration of the distorting effects of this belief than in the term that seeks to describe guerrilla challenges as 'unconventional war'. Conventional war is taken to mean classical warfare between states. Yet statistical assessments of warfare indicate that only 18 to 20 per cent of wars since 1945 can be accurately classified as inter-state wars. Holsti's study suggests that over 75 per cent of the 164 cases of warfare identified since the end of the Second World War involved armed conflict within states.[80] Given the relative lack of inter-state war and the proliferation of violent sub-state actors[81] it is clear that insurgency and civil wars constitute the dominant pattern of warfare over the past 50 years. This, it can be contended, represents the norm. It is unconventional warfare that is the convention.

Of course, from the perspective of Western military planning during the Cold War the emphasis on the spectre of a catastrophic force-on-force clash in Central Europe, possibly with nuclear and chemical weapons, was entirely logical. Dealing with a potential survival-level threat mattered far more than the statistical significance of other wars a continent or more away. Nevertheless, without disputing the prudential desire to prepare a proper defence against a formidable adversary in an age of high-tempo combined arms warfare, it is still legitimate to pose the question in the academic realm about the extent to which, by segregating so-called low-intensity war, strategic analysts could rationalise their avoidance of it. By locking onto nuclear and defence policy issues, they could convince themselves that they were dealing with vital concerns of world survival. 'This seemed to be', according to one Cold War analyst, 'where the action was, literally and academically'.[82]

In a way, the use of the description 'conventional war' in strategic studies literature rationalised the orientation of the discipline towards the concentration on the prospects for inter-state conflict.[83] Such wars were described as 'conventional' – not because they were the convention – but because they were seen as 'more important'. But, one might ask, more important to whom? In

44

truth, the capacity for ethnocentrism in strategic thinking was stark, because the focus of the discipline was not, as Betts rightly observed, in 'war *per se*, than in cataclysmic war among great powers, war that can visit not just benighted people far away, but people like us'.[84] Thus, unlike theorists of counter-insurgency, strategists during the Cold War could ponder the improbabilities of general war between the United States and the Soviet Union, safe in the knowledge that there was little prospect that their theories would ever be challenged in practice. At the same time, by holding forth on nuclear deterrence, arms control and East–West diplomacy, analysts could maintain that these were more important issues than the distractions of actual wars going on elsewhere in the world.

When we reflect upon the evolution of the discipline of strategy the underlying motives for the dismissal of so-called low-intensity conflict as a separate, and less significant, category of war reveal themselves clearly. It becomes evident that most strategic analysts have found it difficult to comprehend two fundamental points: (1) that most wars *do not* involve state actors, and (2) that many wars *do not* necessarily threaten national survival. In other words, the deficiency of strategic studies with regard to the study of low-intensity conflict has nothing to do with the supposedly malign influence of Clausewitz and everything to do with the legacy of twentieth-century warfare that culminated in the titanic struggle for survival in World War II. It is this that accounts for the state-orientated, means-addicted, strategic mentality that was ill at ease in comprehending anything that did not encompass the massive clash of organised armed forces.

The military-intellectual legacy of World War II, of course, transferred easily to the era of superpower confrontation during the Cold War. Indeed, in the nuclear age the survival stakes appeared even higher. Ironically, it was for these reasons that for much of the Cold War era Clausewitzian ideas scarcely registered in strategic studies. If ever they were mentioned it was often to repudiate them as dangerously anachronistic.[85] In the early 1970s Senator William Fulbright claimed: 'There is no longer any validity in the Clausewitzian doctrine of "carrying out of policy by other means". Nuclear weapons have rendered it totally obsolete.'[86] This summed up the essence of most Cold War military and strategic thinking during this era, namely, that in reality it was profoundly un-Clausewitzian.[87] It was the dry, apolitical, technocratic obsessions of nuclear deterrence theories, not Clausewitz – as van Creveld, Keegan, Kaldor, and others wrongly maintain – that held sway in the discipline and which blocked out the study of many other issues in the strategic ambit.

The de-strategisation of war

The narrow disposition of strategic studies was also to a large degree a reflection of official military orthodoxy that prevailed in developed states. In the post Vietnam era military establishments, like their scholarly counterparts, felt uncomfortable with notions of guerrilla wars and counter-insurgency. It was with some relief that in the 1970s they could turn their attention back towards what they did best, which was to plan wars they could win. They could justify their demands for bigger budgets and large equipment procurements by locating their efforts on planning for 'conventional war' as necessitating the essential task of upholding deterrence on the central front in Europe.[88] Other more 'limited' military contingencies were distractions from this supreme duty. Douglas Porch encapsulated the evolving military mentality:

> ... after the experience of two World Wars, together with a Cold War stalemate in Europe, most Western armies viewed small wars as missions to be avoided. Most proved unwilling to alter force structure[s] designed for conventional conflict in Europe to face the challenges of unconventional warfare in distant lands. None of these factors made indigenous resistance unbeatable. It simply meant that small wars remained very much a minority interest in military establishments.[89]

In the policy-making realm the shortcomings of this outlook were revealed in the post Cold War era, when it became evident that large segments of military and political thinking could not comprehend how to deal with contingencies that existed below the 'conventional' threshold. As Paul Beaver put it, military planners had inordinate difficulty contending with 'asymmetric warfare' because traditional 'staff college and command school solutions just do not work'.[90] With the outbreak of warfare in the Balkans following the break up of Yugoslavia in the early 1990s, options for peace enforcement were hampered because the major military powers could not contemplate effective intervention policies other than strategies for total destruction and overthrow.[91] All other contingencies below threats to national survival and major national interests were, in effect, de-strategised.[92] The result was to produce both among politicians and military practitioners a hand-wringing fatalism that could barely countenance passive, and ineffective, humanitarian assistance measures, let alone firmer action.[93] These attitudes almost certainly helped prolong the traumatic war of ethnic cleansing in Bosnia[94] and, arguably even more shamefully, entailed complicity in the Rwandan genocide in 1994.[95]

The de-intellectualisation of strategy

In scholastic circles the impact of the Cold War fixation that conceived intricate theorising about war and peace between the superpowers as the only thing that mattered was no less damaging. The effect was to create a strategic studies discipline that was squeamish and even decadent. Ironically, for all the self-absorption in the minutiae of deterrence and defence policy, along with all the other incidentals surrounding potential war between the superpowers, the discipline was never very interested in war itself.[96] Writers were caught up in the hypotheticals of nuclear conflict that snared even supposedly critical thinkers who were prepared to knock the parameters of strategic studies but rarely tried to expand them.[97] The core of this disciplinary groupthink was captured well by Fred Kaplan when he wrote of the 'compelling illusion' of the seemingly endless discourse on nuclear deterrence: 'Even many of those who recognized its pretence and inadequacy willingly fell under its spell. They continued to play the game because [their closed conception of the discipline led them to believe] there was no other.'[98]

Above all, the Cold War conditioned a discipline of strategy that was often content to see its place as a supporting counsellor to an established defence policy agenda. This passive role in the military-intellectual complex prevented analysts from pursuing those avenues down which their academic vocation should have beckoned them. As Halliday noted, 'in terms of shaping the post-war world, guerrilla warfare, in its revolutionary and counter-revolutionary forms, was at least as influential as nuclear weapons: yet it hardly figured in the orthodox curriculum of strategic studies'.[99] Part of the explanation for this imbalance lay in the fact that analysing nuclear deterrence or national defence policy possessed a more quantifiable empirical base. It was easier to count warheads and tanks, or determine throw-weights and yields, than it was to deal with the murky issues of civil–military co-ordination and the struggle for 'hearts and minds'.[100]

As for revolutions, rebellions, civil wars, and other conflicts between the un-great powers during the Cold War, these took place 'somewhere else', usually in a place called the 'Third World'.[101] These multifariously different conflicts were, it seemed, altogether too complicated for strategists to deal with because, as Betts says, 'the relative salience of concerns about political values, as opposed to material power, is usually greater [in such conflicts] than in international wars'.[102] Therefore, despite tyrannising the lives of far more people post 1945 than all of the collective obsessions of strategists in the Cold War, these wars were often considered to be unworthy of individual attention. By lumping them together under the generic title of wars in the Third World, analysts could excuse their ignorance. Mirroring the impact on military practice, scholarly thinking about such wars could be de-intellectualised. Because such conflicts took place in the backwaters they could be neatly packaged and dismissed by a label.

The post Cold War 'discovery' of low-intensity conflict

Most egregiously of all, hiding away the notion of low-intensity conflict during the Cold War enabled international relations analysts to re-discover this apparently novel phenomenon in the post Cold War world, while at the same time excoriating the 'narrow, statist' outlook of the old discipline of strategy in which they once so enthusiastically participated.[103] A naïve sense of wonderment overcame international relations scholars who, no doubt having got out their atlases to look for work, asserted that in the post Cold War era the incidence and importance of internal warfare would 'spill over national boundaries' and thus 'become more frequent'.[104] 'There will be fewer inter-state wars', according to one commentator, 'but no shortage of low-level conflict within states.'[105]

International relations theorists and strategic analysts regarded such observations as shrewdly perceptive. However, an alternative interpretation is that much of the pre September 11 interest in 'intra-state' wars was the product of Cold War displacement. Were the Iron Curtain and the Berlin Wall still standing today it is doubtful whether international relations scholars would have ever developed any real cognisance of such conflicts. The prosaic reality is that there has been no mass appreciation of the level of ethno-nationalist intra-state warfare except in the first decade of the post Cold War in Eastern Europe. For this to inspire exhortations about the appearance of 'new wars' is itself an indication of the Eurocentric mindset of much contemporary security studies. Vicious civil wars sustained by identity politics, supported by diasporas and waged by paramilitary gangs with a sideline in pecuniary crime have rumbled on from one decade to the next.[106] For all practical purposes the end of the Cold War has been meaningless for most of these wars, as any number of continuing violent struggles, including those in the Basque country, Burma, Colombia, Kashmir, Sudan, and Zaire provide testament. The truth is that these wars and numerous others like them have always constituted the predominant form of warfare post 1945[107] and even pre 1945.[108] Such wars *always have* outnumbered inter-state wars. The key intellectual distinction is that this salient fact was ignored in mainstream strategic studies and international relations thinking for much of the Cold War years, in favour of supposedly more important problems.

Those who now advance the proposition that internal wars are of increasing importance often paid little attention themselves to low-intensity war phenomena in the Cold War years. Now, by seeking to reconstitute this false category of war under different headings such as 'new war', 'ethnic war' or 'complex emergencies', writers reveal their own limited grasp of the history of warfare. It is also of relevance to note that the world's most recent manifestation of 'low-intensity conflict', the 'war against terrorism' initiated after September 11 has, with the overthrow of the Taliban regime in Afghanistan and a war in Iraq, so far proven to be anything but internal or low-intensity.

Low-intensity war and Clausewitzian theory

The fact is that all war, be it 'low-intensity' or otherwise, is inherently the same and can therefore be understood, in its entirety, within the Clausewitzian strategic paradigm in which war is an extension of policy, where the act of violence is intended to fulfil our will. The increased notoriety of conflicts involving non-state actors in the current era does not confound Clausewitzian understandings as his critics maintain. As Jan Honig suggests, Clausewitzian notions are 'easily adaptable to forms of warring social organizations that do not form states . . . any community has its leaders, fighters and common people'.[109] What trips up many strategic and international relations analysts when considering wars that involve non-state actors, causing them inaccurately to see them as an altogether different form of conflict, is that while the objective is the same, the calculus in such wars is often different and more complex. In military clashes that take place between manifestly unequal combatants, be they state or non-state in nature, the interactions in war are somewhat more subtle, but they still fall very much within the Clausewitzian ambit.

War is a reactive environment. It is 'a contest between independent wills'.[110] The will of each combatant is generated by its political and social nature, and responds reciprocally to the actions of its opponents. This establishes one of Clausewitz's important observations that 'wars should never be thought of as something autonomous but always as an instrument of policy'. War will always therefore 'vary with the nature of their motives and of the situations which gave rise to them'.[111] The course of a war will be determined in part by the relative power of each combatant, which will influence how they will choose to fight. Thus, a combatant may decide to avoid or delay open battle with its adversary, engage in evasion, sabotage, hit and run operations, in order to maximise its advantage at any particular point in time. The actions and tactics pursued in war will, consequently, affect its direction and duration. As Clausewitz observed, war always 'moves on its own goal with varying speed'.[112] This reflects the infinite diversity of wars throughout history, be they short, sharp wars between states, like the 1982 Falklands War, to 20-year-long internal struggles within states, such as the Chinese Civil War (1927–49).

Clausewitz noted that war is never an isolated act but consists of a series of engagements, which may, therefore, make certain conflicts particularly protracted.[113] This point recognises that real war is not simply about the crude employment of military might but is often a more calculating environment. This understanding is especially pertinent to conflict between materially disproportionate opponents. Certain kinds of combatants, most obviously those that are clearly materially inferior to their opponent, may wish to manipulate the military instrument, not to destroy the enemy's armed forces but to influence enemy behaviour to facilitate the achievement of political goals. The weaker party may not be able to achieve any tangible military objectives, such as occupying territory or annihilating large segments of the enemy's armed forces. Instead, as Clausewitz explained, 'another military objective must be adopted that will serve the political purposes and symbolise it in peace negotiations'.[114] In this regard, a belligerent may feel, for example, that given its relative inferiority *vis-à-vis* its opponent, a campaign of guerrilla attacks or acts of terrorism to demoralise the enemy is a more appropriate course of action. By such means the weaker belligerent will hope to induce enemy compliance under the threat of coercion rather than physical destruction.

When political actors seek intangible, rather than purely physical, outcomes through military action strategic analysis becomes far more intricate because it requires an acute appreciation of the ambiguities and complexities of the socio-political environment in which these conflicts occur. However, as Eliot Cohen has pointed out, a key problem is often that 'democracies handle the ambiguity of such conflicts very poorly indeed'.[115] Steeped in the traditions of mass clashes of survival and informed by imperatives to win quickly, at low cost, to minimise the impact on society at large in order to make the case for war more palatable for electorates, democracies and their supporting counsellors in the military and strategic studies communities are often repelled by the thought of involvement in 'low-intensity conflicts'.[116] 'The aspect they find most worrying about these conflicts', according to Honig, 'is the seemingly irrational motivations of parties which originate in the murky deepest depths of history.'[117] The unwillingness to discern the roots of 'complex wars' of an internally generated provenance leads strategists into the rhetoric of evasion that obscures the fundamental point that all war is essentially the same.

It is the tactics within war that vary, not the inherent nature of war itself. Guerrilla tactics can be practised by any combatant in any dimension. The inability to understand this basic precept leads analysts into confusion and rhetorical inconsistency. To illustrate, it can be contended that the tactics adopted by Fighter Command during the Battle of Britain in the summer of 1940 represented classic aerial 'guerrilla tactics'.[118] Observers noted at the time that British fighters engaged the Luftwaffe bombers but frequently broke off combat when confronted by German fighter aircraft. Initially, 'These tactics', according to the contemporary journalist William Shirer, 'led many a Messerschmitt pilot to complain that the British Spitfire and Hurricane pilots were cowards, that they fled whenever they saw a German fighter'. However, Shirer continued: 'I suspect now the German pilots understand that the British were not being cowardly but merely smart'.[119] The British were simply designing tactics to play to their strengths, limiting their exposure to losses, while inflicting maximum damage on the enemy. Thereby, the British counteracted the German strategy, which attempted to lure large numbers of the Royal Air Force's fighters off the ground to attack bombing formations.[120] This would have enabled the Germans to concentrate their own fighters to wipe out Britain's air defences. While the British were prepared to see their cities being pounded with bombs, they were not willing to risk the destruction of their fighter formations in great air battles.[121] In this way, as Shirer concluded, while 'the British never risked more than a small portion of their available fighters on any one day, they did send up enough to destroy more German bombers than Goering could afford to lose'.[122]

Likewise, in the naval sphere one could point to commerce raiding and especially the use of submarine warfare as examples of guerrilla tactics at sea. As this and the example of the Battle of Britain demonstrate, they involve all the main principles that we associate with guerrilla activity: the dispersal of one's forces, hit-and-run military actions, the prevention of enemy concentration, and the avoidance of open battle or large confrontations. At the time that these particular tactics were unveiled in World Wars I and II they were regarded as novel, 'unconventional', and sometimes, as we have seen, even cowardly. But these tactics were easily assimilated into mainstream understandings of warfare. Few people would call them guerrilla campaigns. Yet when we see such methods employed on the ground by non-state actors we insist on classifying them as 'guerrilla wars', 'low-intensity wars', 'revolutionary wars', or numerous combinations thereof. What these terms merely underline is the arbitrariness, induced by little more than intellectual laxity, which produces false categorisation, often as a means to explain away the essential unwillingness to go through the laborious task of understanding such wars.

Conclusion: war and only war

This assessment has sought to demonstrate that terms like 'guerrilla warfare' and 'low-intensity war' are fundamentally flawed as analytical abstractions. Guerrilla methods do exist as *tactics* within war, but they do not intrinsically constitute a separate category of war. Gradations of so-called low-intensity war exist only as arbitrary distinctions with little coherent meaning. Their usage does not facilitate understanding but rather undermines the attempt to comprehend the manifold complexity of warfare, often because they have been deployed by academic strategists to compartmentalise particular conflicts about which they feel uncomfortable. What we call low-intensity conflict can only be understood fully within Clausewitzian parameters, which embrace the entire spectrum of war.

The idea that the Clausewitzian paradigm is irrelevant to so-called internal war, guerrilla wars, ethnic war, and the rest is also a serious misapprehension. Critics often overlook the fact that shortly before his death Clausewitz was becoming increasingly cognisant of the importance of non-state military actors, as evidenced by the development of his ideas concerning 'the people in arms', which he recognised sprang from the same social and political sources as all warfare.[123] Moreover, those who misleadingly ascribe to him an obsession with the state are often out to push their own questionable theories about surmounting the state as the primary unit of analysis or trying to set themselves up as competing strategic gurus against Clausewitz.[124] Such agendas are wholly unrelated to the effort to understand the nature of warfare in all its hues and a distraction from the main, longer-term, intellectual problems of strategy in its relationship to so-called low-intensity conflict.

What most of us usually have in mind when we employ terms like guerrilla warfare and low-intensity conflict, is war between grossly unequal combatants, where one side (or sometimes both), be it a state or another type of social organisation, will be predisposed towards utilising a particular set of tactics that enables them to optimise their military position. It is this process of reasoning that leads political actors to deploy the means they do in an attempt to attain their ends within the constraints of the environment in which they find themselves that should be of primary interest to the strategic analyst.

All wars are unique to their time and place. They all have distinctive origins and directions. Because they are multifarious they defy categorisation and cannot be reduced and subsumed under labels like guerrilla war or low-intensity conflict. In understanding war, the unjustly maligned figure of Clausewitz stated correctly that one should not mistake the nature of it by 'trying to turn it into something that is alien to its nature'. He continued: 'That is the first of all strategic questions and the most comprehensive.'[125] As Clausewitz above all recognised, the elemental truth is that, call it what you will – new war, ethnic war, guerrilla war, low-intensity war, terrorism, or the war on terrorism – in the end, there is only one meaningful category of war, and that is *war* itself.

Notes

1 Quoted in Roger Hilsman, *To Move a Nation: The Politics of Foreign Policy in the Administration of John F. Kennedy*, New York: Delta, 1967, p. 413.
2 Morris Janowitz, 'Towards a Redefinition of Military Strategy in International Relations', *World Politics*, 26, 4 (1974), p. 478.
3 Carl von Clausewitz, *On War* (trans. and ed.) Michael Howard and Peter Paret, Princeton, NJ: Princeton University Press, 1984, p. 89.
4 Mary Kaldor, *New and Old Wars: Organized Violence in a Global Era*, Stanford: Stanford University Press, 1999, pp. 1–12.
5 See Steven Simon and Daniel Benjamin, 'America and the New Terrorism', *Survival*, 42, 1 (2000), pp. 59–75; Michael Ignatieff, *Blood and Belonging: Journeys into the New Nationalism*, London: BBC/Chatto & Windus, 1993, pp. 1–11; Benjamin Barber, *Jihad vs. MacWorld: How Globalism and Tribalism are Reshaping the World Order*, New York: Ballantine, 1996, Chapters 15 and 19; and Samuel Huntington, *The Clash of Civilizations and the Remaking of World Order*, New York: Simon & Schuster, 1996, pp. 19–29.
6 Steven Metz, 'Insurgency After the Cold War', *Small Wars and Insurgencies*, 5, 1 (1994), pp. 63–4.
7 See for example Andrew Janos, 'Unconventional Warfare: Framework for Analysis', *World Politics*, 15, 4 (1963), pp. 637–8.
8 See for example Richard Clutterbuck, *Guerrillas and Terrorists*, Athens, Ohio: Ohio University Press, 1977, pp. 22–32.

9 Robin Corbett, *Guerrilla Warfare: From 1939 to the Present Day*, London: Guild Publishing, 1986, pp. 10–21.

10 See for example C. E. Callwell, *Small Wars: Their Principles and Practice*, Lincoln, Nebraska: University of Nebraska Press, 1996, pp. 21–2.

11 See John Shy and Thomas Collier, 'Revolutionary War', in Peter Paret (ed.), *Makers of Modern Strategy: From Machiavelli to the Nuclear Age*, Oxford: Clarendon Press, 1986, p. 817.

12 Ian Beckett, 'The Tradition', in John Pimlott (ed.), *Guerrilla Warfare*, London: Bison, 1985, p. 8.

13 Francis Toase, 'Introduction', in Corbett, *Guerrilla Warfare*, p. 6.

14 Harry G. Summers, 'A War is War is a War is a War', in Loren B. Thompson (ed.), *Low-Intensity Conflict: The Pattern of Warfare in the Modern World*, Lexington, Mass.: Lexington Books, 1989, pp. 27–49.

15 Joint Chiefs of Staff, *Department of Defense Dictionary of Military and Associated Terms*, Washington, DC: Government Publications Office, 1989, p. 212.

16 Summers, 'A War', p. 32.

17 Source: Major Mitchell M. Zais, 'LIC: Matching Forces and Mission', *Military Review*, 66 (1986), pp. 79 and 89. Cited in ibid., p. 32.

18 For an evaluation, including discussions and comparisons between World War II and Vietnam, see David H. Marlowe, *Psychological and Psychosocial Consequences of Combat and Deployment with Special Emphasis on the Gulf War*, Santa Monica, CA: RAND, 2000, esp. pp. 47–63 and 73–114.

19 See Frank W. Weathers, Brett T. Litz and Terence M. Keane, *Military Trauma: Traumatic Stress: From Theory to Practice*, New York: Plenum Press, 1995, pp. 103–28.

20 National Center for PTSD, 'The Legacy of Psychological Trauma of the Vietnam War for Native Hawaiian and American of Japanese Ancestry Military Personnel', US Department of Veterans Affairs <http://www.ncptsd.org/facts/veterans/fs_hawaiian_vets.html>. See also Matthew Friedman, 'The Matsunaga Vietnam Veterans Project', *PTSD Research Quarterly*, 9, 4 (Fall 1998), p. 7.

21 For a discussion of the statistical evidence that suggests that as 'small wars' go, the Northern Ireland conflict was in fact rather a big one, see Brendan O'Duffy and Brendan O'Leary, 'Violence in Northern Ireland, 1969–1989', in John McGarry and Brendan O'Leary (eds), *The Future of Northern Ireland*, Oxford: Clarendon Press, 1990, pp. 318–41.

22 Andrew Mack, 'Why Big Nations Lose Small Wars: The Politics of Asymmetric Conflict', *World Politics*, 26, 1 (1974), p. 186.

23 Clausewitz, *On War*, p. 87.

24 M. L. R. Smith, 'Holding Fire: Strategic Theory and the Missing Military Dimension in the Academic Study of Northern Ireland', in Alan O'Day (ed.), *Terrorism's Laboratory: The Case of Northern Ireland*, Aldershot: Dartmouth Press, 1995, p. 230.

25 Colin Gray, *Strategic Studies and Public Policy: The American Experience*, Lexington: University of Kentucky Press, 1982, p. 124.

26 Peter R. Neumann, *Britain's Long War: British Government Strategy in Northern Ireland, 1968–98*, London: Palgrave Macmillan, 2003, pp. 105–16.

27 See Gilbert Ryle, *The Concept of the Mind*, Chicago: University of Chicago Press, 1949.

28 *The New Lexicon Websters Encyclopedic Dictionary*, Danbury, CT: Lexicon Publications, 1992. p. 777.

29 Clausewitz, *On War*, p. 75.

30 Ibid., p. 75. See also pp. 76–80.

31 C. J. M. Drake, *Terrorists' Target Selection*, London: Macmillan, 1997, pp. 5–15 and 54–73.
32 Peter Sederburg, *Terrorist Myths: Illusions, Rhetoric and Reality*, Englewood Cliffs, NJ: Prentice-Hall, 1989, p. 22.
33 Adrian Guelke, *The Age of Terrorism and the International Political System*, London: IB Tauris, 1997, p. 23.
34 See John Baylis, 'Revolutionary Warfare', in John Baylis *et al.* (eds), *Contemporary Strategy: Theories and Policies*, London: Croom Helm, 1975, pp. 133–44.
35 See the discussion in Michael Walzer, *Just and Unjust Wars: A Moral Argument with Historical Illustrations*, London: Pelican, 1980, pp. 197–206.
36 Smith, 'Holding Fire', pp. 232–3.
37 For a survey of the definitional problems see Alex P. Schmid *et al.*, *Political Terrorism: A New Guide to Actors, Authors, Concepts, Data Bases, Theories and Literature*, Amsterdam: North Holland Publishing, 1988, pp. 1–29.
38 In practice, the 'war on terrorism' denotes a war against the al-Qaeda network. The exact origins of the phrase war on terrorism are unclear, though it was coined almost immediately in the aftermath of the September 2001 attacks by the American news networks and found its way into official American declaratory policy following President George W. Bush's address to the Joint Session of Congress, in which he proclaimed: 'Our war on terror begins with al-Qaeda, but does not end there. It will not end until every terrorist group of global reach has been found, stopped and defeated'. *Address to a Joint Session of Congress and the American People*, Washington DC: Office of the Press Secretary, 20 September 2001. Since that time the expression has entered popular usage to describe the current emphasis of US foreign policy. For a survey see the University of Michigan's Documents Center, 'America's War Against Terrorism', <http://www.umich.edu/govdocs/usterror.html.>.
39 There are numerous examples across military studies literature, from general texts to more specialised studies, which reflect this tendency. For an illustration see Donald Featherstone, *Colonial Small Wars, 1837–1901*, Newton Abbot: David & Charles, 1973, pp. 11–13; Juliet Lodge (ed.), *Terrorism: A Challenge to the State*, Oxford: Martin Robertson, 1981; and Richard A. Preston, Alex Roland and Sydney F. Wise, *Men in Arms: A History of Warfare and its Interrelationships with Western Society*, New York: Harcourt Brace Jovanovich, 1991, pp. 359–85.
40 Smith, 'Holding Fire', p. 231.
41 Harry G. Summers, *On Strategy: A Critical Analysis of the Vietnam War*, Novato, CA: Presidio Press, 1995, p. 73.
42 Summers, 'A War', p. 44.
43 Ibid., p. 45.
44 Bjørn Møller, 'Faces of War', in Håkan Wiberg and Christian P. Scherrer (eds), *Ethnicity and Intra-State Conflict: Types, Causes and Peace Strategies*, Aldershot: Ashgate, 1999, p. 15.
45 See Jan Willem Honig, 'Strategy in a Post-Clausewitzian Setting', in Gert de Nooy (ed.), *The Clausewitzian Dictum and the Future of Western Military Strategy*, The Hague: Kluwer Law International, 1997, p. 118.
46 John Keegan, *A History of Warfare*, New York: Vintage, 1994, p. 58.
47 For a selection of such offerings see, Kaldor, *New and Old War*, pp. 13–30; Keegan, *A History of Warfare*, pp. 20–3; Møller, 'Faces of War', pp. 15–34; Martin van Creveld, *The Transformation of War*, New York: Free Press, 1991, pp. 33–62; Kalevi J. Holsti, *The State, War and the State of War*, Cambridge: Cambridge University Press, 1996, pp. 1–18; and Ralph Peters, 'The New Strategic Trinity', *Parameters*, 28, 4 (1998–9), pp. 73–9.

48 Martin van Creveld, 'What is Wrong With Clausewitz?' in Gert de Nooy (ed.), *The Clausewitzian Dictum and the Future of Western Military Strategy*, The Hague: Kluwer Law International, 1997, p.18.
49 Hayden White, *Metahistory: The Historical Imagination in Nineteenth Century Europe*, Baltimore, Johns Hopkins Press, 1973. White's contention is that all historical writing can be reduced to four figurative expressions: metaphor, metonymy, synecdoche, and irony. For an exposé of the incoherence of this approach see Keith Windschuttle, *The Killing of History*, San Francisco, Encounter Books, 2000, pp. 266–78.
50 Bruce Fleming, 'Can Reading Clausewitz Save Us From Future Mistakes?', *Parameters*, Spring 2004, pp. 75–6.
51 Van Creveld, *The Transformation of War*, pp. 57–8.
52 The British Army, for example, has been thoroughly prepared for 'low-intensity wars' for the best part of two centuries.
53 Azar Gat, *The Origins of Military Thought: From the Enlightenment to Clausewitz*, Oxford, Clarendon, 1989.
54 Christopher Bassford, 'John Keegan and the Grand Tradition of Trashing Clausewitz: A Polemic', *War in History*, 1, 3 (1994), pp. 319–36.
55 Clausewitz, *On War*, p. 87.
56 Ibid., p. 605.
57 Kaldor, *New and Old Wars*, p. 13.
58 Ibid., pp. 13–30.
59 Ibid., pp. 30–68.
60 See Stuart J. Kaufman, *Modern Hatreds: The Symbols and Politics of Ethnic War*, Ithaca, NY: Cornell University Press, 2001. The relationship between ethnicity and modernisation has been known and explicated upon for many years in the comparative politics literature: see for example Robert H. Bates, 'Modernization, Ethnic Competition, and the Rationality of Politics in Contemporary Africa', in Donald Rothchild and Victor Olorunsola (eds), *State versus Ethnic Claims: African Policy Dilemmas*, Boulder, CO: Westview, 1983, pp. 152–71; and Arline McCord and William McCord, 'Ethnic Autonomy: A Socio-Historical Synthesis', in Raymond L. Hall (ed.), *Ethnic Autonomy: Comparative Dynamics, The Americas, Europe, and the Developing World*, New York: Pergamon, 1979, pp. 426–36.
61 See the tract by the head of the People's Liberation Army, Lin Piao, *Long Live the Victory of People's War! In Commemoration of the 20th Anniversary of Victory in the Chinese People's War of Resistance Against Japan*, Peking: Foreign Language Press, 1965, originally published in *People's Daily*, 3 September 1965. It is debatable whether the communist success can be attributed purely to the adherence to this concept of operations. Just as important a factor, if not more so, was the Japanese invasion of China in 1937 and the subsequent eight-year-long Sino–Japanese war, which gravely weakened the Nationalist Kuomintang forces, thus making the communist victory far easier than it otherwise would have been.
62 Lincoln P. Bloomfield, 'Future Small Wars: Must the United States Intervene?', *Orbis*, 12, 3 (1968), p. 672.
63 For a survey see Bruce Hoffman and Jennifer M. Taw, *Defense Policy and Low-Intensity Conflict: The Development of Britain's 'Small Wars' Doctrine During the 1950s*, Santa Monica, CA: RAND, 1991; and Thomas Mockaitis, *British Counterinsurgency, 1919–1960*, London: Macmillan, 1990.
64 The principal British counter-insurgency texts to emerge from this era were: Robert Thompson, *Defeating Communist Insurgency: Lessons from Malaya and Vietnam*, London: Chatto & Windus, 1966; Julian Paget, *Counter-Insurgency*

Campaigning, London: Faber & Faber, 1967; and Frank Kitson, *Low Intensity Operations: Subversion, Insurgency, Peacekeeping*, London: Faber & Faber, 1971.

65 For an exposition see Roger Trinquier, *Modern Warfare: A French View of Counterinsurgency*, London: Pall Mall, 1964. See also David Galula, *Counter-insurgency Warfare*, New York: Praeger, 1964 and Peter Paret, *French Revolutionary Warfare from Indochina to Algeria: The Analysis of a Political and Military Doctrine*, London: Pall Mall, 1964.

66 Alistair Horne, *A Savage War of Peace: Algeria, 1954–1962*, London: Macmillan 1977, pp. 480–504.

67 For some of the key texts on American counter-insurgency thinking see US Marine Corps, *Small Wars Manual* (originally published 1940), Washington DC: Headquarters USMC, 1987; Edward G. Lansdale, *In the Midst of Wars: An American's Mission to Southeast Asia*, New York: Fordham University Press, 1991; Franklin Mark Osanka (ed.), *Modern Guerrilla Warfare: Fighting Communist Guerrilla Movements 1941–1961*, New York: Free Press of Glencoe, 1962; William J. Pomeroy, *Guerrilla and Counter-Guerrilla: Liberation and Suppression in the Current Period*, New York: International Publishers, 1964; T. N. Greene (ed.), *The Guerrilla – and How to Fight Him: Selections from the Marine Corps Gazette*, New York: Praeger, 1962; and Harry Eckstein (ed.), *Internal War: Problems and Approaches*, New York: Free Press of Glencoe, 1964. See also Douglas Blaufarb, *The Counter-Insurgency Era: U.S. Doctrine and Performance, 1950 to the Present*, New York: Free Press, 1977.

68 Summers, 'A War', pp. 39–40.

69 Regis Debray, *Revolution in the Revolution? Armed Struggle and Political Struggle in Latin America*, New York: Grove, 1967.

70 *Focoquismo* or *foco* was the term used to encompass the idea that armed actions could crystallise popular discontent to inspire the masses to rebel. Armed acts could therefore form the 'focus' of the 'revolution', functioning as a substitute for long-term political organisation that characterised Maoist people's war doctrine. It was this strategy that was held to explain the success of the Cuban revolution in 1959, although the underlying brittleness of the Batista regime was often overlooked as an explanatory factor and impeded the wider applicability of the *focoquismo* idea. For the theoretical expositions see R. Debray, *Revolution in the Revolution? Armed Struggle and Political Struggle in Latin America*, New York: Grove, 1987 and Robert Taber, *War of the Flea: A Study of Guerrilla Warfare, Theory and Practice*, London: Paladin, 1970.

71 The reality was that there was rarely any substitute for military force. The Chinese communists took 20 years of bitter struggle before China's civil war concluded with a series of face-to-face battles. In South Vietnam, the failure of the Vietcong's 1968 Tet offensive to inspire a general uprising compelled the North Vietnamese to intervene with standard military formations, culminating in two full-scale invasions in 1972 and 1974. Elsewhere, state authorities were able to concentrate military force against rebel bases in rural areas or burn away urban insurrections through massive repression, most notably in the so-called dirty wars undertaken by Latin American regimes in the 1970s.

72 Gray, *Strategic Studies and Public Policy*, p. 114 and p. 122. It may be argued that 'counter-insurgency faddism' and the 'aura of special forces', lasted only a short time until 1963 when the Green Berets were transferred back to the US Army's command from the CIA. Special forces played only an ancillary role in the Vietnam War, given General Westmoreland's preference for the use of conventional armed forces. See Andrew F. Krepinevich, *The Army and Vietnam*, Baltimore: Johns Hopkins Press, 1986, pp. 35–56.

73 Quoted in Gray, *Strategic Studies*, p. 216. Also see p. 119.
74 Colin Gray, 'What RAND Hath Wrought', *Foreign Policy*, 4 (Fall 1971), pp. 111–29.
75 Richard K. Betts, 'Should Strategic Studies Survive?', *World Politics*, 50, 1 (1997), p. 16.
76 Edward A. Kolodziej, 'What is Security and Security Studies? Lessons from the Cold War', *Arms Control*, 13, 1 (1992), p. 2.
77 The esoteric nature of strategic theorising was something first noted by Hedley Bull. See Hedley Bull, 'Strategic Studies and Its Critics', *World Politics*, 20, 4 (1968), p. 596.
78 Gray, *Strategic Studies*, p. 135.
79 For some good examples of the genre see Paul Wilkinson, *Terrorism and the Liberal State*, London: Macmillan, 1986 and Paul Wilkinson (ed.), *British Perspectives on Terrorism*, London: George Allen & Unwin, 1981.
80 See Tables 2.1 and 2.2 in Holsti, *The State, War and the State of War*, pp. 22–4.
81 By 1983 Peter Janke recorded the existence of 569 violent non-state groups. See Peter Janke, *Guerrilla and Terrorist Organisations: A World Directory and Bibliography*, Brighton: Harvester, 1983.
82 Ken Booth, 'Security and Self: Reflections of a Fallen Realist', in Keith Krause and Michael C. Williams (eds), *Critical Security Studies: Concepts and Cases*, London: UCL Press, 1997, p. 93.
83 During the Cold War years there was only one example of an attempt to locate guerrilla warfare within a general category of 'conventional war'. See Lawrence Freedman, *Atlas of Global Strategy: War and Peace in the Nuclear Age*, London: Macmillan, 1985, pp. 113–40.
84 Betts, 'Should Strategic Studies Survive?', p. 7.
85 See for instance Peter Moody, 'Clausewitz and the Fading Dialectic of War', *World Politics*, 31, 2 (1979), pp. 417–33.
86 J. William Fulbright, 'The Foundations of National Security', in Morton Kaplan (ed.), *Great Issues of International Politics*, Chicago: Aldine, 1974, p. 255.
87 See David A. Baldwin, 'Security Studies and the End of the Cold War', *World Politics*, 48, 1 (1995), p. 130. Also see Gray, *Strategic Studies*, p. 49.
88 Van Creveld, *The Transformation of War*, p. 19.
89 Douglas Porch, 'Introduction to the Bison Books Edition', in Callwell, *Small Wars*, p. xvii.
90 Paul Beaver, 'The Threat to Israel is Not War', *Asian Wall Street Journal*, 24 October 2000.
91 Honig, 'Strategy', pp. 114–19.
92 One may draw a parallel here with the way that Mahanian doctrines 'de-strategised' much naval thinking from the late nineteenth century through to World War II by emphasising that the primary, if not the singular, role of navies was fleet concentration and the seeking of decisive battle. In the early twentieth century the British lawyer turned naval theorist Julian Corbett suggested that navies could more usefully perform a whole range of tasks below the search for decisive fleet engagement, such as amphibious operations, inshore gunfire support, guarding bases, commerce raiding, and so on. For this he was treated as a heretic by the Royal Navy Admiralty, his ideas being officially repudiated up until the 1930s. For a discussion of Corbett's enduring influence see Geoffrey Till, 'Sir Julian Corbet and the Twenty-First Century: Ten Maritime Commandments', in Andrew Dorman *et al.* (eds), *The Changing Face of Maritime Power*, London: Macmillan, 1999, pp. 19–32.
93 Edward Luttwak, 'Give War a Chance', *Foreign Affairs*, 78, 4 (1999), pp. 36–44.

94 Jan Willem Honig and Norbert Both, *Srebrenica: Record of a War Crime*, London: Penguin, 1996, pp. 71–98 and 141–86 as well as James Gow, *Triumph of the Lack of Will: International Diplomacy and the Yugoslav War*, London: Hurst & Co., 1997, pp. 298–331.

95 The allegation centres over the transmission of a fax by the Canadian commander of the UN peacekeeping force in Rwanda, Major General Romeo Dallaire, in January 1994 in which he forewarned of the imminent threat of Hutu extremists to the minority Tutsi population. The cable was ignored by the UN mainly out of the fear of being drawn into the civil conflict. General Dallaire estimated that the despatch of an additional 2,500 troops could have prevented the *Interhamwe* militia from massacring up to a million people. The original fax can be found at the George Washington University's National University Archive <http://www.gwu.edu/~nsarchiv/NSAEBB/NSAEBB53>. The fax reference is: TO: BARIL/DPKO/UNATIONS, NEW YORK, FROM: DALLAIRE/UNAMIR/KIGALI, SUBJECT: REQUEST PROTECTION FOR INFORMANT, 11 January 1994. See also Alec Russell, 'How the West Turned Blind Eye Despite General's "Genocide Fax"', *Daily Telegraph*, 6 April 2004.

96 An anecdotal piece of evidence might suffice to illuminate the point. At a dinner in 1995 to commemorate the thirtieth anniversary of the formation of my own department, the Department of War Studies at King's College London, the guest speaker, and founder of War Studies, Professor Sir Michael Howard, lamented during his speech that, looking back, the one regret he had before he left the College in 1969 was that the department completely ignored the Vietnam war. Apparently, while the war in Indochina was convulsing Western society, the primary concern within the department was examining theories of nuclear deterrence.

97 See, for example, Gwyn Prins, 'Perverse Paradoxes in the Application of the Paradoxical Logic of Strategy', *Millennium*, 17, 3 (1988), pp. 539–51.

98 Fred Kaplan, *The Wizards of Armageddon*, New York: Simon & Schuster, 1983, p. 390.

99 Fred Halliday, *Rethinking International Relations*, London: Macmillan, 1994, p. 126. This neglect was one fully reflected in Halliday's own institution, the Department of International Relations at the London School of Economics. Of course, recognising this deficiency in hindsight is easy. Arguably, there is still no discernible effort to show more understanding of such matters in academia.

100 See Bernard Brodie, 'Why Were We So (Strategically) Wrong?' *Foreign Policy*, 5 (Winter 1971–2), pp. 151–61.

101 For a good example see Caroline Thomas, 'New Thinking About Security in the Third World', in Ken Booth (ed.), *New Thinking About International Security*, London: HarperCollins, 1991, pp. 267–87.

102 Richard Betts, 'Must War Find a Way?', *International Security*, 24, 2 (1999), p. 193.

103 Booth, 'Security', p. 112.

104 Edward A. Kolodziej, 'Renaissance in Security Studies: Caveat Lector!', *International Studies Quarterly*, 36, 4 (1992), p. 422.

105 Ken Booth, 'War, Security and Strategy: Towards a Doctrine for Stable Peace', in Booth (ed.), *New Thinking*, p. 356.

106 See Mats Berdal, 'How "New" Are "New Wars"?, Global Economic Change and the Study of Civil War', *Global Governance*, 9, 4 (2003), pp. 477–502.

107 For a survey of post 1945 civil wars, see Table 1 in Barbara F. Walter, 'Designing Transitions from Civil War: Demobilization, Democratization and Commitments to Peace', *International Security*, 25, 1 (1999), p. 128.

108 See for example Geoffrey Blainey, *The Causes of War*, London: Macmillan, 1988, p. 71 and J. David Singer and Melvin Small, *Resort to Arms: International and Civil Wars, 1816–1980*, Beverly Hills, CA: Sage, 1982.
109 Honig, 'Strategy', p. 110.
110 Bassford, 'John Keegan', p. 329.
111 Clausewitz, *On War*, pp. 87–8.
112 Ibid., p. 87.
113 Ibid., pp. 75–80.
114 Ibid., p. 81.
115 Eliot A. Cohen, 'Looks Like War', *Asian Wall Street Journal*, 16 October 2000.
116 See for example, Colin Powell, *My American Journey*, New York: Ballantine, 1994, p. 544.
117 Honig, 'Strategy', p. 118.
118 For an assessment see Telford Taylor, *The Breaking Wave: The Second World War in the Summer of 1940*, New York, Simon and Schuster, 1967, and Derek Wood and Derek Dempster, *The Narrow Margin: The Battle of Britain and the Rise of Air Power, 1930–1940*, Washington, DC: Smithsonian Institution Press, 1990.
119 William L. Shirer, *Berlin Diary: The Journal of a Foreign Correspondent, 1934–1941*, Boston: Little, Brown & Co., 1941, p. 556.
120 Armand Van Ishoven, *The Luftwaffe in the Battle of Britain*, New York: Charles Scribner's Sons, 1980.
121 See J. F. C. Fuller, *The Second World War, 1939–45: A Strategical and Tactical History*, New York, Duell, Sloan and Pearce, 1954, pp. 83–9.
122 Shirer, *Berlin Diary*, p. 554.
123 Werner Hahlweg, 'Clausewitz and Guerrilla Warfare', in Michael Handel (ed.), *Clausewitz and Modern Strategy*, London: Frank Cass, 1986, pp. 127–33.
124 Irrespective of whether one attributes to Clausewitz a mistaken concern for the state, it is the case that even when warfare does not take place between states, it is often about states. It is about who has control within a state or else an attempt to form a new or separate state out of an existing one. See Honig, 'Strategy', p. 120. For a further discussion see Peter Paret, *Clausewitz and the State: The Man, His Theories, and His Times*, Princeton, NJ: Princeton University Press, 1985, pp. 431–40.
125 Clausewitz, *On War*, p. 596.

References

Baldwin, David A., 'Security Studies and the End of the Cold War', *World Politics*, 48, 1 (1995), pp. 117–41.

Barber, Benjamin, *Jihad vs. MacWorld: How Globalism and Tribalism are Reshaping the World Order*, New York: Ballantine, 1996.

Bassford, Christopher, 'John Keegan and the Grand Tradition of Trashing Clausewitz: A Polemic', *War in History*, 1, 3 (1994), pp. 319–36.

Bates, Robert H., 'Modernization, Ethnic Competition, and the Rationality of Politics in Contemporary Africa', pp. 152–71, in Donald Rothchild and Victor Olorunsola (eds), *State versus Ethnic Claims: African Policy Dilemmas*, Boulder, CO: Westview, 1983.

Baylis, John, 'Revolutionary Warfare', in John Baylis *et al.*, *Contemporary Strategy: Theories and Policies*, London: Croom Helm, 1975, pp. 209–29.

Beaver, Paul, 'The Threat to Israel is Not War', *Asian Wall Street Journal*, 24 October 2000.

Beckett, Ian F. W., 'The Tradition', in John Pimlott (ed.), *Guerrilla Warfare*, London: Bison, 1985, pp. 6–29.

Berdal, Mats, 'How "New" Are "New Wars"? Global Economic Change and the Study of Civil War', *Global Governance*, 9, 4 (2003), pp. 477–502.

Betts, Richard K. 'Should Strategic Studies Survive?', *World Politics*, 50, 1 (1997), pp. 7–33.

—— 'Must War Find a Way?', *International Security*, 24, 2 (1999), pp. 166–98.

Blainey, Geoffrey, *The Causes of War*, London: Macmillan, 1999.

Blaufarb, Douglas, *The Counter-Insurgency Era: U.S. Doctrine and Performance, 1950 to the Present*, New York: Free Press, 1977.

Bloomfield, Lincoln P., 'Future Small Wars: Must the United States Intervene?', *Orbis*, 12, 3 (1968).

Booth, Ken, 'Security and Self: Reflections of a Fallen Realist', in Keith Krause and Michael C. Williams (eds), *Critical Security Studies: Concepts and Cases*, London: UCL Press, 1997, pp. 83–119.

—— 'War, Security and Strategy: Towards a Doctrine for Stable Peace', in Ken Booth (ed.), *New Thinking About International Security*, London: HarperCollins, 1991, pp. 335–76.

Bernard Brodie, 'Why Were We So (Strategically) Wrong?', *Foreign Policy*, 5 (Winter 1971–2), pp. 151–61.

Bush, President George W., *Address to a Joint Session of Congress and the American People*, Washington DC: Office of the Press Secretary, 20 September 2001.

Bull, Hedley, 'Strategic Studies and Its Critics', *World Politics*, 20, 4 (1968), pp. 593–605.

Callwell, C. E., *Small Wars: Their Principles and Practice*, third edn, London: Bison Books, 1996.

Clausewitz, Carl von, *On War*, trans. and ed. Michael Howard and Peter Paret, Princeton, NJ: Princeton University Press, 1984.

Clutterbuck, Richard, *Guerrillas and Terrorists*, Athens, Ohio: Ohio University Press, 1977.

Cohen, Eliot A., 'Looks Like War', *Asian Wall Street Journal*, 16 October 2000.

Corbett, Robin, *Guerrilla Warfare: From 1939 to the Present Day*, London: Guild Publishing, 1986.

Creveld, Martin van, *The Transformation of War*, New York: The Free Press, 1991.

—— 'What is Wrong With Clausewitz?', in Gert de Nooy (ed.), *The Clausewitzian Dictum and the Future of Western Military Strategy*, The Hague: Kluwer Law International, 1997.

Debray, Regis, *Revolution in the Revolution? Armed Struggle and Political Struggle in Latin America*, New York: Grove, 1967.

Drake, C. J. M., *Terrorists' Target Selection*, London: Macmillan, 1997.

Eckstein, Harry (ed.), *Internal War: Problems and Approaches*, New York: Free Press of Glencoe, 1964.

Fleming, Bruce, 'Can Reading Clausewitz Save Us from Future Mistakes?', *Parameters*, Spring 2004, pp. 62–76.

Featherstone, Donald, *Colonial Small Wars, 1837–1901*, Newton Abbot: David & Charles, 1973.

Freedman, Lawrence, *Atlas of Global Strategy: War and Peace in the Nuclear Age*, London: Macmillan, 1985.

Friedman, Matthew, 'The Matsunaga Vietnam Veterans Project', *PTSD Research Quarterly*, 9, 4 (Fall 1998), p. 7

Fulbright, J. William, 'The Foundations of National Security', in Morton Kaplan (ed.), *Great Issues of International Politics*, Chicago: Aldine, 1974.

Fuller, John Frederick Charles, *The Second World War, 1939–45: A Strategical and Tactical History*, New York: Duell, Sloan and Pearce, 1954.

Galula, David, *Counterinsurgency Warfare*, New York: Praeger, 1964.

Gat, Azar, *The Origins of Military Thought: From the Enlightenment to Clausewitz*, Oxford: Clarendon, 1989.

Gow, James, *Triumph of the Lack of Will: International Diplomacy and the Yugoslav War*, London: Hurst, 1997.

Gray, Colin, 'What RAND Hath Wrought', *Foreign Policy*, 4 (Fall 1971), pp. 111–29.

——*Strategic Studies and Public Policy: The American Experience*, Lexington: University of Kentucky Press, 1982.

Greene, T. N. (ed.), *The Guerrilla – and How to Fight Him: Selections from the Marine Corps Gazette*, New York: Praeger, 1962.

Guelke, Adrian, *The Age of Terrorism and the International Political System*, London: IB Tauris, 1997.

Hahlweg, Werner, 'Clausewitz and Guerrilla Warfare', in Michael Handel (ed.), *Clausewitz and Modern Strategy*, London: Frank Cass, 1986, pp. 127–33.

Halliday, Fred, *Rethinking International Relations*, London: Macmillan, 1994.

Hilsman, Roger, *To Move a Nation: The Politics of Foreign Policy in the Administration of John F. Kennedy*, New York: Delta, 1967.

Hoffman, Bruce and Jennifer M. Taw, *Defense Policy and Low-Intensity Conflict: The Development of Britain's 'Small Wars' Doctrine During the 1950s*, Santa Monica, CA: RAND, 1991.

Holsti, Kalevi J., *War, the State, and the State of War*, Cambridge: Cambridge University Press, 1996.

Honig, Jan Willem, 'Strategy in a Post-Clausewitzian Setting', pp. 109–22, in Gert de Nooy (ed.), *The Clausewitzian Dictum and the Future of Western Military Strategy*, The Hague: Kluwer Law International, 1997.

——and Norbert Both, *Srebrenica: Record of a War Crime*, London: Penguin, 1995.

Horne, Alistair, *A Savage War of Peace: Algeria, 1954–1962*, London: Macmillan, 1977.

Huntington, Samuel, *The Clash of Civilizations and the Remaking of World Order*, New York: Simon & Schuster, 1996.

Ignatieff, Michael, *Blood and Belonging: Journeys into the New Nationalism*, London: BBC/Chatto & Windus, 1993.

Ishoven, Armand Van, *The Luftwaffe in the Battle of Britain*, New York: Charles Scribner's Sons, 1980.

Janke, Peter, *Guerrilla and Terrorist Organisations: A World Directory and Bibliography*, Brighton: Harvester, 1983.

Janos, Andrew, 'Unconventional Warfare: Framework for Analysis', *World Politics*, 15, 4 (1963), pp. 636–47.

Janowitz, Morris, 'Towards a Redefinition of Military Strategy in International Relations', *World Politics*, 26, 4 (1974), pp. 471–508.

Kaldor, Mary, *New and Old Wars: Organized Violence in a Global Era*, Stanford: Stanford University Press, 1999.

Kaplan, Fred, *The Wizards of Armageddon*, New York: Simon & Schuster, 1983.

Kaufman, Stuart J., *Modern Hatreds: The Symbols and Politics of Ethnic War*, Ithaca, NY: Cornell University Press, 2001.

Keegan, John, *A History of Warfare*, New York: Vintage, 1994.

Kitson, Frank, *Low Intensity Operations: Subversion, Insurgency, and Peacekeeping*, London: Faber, 1991.

Kolodziej, Edward A., 'Renaissance in Security Studies: Caveat Lector!', *International Studies Quarterly*, 36, 4 (1992), pp. 421–38.

—— 'What is Security and Security Studies? Lessons from the Cold War', *Arms Control*, 13, 1 (1992), pp. 1–31.

Krepinevich, Andrew F., *The Army and Vietnam*, Baltimore: Johns Hopkins Press, 1986.

Lansdale, Edward G., *In the Midst of Wars: An American's Mission to Southeast Asia*, New York: Fordham University Press, 1991.

Lin Piao, *Long Live the Victory of People's War! In Commemoration of the 20th Anniversary of Victory in the Chinese People's War of Resistance Against Japan*, Peking: Foreign Language Press, 1965.

Lodge, Juliet (ed.), *Terrorism: A Challenge to the State*, Oxford: Martin Robertson, 1981.

Luttwak, Edward, 'Give War a Chance', *Foreign Affairs*, 78, 4 (1999), pp. 36–44.

Mack, Andrew, 'Why Big Nations Lose Small Wars: The Politics of Asymmetric Conflict', *World Politics*, 26, 1 (1974), pp. 175–200.

Marlowe, David H., *Psychological and Psychosocial Consequences of Combat and Deployment with Special Emphasis on the Gulf War*, Santa Monica, CA: RAND, 2000.

McCord, Arline and William McCord, 'Ethnic Autonomy: A Socio-Historical Synthesis', in Raymond L. Hall (ed.), *Ethnic Autonomy: Comparative Dynamics, The Americas, Europe, and the Developing World*, New York: Pergamon, 1979.

Metz, Steven, 'Insurgency After the Cold War', *Small Wars and Insurgencies*, 5, 1 (1994), pp. 63–82.

Mockaitis, Thomas R., *British Counterinsurgency, 1919–1960*, London: Macmillan, 1990.

Møller, Bjørn, 'Faces of War', in Håkan Wiberg and Christian P. Scherrer (eds), *Ethnicity and Intra-State Conflict: Types, Causes and Peace Strategies*, Aldershot: Ashgate, 1999, pp. 15–34.

Moody, Peter, 'Clausewitz and the Fading Dialectic of War', *World Politics*, 31, 2 (1979), pp. 417–33.

National Center for PTSD, 'The Legacy of Psychological Trauma of the Vietnam War for Native Hawaiian and American of Japanese Ancestry Military Personnel', US Department of Veterans Affairs. <http://www.ncptsd.org/facts/veterans/fs_hawaiian_vets. html>.

Neumann, Peter R., *Britain's Long War: British Government Strategy in Northern Ireland, 1968–98*, London: Palgrave Macmillan, 2003.

New (The) Lexicon Websters Encyclopedic Dictionary, Danbury, CT: Lexicon Publications, 1992.

O'Duffy, Brendan, and Brendan O'Leary, 'Violence in Northern Ireland, 1968–1989', in John McGarry and Brendan O'Leary (eds), *The Future of Northern Ireland*, Oxford: Clarendon Press, 1990, pp. 318–41.

Osanka, Franklin Mark (ed.), *Modern Guerrilla Warfare: Fighting Communist Guerrilla Movements 1941–1961*, New York: Free Press of Glencoe, 1962.

Paget, Julian, *Counter-Insurgency Campaigning*, London: Faber & Faber, 1967.

Paret, Peter, *Clausewitz and the State: The Man, His Theories, and His Times*, Princeton, NJ: Princeton University Press, 1985.

——*French Revolutionary Warfare from Indochina to Algeria: The Analysis of a Political and Military Doctrine*, London: Pall Mall, 1964.

Peters, Ralph, 'The New Strategic Trinity', *Parameters*, 28, 4 (1999), pp. 73–9.

Pomeroy, William J., *Guerrilla and Counter-Guerrilla: Liberation and Suppression in the Current Period*, New York: International Publishers, 1964.

Porch, Douglas, 'Introduction to the Bison Books Edition', in C. E. Callwell, *Small Wars: Their Principles and Practice*, Lincoln, Nebraska: University of Nebraska Press, 1996, pp. v–xviii.

Powell, Colin, *My American Journey*, New York: Ballantine, 1994.

Preston, Richard A., Alex Roland and Sydney F. Wise, *Men in Arms: A History of Warfare and its Interrelationships with Western Society*, New York: Harcourt Brace Jovanovich, 1991.

Prins, Gwyn, 'Perverse Paradoxes in the Application of the Paradoxical Logic of Strategy', *Millennium*, 17, 3 (1988).

Russell, Alec, 'How the West Turned Blind Eye Despite General's "Genocide Fax"', *Daily Telegraph*, 6 April 2004.

Ryle, Gilbert, *The Concept of the Mind*, Chicago: University of Chicago Press, 1949.

Schmid, Alex P. *et al.*, *Political Terrorism: A New Guide to Actors, Authors, Concepts, Data Bases, Theories and Literature*, Amsterdam: North Holland Publishing, 1988.

Sederburg, Peter, *Terrorist Myths: Illusions, Rhetoric and Reality*, Englewood Cliffs, NJ: Prentice-Hall, 1989.

Shirer, William L., *Berlin Diary: The Journal of a Foreign Correspondent, 1934–1941*, Boston: Little, Brown, 1941.

Shy, John and Thomas Collier, 'Revolutionary War', pp. 815–62, in Peter Paret (ed.), *Makers of Modern Strategy: From Machiavelli to the Nuclear Age*, Oxford: Clarendon Press, 1986.

Simon, Steven and Daniel Benjamin, 'America and the New Terrorism', *Survival*, 42, 1 (2000), pp. 59–75.

Singer J., David and Melvin Small, *Resort to Arms: International and Civil Wars, 1816–1980*, Beverly Hills, CA: Sage, 1982.

Smith, M. L. R., 'Holding Fire: Strategic Theory and the Missing Military Dimension in the Academic Study of Northern Ireland', in Alan O'Day (ed.), *Terrorism's Laboratory: The Case of Northern Ireland*, Aldershot: Dartmouth Press, 1995.

Summers, Harry G., *On Strategy: A Critical Analysis of the Vietnam War*, Novato, CA: Presidio Press, 1995.

——'A War is War is a War is a War', pp. 27–49, in Loren B. Thompson (ed.), *Low-Intensity Conflict: The Pattern of Warfare in the Modern World*, Lexington, Mass.: Lexington Books, 1989.

Taber, Robert, *War of the Flea: A Study of Guerrilla Warfare, Theory and Practice*, London: Paladin, 1970.

Taylor, Telford, *The Breaking Wave: The Second World War in the Summer of 1940*, New York: Simon and Schuster, 1967.

Thomas, Caroline, 'New Thinking About Security in the Third World', in Ken Booth (ed.), *New Thinking About International Security*, London: HarperCollins, 1991, pp. 267–89.

Thompson, Robert, *Defeating Communist Insurgency: Experiences from Malaya and Vietnam*, London: Chatto & Windus, 1966.

Till, Geoffrey, 'Sir Julian Corbet and the Twenty-First Century: Ten Maritime Commandments', in Andrew Dorman *et al.* (eds), *The Changing Face of Maritime Power*, London: Macmillan, 1999, pp. 19–32.

Toase, Francis, 'Introduction', in Robin Corbett, *Guerrilla Warfare: From 1939 to the Present Day*, London: Guild Publishing, 1985, pp. 6–9.

Trinquier, Roger, *Modern Warfare: A French View of Counterinsurgency*, London: Pall Mall, 1964.

US Joint Chiefs of Staff, *Department of Defense Dictionary of Military and Associated Terms*, Washington, DC: Government Publications Office, 1989.

US Marine Corps, *Small Wars Manual*, Washington DC: Headquarters USMC, 1987.

Walter, Barbara F., 'Designing Transitions from Civil War: Demobilization, Democratization and Commitments to Peace', *International Security*, 25, 1 (1999), pp. 127–55.

Walzer, Michael, *Just and Unjust Wars: A Moral Argument with Historical Illustrations*, London: Pelican, 1980.

Weathers, Frank, W., Brett T. Litz and Terence M. Keane, *Military Trauma: Traumatic Stress: From Theory to Practice*, New York: Plenum Press, 1995.

White, Hayden, *Metahistory: The Historical Imagination in Nineteenth Century Europe*, Baltimore: Johns Hopkins Press, 1973.

Windschuttle, Keith, *The Killing of History*, San Francisco: Encounter Books, 2000.

Wilkinson, Paul, *Terrorism and the Liberal State*, London: Macmillan, 1986.

——(ed.), *British Perspectives on Terrorism*, London: George Allen & Unwin, 1981.

Wood, Derek and Derek Dempster, *The Narrow Margin: The Battle of Britain and the Rise of Air Power, 1930–1940*, Washington, DC: Smithsonian Institution Press, 1990.

Zais, Major Mitchell M., 'LIC: Matching Forces and Mission', *Military Review*, 66, 8 (1986), pp. 89–99.

3

THE CONCEPT OF
CONVENTIONAL WAR
AND ARMED CONFLICT
IN COLLAPSED STATES

Isabelle Duyvesteyn

War has become mainly a feature of the developing world.[1] In order to analyse and explain these wars, several concepts have been prominently used. One of those concepts has been irregular warfare, which stresses factors such as indirect fighting techniques and low technology weaponry. Another recently used label is chaos and barbarity, to describe what has been going on in such diverse conflict theatres as the Balkans and the Horn of Africa. The concept of conventional war has without much consideration been marginalised and sometimes even neglected as a concept for analysis, in particular in wars occurring in collapsed states. This is not to suggest that conventional wars have not been fought in the developing world. This is clearly not the case. One only has to think, as an example, of the conflict between Ethiopia and Eritrea, in which the warring parties used trench warfare. The arguments in this chapter will show the much wider relevance of the conventional war concept.

The aim of the chapter is to demonstrate that important features of conventional warfare are present in the wars that until now have been categorised as irregular. An operational centre of gravity, a distinction between combatant and civilian, and substantial numbers of openly operating fighters are characteristics of conventional war. This can also be detected in so-called irregular or chaotic wars. I shall first outline the ideas of the dominant approaches to armed conflict since the end of the Cold War. This will be followed by an account of what conventional warfare is and how the important features of this type of war can be observed in wars in collapsed states.

While most armed conflicts today are fought in the developing world, these wars are in the majority internal or civil wars.[2] They take place within states as opposed to between states, even though many of these internal wars have a

65

tendency to spill over into the territory of neighbouring states. Transnational wars or conflict complexes are the terms used to describe this phenomenon.[3] Africa and Asia are the continents most plagued by this type of war.[4] Since the end of the Cold War there has been increased attention to these internal wars; in particular, warfare in territories where state structures are no longer functioning has received widespread attention.[5]

In order to describe the ways military instruments were used in these wars, the terms chaos and irregular war have been prominently applied. Some observers and scholars of armed conflicts have favoured an approach that described armed conflict as irrational, as an expression of primordial tendencies that had been buried for the duration of the Cold War and which re-emerged with force in the early 1990s.[6] This barbarity thesis received widespread attention, at least in the popular press. However, among experts this point of view did not become commonplace. The stress on irrationality was very unsatisfactory for scientists. The ultimate consequence of this line of reasoning was that, if the conflict is impossible to comprehend, the outside world can hardly do anything to mediate.

Apart from chaos, warlordism and banditry have been used to describe these wars. They share an important limitation for this discussion in that these terms focus more on the actors involved than on how they fight war or confront their enemy. Warlords and their rule, which is also called warlordism, have characteristically operated in situations in which state or centralised power was weak.[7] Warlordism has been studied in most detail for the rise of individual military leaders in China at the beginning of the twentieth century.[8] Warlords are generally considered to be actors who are in control of a piece of territory with a monopoly over the sources of power. The term warlord has been applied to Africa to analyse the nature of local rulers.[9] Recently the faction leaders in Somalia, in particular, have been called warlords.[10] This application is rather problematic because the Somali faction leaders were not clearly in charge of a defined piece of territory and neither did they possess a monopoly over the sources of power. In particular, military and economic power, in the forms of armaments and food aid, were highly contested.

The term banditry has also been applied and seems very attractive because of the stress on enrichment and plunder, which has constituted an important activity during many African wars.[11] As with warlordism, this term describes the actors and their organisation more than the way in which they fight war. It should not be forgotten that bandits prefer to operate in circumstances of insecurity and a lack of law enforcement. Wartime can create these circumstances. Both warlords and bandits can use military strategies, such as irregular or conventional war, to conduct their military operations. Other activities, such as robbing and plunder, will be discussed below, but are not considered the main factors in the armed interactions of the different factions involved in the wars under consideration.[12]

Another point of view, popular among general observers and academic scholars alike, has been that these kinds of conflicts can be explained by familiar concepts of irregular warfare. Guerrilla war, insurgency and low-intensity conflict have been terms used for analysis in this respect. Irregular war is usually twinned with regular war. It is a rather misleading term because what was irregular seems to become more and more regular. Unconventional war, as the opposite of conventional war, is a problematic term as well because, according to some army doctrines, unconventional war refers specifically to the methods used, which can include nuclear, biological and chemical weapons.[13] Conventional war is also considered to be different from guerrilla and insurgency war. 'Guerrilla' is a word derived from the Spanish *guerra* (or 'war') and means small war. While the history of small war has long antecedents, dominant in the thinking about this kind of war seems to be the work of revolutionary guerrilla theorists such as Mao Tse-tung and Vo Nguyen Giap.[14] The age of the revolutionary guerrilla and the struggle of communist versus capitalist is clearly past its heyday. The question is whether these labels are the most appropriate to use in describing the wars under consideration here. A last term of importance that has been used is low-intensity conflict. While this term is infelicitous in itself because most of these conflicts are anything but low in intensity, there is further room for confusion. Some military doctrines have chosen low-intensity conflict in order to describe a category of military operations that is carried out on a level below full-scale war. Activities such as peacekeeping, disaster relief and counter-drug operations are included.[15]

In order to describe the phenomenon of war that is distinct from conventional war, the term guerrilla will be used.[16] The definitions of both guerrilla and conventional war will be discussed in more detail below. The main question of concern here is whether traditional concepts of war really are out of place in the analysis of wars in collapsed states such as Liberia, Sierra Leone and Somalia. These cases can be seen as counter-intuitive. In this kind of war especially we would expect to encounter the practices of irregular warfare, because irregular warfare is generally regarded as an instrument of the weak and poor, while conventional war is seen as an instrument of the strong and wealthy. State collapse and unruly armed forces are not associated with conventional warfare. The reasons why conventional war is more appropriate than has hitherto been realised in analysing war in the case of state collapse will be elaborated in the rest of this chapter, with the main arguments being illustrated with evidence mostly from the war in Somalia (1991–7).[17]

Guerrilla warfare

Guerrilla warfare is a concept that is used to describe a strategy or rather a part of a strategy employed in warfare but it can also be applied as a term that signifies a tactic of war.[18] According to the levels of strategy, the tactical level is concerned with the meeting of men and matériel, while the operational level sees the meeting of the opponents' war plans. The strategic level, as the highest level of strategy, incorporates the overall aims of the warring parties. Thus a tactical strike can involve an attack on a bridgehead, a power installation or the life of a politician. An operational plan can involve a concerted attack against the opponent's capital, its main army strongholds or a contested piece of territory. The strategic plan might be to topple a regime or to capture territory. According to the first approach to guerrilla warfare as part of a strategy of war, military force is used in order to achieve a strategic goal. As a tactic guerrilla warfare is confined to the lower levels of strategy.

Revolutionary guerrilla war

Revolutionary guerrilla war was a popular term during the Cold War to describe communist inspired struggles against governments mostly in the developing world. The ultimate aim was to take over power from the government by means of a communist revolution. One of the most important theorists on revolutionary guerrilla war has been Mao Tse-tung.[19] Mao's ideas were formulated on the basis of his experiences in China in the 1930s. His theory of revolutionary war consists of three stages. In stage one of his prescription for guerrilla war, fighters or guerrillas start operating from remote areas in terrain that is difficult to enter. The aim in this phase is to establish bases from which the guerrillas can extend their operations. The guerrillas carry out acts of sabotage, hit and run strikes and other under-mining activities, designed to disrupt the functioning of the state and economy.

In stage two, the guerrilla bases are extended to other areas with more people. The guerrillas continue to attack government strongholds and symbols, but direct confrontations with the regular armed forces are avoided. In stage three, the guerrilla base areas are linked together and the government is confronted directly. Here the guerrilla force transforms into a conventional army and a full conventional war can be fought. Few guerrilla movements have reached this last stage. When they did, such as in Angola, they were often not very successful.[20]

There are bottom–up explanations for guerrilla war and top–down ones. A bottom–up explanation focuses on the traditional attributes of a guerrilla movement, such as the rising of the masses due to disenfranchisement and dissatisfaction with the affairs of the state. A top–down explanation draws attention to the role of a small group or leadership taking up and encouraging existing but latent dissatisfaction and grievances among the population. Disadvantaged groups or populations, or town and countryside dichotomies are tapped into to help the guerrilla war gain momentum.[21] In most cases it can be expected that these two explanations are complementary rather than mutually exclusive.

The logic of the revolutionary guerrilla is to achieve their strategic aims by concentrating on the tactical level of strategy. This has several implications, which can be seen as characteristic of guerrilla war. In the first phase of this type of warfare, only a small number of men is necessary to carry out these tactical strikes, sometimes requiring only one individual to place a bomb or pull a trigger. To successfully hurt the enemy where he is weakest, great effects can be attained by surprise. A surprise attack by unidentified perpetrators is an important instrument to contribute to the aim of weakening the state. This implies that the combatants do not identify themselves. They hide among the population. A distinction between civilians and combatants can thus not be drawn.

Several conflicts fought during the period of the Cold War accorded with this characterisation. Examples include not only Angola, but also Vietnam and Mozambique. The processes involved in putting into practice the prescriptions of revolutionary guerrilla war were diverse. Specific elements were either conveniently forgotten or pragmatically introduced. The support of the population was not always secured: there were operations that clearly antagonised the public; and outside support was sought in order to increase the chances of success in the war, though Mao had stressed self-reliance. These are just two examples of how the theory and the practice of guerrilla war could diverge.

Nowadays, the framework of the Cold War, in which the revolutionary guerrilla ideas found many followers, has disappeared. The question therefore arises as to whether the revolutionary guerrilla war concept still has explanatory value for present-day military practices in developing states. Many authors have answered this question positively. They continue to apply the term guerrilla war to the different struggles that have been fought since the early 1990s, including those in collapsed states.[22] However, at least three important objections can be raised against this present-day perspective on guerrilla war. These objections render its application to the conflicts in the developing world problematic.

First, an important characteristic of guerrilla warfare is the role of the state. Guerrilla forces, in the understanding of revolutionary war, operate against a state or state actor. That many armed factions do not operate against state actors has been amply demonstrated by the striking cases of state collapse since the end of the Cold War.[23] However, even if the lack of a state opponent is disregarded, this does not save the concept of the revolutionary guerrilla war.

A second problematic element of the concept is the aim of the struggle. Revolutionary change is supposed to be the defining factor of this approach to guerrilla war. Today the ideological political content of the warring factions is fundamentally different.[24] Neither Marxist nor Leninist nor

Maoist thought prevails in the armed factions that are fighting in the wars under consideration.[25] While most would agree that the underpinning of ideological political thought is very thin in the case of Somalia, rescue attempts have been made. Some observers have opted simply to replace political ideology with other motivations for which the fighters enter the battlefield. Steven Metz, for example, has distinguished two new types of guerrilla insurgency: spiritual and commercial.[26] Spiritual insurgency is concerned with problems in the process of modernisation and lack of justice. This form of insurgency is, according to Metz, linked to its predecessor of revolutionary insurgency because it is aimed at a regime or the national state – but this has already been found problematic. Commercial insurgency is said to be new and concerned with the acquisition of wealth; personal wealth especially is the defining factor of this kind of insurgency.

Important motivations that have recently been ascribed to the armed factions fighting in wars in the developing world are not only personal benefit and wealth motives but also concerns about ethnic, clan and religious identity. Furthermore, environmental factors have been awarded large-scale influence.[27] Though it is problematic to attach such mono-causal labels to explain these wars, the exercise of replacing one set of goals with another underlines the widespread conviction that guerrilla warfare and insurgency are useful concepts for analysis.

However, it is not only questionable whether the ideological motivations can simply be replaced by monetary or spiritual ones to save these concepts. It is also questionable whether the warring factions aimed at a revolution and at breaking down state structures. These were already weak to start with and it is doubtful whether they actually used the strategic guerrilla war concept in order to achieve their aims. Did these warring factions go through the development of hit and run strikes, the establishment and extension of base areas and the final conventional confrontation of the enemy in order to realise monetary or spiritual goals? It is questionable whether faction leader Aidid in Somalia actually used this guerrilla war vocabulary in a flat and sparsely vegetated terrain that was highly unsuited for guerrilla operations. Initially the confrontations with the Somali government army took place in the open field or in urban terrain.[28] Subsequently, major confrontations took place between rival faction leaders, with heavy shelling and bombardments with high-calibre guns in and around the major towns, such as Mogadishu, Kismayo and Baidoa. Is this the third phase of Mao's revolutionary guerrilla war, namely conventional war, and did they ever go through phase one and two?

A third objection to the application of the revolutionary guerrilla concept to recent wars in the developing world is the fact that increased urbanisation in the developing world has led to urban environments becoming more and more important in the conduct of warfare. Conflicts are often fought in an urban setting.[29] One only has to think of the fierce confrontations in and around Mogadishu in the case of Somalia, which left the city in shambles in the course of 1991 and early 1992. This urban environment is anathema to guerrilla war in both the strategic revolutionary understanding and the tactical approach, which will be discussed shortly. The term urban guerrilla is a contradiction in terms due to the logic of the occupation of a base area in the understanding of revolutionary war.[30] How is this to be realised in a heavily built up area? Also, the fighter involved in a war in an urban setting is not able to operate in secret in order to establish a hold in the same manner as is done in the base areas, unless the fighters carry out attacks against individuals and installations, which should be more accurately called terrorism. This point will be further elaborated below. Most important here is that the distinction between the terrorist and the guerrilla disappears.

Guerrilla tactics

The second approach to guerrilla war, as a tactic rather than as a part of a comprehensive strategy, also presents a popular point of view for describing recent wars on the African continent. The methods of fighting forces in developing states, such as in the cases of Liberia, Sierra Leone and Somalia, are characterised by the apparent absence of an operational plan and the concentration on seemingly tactical confrontations of short duration. Before the period of the Cold War, guerrilla tactics had been a tried and tested method of waging war.[31] Guerrilla tactics here is a concept that emphasises the concentration of the fighters on the weaknesses of the opponent, while avoiding its strength. In this perspective it is as old as the phenomenon of war itself.[32]

However, this description of guerrilla tactics as the concentration on the enemy's weaknesses and avoiding its strong points invites confusion. Could this not just as well be part of conventional manoeuvre warfare, which uses the same principles? Furthermore, conventional armies often possess Special Forces, which carry out subversion and obstruction operations in order to hamper the operation of the enemy fighters. These forces operate together. Could this not just as well be, in the case of the wars in collapsed states, but a minor aspect of the activities of wars instead of the whole picture?

Another problematic aspect, as already noted, is the fact that when guerrillas concentrate just on the tactics, the distinction between guerrilla and terrorism becomes blurred. When is a tactical strike a guerrilla hit-and-run action to hurt the enemy and when is it a terrorist attack? This approach does not rescue the explanatory and analytical value of the guerrilla concept either.

This section has attempted to make clear that the application of the term guerrilla, in both meanings of the term, to wars in developing states since the end of the Cold War poses several problems. The concept seems to have been stretched to such limits that it has lost its clear analytical and explanatory value. It can be questioned whether the concept is not used because of a lack of alternatives, rather than because there is a clear positive match between the concept and the recent practice of warfare. Furthermore, it can be questioned whether the term guerrilla has acquired a derogatory meaning, similar to the political use of the term terrorist, to describe opponents of a varying but difficult to comprehend nature in the developing world.

Conventional warfare

There are several features of war in collapsed states already highlighted above that make the application of the concept of conventional war seem unattractive too. First, in this perspective the presence of non-state actors seems also problematic. Conventional war is often associated with the state. It is a type of warfare that is fought by states against other states. Second, conventional war is aimed at the destruction of the enemy's forces, its material capacity to pursue war further, and its will to do so.[33] Conventional war, as distinct from guerrilla war, is characterised by a clear operational centre of gravity. On the operational level of strategy the armed interactions show a focal point to which all effort is directed. However, these features seem to be lacking in the wars in collapsed states. The actors do not represent states and they do not seem to confront each other directly, let alone aim for the destruction of their opponents.

There are other features that make the application of the concept of conventional war unattractive. The use of small arms and the occurrence of looting and plunder have been prominent in recent conflicts. Small arms as the weapon of choice in these wars have received a lot of attention because of their widespread use.[34] The presence and availability of small arms is seen as an important factor in sustaining war.[35] Most small arms were imported to developing countries during the Cold War. Weapons have been sold, stolen or simply lost track of. Unlike the registry for heavy weapons purchases, until recently such a monitoring system did not exist for small arms. Not only are these weapons easy to operate, they can also be highly effective.

However, small weapons do not make conventional war impossible. Small arms can be used openly. They can be deployed in an operational plan towards an operational goal in commanded and coordinated actions. Heavy weapons and advanced technology are neither necessary nor sufficient conditions for conventional war. Conventional battle is not only a phenomenon of the modern age. In pre-modern Europe, for example, these kinds of battles were also fought.

Looting and plunder have also been prominent features of recent wars, such as in the Democratic Republic of Congo, Liberia and Sierra Leone. In these conflicts, in which such aspects featured prominently, a close link between the armed forces and business undertakings has been noted.[36] There are states in which war and economics are extremely tightly knit.[37] Looting during warfare can become institutionalised, especially when no alternatives are found to maintain the armed forces. In Somalia there were examples of traders and rebel leaders co-operating. Some traders had an interest in maintaining high food prices. They asked fighters to fire at ships bringing food aid into the country in order to prevent food being unloaded, which could bring down the prices on the market. When the shortage of food drove up the prices on the market, more wanted to share in the profit and therefore the number of attacks rose.

Looting food in the case of Somalia significantly contributed to starvation. The famine in Somalia was in the first place caused by the war that plagued the country.[38] The forces of nature, such as drought, that occurred at the same time in Somalia then contributed to famine. Natural disasters do not necessarily lead to famine. Human actions are largely responsible for the outbreak of such a calamity.[39] War or lack of government control, for example, can be the reason for the population not being able to obtain food. Even when drought occurs, the mechanisms of exchange and trade can assure that food is available, especially when traders see that their goods will be in demand. Starvation is the result of actively withholding food from groups of people. For the Somali rebel groups, control over food became a war-fighting instrument. The control over aid strengthened the warring side, and it weakened the opponent when food provision among its forces was hampered. Examples of other wars in which the instrument of starvation was used have occurred in Angola, Biafra, Eritrea, and Sudan.[40]

However, these features of looting and starvation have accompanied warfare over the centuries in all parts of the world and do not disqualify a war from being conventional.[41] Warfare is simply not a clean business, as we sometimes tend to forget given that there are international conventions in place to protect, for instance, the rights of combatants and civilians. Plunder has been a common phenomenon associated with war. The link between warfare and looting operated because war leaders did not have any available means to feed, clothe and house the fighters. Therefore, both fighters and regular soldiers were forced to help themselves. Neither looting, nor plunder, nor starvation, are new phenomena. What these observations on the wars in Africa have tended to overlook is the fact that such features are frequent companions of wars. Perhaps it is because these features seem to make up the majority of the activity that goes on in the battle theatre that they tend to stand out. Another factor is that this is not the way Western audiences expect or prefer to see wars conducted.

There seems to be a strong bias towards regarding conventional war as Western war, such as an armed confrontation between the Soviet Union and the United States, for which the world had been preparing during the many decades of the Cold War.[42] Conventional war is supposed to be techno-logically advanced and relatively clean, with no room for plunder, cruelty or starvation. This is in stark contrast to the ways many wars, recently in Africa and in the more distant past in Europe, have been fought. In Europe in the early modern period, even during the Napoleonic wars, the armed forces often lived off the land, appropriating anything they needed in order to remain a fighting force.[43] This not only involved plunder but was also accompanied by acts of cruelty and starvation. Even during the last major war in Western Europe these phenomena were present. These features therefore do not disqualify war from being conventional.

What then are the main features of conventional war? Conventional war is usually defined as a kind of war in which the political and military spheres are separated, the fighters operate openly, the command structure with ranks and a hierarchy is centralised, leading to coordinated operations, and these operations are carried out by large numbers of recruits. In order to assess the essentials of conventional war, they should be clearly distinguished from guerrilla war.

However, distinguishing between the political and military spheres is a confusing business. It is true that in a revolutionary guerrilla war the political and military spheres are closely fused. The fighters, who to the enemy look like civilians, may be indoctrinated with communist propaganda. Propaganda agents tend to be present in every level of the organisation, including the smallest unit or cell. The fact that these agents could be identified points to a separation of the political and military spheres. At the top of the communist organisation the military and political spheres existed as separate entities, but were also integrated, often in the form of a strong leader, in order to conduct the revolutionary war.

Another potential distinguishing factor that could create confusion is the centralised command structure, with its attendant features of ranks, hierarchy and coordination. In revolutionary guerrilla organisations these features can also be found. For example, in Mao's prescription for the successful conduct of a guerrilla war, this element was deemed essential. According to Mao's prescriptions, 'In guerrilla base areas, the command must be centralized for strategical purposes and decentralized for tactical purposes'.[44] A sound organisation was important for the success of the war.

For the present discussion, conventional war may be distinguished from guerrilla war in at least three crucial respects. First, the centre of gravity: conventional and guerrilla war have centres of gravity on different levels of strategy, tactical and operational respectively. Second, the distinction between combatants and noncombatants is absent in guerrilla warfare and clearly present in conventional warfare. Third, the operations are carried out by a large number of fighters, who operate in the open in conventional war, as opposed to secret operations of a small number of men or even individuals operating single-handedly in revolutionary guerrilla war. This is also the dividing line between phase three of revolutionary guerrilla war, which consists of conventional war, and the preceding phases. These features, as will be argued here, are also observable in conflicts in collapsed states.

Operational centre of gravity

An operational centre of gravity is observable in conflicts that at first seem to have more in common with guerrilla war. An operational centre of gravity is generally an object towards which concerted military force is directed. As described above, this can be the armed forces of the opponent, a particular part of its territory or its government or capital. It is distinct from the tactical centre of gravity, which is usually diverse and of a smaller nature, such as bridgeheads, power installations or the lives of politicians. As already noted, cities are an important focus for armed conflict in the developing world. This is confirmed upon closer inspection of several wars in the former Third World, including the case of Somalia.

The field of conflict geography yields particularly interesting insights. The capital is often the special focus of armed interactions.[45] In historical perspective, the capital in many African states has had strong binding powers. Lack of physical control over the hinterland for varying reasons, among others lack of interest or excessive expense, meant that the capital functioned to bind the state together during both colonial times and in the post-colonial era.[46] In the case of Somalia, the fiercest fighting, the use of heavy weapons and consequently the greatest destruction have been witnessed in Mogadishu and other large towns in the south of the country. They can be identified as important centres of gravity in the armed interactions of the warring parties, not only in their focus but also in the time and energy invested in the confrontations over these objectives.

Operations in city environments have several implications. Revolutionary guerrilla war is impossible because the logistics of operating from base areas is difficult in built-up areas. Guerrilla tactics, as used in urban surroundings, result more often than not in terrorism or sniper activity. Not only the presence of the fighters confirm the city as the centre of gravity; also their actions there underline its importance. The operations of the fighting forces in Mogadishu, and also in the Liberian and Sierra Leonean capitals to name but a few, were clearly identifiable. On reading descriptions of the confrontations one can only conclude that the fighters were aware of the presence of the enemy and fired in their direction. Suburbs, particular strongholds, such as the city's air and seaports, were repeatedly the focus of armed confrontations in which the available heavy armaments were used. A distinguishable battle theatre was present. Furthermore, it was impossible to control terrain in the cities without identifying oneself. This control remained elusive because in many cases the weaponry the fighters could use, dominated by small arms, could not achieve lasting dominance over the opponent. Whenever heavy weaponry became available, through capture, donation or trade, it was used to inflict damage on the opponent in or around urban centres. These were the centres of gravity towards which the military force of the fighters was directed, and there the largest destruction was witnessed. An operational centre of gravity can thus be identified around which the fighters' actions converged.

The distinction between combatants and noncombatants

The second important characteristic of conventional war, the distinction between combatants and noncombatants, can also be observed in collapsed states such as Somalia. This is contrary to the mainly Western complaints that this distinction was difficult to draw. It may well be the case that the problems United States forces encountered in Somalia from failing to clearly distinguish between friend and foe have dominated the discussion. It should not be forgotten, however, that the methods the Somali used against the intervention forces were markedly different from those used against each other. One example was the tactic of swarming, in which women and children were used in large numbers. The fighters would hide among these large crowds of people. In this way the fighters could make advances or attack particular targets. The peace-keeping soldiers, as the Somalis knew very well, had strict instructions to fire only in self-defence and to refrain from harming civilians. This Somali tactic made the identification of noncombatant civilians very difficult for the peace-keepers.

However, in drawing attention to local culture and sensitivities, there are important ways in which a distinction between fighter and civilian could be drawn. Physical attributes and behaviour towards their environment and towards other fighting groups are important in this respect.

Physical attributes, not only regular army uniforms but also disguises and references to local cultural practices, made the fighters stand out from the rest of the population. Army uniforms or parts of army accoutrements were on visible display in the wars under consideration.[47] The fact that these were important and highly coveted can be illustrated by several developments. In the case of Somalia, the military leaders apparently had the ambition to provide their men with army fatigues when their finances allowed.[48] More common than complete or parts of army uniforms were other physical means of distinction such as arm or headbands. In particular, in the first phase of the wars the Somali fighters were described as wearing white headbands and the Liberian fighters, the Black Scorpions, used black armbands as means of identification.[49]

Apart from these more common means of distinction and notably in the conflicts in West Africa, factors relating to local culture played a role. There was the practice of initiation rites for young boys and young men. In order to become men their bodies were marked or tattooed. This practice of the forcible tattooing of the fighters was widespread in Liberia and Sierra Leone.[50] Tattoos were a way of recognising fighters. Another aspect of local culture, such as the use of disguises, played a role. In Liberia the fighters were described as 'kitted out for battle in women's wigs and dresses. One wore a flowery lavatory seat cover on his head. One fighter sauntered down the road in Pan Am airline socks.'[51] These disguises were a well-known feature of local beliefs in spiritual power. Masks, the use of white clay and painted faces were practices associated with spiritual leaders and were now copied on a large-scale by the fighters. These adornments could scare the enemy and would provide spiritual protection through close contact with the spiritual world.[52] During the two wars civilians did not share this practice of dressing up and therefore a distinction could be drawn.

More important than the physical attributes of the fighters was their behaviour towards their environment. This also points, in an important measure, to a distinction between combatants and noncombatants. The fighters lived off the land. Logistical apparatuses to feed the fighters were often non-existent. In order to obtain food, the fighters had to get this from the local population. They thus could not remain anonymous. The appropriation of food often went hand in hand with coercion of the local residents. This obviously made them stand out.

Furthermore, as noted, the fighting in urban environments called for open engagements. This caused the local population to know where the fighters were active.[53] In Somalia, for example, Aidid and his men were not hiding in the bush. People knew where the fighters were operating.[54] When the means were available and the necessity shown, Aidid sought out his opponents in the open. Some factions used the opposite of surprise attacks. The simple announcement of attacks made people flee in fear, which meant advances of the rebel forces without much expenditure of power. Striking examples are also found in the wars in Liberia and Sierra Leone.[55]

Contributing factors to this noticeable behaviour towards their environment were the fighters' different accents and manners. Important details, such as the fact that the fighters often came from the countryside, where the main recruitment drives took place, while they were fighting in the cities, were important. Therefore the fighters spoke different dialects from the local population living in the areas where they were operating. Special care was taken to ensure that the fighters did not operate in or were not able to return to their home regions. In the case of Liberia, it was common practice that fighters were forced to kill a relative, not only to show their prowess as a fighter but also to cut off any route home.[56]

Apart from physical distinctions and the behaviour of the fighters towards the population, their behaviour towards the other fighting groups also points to a distinction between fighters and civilians. On closer inspection, cease-fires were possible and did at times hold relatively well. An important example in the case of Somalia was the cease-fire concluded under United Nations auspices in March 1992, after which the first peace-keeping mission was sent to the country. The fact that this cease-fire held for some time in Mogadishu indicated that the fighters were able to distinguish between friend and foe. They knew against whom to hold their fire. Furthermore, the fact that the war leaders were able to elicit such compliance from their fighters points to the command they were able to establish over them.[57] On the basis of this compliance, the Somali factions concluded not only cease-fires but also formed alliances. Aidid cooperated with almost all other factions when it was to his advantage. The enemy of my enemy was indeed considered a friend. The fact that these alliances were concluded can only point to their relative usefulness and the success that attended them. If it was not in their interest, why would the war leaders form such coalitions? If on the battlefield they proved to be a failure the logic of concluding them would also disappear. In short, the fighters knew whom they were fighting against.

A last important argument for the distinction between fighters and civilians is the fact that outsiders could also draw conclusions to this effect. The aid agencies that were present in these diverse battle zones concluded that as a proportion of the total fatalities, civilians numbered very high.[58] The fact that such conclusions could be reached by the organisations, which also argued that the distinction was difficult, can only lead to the conclusion that distinctions were possible in one way or another.[59] As a proportion of war casualties, civilian deaths have been on the increase in the twentieth century. While this might be seen as an undesirable development, it should not cloud judgements on what is going on in these wars and on the fact that the distinctions at least by the local population could be drawn.

Number of fighters

The third characteristic of conventional war is the number of fighters who operate in the open. This type of warfare relies on large numbers of combatants who are not part of a clandestinely operating organisation acting in secret. On close inspection of the wars under consideration, not only can an important centre of gravity be detected but this centre of gravity is also repeatedly fought over with the use of large numbers of fighters. This points to the importance that is attached to this centre and the strength of the desire to gain control over it. Control can only be achieved by physical occupation and such an occupation requires a large number of troops. All the warring factions under consideration at one time or other commanded large numbers of fighters. In Somalia, chasing out the president in 1990–1 required a large number of fighters. When important operations focused on urban centres, these could not be taken by stealth alone. The recruitment of a large number of fighters did not prove problematic for the factions. Local and regional opposition to the Somali regime initially proved a fruitful force for the war leaders to appeal to.[60] Using a favourable season, when the cattle herders could leave the cattle in the care of youngsters, and a favourable location, such as areas with a history of dissidence, also helped recruit fighters. Appeals to clan identity contributed to the formation of the Somali armed factions, even though factions were not always clearly clan organisations. Exploiting such factors, the factions could recruit a large number of fighters.

In the environment of a collapsed state, armed factions became very attractive as a source of security, gainful employment and food. There were very few alternatives to which the population could turn. This contributed to the continued support that the population lent to the warring factions. An example of the use of large numbers of fighters was the attack on the American troops who raided the Olympic Hotel in October 1993 looking for Aidid. The tragic consequence of the resulting firefight, which lasted for hours, was the loss of 18 American lives and the subsequent withdrawal of the intervention troops.

There seem to be strong biases toward regarding conventional war as a form of war that is Western, modern, uses high-technology weapons, and is relatively clean. There are strong prejudices at work in the preferred way of seeing this kind of war. Such prejudice does injustice to some striking conventional features of wars in the developing world that hitherto have been categorised as guerrilla struggles. In these wars too not only was there a centre of gravity and a distinction between combatants and noncombatants, but also a large number of fighters were engaged.

It should, however, be noted that conventional battles were not continuous. There were long pauses between conventional confrontations caused by the absence of need to engage the enemy or weakness of the fighting forces. During these episodes other features, such as starvation and plunder, were prominent. These could contribute to the weakening of the enemy without risking the full force of the faction. But this does not mean that conventional war was not the main strategy chosen to fight the war. Drawing on historical analogies, battles were conducted when the necessity arose, such as threats to strengths and positions, and when the circumstances were favourable, such as the season or the weather. This was also the case in the conflicts this chapter has focused on.

Conclusion

Conventional war and guerrilla war are concepts used to describe and analyse the most important ways and means of warfare. Furthermore, they have been put into practice by military forces all around the world. They cover the wide range of ideas on how armed interactions are conducted and form part of the overall phenomenon of war.[61] While there seems no reason to discard the concepts themselves in distinguishing war activities, this chapter has questioned, on the basis of empirical evidence, the applicability of the term guerrilla warfare to war in a certain environment, namely collapsed states.

This chapter has sought to demonstrate that first, guerrilla war is a problematic concept to use in understanding wars in collapsed states, and second, that while the idea of conventional war is subject to Western bias, it is more appropriate for understanding these wars than has hitherto been realised. Essential characteristics of this kind of war can also be present in those wars in cases of state collapse that have mainly been seen as guerrilla struggles, if not as chaos and barbarity. Guerrilla war is problematic because of the absence of state actors and ideological aims and because of the urban environment in which war often occurs. Conventional war is appropriate because an operational centre of gravity can be detected, a distinction can be made between combatants and noncombatants, and because large numbers of fighters can be called upon.

The failure to recognise the true nature of contemporary conflict has often been seen as the number one factor in explaining why it is so difficult to achieve success in intervention operations in this kind of war. In particular, the conventional orientations of Western armed forces have been criticised as hampering the formulation of a proper answer to these so-called irregular threats. This chapter has not argued that the armed forces were right after all to maintain a conventional posture. First and foremost, not all peace operations aim to get involved in the armed interactions of the warring parties. Most often they are sent to deal with the symptoms of the problems rather than of their root causes. It is thus questionable if they need to be prepared to engage in or willing to respond to the type of warfare that the warring parties are fighting.

Second, in case the intervention forces are sent to engage with the warring parties, a conventional answer is not necessarily the right one. Other factors than the military may be more important in influencing the operation of the warring faction. Cutting their supply routes and hampering the operation of the factions might be quicker ways to achieve success. These suggestions can be seen as part of the counter-insurgency repertoire and are thus not always conventional in character. To deal effectively with these wars, an all-inclusive approach that takes into account all the elements that fuel the conflict should be considered.

It is clear that these issues deserve further investigation in order to develop proper responses to emergencies in collapsed states. The first step in achieving this is to correctly analyse the interactions in these wars, including their conventional features.

Notes

1 Parts of this chapter are based on the author's PhD thesis, which was completed in October 2002 at the War Studies department of King's College, London and published as *Clausewitz and African War, Politics and Strategy in Liberia and Somalia*, London: Frank Cass, 2005.
2 Errol A. Henderson and J. David Singer, 'Civil War in the Post-Colonial World, 1946–92', *Journal of Peace Research*, 37, 3 (2000), pp. 275–99.

3 Peter Wallensteen and Margareta Sollenberg, 'Armed Conflict and Regional Conflict Complexes, 1989–1997', *Journal of Peace Research*, 35, 5 (1998), pp. 621–34.

4 <http://www.sozialwiss.uni-hamburg.de/publish/Ipw/Akuf/archiv_afrika.htm# Trends>, website last consulted 10 February 2003.

5 According to some this might be the wave of the future, e.g. Somalia, Afghanistan. Raymond W. Copson, *Africa's Wars and Prospects for Peace*, Armonk, NY: M. E. Sharpe, 1994, p. 157.

6 Robert D. Kaplan, 'The Coming Anarchy: How Scarcity, Crime, Overpopulation, and Disease are Rapidly Destroying the Social Fabric of our Planet', *Atlantic Monthly*, 273 (February 1994), pp. 44–76.

7 Paul B. Rich (ed.), *Warlords in International Relations*, Basingstoke: Macmillan, 1999 and John Mackinlay, 'Warlords', *Rusi Journal*, 143, 2 (1998), pp. 24–32.

8 Warlords came to prominence around the end of Chinese imperial rule (1916–27). See Edward A. McCord, *The Power of the Gun: The Emergence of Modern Chinese Warlordism*, Berkeley, CA: University of California Press, 1993; James E. Sheridan, *Chinese Warlord: The Career of Feng Yu-hsiang*, Stanford, CA: Stanford University Press, 1966; and Diana Lary, *Warlord Soldiers: Chinese Common Soldiers, 1911–1937*, Cambridge: Cambridge University Press, 1985.

9 In the past, the cases of Chad and Mozambique at the end of the 1970s and early 1980s have been important examples: Roger Charlton and Roy May, 'Warlords and Militarism in Chad', *Review of African Political Economy*, 45/46 (1989), pp. 12–25 and Colin Darch 'Are There Warlords in Provincial Mozambique? Questions of the Social Base of MNR Banditry', *Review of African Political Economy*, 45/46 (1989), pp. 34–49.

10 For a comparison of African warfare with warlordism, see for example William Reno, *Warlord Politics and African States*, Boulder, CO: Lynne Rienner, 1998.

11 E. J. Hobsbawm, *Bandits*, London: Trinity, 1969. The phenomenon of banditry was prevalent in the Middle Ages but has continued to exist throughout history. For an application of Hobsbawm's ideas about banditry to Africa, see Ralph A. Austin, 'Social Bandits and Other Heroic Criminals: Western Models of Resistance and their Relevance for Africa', in Donald Crummey (ed.), *Banditry, Rebellion and Social Protest in Africa*, London: James Currey, 1986, pp. 89–108.

12 Excluded also are globalisation arguments, which provide another explanatory framework with less emphasis on the military factors that are the focus here. See for example Mary Kaldor, *New and Old Wars: Organized Violence in a Global Era*, Cambridge: Polity, 1999.

13 See for example Dutch military doctrine: *Koninklijke Landmacht, Militaire Doctrine*, Den Haag: SDU, 1996.

14 Mao Tse-tung, *On Guerrilla Warfare*, tr. Samuel Griffith, New York: Praeger, 1965 and Russel Stetler (ed.), *The Military Art of People's War: Selected Writings of General Giap Vo Nguyen*, New York: Monthly Review, 1970. See also John Shy and Thomas W. Collier, 'Revolutionary War', in Peter Paret (ed.), *Makers of Modern Strategy: From Machiavelli to the Nuclear Age*, Oxford: Clarendon, 1986, pp. 815–62; Ernesto Che Guevara, *Guerrilla Warfare*, Lincoln, Neb.: University of Nebraska Press, 1998; Steve Lewis, 'Che Guevara and Guerrilla Warfare: Training for Today's Nonlinear Battlefields', *Military Review*, 81, 5 (2001), pp. 98–101.

15 See for example US *Army Field Manual FM 100-20/AFP3-20*, Washington, DC: Headquarters Departments of the Army and the Air Force, 1990. For a discussion of the problems attached to low-intensity concepts, see Christopher Bellamy, 'If You Can't Stand the Heat: New Concepts of Conflict Intensity', *RUSI Journal*, 143, 1 (1998), pp. 25–31.

16 This choice for analytical purposes is not to suggest that this is the one and only way to distinguish these different kinds of war. See for this discussion David Fastabend, 'The Categorization of Conflict', *Parameters*, 27, 2 (1997), pp. 75–87.

17 For a short history of the conflict see Daniel Compagnon, 'Somali Armed Movements: The Interplay of Political Entrepreneurship and Clan-Based Factions', in Christopher Clapham (ed.), *African Guerrillas*, Oxford: James Currey, 1998, pp. 73–90.

18 Ian F. W. Beckett, *Encyclopedia of Guerrilla Warfare*, Santa Barbara, CA: ABC-CLIO, 1999 and Anthony James Joes, *Guerrilla Warfare: A Historical, Biographical and Bibliographical Sourcebook*, Westport, Conn.: Greenwood, 1996.

19 Mao Tse-tung, *On Guerrilla Warfare*.

20 Alex de Waal, 'Contemporary Warfare in Africa', in Mary Kaldor and Basker Vashee (eds), *Restructuring the Global Military Sector, I New Wars*, London: Pinter, 1997, pp. 287–332, p. 299.

21 Norma Kriger, *Zimbabwe's Guerrilla War: Peasant Voices*, Cambridge: Cambridge University Press, 1992.

22 See for example Clapham, *African Guerrillas* and De Waal, 'Contemporary Warfare in Africa'.

23 This is not to suggest that the state has become irrelevant for warfare, as some have suggested. See Martin van Creveld, *The Transformation of War*, New York: Free Press, 1991.

24 However, Larry Cable argues that modern-day insurgents, including those operating in the early 1990s, strive for 'political authority over a specified population in a defined geographic venue'. Larry Cable, 'Reinventing the Round Wheel: Insurgency, Counter-insurgency, and Peacekeeping Post Cold War', *Small Wars and Insurgencies*, 4, 2 (1993), pp. 228–62. For the argument that nineteenth century guerrillas, even during the Napoleonic wars, were also marked by ideology, see John Broom, 'The Counterinsurgency Paradox', *Military Review*, 77, 4 (1997), pp. 42–50.

25 Notwithstanding this observation, there are still some factions aiming to promote these objectives such as the currently active Maoist fighters in Nepal and the Shining Path Movement in Peru.

26 Stephen Metz, 'Insurgency after the Cold War', *Small Wars and Insurgencies*, 5, 1 (1994), pp. 63–82.

27 Isabelle G. B. M. Duyvesteyn, 'Contemporary War: Ethnic Conflict, Resource Conflict or Something Else?', *Civil Wars*, 3, 1 (2000), pp. 90–114.

28 John Drysdale, *Whatever Happened to Somalia?*, London: Haan, 1995.

29 Jean-Luc Marret, *Cities and Infra-state Conflicts*, Camberley: Conflict Studies Research Centre, 2001.

30 Walter Laqueur, *The New Terrorism: Fanaticism and the Arms of Mass Destruction*, London: Phoenix, 2001, pp. 8–9.

31 Anthony James Joes, *Guerrilla Conflict Before the Cold War*, Westport, Conn.: Praeger, 1996 and Robert Asprey, *War in the Shadows: The Classic History of Guerrilla Warfare From Ancient Persia to the Present*, London: Little Brown, 1994.

32 See for example Sun Tzu, *The Art of War*, Ware: Wordsworth, 1993.

33 See, among others, Carl von Clausewitz, *Vom Kriege: Hinterlassenes Werk*, Bonn: Dümmler, 1952.

34 SIPRI Yearbook 1999, *Armaments Disarmament and International Security*, Oxford: Oxford University Press, 1999, pp. 506–16.

35 Cassidy Craft, *Weapons for Peace, Weapons for War: The Effects of Arms Transfers on War Outbreak, Involvement and Termination*, New York: Routledge, 1999 and John Sislin and Frederic S. Pearson, *Arms and Ethnic Conflict*, London: Rowman and Littlefield, 2001.

36 Alex de Waal, 'Contemporary Warfare in Africa: Changing Context and Changing Strategies', *IDS Bulletin*, 27, 3 (1996), pp. 6–16, p. 8. See also Janet Roitman, 'The Garrison-Entrepôt', *Cahiers d'Études Africaines*, 38, 150–2 (1998), pp. 297–329.

37 On Liberia, see for example, Stephen Ellis, *The Mask of Anarchy*, London: Hurst, 1999, p. 289 and François Jean and Jean Christophe Rufin (eds), *Économie des Guerres Civiles*, Paris: Hachette, 1996.

38 Alex de Waal, *Famine Crimes: Politics and the Disaster Relief Industry in Africa*, Oxford: James Currey, 1997.

39 Jean Drèze, Amartya Sen, and Athar Hussein (eds), *The Political Economy of Hunger, 1 Entitlement and Well-Being*, Oxford: Clarendon, 1995 and Amartya Sen, *War and Famines: On Divisions and Incentives*, Paper 33, Development Research Programme, London: London School of Economics, 1991.

40 See for example David Keen, *The Benefits of Famine: A Political Economy of Famine and Relief in South-Western Sudan, 1983–1989*, Princeton, NJ: Princeton University Press, 1994.

41 For a discussion of the role of food as an instrument of war, see also Gayle E. Smith, 'Relief Operations and Military Strategy', in Thomas C. Weiss and Larry Minear (eds), *Humanitarianism Across Borders: Sustaining Civilians in Times of War*, Boulder, CO: Lynne Rienner, 1993, pp. 97–116.

42 See for example the concept of the AirLand Battle: US Army, Training and Doctrine Command, *AirLand Battle 2000*, Washington, DC: Department of the Army, 1981.

43 For a comparison of the Thirty Years' War and contemporary wars, see Herfried Münkler, *Die neuen Kriege*, Reinbek: Rowohlt, 2002.

44 Mao Tse-tung, *On Guerrilla Warfare*, p. 114.

45 As argued elsewhere, this operational centre overlapped with the political goal of the warring factions, which was control over the political centre in order to gain international recognition, power and legitimacy. See Duyvesteyn, 'Contemporary War'.

46 Jeffrey Herbst, *State and Power in Africa: Comparative Lessons in Authority and Control*, Princeton, NJ: Princeton University Press, 2000. For the case of Zaire/Democratic Republic of Congo and Sierra Leone, see Mika Vehnämäki, 'Diamonds and Warlords: The Geography of War in the Democratic Republic of Congo and Sierra Leone', *Nordic Journal of African Studies*, 11, 1 (2002), pp. 48–74.

47 De Waal, 'Contemporary Warfare in Africa', p. 292.

48 Human Rights Watch, *Somalia Faces the Future: Human Rights in a Fragmented Society*, New York: Human Rights Watch, 1995, p. 46.

49 Peter Biles, 'Somali President Appeals for Cease-fire in Capital', *Guardian*, 3 January 1991.

50 Paul Richards, *Fighting for the Rainforest: War, Youth and Resources in Sierra Leone*, Oxford; James Currey, 1996, p. 5.

51 Matthew Campbell, 'Rebels Deal Out Death on Road to Monrovia', *Sunday Times*, 12 August 1990. See also Mary Moran, 'Warriors or Soldiers? Masculinity and Ritual Transvestism in the Liberian Civil War', in Constance R. Sutton (ed.), *Feminism, Nationalism and Militarism*, Arlington, VA: Association for Feminist Anthropology/American Anthropological Association, 1995, pp. 73–88.

52 Ellis, *The Mask of Anarchy*.
53 For accounts by local residents witnessing the rebel actions, see for example, Mariam Arif Gassem, *Hostages: The People who Kidnapped Themselves*, Nairobi: Central Graphic Services, 1994 and Joseph Njoh, *Through the Liberian Storm*, London: Minerva, 1996.
54 See also for the case of the war in Zaire/Democratic Republic of Congo: Human Rights Watch, *Zaire: Transition, War and Human Rights*, New York: Human Rights Watch, 1997.
55 De Waal, 'Contemporary Warfare in Africa', p. 315.
56 Human Rights Watch, *Easy Prey: Child Soldiers in Liberia*, New York: Human Rights Watch, 1994.
57 Jean Hélène, 'Somalie: l'inquiétude des organisations humanitaires', *Le Monde*, 28 November 1992.
58 See for example Human Rights Watch, *Somalia Faces the Future*, p. 23.
59 This paradoxical argument can also be seen in Human Rights Watch, *Somalia Faces the Future*.
60 As an example of an earlier phase in the Somali war, before the collapse of the state, a local commander explained the problems of recruitment as follows: 'I start by planning an attack with 60 men, and soon I have 3,000. And there is no way of telling them not to go. So, in those narrow mountain passes [in the north of Somalia], I lose every effect of surprise; we are too crowded together; the artillery hits us with full force; everybody attacks without orders. They shoot tremendous amounts of ammunition and nothing much gets done. Then, after we get back to base, they all disappear to go back to the bush.' Gérard Prunier, 'A Candid View of the Somali National Movement', *Horn of Africa*, 13 and 14, 3, 4, 1 and 2 (1990/1991), pp. 107–20, p. 113.
61 See also the chapter by Mike Smith in this volume.

References

Asprey, Robert B., *War in the Shadows: The Classic History of Guerrilla Warfare From Ancient Persia to the Present*, London: Little Brown, 1994.

Austin, Ralph A., 'Social Bandits and Other Heroic Criminals: Western Models of Resistance and their Relevance for Africa', in Donald Crummey (ed.), *Banditry, Rebellion and Social Protest in Africa*, London: James Currey, 1986, pp. 89–108.

Beckett, Ian F. W., *Encyclopaedia of Guerrilla Warfare*, Santa Barbara, CA: ABC–CLIO, 1999.

Bellamy, Christopher, 'If You Can't Stand the Heat: New Concepts of Conflict Intensity', *RUSI Journal*, 143, 1 (1998), pp. 25–31.

Broom, John, 'The Counterinsurgency Paradox', *Military Review*, 77, 4 (1997), pp. 42–50.

Cable, Larry, 'Reinventing the Round Wheel: Insurgency, Counter-Insurgency, and Peacekeeping Post Cold War', *Small Wars and Insurgencies*, 4, 2 (1993), pp. 228–62.

Charlton, Roger and Roy May, 'Warlords and Militarism in Chad', *Review of African Political Economy*, 45/46 (1989), pp. 12–25.

Clapham, Christopher (ed.), *African Guerrillas*, Oxford: James Currey, 1998.

Clausewitz, Carl von, *Vom Kriege: Hinterlassenes Werk*, Bonn: Dümmler, 1952.

Compagnon, Daniel, 'Somali Armed Movements: The Interplay of Political Entrepreneurship and Clan-Based Factions', in Christopher Clapham (ed.), *African Guerrillas*. Oxford: James Currey, 1998, pp. 73–90.

Copson, Raymond W., *Africa's Wars and Prospects for Peace*. Armonk, NY: M. E. Sharpe, 1994.

Craft, Cassidy, *Weapons for Peace, Weapons for War: The Effects of Arms Transfers on War Outbreak, Involvement and Termination*, New York: Routledge, 1999.

Creveld, Martin van, *The Transformation of War*, New York: The Free Press, 1991.

Darch, Colin, 'Are There Warlords in Provincial Mozambique? Questions of the Social Base of MNR Banditry', *Review of African Political Economy*, 45/46 (1989), pp. 34–49.

Drèze, Jean, Amartya Sen, and Athar Hussein (eds), *The Political Economy of Hunger: Vol. 1 Entitlement and Well-Being*, Oxford: Clarendon, 1995.

Drysdale, John, *Whatever Happened to Somalia?*, London: Haan, 1995.

Duyvesteyn, Isabelle, *Clausewitz and African War: Politics and Strategy in Liberia and Somalia*, London: Frank Cass, 2004.

——'Contemporary War: Ethnic Conflict, Resource Conflict or Something Else?', *Civil Wars*, 3, 1 (2000), pp. 92–116.

Ellis, Stephen, *The Mask of Anarchy*, London: Hurst, 1999.

Fastabend, David, 'The Categorization of Conflict', *Parameters*, 27, 2 (1997), pp. 75–87.

François, Jean and Jean Christophe Rufin (eds), *Économie des Guerres Civiles*, Paris: Hachette, 1996.

Gassem, Mariam Arif, *Hostages: The People Who Kidnapped Themselves*, Nairobi: Central Graphic Services, 1994.

Guevara, Ernesto Che, *Guerrilla Warfare*, Lincoln, Neb.: University of Nebraska Press, 1998.

Henderson, Errol A. and J. David Singer, 'Civil War in the Post-Colonial World, 1946–92', *Journal of Peace Research*, 37, 3 (2000), pp. 275–99.

Herbst, Jeffrey, *State and Power in Africa: Comparative Lessons in Authority and Control*, Princeton, NJ: Princeton University Press, 2000.

Hobsbawm, Eric J., *Bandits*, London: Trinity, 1969.

Human Rights Watch, *Zaire: Transition, War and Human Rights*, New York: Human Rights Watch, 1997.

——*Somalia Faces the Future: Human Rights in a Fragmented Society*, New York: Human Rights Watch, 1995.

——*Easy Prey: Child Soldiers in Liberia*, New York: Human Rights Watch, 1994.

James Joes, Anthony, *Guerrilla Warfare: A Historical, Biographical and Bibliographical Sourcebook*, Westport, Conn.: Greenwood, 1996.

——*Guerrilla Conflict Before the Cold War*, Westport, Conn.: Praeger, 1996.

Kaldor, Mary, *New and Old Wars: Organized Violence in a Global Era*, Cambridge: Polity Press, 1999.

Kaplan, Robert D., 'The Coming Anarchy: How Scarcity, Crime, Overpopulation, and Disease are Rapidly Destroying the Social Fabric of our Planet', *Atlantic Monthly*, 273 (1994), pp. 44–76.

Keen, David, *The Benefits of Famine: A Political Economy of Famine and Relief in South-Western Sudan, 1983–1989*, Princeton, NJ: Princeton University Press, 1994.

Kriger, Norma, *Zimbabwe's Guerrilla War: Peasant Voices*, Cambridge: Cambridge University Press, 1992.

Laqueur, Walter, *The New Terrorism: Fanaticism and the Arms of Mass Destruction*, London: Phoenix, 2001.

Lary, Diana, *Warlord Soldiers: Chinese Common Soldiers, 1911–1937*, Cambridge: Cambridge University Press, 1985.

Lewis, Steve, 'Che Guevara and Guerrilla Warfare: Training for Today's Nonlinear Battlefields', *Military Review*, 81, 5 (2001), pp. 98–101.

Mackinlay, John, 'Warlords', *Rusi Journal*, 143, 2 (1998), pp. 24–32.

Mao Tse-tung, *On Guerrilla Warfare*, tr. Samuel Griffith, New York: Praeger, 1965.

Marret, Jean-Luc, *Cities and Infra-State Conflicts*, Camberley: Conflict Studies Research Centre, 2001.

McCord, Edward A., *The Power of the Gun: The Emergence of Modern Chinese Warlordism*, Berkeley, CA: University of California Press, 1993.

Metz, Steven, 'Insurgency After the Cold War', *Small Wars and Insurgencies*, 5, 1 (1994), pp. 63–82.

Moran, Mary, 'Warriors or Soldiers? Masculinity and Ritual Transvestism in the Liberian Civil War', pp. 73–88 in Constance R. Sutton (ed.), *Feminism, Nationalism and Militarism*, Arlington, VA: Association for Feminist Anthropology/American Anthropological Association, 1995.

Münkler, Herfried, *Die Neuen Kriege*, Reinbek: Rowohlt, 2002.

Njoh, Joseph, *Through the Liberian Storm*, London: Minerva, 1996.

Prunier, Gérard, 'A Candid View of the Somali National Movement', *Horn of Africa*, 13 and 14, 3, 4, 1 and 2 (1990/1991), pp. 107–20.

Reno, William, *Warlord Politics and African States*, Boulder, CO: Lynne Rienner, 1998.

Rich, Paul B. (ed.), *Warlords in International Relations*, Basingstoke: Macmillan, 1999.

Richards, Paul, *Fighting for the Rainforest: War, Youth and Resources in Sierra Leone*, Oxford: James Currey, 1996.

Roitman, Janet, 'The Garrison-Entrepôt', *Cahiers d'Études Africaines*, 38, 150–2 (1998), pp. 297–329.

Royal Netherlands Army, *Militaire Doctrine (LDP I)*, The Hague: Koninklijke Landmacht (Royal Netherlands Army), 1996.

Sen, Amartya, *War and Famines: On Divisions and Incentives*, Paper 33 Development Research Programme. London: London School of Economics, 1991.

Sheridan, James E., *Chinese Warlord: The Career of Feng Yu-hsiang*, Stanford, CA: Stanford University Press, 1966.

Shy, John and Thomas Collier, 'Revolutionary War', in Peter Paret (ed.), *Makers of Modern Strategy: From Machiavelli to the Nuclear Age*, Oxford: Clarendon Press, 1986, pp. 815–62.

SIPRI, *Yearbook 1999, Armaments Disarmament and International Security*, Oxford: Oxford University Press, 1999.

Sislin, John and Frederic S. Pearson, *Arms and Ethnic Conflict*, London: Rowman and Littlefield, 2001.

Smith, Gayle E., 'Relief Operations and Military Strategy', in Thomas C. Weiss and Larry Minear (eds), *Humanitarianism Across Borders: Sustaining Civilians in Times of War*, Boulder, CO: Lynne Rienner, 1993, pp. 97–116.

Stetler, Russel (ed.), *The Military Art of People's War: Selected Writings of General Giap Vo Nguyen*, New York: Monthly Review, 1970.

Sun-Tzu, *The Art of War*, Ware: Wordsworth, 1993.

US Army Training and Doctrine Command, *AirLand Battle 2000*, Washington, DC: Department of the Army, 1981.

US Army and Air Force, *FM 100-20/AFP3-20*, Washington, DC: Headquarters Departments of the Army and the Air Force, 1990.

Vehnämäki, Mika, 'Diamonds and Warlords: The Geography of War in the Democratic Republic of Congo and Sierra Leone', *Nordic Journal of African Studies*, 11, 1 (2002), pp. 48–74.

Waal, Alex de, 'Contemporary Warfare in Africa', in Mary Kaldor and Basker Vashee (eds), *Restructuring the Global Military Sector, Vol. I New Wars*, London: Pinter, 1997, pp. 287–332.

—— *Famine Crimes: Politics and the Disaster Relief Industry in Africa*, Oxford: James Currey, 1997.

—— 'Contemporary Warfare in Africa: Changing Context and Changing Strategies', *IDS Bulletin*, 27, 3 (1996), pp. 6–16.

Wallensteen, Peter and Margareta Sollenberg, 'Armed Conflict and Regional Conflict Complexes, 1989–1997', *Journal of Peace Research*, 35, 5 (1998), pp. 621–34.

4

WARFARE IN CIVIL WARS

Stathis N. Kalyvas*

Introduction

The aim of this chapter is threefold. First, I argue that the study of civil wars must incorporate a solid theoretical understanding of warfare; second, I introduce a distinction between three different types of civil war based on how they are fought and trace the origins of each type; third, I explore the effects of these types of warfare on the patterns of violence in civil wars. The purpose of the chapter is primarily conceptual and 'theory-generating' rather than 'theory-testing'.

Accordingly, the chapter is divided into three sections. Section 1 discusses the necessity of incorporating a theory of warfare into the social-scientific research on civil strife. It then identifies three types of warfare that characterise civil wars. Two are well known: conventional and irregular warfare; the third one tends to be mischaracterised: I call it 'symmetric non-conventional' warfare. I trace the origins of each type to three distinct processes: failed military coups or secessions in federal states tend to produce civil wars fought via conventional warfare; peripheral or rural insurgencies tend to give rise to civil wars fought via irregular war; and state collapse leads to civil wars fought in a 'symmetric' but 'non-conventional' way. I argue that this distinction may move us beyond imprecise but popular typologies, of the 'old war' versus 'new war' type. Section 2 relies on a brief discussion of seven cases to illuminate the empirical links between warfare and violence; the cases were chosen to maximise the variety of warfare type and the ethnic/non-ethnic dimension: Algeria 1954–62, Angola 1961–75, Lebanon 1975–90, Liberia 1987–2003, Nigeria–Biafra 1967–70, Oman 1965–75, and Spain 1936–39. Last, in section 3 I explore the theoretical links between warfare and violence. I identify three theoretical accounts of violence. The *sociological* thesis connects violence to deep prewar divisions and conflicts; the *Hobbesian* thesis imputes causal force to the collapse of order and anarchy; and the *military* thesis points to vulnerability as the causal mechanism behind mass civilian victimisation. I conclude with methodological observations about the links between these arguments and the type of warfare practised in civil wars.

Warfare in civil wars: three types

It is not an exaggeration to say that warfare has generally been absent from the social-scientific study of civil wars and revolutions. The great majority of research in the social sciences has privileged instead the study of social and political factors that are thought to affect the onset or termination of civil wars and revolutions. In overlooking warfare, social scientists have made a mistake that mirrors another well-known error, namely the reduction of civil wars (and wars in general) to the exhaustive treatment of their military details – their tactics, techniques and firepower, while their political and social content is ignored. As a result, the study of war has been marginalised and relegated to specialised (typically descriptive) case studies, while the politics of civil wars are often treated as if they were no different from regular politics during times of peace, when people make choices much as they would do in the context of electoral politics – rather than situations deeply embedded in and shaped by armed combat.

However, as Mao Zedong observed, 'war has its own particular character-istics and in this sense it cannot be equated with politics in general'.[1] Indeed, the importance of warfare in structuring politics, altering the social and economic environment, shaping individual and collective incentives, and defining who the relevant political actors are, cannot be underestimated. This is particularly the case for micro-level research that seeks to uncover the mechanisms of recruitment, defection and violence. Viewed from this perspective, war is a social and political environment fundamentally different from peace in at least two crucial ways. First, it entails far more constraints and far less consent; second, the stakes are incomparably higher for the individuals involved. It is one thing to vote for a party, and another to fight (and possibly die) for it. In times of war, 'the ambiguity that normally characterize[s] everyday common sense and practice [is] simply no longer acceptable: one [has] to choose between one of two sides'.[2] During the American Civil War, 'normal expectations collapsed, to be replaced by frightening and bewildering personal and cultural chaos. The normal routes by which people solved problems and channeled behavior had been destroyed. ... Ordinary people, civilians as well as soldiers, were trapped by guerrilla war in a social landscape in which almost nothing remained recognizable or secure.'[3] In short, the key contribution of war is the primacy of violence as a resource, 'the virtual equation of power and injury'.[4] Again, as Mao Zedong put it, 'politics is war without bloodshed while war is politics with bloodshed'.[5]

The implications of overlooking warfare and subsuming it under the political conflict with which it is associated are considerable. Phenomena such as collective action, mobilisation and violence are automatically and exclusively linked to the prewar political and social dynamics that are posited to have motivated the conflict in the first place. The civilian behaviour and collective identities that inform the war are, likewise, seen as reflections of prewar conflicts; civilian collaboration with an insurgent political actor easily becomes interpreted as an indicator of civilian preference and support for this actor; individual participation in an insurgent army may be misleadingly interpreted as a risky choice and raise the spectre of the collective action problem, when in fact non-participation may turn out to have been much riskier. Hence a focus on warfare is essential in understanding how civil wars endogenously affect (and even transform) the strategies and identities of the political actors as well as the individuals involved in the war. At the same time, the analysis of warfare makes sense only if it is ultimately integrated into a comprehensive treatment of civil war.

Any discussion of warfare and civil war must begin by stressing the essential distinction between *type of war* and *type of warfare*. Wars can be classified in many useful ways: some stress the primary actors involved (e.g. international or domestic), their goals (e.g. offensive or defensive), their worldviews and societal projects ('greed and grievance'), and so on.[6] In contrast, the analysis of warfare begins from the form and type of warfare used in a given war.

A common empirical observation in the descriptive literature on civil wars is that most of them are fought by means of irregular ('guerrilla') rather than conventional warfare. A few civil wars mix irregular and conventional warfare (e.g. Russia, China, Vietnam), while a very small number are fought fully or predominantly as conventional wars (e.g. Spain). All in all, conventional civil wars are 'rare instances appearing only under specific and rather exceptional circumstances'.[7] In contrast, almost all interstate wars are fought conventionally.[8] In short, there is a high degree of overlap between civil and non-conventional war on the one hand, and interstate and conventional war, on the other. It follows that any analysis of civil war must incorporate a thorough understanding of non-conventional forms of warfare.

The distinction between irregular and conventional war is common and widely accepted, though the terminology varies. Like all distinctions, it is an ideal-typical one with the two types' edges blending into each other;[9] nevertheless, it remains an essential one. The existing terminological and conceptual confusion and the difficulties of operationalisation should not be taken to imply that irregular war is just a figment of some authors' imagination.[10]

Conventional warfare entails face-to-face confrontations between regular armies across clear frontlines. This type of warfare requires a commonly shared perception of a balance of power between the two sides. In the absence of some kind of mutual consent (which entails some reasonable belief in future victory), no conventional battle can take place.[11] On the other hand, irregular war is a type of warfare that requires a choice by the strategically weaker side 'to assume the tactical offensive in selected forms, times, and places'[12] – in other words, to refuse to match the stronger side's expectations

Table 1 Types of warfare in civil war

		Resource level of incumbents	
		High	Low
Parity between the actors	Yes	Conventional	Symmetric non-conventional
	No	Irregular	

in terms of the conventionally accepted basic rules of warfare. A stylised description of irregular war goes as follows: the state (or *incumbent*) fields regular troops and is able to control urban and accessible terrain, while seeking to militarily engage its opponents in peripheral and rugged terrain; challengers (rebels or *insurgents*) 'hover just below the military horizon', hiding and relying on harassment and surprise, 'stealth and raid'.[13] Such wars often turn into wars of attrition, with insurgents seeking to win by not losing while imposing unbearable costs on their opponent.[14] As a Vietnamese communist told an American official in 1975: 'One side is not strong enough to win and the other is not weak enough to lose'.[15] There are many variations on this stylised scenario, involving outside intervention or assistance that may lead the insurgents to gradually switch from irregular war to conventional war (e.g. China); conversely, the progressive deterioration of the state may force incumbents to opt for irregular war as well (e.g. Liberia).

In short, irregular warfare is a manifestation of military *asymmetry* between actors – both in terms of their respective power and their ensuing willingness to fight on the same plane: the weaker actor refuses to directly face the stronger one. The main empirical indicator of irregular war is the dearth of large-scale direct military confrontations or 'set battles' and the absence of frontlines. Contrary to what is sometimes claimed or implied,[16] irregular war is not wedded to a specific cause (revolutionary, communist or nationalist) but can be deployed to serve a very diverse range of goals. Of course, asymmetry is not an exclusive feature of irregular war; it is also compatible with other forms of violence, including 'terrorism'.

While asymmetry is predominantly expressed in irregular war, the converse is not the case, as often implied: symmetry (or parity) is not synonymous to conventional war. Rather, it is possible to point to a type of warfare that often gets confused with irregular war, which I call 'symmetric non-conventional warfare.' This type of warfare is often described as 'primitive' or 'criminal' war[17] and entails irregular armies on both sides in a pattern resembling pre-modern war.[18] Table 1 maps the three types along the two dimensions of parity between the actors and the resources of the incumbents.

What are the origins of these three types of warfare? I offer the following conjecture. Conventional civil war emerges either out of failed military coups or attempts at secession in federal or quasi-federal states;[19] irregular war results from peripheral or rural insurgencies; last, 'symmetric non-conventional warfare' can be observed in civil wars that accompany processes of state collapse. I shall now briefly discuss each process.

Conventional civil wars take place when an existing army splits, either because of a failed coup (e.g. the Spanish Civil War) or because a unit of a federal or quasi-federal state, which can claim control over a substantial part of the state's armed forces, attempts to secede (e.g. the American Civil War, the Biafran War).[20] High levels of external support or external intervention in favour of the rebel side may turn an irregular war into a conventional one: this was the case during the late phases of the Chinese Civil War and the Vietnam War. The relative dearth of conventional civil wars can now be explained by the lack of resources on the rebel side.

Irregular civil wars emerge incrementally and often slowly from a state's periphery. They entail a slow and patient process of state-building by an insurgent organisation.[21] Geography plays a key role in their onset and conduct. An extensive body of research exists on this type of war. Examples include civil wars in Malaya, Mozambique during the Portuguese colonisation, Kashmir, Aceh (Indonesia), and elsewhere.

Symmetric non-conventional wars are much less studied and understood: this is where the haphazard use of the term 'guerrilla war' can be particularly misleading. These wars are fought on both sides by irregular armies following a process of state collapse that reflects the fundamental weakness and eventual implosion of the incumbent actor. This entails the disintegration of the state army and its replacement by rival militias, which typically equip themselves by plundering the arsenal of the disbanded army.[22] Several ground-level descriptions of these wars point to similarities with irregular warfare (most notably the absence of regular armies), but they also emphasise key features that set the two apart. This type of warfare differs from conventional civil war because it lacks regular armies and set battles. From an analytical as well as an empirical point of view, it is the presence of frontlines that endows this type of warfare with its distinct feature *vis-à-vis* irregular warfare and provides the most cogent way to differentiate it from the latter. The presence of frontlines, which take various forms (including roadblocks and checkpoints), has been stressed in many descriptions of symmetric non-conventional wars.[23] Examples include the Lebanese Civil War, the wars in Congo-Brazzaville, Liberia, and Mozambique during independence, and most civil wars that erupted in the wake of the Soviet Union's collapse.

Empirical links between warfare and violence

Wars vary enormously across many dimensions and the sources of this variation are highly complex. Clausewitz remarked that the conduct of war is determined by the nature of societies, 'by their times and prevailing conditions'; in other words, he pointed to their underlying sociology. The same variation can be observed in civil wars. However, while the sociology of wars has made substantial progress in the course of the last decades,[24] the same cannot be said about civil wars – an indicator of the more general lag in the study of civil wars as compared to interstate ones. Recent research on civil wars is quickly closing the gap, but this research focuses primarily on the determinants of civil war onset, duration and termination, and its effects, rather than civil war *per se*.

The variation in the intensity of violence within civil wars is perplexing. The form and intensity of violence used by the Russian Reds and Whites during the Russian Civil War; the Serbs, Moslems and Croats in Bosnia; or the various competing factions in Liberia, vary significantly across many dimensions. In some civil wars, the majority of abuses are committed by the incumbents (e.g. Guatemala); in some, there appears to be a balance between incumbents and insurgents (e.g. Peru); and in some others, insurgents seem to carry out the worst atrocities (e.g. Sierra Leone, Mozambique).

The same is true about violence across civil wars. Consider Northern Ireland. Although British authorities have committed human rights abuses, including the systematic practice of torture, they 'have not ruthlessly and brutally suppressed the population which explicitly or tacitly supports insurrection in the manner experienced by Algerian Muslims, Afghan peasants, Iraqi Kurds, Kashmiri Muslims, Palestinian Muslims and Christians, South African blacks, Sri Lankan Tamils, and Vietnamese peasants'.[25] As an IRA member was told after his arrest by the security forces: 'If this was Beirut we would just take you out into that yard and shoot you'.[26] Likewise, the IRA 'sought to avoid any operations that had obviously sectarian overtones: a policeman could be justified as a legitimate target, his non-combatant Protestant family could not'.[27] In short, the conflict in Northern Ireland has been characterised by considerable reciprocal restraint.[28] Such restraint has been absent in many other civil wars. How to explain this variation?

The causes of the cross-national variation in levels, types and practices of violence are multiple and complex, as remarked by Ernesto 'Che' Guevara:

> The enemies of the people act in a more or less intensely criminal fashion according to the specific social, historic and economic circumstances of each place. There are places where the flight of a man into the guerrilla zone, leaving his family and his house, does not provoke any great reaction. There are other places where this is enough to provoke the burning or seizure of his belongings, and still others where the flight will bring death to all members of his family.[29]

Cross-national variation includes the specific profile of political actors and their political ideology;[30] their organisational structure, underlying social basis, and military culture;[31] their resources; their national and local leadership and strategies;[32] the type of challenges they face; the domestic and international context in which they operate (including prevailing international norms of war);[33] the specific internal and technological dynamics of the war; the degree of militarisation of the conflict; and factors such as geography and climate. It is plausible to surmise that all these factors have an impact on violence.

Given the current state of the theoretical and empirical knowledge, specifying and testing cross-national models to explain this variation in violence remains challenging, to say the least. Conceptual clarification and theoretical development seem to be the wisest starting points. Elsewhere, I take an analytic approach and specify the microfoundations of selective violence.[34] Here, I take a more inductive approach and explore whether a better understanding of how civil wars are fought can help explain why their violence diverges so much.

I shall review seven civil wars covering the entire range of warfare as identified in this chapter, in order to explore whether they correlate with particular patterns of violence. The relation between warfare and violence is not a trivial issue because most victims of civil wars are civilians rather than soldiers. These cases were chosen randomly to vary their political and social basis (ethnic and non-ethnic, secessionist and non-secessionist). They are: Algeria 1954–62, Angola 1961–75, Lebanon 1975–90, Liberia 1987–2003, Nigeria–Biafra 1967–70, Oman 1965–75, and Spain 1936–9. Obviously this is not intended as an exhaustive discussion but rather as a very rough and tentative first-cut overview based mainly on ground-level descriptions.

Conventional civil wars

One of the best known (and most studied) conventional civil war is the Spanish Civil War, which caused a substantial number of civilian casualties. A striking fact is that the greatest amount of violence against civilians took place in the initial months of the war when high uncertainty and the presence of real or suspected 'fifth-columnists' (a term invented during that war) behind one's back subverted the logic of frontlines.[35] Once the frontline was stabilised, fatality rates declined.[36] In other words, violence was used to eliminate known opponents and terrorise their potential sympathisers so as to secure the army's rear and ensure that a proper conventional war could be fought. Once the frontlines were stabilised, rates of violence went down and rival supporters were given the opportunity to switch sides.

A more recent conventional civil war was the Biafran War (1967–70), the result of the attempt by the Southern Igbo leadership to secede from Nigeria. The Igbo leadership opted against waging a guerrilla war and relied instead on those segments of the national army that had joined the secession to fight a conventional war. Though there were reports of massacres of civilians, this does not seem to have been the predominant form of violence. In fact, massacres (in the context of mass riots) preceded the war and served as one of its justifications, but stopped while the war was still ongoing. By far, most civilian fatalities resulted from the blockade imposed by the Nigerian Army: they were indirect rather than direct victims.

These two cases suggest that after crossing an initial threshold, conventional civil wars tend to produce violence that resembles the patterns observed in most modern interstate conventional wars: fatalities tend to be primarily military rather than civilian, and civilian fatalities tend to be indirect ('collateral') rather than direct. Hence, it is possible to state that the form of warfare correlates with the patterns of fatalities, with the causal arrow apparently going from the former to the latter. At the same time, just turning the war into a conventional conflict may require high levels of violence in the initial stages if the population is intermixed, i.e. when people of questionable loyalty happen to live on the wrong side of the frontline. This suggests the saliency of individual identities (they credibly signal certain courses of action) and their concomitant visibility.[37]

Irregular civil wars

The war of Algerian independence (1954–62) was a classic war of decolonisation fought as an insurgency, that is to say via irregular warfare. It was a civil war both in strict terms (Algeria was under French jurisdiction, hence this was a domestic conflict) and in a more general sense (Muslim Algerians fought on both sides and the French were also divided, with many leftists taking the side of the independentists). Violence against civilians was plentiful and exercised by both sides. The Algerian National Liberation Front (FLN) used violence against French settlers and local competitors, but mainly against ordinary Algerian peasants who for one reason or another refused to collaborate. For instance, the massacre of 123 people (71 of whom were Europeans) on 20 August 1955 in the coastal city of Philippeville was intended to stir up mass support for the revolution by creating a climate of intercommunal tension and induce a mindless repression by the French, which would bring international opprobrium while pushing Algerians to join the FLN.[38] After this and similar tactics failed, the FLN resorted to the systematic use of terrorism, targeting the civilian population, whether it was Algerian Muslims who were known to be 'friendly' to France, or Europeans. As a pro-FLN author recalls, 'it is legitimate to say that it was the violence of terrorism that jolted a good number of us out of our complacency and our reluctance to think about things'.[39] However, while the FLN could easily intimidate the countryside, it was having difficulty organising the population in urban areas, where it eventually resorted to tactics such as random bombing. This led to the famous battle of Algiers, which ended with a French victory. On the other side, the French tried various tactics in the countryside, ranging from collective punishment to mass population displacement. While they won in narrowly military terms, they were unable to sustain the political and economic cost of the war and were forced to negotiate an end to the conflict.

The Algerian case provides a snapshot of two functions of violence: the demonstration or signalling function, whereby violence is used to signal capability, induce mobilisation and attract international attention, and the terrorist function, whereby violence is used to deter civilians from collaborating with the enemy. The outcome is suggestive: high levels of violence from both sides. What is particularly interesting is that although one would expect the violence to follow the ethnic divide (native/Muslim versus settler/Christian), it did not: intra-ethnic violence appears to have been more common than inter-ethnic violence, in a pattern that appears common to many civil wars that are fought via irregular warfare.[40]

The Angolan war of independence (1961–75) is similar to the Algerian war: a decolonisation conflict fought irregularly. The war began on 4 February 1961 with initial attacks by the independentist MPLA, aimed at freeing political prisoners held by the Portuguese. The immediate Portuguese retaliation was severe: 3,000 Angolan civilians were killed in the streets and in their homes in Luanda, and 5,000 more civilians were massacred in the Malange district. Further, the Portuguese mobilised an army of 80,000, organised local militias and armed the white settler population. Villagers were reportedly napalmed and survivors were executed on the spot. Prairie fires were ignited to prevent the escape of refugees, tens of thousands of whom streamed toward the borders, seeking sanctuary in the Congo.[41] Little occurred during the next three years as the MPLA regrouped and opened a new front in 1964 near the Congo border. The MPLA opened a third front in 1966. There were many rumours of Portuguese atrocities, but the insurgents also proved very brutal, both against white settlers and the native population.[42] The Angolan case matches the Algerian one in that when violence began it contained a strong demonstration effect along ethnic lines, but then switched to terrorisation and assumed a substantial intra-ethnic character.

Less known is the war in Oman (1965–7), which was fought mainly in the Dhofar region of Southwestern Oman. Although the British played an active role, this was more of a domestic insurgency fuelled by the Cold War than a classic decolonisation war. For both sides, the insurgents and the Sultan's forces and their British allies, the war was one of attrition, described as a war 'for the hearts and minds' of the local population, the Jabalis.[43] The insurgents tried several times to open another front in Northern Oman but were unsuccessful each time. This resulted in the fighting being concentrated strictly in the Dhofar region, which although hard to navigate, was a relatively small area in which the government forces were soon able to construct large barricades blocking supply routes to the insurgents (most notably the Hornbeam line). Their main objective was 'to isolate the insurgent both physically and politically from the population'. To achieve this objective, they burned villages that were not pro-Sultan and hung up the corpses of insurgent fighters to rot in the centre of Dhofar towns.[44] Additionally, the government organised the so-called *firqat*, groups of defectors from the insurgents who were assigned to fight in the mountainous terrain of Dhofar, where government troops were not performing. The *firqat* were organised on a tribal basis and assigned to their tribal area, which resulted in better information connections.[45] The insurgents were almost eradicated by the war's end. This war differs from the previous two in that the insurgents were eventually defeated. Violence, however, was plentiful, featuring both an intra-ethnic and terrorist character.

All three cases of irregular war suggest that while the signalling character of violence cannot be ignored, violence was primarily used to terrorise the population and shape its behaviour. In other words, violence is a key resource in irregular wars: it displays a strategic logic, as suggested by its intra-ethnic dimension. What distinguishes irregular civil wars from conventional ones (and possibly from symmetric non-conventional ones) is the willingness of at least one actor to be discriminating, i.e. to try to separate those among the population allegedly supporting their rival actively and systematically from those who do not – and in doing so, to shape the population's incentives.

Symmetric non-conventional civil wars

I now turn to the last type of warfare and examine two cases, Lebanon and Liberia. Unlike most irregular wars, the Lebanese Civil War (1975–90) was equally (if not more) urban as it was rural. A key aspect of this war was the presence of visible boundaries separating sectarian enclaves controlled by various militias. Initially, the frontline at the centre of Beirut shifted for months until it finally settled down and remained pretty much fixed for the rest of the war, dividing the city between eastern and western sectors along the notorious Green Line. The war went through at least five different phases. The first phase lasted one year (1975–6), entailed heavy fighting and eventually ended with a 'ceasefire'. Subsequently, the war was characterised by sniper-style, sporadic fighting between militias (1976–82). The Israeli invasion of Lebanon brought additional complications and provoked an escalation both in terms of fighting and violence (1982–5). This was followed once more by sporadic militia violence (1985–9) and the so-called rebellion of General Aoun (1989–90), which was accompanied by heavy shelling. Violence was considerable with a lot of looting, but it fluctuated wildly and was not easily traceable. 'Uncontrolled elements' (*anassir ghair bundabita*) were allegedly responsible for much (apparently random) violence against civilians. However, many civilians suspected that these men were merely a good excuse for useful activities that could not be openly condoned but were centrally planned and organised by the competing factions.[46] It is estimated that no more than 10 per cent of the casualties involved combatants, and combat was rare.[47] Violence was widely reported as being practised along ethnic lines, though reliable data are lacking.

Similar features emerge from descriptions of the civil war in Liberia (1987–2003): the violence was considerable, allegedly motivated by ethnic hatred and taking place under territorial segmentation defined by frontlines. The government army quickly turned into an undisciplined ethnic militia, practically indistinguishable from competing ones. Massacres and torture were common and practised by all sides.[48] One of the most vicious attacks of the entire war was the massacre of over 500 civilians that took place on 5–6 June 1993, targeting mostly women and children at a displaced persons camp outside Harbel. Augustine Mahiga, UN High Commissioner for Refugees, described the massacre as follows: 'They cut throats, they cut heads, threw out brains, opened stomachs and threw out intestines, broke legs, and shot so many bullet wounds that you cannot understand why'.[49] Like the Lebanese Civil War, the Liberian one produced mass civilian displacement and ethnic segregation.

While the Liberian war has been described as a 'new' civil war, the same is not the case for Lebanon. Yet the two wars display considerable similarities: state collapse, seemingly gratuitous violence across ethnic lines, and expulsion of populations rather than attempts to win them over. The type of warfare appears to correlate with the patterns of violence and suggests violence that is, on its surface, more ethnically-motivated and indiscriminate than the violence of irregular wars.

A first point is that the features of 'new' civil wars are not new.[50] Put otherwise, the imprecise 'new civil war' category may, in fact, be capturing a specific type of warfare, namely symmetric non-conventional warfare.[51] A second point is that the seemingly ethnic and indiscriminate character of the violence (assuming this observation survives systematic empirical research) may represent a lack of resources for collecting finer-grained information, also reflected in the absence of an incumbent actor, rather than motivations that are inherently more 'ethnic' or violent, or related to globalisation, etc.

Certain hypotheses about the cross-national variation of violence can be derived. When both political actors enjoy access to informational resources they will try to be discriminating. If one actor has informational resources while the other lacks them, we should observe a skewed pattern of violence with one actor being selective and the other indiscriminate. Last, if both sides lack informational resources, violence should be indiscriminate on both sides. If this is correct, it would mean that warfare is a proximate or intermediate variable between information and violence.[52]

Theoretical links between warfare and violence

Having proposed this conjecture, I identify three theoretical accounts of violence. The first one (which I call the *sociological* thesis), connects violence to deep prewar divisions and conflicts (also referred to as 'polarisation'). In this view, both violence and warfare are just an expression of these pre-existing conflicts; in fact, warfare is a simple intervening variable between polarisation and violence that does not deserve to be studied other than on narrow empirical grounds. The second account (the *Hobbesian* thesis) imputes causal force to the collapse of order that tends to characterise civil wars; warfare under these conditions tends to be inherently barbaric because of the absence of the structures and authorities that have either the incentive or the predisposition to civilise war. Finally, the third account (the *military* thesis) points to vulnerability as the causal mechanism behind mass civilian victimisation. This is the thesis that places most causal force squarely on warfare, though it appears to be misspecified.

The main theorist of the polarisation thesis, Carl Schmitt, stressed the heavily ideological character of the 'national liberation' movements of the decolonisation and Cold War era with deep divisions.[53] In his 'theory of the partisan', he argued that the 'limited and domesticated' hostility of conventional war turned into the 'real hostility' of partisan warfare because of ideological enmity – an insight that is found in many subsequent works and has been adapted specifically to deal with ethnic conflict.[54] However, Schmitt was generalising from a particular historical period and failed to recognise that violence and irregular war have a broader historical connection. Contrary to what was widely believed in the 1960s, irregular war was not invented by Mao Zedong or Che Guevara. As a practice it is as old as warfare, while its theorisation as a military doctrine goes back to the late eighteenth century;[55] the fact that irregular war has survived the end of the Cold War is another indicator of its instrumental (as opposed to ideological) character. In addition, the obvious limitation of this thesis is that it cannot explain the extreme violence of the many civil wars that are not motivated by ideology (even when religion and ethnicity are taken to be ideological differences). Indeed, most symmetric non-conventional wars appear to be highly violent even though they do not seem to be motivated by ideological precepts. Formulated in a falsifiable way, this argument predicts that the deeper the divisions (or the more acute the degree of *polarisation*), the higher the level of violence. The evidence is scant and mixed. From an impressionistic point of view it seems difficult to account for the extreme violence of many recent civil wars in Africa by pointing to patterns of prewar polarisation. I know of only two studies that examine the link between polarisation and violence in a systematic way. Ledesma Vera provides some tentative results that show a relation between levels of prewar polarisation and levels of violence across villages of Aragón during the Spanish Civil War.[56] In a recent paper, Chacón (2003) finds that prewar polarisation as measured by electoral returns at the municipal level in Colombia is a good predictor of violence during the first phase (1946–50) of the civil conflict in that country, known as *Violencia*. This was a period during which the conflict was not militarised and looked a lot like a generalised riot. However, polarisation ceases to be a good predictor of violence in the second period of the *Violencia* (1958–63), once the situation evolved into a militarised conflict. During this period, geographical and military variables appear much more significantly related to violence.[57] This finding supports the conjecture that in a militarised conflict, warfare has an effect on violence that is independent of polarisation.

The Hobbesian thesis, in the form of an argument stressing the 'medievalisation' or criminalisation of war, emerged to tackle various problems with the sociological account. Because irregular warfare presupposes a relative absence of formal structures, it causes a breakdown in military discipline, thus turning war into a cover for decentralised looting, banditry and all kinds of violence against civilians. The absence of professional armies indicates the disappearance of the 'warriors' honour' and its replacement with barbarism.[58] According to van Creveld, contemporary guerrilla wars 'from Colombia to the Philippines' are nothing more than 'the work of ragtag bands of ruffians out for their own advantage, hardly distinguishable from the *ecorcheurs* ('skinners') who devastated the French countryside during the Hundred Years' War'.[59] The weakness of this argument is obviously its failure to account for the violence of conventional civil wars. Formulated in a falsifiable way, this argument predicts that the more irregular the armies, the higher the violence. In Selesky's formulation: 'The greater the distance away from centralised monitoring, and probably also the smaller the numbers involved, the greater the opportunity for men to use violence to settle some personal score which may or may not have anything to do with the goals of the society that has authorised them to use purposeful violence in the first place.'[60] However, empirical support for this contention appears limited. For instance, we know that in many civil wars (e.g. El Salvador, Guatemala) the greatest amount of violence is produced by highly disciplined regular armies rather than insurgent irregulars. The behaviour of the Nazi and Japanese armies in occupied countries during the Second World War is another obvious case. In terms of systematic evidence, it turns out that during the English Civil War atrocities were more common during times and in areas where professional armies operated, rather than where local militias held sway.[61] The single worst massacre in Bosnia, in Srebrenica, was executed in a highly organised fashion by regular troops rather than paramilitary thugs. Recent econometric analysis of evidence from Africa also seems to support the contention that violence against civilians is used to achieve military advantage as opposed to loot and prey.[62]

Last, the military thesis, stressed in many studies of guerrilla warfare, contends that violence results primarily from the acute feeling of vulnerability that combatants experience in the context of irregular war. According to the psychological version of the argument, the absence of frontlines and the presence of the enemy behind one's back cause uncertainty, fear and even panic, often reaching 'endemic' proportions.[63] In turn, this facilitates trigger-happy reactions, particularly among troops that lack training for irregular war.[64] Violence by disciplined troops, such as the massacre of Vietnamese peasants by US servicemen in My Lai, is often linked to these processes.[65] The problem with this account is that it privileges expressive motivations and conflates levels of analysis. We know that armies do not just behave expressively: there are several incentives at various levels that typically constrain the indiscriminate expression of emotions (such as fear) from the rank and file.

The rationalist variant of vulnerability appears more satisfactory: it links violence specifically to an army's inability to identify the enemy. In an environment where it is impossible to tell civilian and enemy combatant apart, it pays to err on the side of violence. Hence the inevitable 'dirty violence' of counterinsurgency. If the enemy refuses to fight in standard ways and if they prove 'difficult to subdue using the techniques of "civilised" war, then uncivilised means must be used instead.[66] In short, it is not just that combatants kill people haphazardly out of sheer frustration (though this may well be the case on the ground and at the level of individual motivations), but that violence addresses a basic problem of irregular war. Note that, in spite of its application, this argument applies equally to both incumbents and insurgents, since the latter face a similar identification problem with informers and suffer from betrayal and infiltration. Formulated as a testable hypothesis, this argument would make violence a function of the degree of vulnerability that a military actor faces. Evidence from the Spanish Civil War, where it is possible to hold other factors constant while varying vulnerability, tends to support this argument: recall that most of the violence against civilians during that war took place in the initial months of the war under high uncertainty and fluidity. At the same time, the vulnerability argument predicts that violence will reach its highest level in the most contested areas, where political actors are most vulnerable. However, there is empirical evidence suggesting that this is not necessarily the case.[67] A better version of the rationalist variant of the military thesis awaits specification.

An obvious connection between the theoretical discussion and the empirical examination of warfare is the observation that each mechanism is related to a different type of warfare. Thus, irregular warfare causes violence via military vulnerability, symmetric non-conventional warfare produces violence via anarchy, while the violence in conventional warfare reflects prewar polarisation. Put otherwise, the sociological thesis 'explains' the violence of conventional civil wars, the military thesis 'explains' the violence of irregular civil wars, and the Hobbesian thesis 'accounts' for the violence of symmetric non-conventional war. However, such a fit would also suggest that each theoretical account selects the empirical cases from which it is derived. Since we are concerned about the direction of causality between warfare and violence, this observation means that each theoretical account is biased. The only way out of this methodological dead-end is to operationalise and test the three theoretical arguments by deriving their testable implications.

To summarise the main points of this chapter. On the substantive front, I stress the importance of focusing on information (and the resources necessary for its collection and assessment) as a crucial variable in the study of civil war and violence, and suggest the need to identify the factors that account for variation in the availability of information both across and within wars. On the theoretical front, I argue in favour of the incorporation of a theoretical understanding of warfare into the social-scientific investigation of civil wars. Last, on the methodological front, I hope to have demonstrated the necessity of combining ground-level empirical analysis and abstract theoretical reflection rather than thinking of them as divorced or mutually exclusive.

Notes

* I would like to thank Rhea Myerscough for research assistance.
1 Bruno Shaw, 'Selections from Selected Works of Mao Tse-Tung', in Sam C. Sarkesian (ed.), *Revolutionary Guerrilla Warfare*, Chicago: Precedent Publishing, 1975, p. 223.
2 Ted Swedenburg, *Memories of Revolt: The 1936–1939 Rebellion and the Palestinian National Past*, Minneapolis: University of Minnesota Press, 1995, p. 170.
3 Michael Fellman, *Inside War: The Guerrilla Conflict in Missouri During the American Civil War*, New York: Oxford University Press, 1989, p. xvi.
4 Mary Elizabeth Berry, *The Culture of Civil War in Kyoto*, Berkeley: University of California Press, 1994, p. xix.
5 Quoted in Shaw, *Selections*, pp. 223–4.
6 Jan Angstrom, 'Towards a Typology of Internal Armed Conflict: Synthesising a Decade of Conceptual Turmoil', *Civil Wars*, 4, 3 (2001), pp. 93–116.
7 Jean-Pierre Derriennic, *Les Guerres Civiles*, Paris: Presses de Sciences Po, 2001, p. 166. Smith challenges this point, but he does so on the basis of three examples only. See M. L. R. Smith, 'Guerrillas in the Mist: Reassessing Strategy and Low Intensity Warfare', *Review of International Studies*, 29 (2003), p. 22.
8 The very few irregular interstate wars consist mostly of low-intensity border skirmishes, such as the Libya–Chad war and the war between Belize and Guatemala. See Robert E. Harkavy and Stephanie G. Neuman, *Warfare and the Third World*, New York: Palgrave, 2001, pp. 18–19.
9 For example, the Russian and Chinese civil wars entailed weak regular armies operating in huge territory under conditions approximating irregular war. See Orlando Figes, *A People's Tragedy: The Russian Revolution, 1891–1924*, New York: Penguin 1996, p. 557.
10 As claimed by Smith, 'Guerrillas in the Mist', p. 20.
11 André Beaufre, *La guerre révolutionnaire: Les formes nouvelles de la guerre*, Paris: Fayard, 1972, p. 12.
12 Samuel P. Huntington, 'Guerrilla Warfare in Theory and Policy', in Franklin Mark Osanka (ed.), *Modern Guerrilla Warfare. Fighting Communist Guerrilla Movements, 1941–1961*, New York: The Free Press, 1962, p. xvi.
13 Anna Simons, 'War: Back to the Future', *Annual Reviews of Anthropology*, 28 (1999), p. 84; Fellman, *Inside War*, p. 23.

14 Thomas H. Henriksen, *Revolution and Counterrevolution: Mozambique's War of Independence, 1964–1974*, Westport: Greenwood Press, 1983, p. 141; John Shy, *A People Numerous and Armed: Reflections on the Military Struggle for American Independence*, New York: Oxford University Press, 1976, p. 12.

15 Quoted in Thomas C. Thayer, *War Without Fronts: The American Experience in Vietnam*, Boulder, CO: Westview Press, 1985, p. 97.

16 For example by Carl Schmitt, *Théorie du Partisan*, Paris: Flammarion, 1992.

17 Mueller contrasts this type of war to 'disciplined warfare'. See John Mueller, 'Hatred, Violence, and Warfare: Thugs as Residual Combatants', paper presented at the 2001 Annual Meeting of the American Political Science Associated, 30 August–2 September.

18 Timothy Earle, *How Chiefs Come to Power: The Political Economy in Prehistory*, Stanford: Stanford University Press, 1997, p. 108.

19 By 'quasi-federal' states I mean states that have devolved a substantial degree of their military authority, particularly through the creation of extensive local and regional militias.

20 The Russian Civil War took place after the Bolshevik coup failed to establish control over the entire territory of the Russian Empire while the civil war in Bosnia is a variant of attempted secession. See Susan L. Woodward, *Balkan Tragedy. Chaos and Dissolution After the Cold War*, Washington, DC: The Brookings Institution, 1995, p. 272.

21 A key condition for the emergence of irregular war appears to be a combination of low GDP, dispersed rural settlement and rough terrain. See James D. Fearon and David D. Laitin, 'Ethnicity, Insurgency, and Civil War', *American Political Science Review*, 97, 1 (2003).

22 For example Valery Tishkov, 'Ethnic Conflicts in the Former USSR: The Use and Misuse of Typologies and Data', *Journal of Peace Research*, 36, 5 (1999), p. 585. The process of disintegration is often swift, though sometimes it may be slower.

23 Gladys Mouro, *An American Nurse Amidst Chaos*, Beirut: American University of Beirut, 1999, p. 32; Lina Mikdadi Tabarra, *Survival in Beyrut: A Diary of Civil War*, London: Onyx Press, 1979, p. 11; Rémy Bazenguissa-Ganga, 'The Spread of Political Violence in Congo-Brazzaville', *African Affairs*, 98, 390 (1999), pp. 37–54; Stephen Ellis, *The Mask of Anarchy: The Destruction of Liberia and the Religious Dimension of an African Civil War*, New York: New York University Press, 1999; Christian Geffray, *La cause des armes au Mozambique: Anthropologie d'une guerre civile*, Paris: Karthala, 1990, pp. 128, 206; Anthony Loyd, *My War Gone By, I Miss it So*, New York: Penguin, 2001; Michael Ignatieff, *The Warrior's Honor: Ethnic War and the Modern Conscience*, New York: Henry Holt and Company, 1998; V. Tishkov, *Ethnic Conflicts in the Former USSR*, p. 576; Thomas Goltz, *Azerbaijan Diary. A Rogue Reporter's Adventures in an Oil-Rich, War Torn, Post-Soviet Republic*, Armonk: M. E. Sharpe, 1998; Catherine Dale, 'The Dynamics and Challenges of Ethnic Cleansing: The Georgia–Abkhazia Case', *Refugee Survey Quarterly*, 16, 3 (1997), pp. 80–1.

24 The classic text is Gaston Bouthoul, *Traité de polémologie. Sociologie des guerres*, Paris: Payot, 1970. Recent advances include contributions from what is known as the 'new military history' field. Ironically, there seems to be a dearth of theorising about warfare in the field of International Relations.

25 Brendan O'Leary and John McGarry, *The Politics of Antagonism: Understanding Northern Ireland*, London: The Athlone Press, 1993, p. 19.

26 Eamon Collins (with Mick McGovern), *Killing Rage*, New York: Granta Books, 1999, p. 188.

27 Ibid., p. 295.

28 Kevin Toolis, *Rebel Hearts: Journeys Within the IRA's Soul*, New York: St Martin's Griffin, 1997, p. 21.
29 Ernesto Che Guevara, *Guerrilla Warfare*, Lincoln: University of Nebraska Press, 1998, pp. 75–6.
30 Omer Bartov, *Hitler's Army: Soldiers, Nazis, and War in the Third Reich*, New York: Oxford University Press, 1992; François Furet, *Interpreting the French Revolution*, Cambridge: Cambridge University Press, 1981. Note, however, that ideology often fails to fit with observed violence. Communist violence was centralised and bureaucratic in the Russian and Greek Civil Wars, but decentralised and 'anarchic' in the Finnish and Spanish Civil Wars.
31 Jonathan E. Gumz, '*Wehrmacht* Perceptions of Mass Violence in Croatia, 1941–1942', *The Historical Journal*, 44, 4 (2001), pp. 1015–38.
32 Ben Shepherd, 'Hawks, Doves and *Tote Zonen*: A Wehrmacht Security Division in Central Russia, 1943', *Journal of Contemporary History*, 37, 3 (2002), pp. 349–69.
33 James Ron, 'Boundaries and Violence: Repertoires of State Action Along the Bosnia/Yugoslavia Divide', *Theory and Society*, 29 (2000), pp. 609–40.
34 Stathis N. Kalyvas, *The Logic of Violence in Civil War*, manuscript, Yale University, 2004.
35 The most recent reference work on this topic is Santos Juliá (ed.), *Victimas de la guerra civil*, Madrid: Temas de Hoy, 1999.
36 José Luis Ledesma Vera, 'Espacios de Poder, Violencia y Revolución: Una Perspectiva Política de la Represión en el Aragón Republicano Durante la Guerra Civil', in Antonio Morales Moya (ed.), *El Difícil Camino a la Democracia*, Madrid: Sociedad Estatal España Nuevo Milenio, 2001, p. 256; Enric Ucelay da Cal, 'La guerre civile espagnole et la propagande franco–belge de la Première Guerre mondiale', in Jean-Clément Martin (ed.), *La guerre civile entre histoire et mémoire*, Nantes: Ouest Éditions, 1995, p. 84.
37 Note, however, that the small number of conventional civil wars suggests that only a limited subset of civil wars where one finds high levels of polarisation and visible identities turn conventional.
38 Mouloud Feraoun, *Journal 1955–1962: Reflections on the French–Algerian War*, Lincoln, NE: University of Nebraska Press, 2002, xvii.
39 Ibid., p. 44.
40 Stathis N. Kalyvas, 'The Logic of Violence in Civil War: Ethnic and Non-Ethnic Civil Wars', unpublished paper, The University of Chicago, 2002.
41 Don Barnett and Roy Harvey, *The Revolution in Angola: MPLA, Life Histories, and Documents*, New York: The Bobbs-Merrill Company, 1972, p. 2.
42 Ibid., pp. 119, 200; Al J. Venter, *The Terror Fighters: A Profile of Guerrilla Warfare in Southern Africa*, Cape Town: Purnell, 1969, p. 112.
43 Fred Halliday, *Mercenaries: Counter-Insurgency in the Gulf*, Nottingham, UK: Russell Press, 1977, p. 48.
44 Ibid., pp. 49–54.
45 John Akehurst, *We Won a War: The Campaign in Oman, 1965–1975*, Wilton, Salisbury, Wiltshire: Michael Russell Publishing, 1982, p. 77.
46 Jean Said Makdisi, *Beirut Fragments: A War Memoir*, New York: Persea Books, 1990, p. 58.
47 Jonathan C. Randal, *Going All the Way: Christian Warlords, Israeli Adventurers, and the War in Lebanon*, New York: The Viking Press, 1983, p. 76.
48 Ellis, *The Mask of Anarchy*, p. 80 ff.
49 *The Independent*, 7 June, 1993.
50 Stathis N. Kalyvas, '"New" and "Old" Civil Wars: A Valid Distinction?', *World Politics*, 54, 1 (2001).

51 But note that not all recent civil wars are symmetric non-conventional ones. The Colombian Civil War is a case in point.

52 Obviously, this begs the question of what determines the distribution of informational resources in the first place. I will leave this question aside for now.

53 Schmitt, *Théorie du Partisan.*

54 For example Kalevi J. Holsti, *The State, War, and the State of War*, Cambridge: Cambridge University Press, 1996, p. 39.

55 Walter Laqueur, *Guerrilla Warfare: A Historical and Critical Study*, New Brunswick, NJ: Transaction, 1998.

56 Ledesma Vera, *Espacios de Poder, Violencia y Revolución*, pp. 249–68.

57 Mario Chacón Barrero, *Dinámica y Determinantes de la Violencia Durante 'La Violencia': Una Aproximación Desde la Econometria Espacial*, unpublished paper, Universidad de los Andes, 2003.

58 Ignatieff, *The Warrior's Honor*; Mueller, *Hatred, Violence, and Warfare.*

59 Martin van Creveld, *The Transformation of War*, New York: The Free Press, 1991, p. 60.

60 Harold E. Selesky, 'Colonial America', in Michael Howard, George J. Andreopoulos, and Mark R. Shulman (eds), *The Laws of War: Constraints on Warfare in the Western World*, New Haven: Yale University Press, 1994, p. 85.

61 Will Coster, 'Massacre and Codes of Conduct in the English Civil War', in Mark Levene and Penny Roberts (eds), *The Massacre in History*, New York: Berghahn Books 1999, p. 95.

62 Paul Azam and Anke Hoeffler, 'Violence Against Civilians in Civil Wars: Looting or Terror?', *Journal of Peace Research*, 39, 4 (2002), pp. 461–85.

63 Matthew Cooper, *The Nazi War Against Soviet Partisans, 1941–1944*, New York: Stein and Day, 1979, p. 92.

64 Dave Grossman, *On Killing: The Psychological Cost of Learning to Kill in War and Society*, Boston: Little, Brown, and Company, 1995.

65 Michael Bilton and Kevin Sim, *Four Hours in My Lai*, New York: Penguin, 1992.

66 Selesky, 'Colonial America', pp. 61–2.

67 Stathis N. Kalyvas, *The Logic of Violence in Civil War.*

References

Akehurst, John, *We Won a War: The Campaign in Oman, 1965–1975*, Wilton, Salisbury, Wiltshire: Michael Russell Publishing, 1982.

Angstrom, Jan, 'Towards a Typology of Internal Armed Conflict: Synthesising a Decade of Conceptual Turmoil', *Civil Wars*, 4, 3 (2001), pp. 93–116.

Azam, Paul and Anke Hoeffler, 'Violence Against Civilians in Civil Wars: Looting or Terror?', *Journal of Peace Research*, 39, 4 (2002), pp. 461–85.

Barnett, Don and Roy Harvey, *The Revolution in Angola: MPLA, Life Histories, and Documents*, New York: The Bobbs-Merrill Company, 1972.

Bartov, Omer, *Hitler's Army: Soldiers, Nazis, and War in the Third Reich*, New York: Oxford University Press, 1992.

Bazenguissa-Ganga, Rémy, 'The Spread of Political Violence in Congo-Brazzaville', *African Affairs*, 98, 390 (1999), pp. 37–54.

Beaufre, André, *La guerre révolutionnaire. Les formes nouvelles de la guerre*, Paris: Fayard, 1972.

Berry, Mary Elizabeth, *The Culture of Civil War in Kyoto*, Berkeley: University of California Press, 1994.

Bilton, Michael and Kevin Sim, *Four Hours in My Lai*, New York: Penguin, 1992.

Bouthoul, Gaston, *Traité de polémologie. Sociologie des guerres*, Paris: Payot, 1970.

Chacón Barrero, Mario, *Dinámica y Determinantes de la Violencia Durante 'La Violencia': Una Aproximación Desde la Econometria Espacial*, unpublished paper, Universidad de los Andes, 2003.

Che Guevara, Ernesto, *Guerrilla Warfare*, Lincoln: University of Nebraska Press, 1998.

Collins, Eamon (with Mick McGovern), *Killing Rage*, New York: Granta Books, 1999.

Cooper, Matthew, *The Nazi War Against Soviet Partisans, 1941–1944*, New York: Stein and Day, 1979.

Coster, Will, 'Massacre and Codes of Conduct in the English Civil War', in Mark Levene and Penny Roberts (eds), *The Massacre in History*, New York: Berghahn Books, 1999, pp. 89–105.

Creveld, Martin van, *The Transformation of War*, New York: The Free Press, 1991.

Dale, Catherine, 'The Dynamics and Challenges of Ethnic Cleansing: The Georgia–Abkhazia Case', *Refugee Survey Quarterly*, 16, 3 (1997), pp. 77–109.

Derriennic, Jean-Pierre, *Les Guerres Civiles*, Paris: Presses de Sciences Po, 2001.

Earle, Timothy, *How Chiefs Come to Power: The Political Economy in Prehistory*, Stanford: Stanford University Press, 1997.

Ellis, Stephen, *The Mask of Anarchy: The Destruction of Liberia and the Religious Dimension of an African Civil War*, New York: New York University Press, 1999.

Fearon, James D. and David D. Laitin, 'Ethnicity, Insurgency, and Civil War', *American Political Science Review*, 97, 1 (2003), pp. 75–86.

Fellman, Michael, *Inside War: The Guerrilla Conflict in Missouri During the American Civil War*, New York: Oxford University Press, 1989.

Feraoun, Mouloud, *Journal 1955–1962: Reflections on the French–Algerian War*, Lincoln, NE: University of Nebraska Press, 2002.

Figes, Orlando, *A People's Tragedy: The Russian Revolution, 1891–1924*, New York: Penguin, 1996.

Geffray, Christian, *La cause des armes au Mozambique: Anthropologie d'une guerre civile*, Paris: Karthala, 1990.

Grossman, Dave, *On Killing: The Psychological Cost of Learning to Kill in War and Society*, Boston: Little, Brown, and Company, 1995.

Goltz, Thomas, *Azerbaijan Diary. A Rogue Reporter's Adventures in an Oil-Rich, War Torn, Post-Soviet Republic*, Armonk: M. E. Sharpe, 1998.

Gumz, Jonathan E., '*Wehrmacht* Perceptions of Mass Violence in Croatia, 1941–1942', *The Historical Journal*, 44, 4 (2001), pp. 1015–38.

Halliday, Fred, *Mercenaries: Counter-Insurgency in the Gulf*, Nottingham, UK: Russell Press, 1977.

Harkavy, Robert E. and Stephanie G. Neuman, *Warfare and the Third World*, New York: Palgrave, 2001.

Henriksen, Thomas H., *Revolution and Counterrevolution: Mozambique's War of Independence, 1964–1974*, Westport: Greenwood Press, 1983.

Holsti, Kalevi J., *The State, War, and the State of War*, Cambridge: Cambridge University Press, 1996.

Huntington, Samuel P., 'Guerrilla Warfare in Theory and Policy', in Franklin Mark Osanka (ed.), *Modern Guerrilla Warfare. Fighting Communist Guerrilla Movements, 1941–1961*, New York: The Free Press, 1962, pp. xv–xxii.

Ignatieff, Michael, *The Warrior's Honor: Ethnic War and the Modern Conscience*, New York: Henry Holt and Company, 1998.

Juliá, Santos (ed.), *Victimas de la guerra civil*, Madrid: Temas de Hoy, 1999.

Kalyvas, Stathis N., *The Logic of Violence in Civil War*, unpublished manuscript, Yale University, 2004.

Kalyvas, Stathis N., 'The Logic of Violence in Civil War: Ethnic and Non-Ethnic Civil Wars', unpublished paper, The University of Chicago, 2002.

Kalyvas, Stathis N., '"New" and "Old" Civil Wars: A Valid Distinction?', *World Politics*, 54, 1 (2001), pp. 99–118.

Laqueur, Walter, *Guerrilla Warfare: A Historical and Critical Study*, New Brunswick, NJ: Transaction, 1998.

Ledesma Vera, José Luis, 'Espacios de Poder, Violencia y Revolución: Una Perspectiva Política de la Represión en el Aragón Republicano Durante la Guerra Civil', in Antonio Morales Moya (ed.), *El Difícil Camino a la Democracia*, Madrid: Sociedad Estatal España Nuevo Milenio, 2001, pp. 249–68.

Loyd, Anthony, *My War Gone By, I Miss it So*, New York: Penguin, 2001.

Makdisi Jean Said, *Beirut Fragments: A War Memoir*, New York: Persea Books, 1990.

Mouro, Gladys, *An American Nurse Amidst Chaos*, Beirut: American University of Beirut, 1999.

Mueller, John, 'Hatred, Violence, and Warfare: Thugs as Residual Combatants', paper presented at the 2001 Annual Meeting of the American Political Science Associated, 30 August–2 September 2001.

O'Leary, Brendan and John McGarry, *The Politics of Antagonism: Understanding Northern Ireland*, London: The Athlone Press, 1993.

Randal, Jonathan C., *Going All the Way: Christian Warlords, Israeli Adventurers, and the War in Lebanon*, New York: The Viking Press, 1983.

Ron, James, 'Boundaries and Violence: Repertoires of State Action Along the Bosnia/Yugoslavia Divide', *Theory and Society*, 29 (2000), pp. 609–40.

Selesky, Harold E., 'Colonial America', in Michael Howard, George J. Andreopoulos, and Mark R. Shulman (eds), *The Laws of War: Constraints on Warfare in the Western World*, New Haven: Yale University Press, 1994, pp. 59–85.

Shaw, Bruno, 'Selections from Selected Works of Mao Tse-Tung', in Sam C. Sarkesian (ed.), *Revolutionary Guerrilla Warfare*, Chicago: Precedent Publishing, 1975, pp. 205–35.

Schmitt, Carl, *Théorie du Partisan*, Paris: Flammarion, 1992.

Shepherd, Ben, 'Hawks, Doves and *Tote Zonen*: A Wehrmacht Security Division in Central Russia, 1943', *Journal of Contemporary History*, 37, 3 (2002), pp. 349–69.

Shy, John, *A People Numerous and Armed: Reflections on the Military Struggle for American Independence*, New York: Oxford University Press, 1976.

Simons, Anna, 'War: Back to the Future', *Annual Reviews of Anthropology*, 28 (1999), pp. 73–108.

Smith, M. L. R., 'Guerrillas in the Mist: Reassessing Strategy and Low Intensity Warfare', *Review of International Studies*, 29 (2003), pp. 19–37.

Swedenburg, Ted, *Memories of Revolt: The 1936–1939 Rebellion and the Palestinian National Past*, Minneapolis: University of Minnesota Press, 1995.

Tabbara, Lina Mikdadi, *Survival in Beyrut: A Diary of Civil War*, London: Onyx Press, 1997.

Thayer, Thomas C., *War Without Fronts: The American Experience in Vietnam*, Boulder, CO: Westview Press, 1985.

Tishkov, Valery, 'Ethnic Conflicts in the Former USSR: The Use and Misuse of Typologies and Data', *Journal of Peace Research*, 36, 5 (1999), pp. 571–91.

Toolis, Kevin, *Rebel Hearts: Journeys Within the IRA's Soul*, New York: St Martin's Griffin, 1997.

Ucelay da Cal, Enric, 'La guerre civile espagnole et la propagande franco-belge de la Première Guerre mondiale', in Jean-Clément Martin (ed.), *La guerre civile entre histoire et mémoire*. Nantes: Ouest Éditions, 1995, pp. 77–90.

Venter, Al J., *The Terror Fighters: A Profile of Guerrilla Warfare in Southern Africa*, Cape Town: Purnell, 1969.

Woodward, Susan L., *Balkan Tragedy. Chaos and Dissolution After the Cold War*, Washington, DC: The Brookings Institution, 1995.

5

A DIFFERENT KIND OF WAR?

September 11 and the United States' Afghan war*

Colin McInnes†

> This will be a different kind of conflict against a different kind
> of enemy.
>
> President George W. Bush, 15 September 2001.[1]

The terrorist attacks against the United States on September 11 2001 and the US response have been widely described as heralding a new kind of war.[2] For over a decade previous to September 11, however, a body of literature was developing concerning what Martin van Creveld has called 'the transformation of war' and Mary Kaldor 'new wars'.[3] Although this literature is fairly disparate, it is united in arguing that during the 1990s a new kind of warfare began to emerge (or, for some, had already emerged). For much of the twentieth century war in the West had been dominated by the experience and the fear of total war. Even so-called 'limited wars' fought by Western powers outside Europe were fought in the shadow of total war. By the end of the Cold War, however, a consensus was emerging that major war between Western powers was obsolete and that the era of total war was over.[4] The West still engaged in military operations on a regular basis but their character was fundamentally different.

What this chapter addresses is whether September 11 and its immediate aftermath – the US campaign in Afghanistan, Operation Enduring Freedom – confirmed those trends, which were emerging in the 1990s, or whether it really did constitute a different kind of war. Some caution must be used, not only due to the temporal proximity to the two events but also in generalising from such a limited base. Not least it is uncertain how the wider US-led 'war against terrorism' will develop. Nevertheless, September 11 and Operation Enduring Freedom can be usefully compared with the 'new wars' of the 1990s.

To do this, I adopt a four-point framework based on key features of Western military operations in the 1990s.[5] The first of these is that wars no longer spread geographically but were localised, not only in terms of the fighting but in their impact as well. As a result the West intervened in conflicts *without* the risk of war spreading to the West itself. NATO's intervention in Kosovo, American intervention in Somalia and Haiti, even coalition operations in the Gulf, did not lead to the war spreading to the West, nor was this risk seen as a serious possibility. In part the inability of local conflicts to escalate into more general war was because there was no global conflict into which they could be subsumed. During the Cold War, local conflicts such as those in the Horn of Africa, the Middle East and South-East Asia acquired global dimensions due to superpower rivalry. But the lack of a global conflict in the 1990s meant that there was no wider context for escalation. Wars also lacked escalatory potential due to the lack of military capabilities. Not only was the United States the sole military superpower, meaning that any conventional military conflict with it would almost certainly end in defeat, but few states possessed the capability to launch attacks outside their own region. The threat of long-range missiles developed by so-called rogue states was still some way off (nevertheless prompting a revival of interest in strategic defences), while terrorism appeared confined to the 'threat within'.

The second element in the transformation of war concerns the nature of the enemy. In the age of total war the enemy was the opposing state and its people. Propaganda demonised not only enemy leaders but also enemy soldiers and society *en masse*. A 'literature of atrocity' appeared with the purpose of dehumanising the enemy.[6] On the Eastern Front in the Second World War, the Germans *en masse* were seen as the enemy by the Soviets; for Germany the Jewish people were to be eradicated in their entirety; while the willingness of the British to bomb German cities (and to a lesser extent, German bombing of British cities) suggests that the people were considered to be the enemy. During the 1990s however, the enemy was no longer portrayed as the state but as a regime or even an individual leader. The comments of President Clinton during the Kosovo crisis are typical:

> Our quarrel is not with the Serbs in Serbia, it is not with the Serbs in Kosovo, it is not with Serbian Americans; it is with the leadership who believes it is alright to kill people and to uproot them and to destroy their family records and to erase any record of their presence in a land simply because of their ethnic heritage.[7]

In Britain, the Foreign Secretary Robin Cook made a similar point in a message to the Serb people:

> [NATO's bombing] is not intended against the Serbian people. It is not intended to undermine your country . . . our objective has been to strike against the power-base of President Milosevic . . . I bitterly regret having to enter into conflict with your country. It started because President Milosevic chose to ignore our warnings and

conduct the most awful cruelty in Kosovo. It can end when he calls a halt to that cruelty, and lets the people of Kosovo, and the people of Yugoslavia, have the peaceful and prosperous future they deserve.[8]

In this shift from counter-state to counter-regime, Western politicians explicitly distance themselves from presenting the people – Serbs, Somalis, Iraqis or whomever – as the enemy. Indeed the people are often presented as suffering under a repressive regime. The target therefore is not the state but the leadership, what it values and its ability to maintain a grip on power.

Third, and closely related to this, was the attempt to minimise collateral damage. Considerable efforts were made to avoid causing collateral damage, efforts which were much publicised by Western leaders. US Secretary of Defense William Cohen commented about the 1998 air strikes against Iraq, for example, that 'We've taken great care to minimize casualties amongst innocent civilians in our strikes. . . . To the extent that there are civilian casualties, only Saddam and his brutally destructive regime are to blame.'[9] After the first night of NATO bombing in the Kosovo conflict, Prime Minister Tony Blair reported 'we have done everything we can to minimise civilian damage'.[10]

Despite the effort given over to minimising collateral damage, mistakes still occurred. The strong reaction to such mistakes was in part due to raised expectations – that when the rhetoric of precision was coupled to powerful images of bombs hitting targets with unnerving accuracy, an expectation developed that collateral damage should not occur. This however can only be a partial explanation. After all, it was not the West that suffered from collateral damage but the enemy. Part of the explanation therefore has to do with the changed identification of the enemy. If the enemy was no longer the people but a regime or leadership, then bombs that missed did not hit the 'enemy' but innocent civilians. In the Second World War there were few qualms about causing collateral damage because ultimately it was still the enemy that suffered. But when bombs missed their targets in Belgrade or Baghdad in the 1990s, it was the innocent and the vulnerable that suffered. Another part of the explanation is that a tacit bargain had been struck, whereby if the enemy population was no longer targeted, then Western society similarly should not be placed at risk. If the West attacked civilian targets or caused collateral damage, then this might have made Western society a legitimate target; such actions would have invited retaliation in kind. But by avoiding enemy civilians and minimising collateral damage, the West may, consciously or not, have been encouraging the enemy to reciprocate and create a norm of non-combatant immunity.[11]

Finally, if society participated in war during the age of total war, then in these new wars it had no such desire. Instead, society spectated. Wars were no longer fought by nations in arms, rather they were fought by representatives on the field of battle. War was no longer an obligation of citizenship but the business of professionals. Those involved had chosen to be so through a career choice and accepted unlimited liability as part of their professional contract. By making war the business of professionals, Western societies absolved themselves from some of the responsibility of placing them in harm's way. For those involved, war was their chosen occupation and death and injury an occupational hazard. The social contract that formed part of Clausewitz's trinitarian perspective on war was replaced by a business relationship.[12] The costs of war were also reduced by the comparatively small numbers involved, usually a few thousand.[13] Wars were fought by a small fraction of the West, limiting not only exposure to suffering but also the sense of participation and shared endeavour. But even though the numbers involved were small the political impact of casualties might nevertheless be considerable: the military may be our representatives, but they are *our* representatives. In Bosnia and Somalia, each American soldier was politically significant and as a consequence their exposure to risk was also minimised.[14]

September 11

At 08.45 local time on September 11 2001, a hijacked American Airlines passenger jet was flown into the north tower of the World Trade Center in New York City. Eighteen minutes later a second hijacked aircraft was flown into the south tower. Just under an hour after the first attack, a third hijacked aircraft was flown into the Pentagon in Washington DC, causing part of it to collapse. At 10.05 the south tower of the World Trade Center collapsed, followed at 10.28 by the north. At 10.10 a fourth hijacked aircraft crashed in Somerset County, Pennsylvania, south of Pittsburgh.[15] It was immediately apparent that the death toll from these concerted attacks would be high, the shock compounded by the fact that the vast majority would be ordinary citizens working in two of the West's major cities. The peculiarly evocative images – of a clear blue sky, gleaming aircraft, white buildings, the black smoke and red fireballs from impact; of the almost graceful collapse of both towers; of the survivors, some barely recognisable as human beings, emerging from the devastation; of the cloud of dust and debris obscuring the lower half of Manhattan – were transmitted globally by a media quickly on the scene. Almost as evocative was the rhetoric that followed, not least the analogies with Pearl Harbor, suggesting a fundamental transformation in American foreign policy as well as in the nature of threats faced by the United States.[16]

To a certain extent such attacks had been presaged. In 2000 the US National Commission on Terrorism had reported that 'Today's terrorists seek to inflict mass casualties, and they are attempting to do so both overseas and on American soil.'[17] In April 2001, the US State Department began its report *Patterns of Global Terrorism* by arguing that 'terrorism continues to pose a clear and present danger to the international community'.[18] Both reports cited the Taliban regime in Afghanistan as a sponsor of terrorism, while the

State Department's *Patterns of Global Terrorism* report specifically mentioned Osama bin Laden.[19] Prior to September 11, at least one FBI agent had raised concerns over Middle Eastern enrolments at US flight schools and just weeks before September 11 the President himself received a briefing on the possibility of an imminent attack.[20] Attacks against US targets were also hardly new, particularly the 1998 attacks against embassies in East Africa (which killed 224 people, including 12 Americans, and injured perhaps 5,000 more), the 12 October 2000 attack against the USS *Cole* (which killed 17 US sailors) and the thwarted attack over the Millennium. Nor was the attempted hijacking of US aircraft new – in 1995 a conspiracy to hijack 11 US aircraft simultaneously over the Pacific had also been thwarted. Most tellingly the World Trade Center had itself been a target of terrorist attack in 1993, with six killed and over a thousand wounded.[21] To a certain extent, what was surprising on September 11 2001 was the means used – the National Commission on Terrorism, for example, had identified a number of possible means of terrorist attack, including bio-terrorism and cyber attacks, but not hijacked aircraft being flown into landmark buildings.[22] But perhaps most shocking was the combination of the scale of the loss of civilian life, the fact that this was accomplished in the West itself (and particularly in the United States) and the live television coverage – on September 11 most of the world became spectators of terrorism.

Was this war? Initially there was confusion within the Bush Administration over whether the attacks constituted an act of war. US Attorney General Ashcroft on September 11 talked of bringing 'the people responsible for these acts, these crimes, to justice'.[23] On the same day Secretary of Defense Rumsfeld, asked if he considered the attacks to be acts of war, replied 'What words the lawyers will use to characterize it is for them'.[24] In his address to the nation that evening, however, the President talked of 'the war against terrorism'.[25] The next day he referred to the attacks as acts of war,[26] a message repeated in his address to the Joint Session of Congress on 20 September.[27] Speaking on 14 September in the House of Commons, the Prime Minister appeared somewhat more circumspect, couching the act in criminal terms and talking of 'bringing those responsible to account'.[28] But over the weekend, in an interview with CNN, he too talked of war: 'the fact is that we are at war with terrorism . . . it is a war, if you like, between the civilised world and fanaticism'.[29]

September 11 and the transformation of war

The events of September 11 were shocking in part because they appeared to break the pattern of war established by the West in the 1990s. In the previous decade, war had become something conducted at a safe distance. But on September 11 the attacks were at the heart of the West, against the capital of the United States and against one of its most famous and most visited cities.

The President told Congress on 20 September, 'Our Nation has been put on notice: We are not immune from attack'.[30] A new sense of vulnerability emerged,[31] apparent in the reaction to the anthrax attacks a few weeks later, and quickly led to a range of homeland defence measures, including the creation of the Office of Homeland Security under Governor Tom Ridge and a $20bn package of measures to promote homeland security.[32] Nor was this seen as simply an attack on the United States. Not only were citizens of over 80 other nations killed in the attacks of September 11,[33] but the attacks were portrayed more broadly as attacks upon 'the free world', or more usually 'the civilised world'.[34] The implication was clear: it was not simply the United States that was now vulnerable and which might be attacked on its own soil.

If the West's wars in the 1990s had been localised and fought away from the West, then they had also been portrayed as wars against regimes or leaders. Targeting policies had accordingly attempted to minimise civilian deaths, particularly collateral damage. In some senses the attacks of September 11 were also against leadership targets: they were against the United States, the leader of the free world; two of the aircraft were targeted at symbols of US global financial leadership; and one aircraft was targeted at the headquarters of the US military. But this was not discriminate targeting against regimes; it was indiscriminate, with no attempt to minimise civilian deaths. In his 1998 *fatwa*, Osama bin Laden had stated that 'The ruling to kill the Americans and their allies – *civilians and military* – is an individual duty for every Muslim who can do it in any country in which it is possible to do it'.[35] Nor did the attacks appear to be geared to the downfall of a regime: the target was at best US 'leadership' in a vague sense. Conceivably the downfall of the West was an aim, but this remained unclear. Osama bin Laden's *fatwa*, for example, had called for more specific goals relating to Islam's holy sites as well as the more general injunction that the enemies of Islam be rendered unable to threaten Muslims.[36]

September 11 also departed from the pattern of warfare established by the West in terms of collateral damage. Whereas the West had taken great pains to avoid unnecessary civilian deaths – albeit not always successfully – the terrorist attacks either did not accept any distinction between legitimate targets and collateral damage, or did not care about it. As the Prime Minister's Official Spokesman, Alastair Campbell, bluntly put it: 'These people had no regard for human life'.[37] Nick Wheeler has written, 'What shocked the world about the events of September 11 was that the perpetrators of this act deliberately set out to kill innocent civilians'.[38] This stood in stark contrast to the manner in which the West had presented its campaigns in the late 1990s, when efforts had been made to minimise civilian suffering and both President Clinton and Prime Minister Blair had apologised for the suffering that had occurred.[39] Almost a year after the attacks of September 11, however, estimates of those killed ran at 3,062, the overwhelming majority of them civilians.[40] According to official US sources, approximately 2,000 children lost a parent on September 11; one business alone lost 700 civilian employees, leaving 50 pregnant widows.[41] Francois Heisbourg was not alone in wondering what the purpose of this was; for Heisbourg, the attacks were 'not political in the Clausewitzian sense'.[42] This appeared instead to be some new form of warfare, which went beyond not only traditional understandings of instrumental force, but acceptable norms of conduct in war. Adam Roberts concluded that 'The attacks of September 11 should be regarded as falling within the legal category of "crimes against humanity", which encompasses widespread or systematic murder against any civilian population'.[43]

The final area of change concerned the risk to Western society. The wars of the 1990s had presented virtually no direct risk to the majority of Western society. But on September 11 that all changed. Suffering was not limited to those directly involved but spread throughout the United States. As Secretary of Health Thompson put it, 'Every single American lost something today . . . America and all of its citizens share tonight in the grief that has been caused'.[44] Perhaps most revealing was the sense that life as normal had been interrupted by a new form of insecurity. Although the President attempted to reassure the American people on September 11 that the US was still 'open for business',[45] the next day he stated that 'it is not business as usual'.[46] In his address to the Joint Session of Congress on 20 September, President Bush was aware that life had not returned to normal and showed no signs of doing so quickly: 'It is my hope that in the months and years ahead, life will return almost to normal'.[47] There is a strong sense that society had been directly affected by the events of September 11. The majority of Americans may have been spectators to the events on the day itself, but they participated in the suffering. These terrorist acts created not only spectacular images but also rendered the West empathic spectators: that in watching the destruction, the citizens of the West were made aware of their vulnerability to subsequent acts. The attacks on the World Trade Center in particular produced feelings of empathy: these were ordinary citizens working in one of the most-famous buildings of one of the most-visited cities of the West. Being a spectator was used by the terrorists not to distance the citizens of the West from the attacks, but to bring them closer.

Does this mean that September 11 changed war for the West? There are three possible reasons why it did not. First, the attacks on September 11 were not carried out by the West but by its enemies. Therefore, although the *experience* of that day may have been different for those living in the West from, for example, the war in Kosovo, it tells us little about how the West will *conduct* subsequent military operations. This is the focus of the section below. Second, the outrage over September 11 suggests the potency of the framework outlined above. Just as not all wars in the age of total war were 'total',[48] so not all wars in the current age need conform fully to the framework; but when they do not, and in such an extreme manner, then the reaction may be one of outrage. Thus Osama bin Laden and al-Qaida were quickly portrayed as evil precisely because they did not conform to Western ideas of how war should be fought: in rather simplistic terms, it was a case of 'bad guys cheat', or of not fighting fair. The worldwide, near universal condemnation that followed the attacks suggested that norms had been broken and that there was a desire to maintain these not dispense with them. Third, September 11 has been described as an 'asymmetric' attack.[49] This form of warfare attempts to deny the enemy a war fought along its preferred lines, offering instead challenges and situations that it finds uncomfortable or unfamiliar. It is often a strategy of the weak against the strong, where they exploit what few advantages they have to create something unexpected, to which an enemy has difficulty responding. US strategic preferences are not simply for a Gulf War-type conflict – of a 'proper' war involving large scale operations against regular forces in a defined theatre of war, where overwhelming US material superiority can be brought to bear.[50] More broadly it is for the sort of war identified above, fought away from the West against regimes, not affecting Western societies and causing minimal loss of life. September 11 was an asymmetric attack because it was a negative image of the framework discussed above. The pattern of war developed by the West set the agenda for asymmetric attacks against the West.

The Afghan campaign: Operation Enduring Freedom

The US military response to September 11 began on 7 October 2001. The aims of the campaign in Afghanistan were initially unclear. Two distinct options emerged. The first involved punishing the Taliban for harbouring and collaborating with al-Qaida, and was intended to coerce the regime into bringing those involved to justice.[51] The second was to topple the Taliban regime and open up the way for an alternative government that would allow the United States direct access to al-Qaida hideouts in Afghanistan. By the eve of the campaign, the Taliban's failure to cooperate with US demands had effectively undermined the first option and the United States appeared to be seeking the removal of the regime, both as an act of punishment but also as a deterrent to other states harbouring terrorists.[52] Planning began on 12 September when Secretary of Defense Rumsfeld ordered the preparation of 'credible military options' to respond to international terrorism. Key to this was US Central Command under General Tommy R. Franks, which was tasked with preparing a warplan for operations in Afghanistan. Franks' concept of operations was presented to President Bush on 21 September and reflected very much the regime removal option. It proposed that 'US Central Command . . . would destroy the Al Qaida [sic] network inside Afghanistan along with the illegitimate Taliban regime which was protecting and harbouring the terrorists'.[53] More detailed plans for combat operations, including target sets and force requirements, were presented to Secretary Rumsfeld on 1 October and were authorised by the President the next day. The plan involved 'multiple lines of operation' to be conducted simultaneously rather than sequentially and included targeting the leadership of al-Qaida and the Taliban, attacking the Taliban military, and delivering humanitarian aid. Crucially, Franks' strategy was to avoid 'invading' Afghanistan and to work with rather than against the people – though the extent of such cooperation in the initial stages of the campaign was not obviously great.[54] Although US ground troops were inserted early on, these were limited in number and drawn from special forces. Operating with the opposition United Front (or 'Northern Alliance'), their role appeared primarily to be one of intelligence gathering and targeting precision-guided munitions launched from US aircraft. A larger ground presence would not only have been problematic, given the lack of host-nation support in the region (both Muslim Pakistan and the former Soviet republics neighbouring Afghanistan would have had substantial political problems in acting as a base for a US ground force), but also would have raised fears of a protracted involvement similar to that following the Soviet Union's 1979 invasion.[55]

The operation began with air strikes against selected military targets, and expanded to include strikes against political and infrastructure targets as well as al-Qaida bases. Air strikes were complemented by special forces operations and an ambitious raid by US ground forces against the Kandahar compound of the Taliban's leader, Mullah Omar. US strategy appeared to be attempting to split the already divided Taliban both by strategic strikes and also by affecting its military capabilities, most particularly in the north against the United Front.[56] By the end of October, however, little appeared to have been achieved. Critics of the campaign became increasingly vocal: the United Front had failed to take the key northern town of Mazar-e Sharif; Taliban support appeared strong in both Afghanistan and areas of neighbouring Pakistan; and a number of targeting mistakes had led to questions over the conduct of the campaign. Although in retrospect the Taliban was under increasing pressure, caught between maintaining its military front in the north and retaining control elsewhere in Afghanistan, the impression elsewhere was of a campaign getting nowhere fast.[57] It was in this context that in the final week of October, US strategy shifted towards one of 'brute force'.[58] B-52 bombers began carpet-bombing Taliban positions in support of United Front ground operations. In November the air attacks intensified, on 7 November reaching 120 attack sorties a day.[59]

The sudden collapse of the Taliban, however, was largely unexpected.[60] On 9 November the key northern town of Mazar-e Sharif fell to United Front troops. The Taliban attempted to retreat south to the source of their political power in the Kandahar region. Command and control however broke down catastrophically and the retreat became a rout, characterised by a succession of defections. On 12 November United Front forces broke onto the Shomali Plain and the next day entered the capital, Kabul. After an agreement signed in Bonn on 5 December, an interim authority was established under

Hamid Karzai, and on 20 December UN Security Council Resolution 1386 authorised the establishment of the International Security Assistance Force (ISAF) under British command. The Taliban attempted to make a stand in Kandahar, but abandoned its home base there on 7 December. A week later US Marine Corps armoured troops moved in to establish control of the airport.

The collapse of the Taliban was probably a result of a number of factors, not least the synergy between US air power and United Front ground offensives. But the inherent weaknesses of the Taliban regime also probably played a part. The Taliban was a loose coalition that had failed to grow out of its regional roots. As a result it found itself overextended, lacking popular support and prone to division. When placed under pressure, it began to collapse within itself. It then decided to fall back and regroup around Kandahar. This proved to be a strategic error. Adopting a positional defence made it vulnerable to US air power, while it misjudged the US political aims in hoping for some form of accommodation. The US by now was interested in nothing short of the total overthrow of the Taliban. It was only with the fall of Kandahar that the Taliban fell back on the strategy it was best equipped for and the US least able to deal with, one of guerrilla warfare.[61]

With the collapse of Taliban resistance in Kandahar and the establishment of an interim authority in Kabul, most of Afghanistan entered a period of post-conflict reconstruction. For the United States, however, the conflict continued, though its nature had changed. General Franks described the mission as now being to 'locate and destroy remaining pockets of Taliban and Al Qaida [sic] fighters and to search for surviving leadership'.[62] For Franks, much work still needed to be done and some of it very dangerous.[63] This resulted in some tension between the Afghans and the United States, especially over continued aerial bombardment. It also led to some instances of US air power being misled by local intelligence and used by warlords to settle old scores.[64] The overall pattern that emerged was described by Franks as one of a general low level of activity with occasional 'spikes' of more intense activity.[65] US ground forces began to play an increasingly significant role in combat operations, including a pitched battle in mid December at Tora Bora, south of Jalalabad.[66] More significant however was Operation Anaconda, which began on 2 March in a 70 square-mile rough mountainous area of the Paktia province around Shah-I-Kot. The operation involved around 2,000 coalition ground troops, including 800–900 Americans, against Taliban and al-Qaida forces estimated as several hundred strong. Franks described the close-quarter fighting as 'very scary', not helped by the difficult conditions, and a number of American soldiers were killed in the fighting.[67] Although there was some speculation that the United States had allowed Taliban and al-Qaida fighters to gather there so that they could conduct a single decisive battle rather than a series of smaller 'cat and mouse chases',[68] subsequent operations (including Operation Snipe beginning on 29 April and

Operation Condor in May 2002[69]) suggested that this phase of the conflict was still far from over. Nevertheless, in the first three months of Operation Enduring Freedom the United States had succeeded in removing the Taliban regime from power. Al-Qaida activities had been severely disrupted, though the organisation had not been destroyed: it had lost the ability to operate out of a friendly state and at least 11 training camps as well as other facilities in Afghanistan; at least eight of the top al-Qaida leaders were believed dead, although both Osama bin Laden and the Taliban leader Mullah Omar were probably still alive and on the run; and some 3,000–4,000 Taliban troops had been killed, along with several hundred 'Afghan Arabs' associated with al-Qaida.[70]

The war in Afghanistan: back to the future

The conduct and experience of Operation Enduring Freedom bore many of the hallmarks of Western military operations from the 1990s. Not least, the war was fought in Afghanistan with no direct engagement by Western society at large. In three important respects, however, Enduring Freedom was not as localised as previous Western military operations.

First, not only were some of the bombing missions flown from bases in the continental United States (as had been the case in Kosovo[71]), but the operation was commanded and controlled from CENTCOM's base in Tampa, Florida. During Operation Desert Storm, Frank's predecessor General Norman Schwarzkopf had been based in Saudi Arabia; but for Afghanistan operations were controlled at arms' length from within the United States.[72] This was partly due to the smaller footprint involved, but also a result of advances in technology that allowed Franks not only to video-teleconference with local commanders, but to 'see' the battlefield with 'unparalleled situational awareness'.[73] Second, the US appeared committed to widening the war to a more general attack on terrorism and states supporting terrorists. In his 29 January 2002 State of the Union Address, President Bush stated that 'Our second goal [in the war against terror] is to prevent regimes that sponsor terror from threatening America or our friends and allies with weapons of mass destruction'. The President went on to explicitly identify Iran, Iraq and North Korea as constituting 'an axis of evil'.[74] Implicit was the threat that military actions might be considered against these states. A few days earlier, Secretary of Defense Rumsfeld had been even more explicit: 'if we have to go into 15 more countries, we ought to do it'.[75] Third, a real fear remained that September 11 would not be the last attack on American soil. In May 2002, Vice-President Dick Cheney gave a high-profile warning that another terrorist attack was 'almost certain'.[76] At the time Cheney was almost certainly aware of the arrest of Abdullah al-Muhajir on suspicion of planning a terrorist attack in the United States using a 'dirty bomb', an arrest only made public in June.[77] Therefore although conventional military operations might be fought elsewhere, asymmetric attacks could be conducted against the United States itself, as well as its allies. Importantly, whereas asymmetric responses in previous conflicts were limited to the theatre of operations (such as the use of Western hostages as a 'human shield' and the release of oil into the Persian Gulf by Saddam during the Gulf War, and ethnic cleansing prompting a mass exodus in Kosovo by the Milosevic regime[78]), after September 11 this no longer appears to be the case.

Operation Enduring Freedom was also similar to operations of the 1990s in that the enemy was couched in terms of a regime (and, in this instance, the terrorists it harboured) rather than the state and the people. Thus the debate over campaign objectives was whether to coerce or remove the regime in Afghanistan,[79] while leaders on both sides of the Atlantic emphasised that the enemy was not the Afghan people but the Taliban regime and al-Qaida.[80] As with previous operations, the Western narrative was of a people oppressed by a regime, and it was that regime which was the target of military operations. Thus President Bush stated to the Joint Session of Congress that 'America is a friend of the Afghan people',[81] while General Franks talked of 'America's compasssion for the suffering Afghan people'.[82] In case anyone was in any doubt of the oppressed nature of the Afghan people, the Administration detailed how 'Afghanistan's people have been brutalized'.[83] As Nick Wheeler has pointed out, however, there were limits to this compassion: the humanitarian aid dropped by air at the beginning of the campaign was dismissed by aid workers as a propaganda stunt; the US was unwilling to commit to the ISAF despite the wishes of the interim authority; and warlords among the United Front allies were reported as being responsible for human rights abuses against Pashtun civilians in the north.[84] Such limits had of course been seen in previous Western interventions, most recently in the unwillingness of NATO to commit to an opposed ground entry in Kosovo, and the height at which NATO aircraft operated in that conflict in order to avoid the risk from hand-held SAMs. What matters here though is that the narrative of oppression is much the same as for previous operations, and that the campaign objectives and enemy imaging were couched in terms of the regime rather than the Afghan people.

A third area of similarity concerned the attention paid to minimising collateral damage. General Franks has repeatedly asserted that 'this has been the most accurate war ever fought in this nation's history'.[85] Secretary of Defense Rumsfeld went further: 'no nation in human history has done more to avoid civilian casualties than the United States has in this conflict'.[86] To ensure this low level of civilian deaths, not only was a very high proportion of precision-guided munitions used[87] but there was also tight control over the targeting process, such that some Air Force commanders became frustrated that concerns over civilian casualties were hindering military operations.[88] Nevertheless Carl Connetta estimated that the campaign 'directly claimed the lives of 1,000 Afghan civilians, probably added more than another 3,000 deaths to the toll of the country's humanitarian crisis, and certainly produced 500,000 new refugees and displaced persons'.[89] Deliveries of aid and food were also disrupted at the local level for two to three months in late 2001, causing further suffering.[80] Indeed Connetta argues that the rate of civilians killed per bomb dropped was higher than in Kosovo.[91] Higher estimates of civilian deaths released by the Taliban regime were quickly discounted as unreliable, though those produced by the US academic Marc Herold received considerably more attention. Herold claimed that up to 4,000 Afghan civilians had been killed by US bombing raids between 7 October 2001 and 1 January 2002, and that the US 'directly targeted certain civilian facilities deemed hostile to its war intent'.[92] Although Herold's data has been criticised as lacking in rigour,[93] it is nevertheless clear that a substantial number of Afghans died as a result of US bombing raids, not least in a series of high-profile 'mistakes'. These included the bombing of a UN de-mining facility, an attack on a Red Cross food convoy and the double bombing of a Red Cross food distribution centre. Nor did controversy end with the fall of Kabul: on 29 December an attack purportedly on Taliban and al-Qaida leaders in the village of Qalai Niazi killed up to 107 villagers; a convoy of tribal elders *en route* from Paktia to the inauguration of the interim authority was mistakenly attacked by US aircraft, killing up to 65; on 1 July, during Operation Full Throttle, 48 civilians were killed and 117 wounded in attacks on villages in the home province of Mullah Omar.[94]

Attacks such as these prompted expressions of concern from within Afghanistan, including from some within the new government, as well as from US allies in the Coalition.[95] In response to these criticisms the Bush Administration deployed several arguments: that some civilian deaths were inevitable in war, though regrettable, but that the United States had worked harder than any previous belligerent to minimise such deaths; that the Taliban deliberately placed civilians at risk by deploying military assets in civilian buildings, including mosques and by using villages as human shields; that leadership targets and in particular al-Qaida targets were often located in residential areas, making collateral damage more likely; and that ultimate responsibility for civilian deaths lay not with the United States but with those who started the war.[96] Additional, less readily acknowledged reasons may have included the particular weapons and aircraft used being less accurate than in Kosovo; the poor and unreliable nature of some of the intelligence; the problem of how to respond rapidly but with certainty to targets of opportunity (particularly once the Taliban was on the run and became intermingled with refugee flows); and difficulties in targeting small groups of guerrilla fighters mingling with the civilian population.[97] Some remained unconvinced that the United States had done enough to meet some of the more stringent criteria for a 'just' or 'humanitarian' war;[98] nevertheless it is clear that the rhetoric emphasised a concern over minimising civilian casualties, that a major attempt had been made to limit non-combatant deaths, and that Connetta's figure of 1,000 to 1,300 accidental civilian deaths in the first few months stands in stark contrast not only to the deliberate targeting of civilians on September 11, but to civilian deaths in the era of total war.[99]

Finally, Operation Enduring Freedom also demonstrated a high level of concern for the lives of Coalition, and particularly US service personnel. That this would be the case was not necessarily immediately apparent from the initial bravado of Administration officials. After meeting his top national security advisers at Camp David on 15 September, President Bush stated: 'The United States will do what it takes to win this war'. Attorney General Ashcroft echoed these sentiments: 'we're going to get them, no matter what it takes'.[100] Two days later at the Pentagon, the bullish mood was still with the President, stating that the United States was 'ready to defend freedom at any cost'.[101] But four months on Congress was praising General Franks for the low loss of life in Afghanistan.[102] Indeed, by early January only two US service personnel had lost their lives due to enemy fire (one of whom was a CIA operative);[103] and although the loss of life began to increase as the United States became more directly involved in ground operations, the rate of increase was still slow.[104] Central to this was General Franks' decision not to invade Afghanistan but to rely on the combination of US air power and United Front ground forces, supported by limited numbers of coalition special forces on the ground.

Finding willing local allies appeared to be developing as a feature of US operations, allowing fewer US forces to be placed in exposed and dangerous situations on the ground. As a number of commentators have pointed out, the precedent for cooperation with the United Front lay with the KLA in Kosovo.[105] However, the parallel is not exact. In particular, NATO's relationship with the KLA was at best at arm's length, whereas in Afghanistan the US coordinated its operations with the United Front. The United Front had a status the KLA never enjoyed and became an integral element of US strategy in Afghanistan.[106] More important for the general point, however, is that it is not clear that reliance on local ground forces was a preferred strategic option. The initial degree of coordination between the United States and the United Front was quite limited, and it was only with the change in strategy to one of brute force in late October 2001 that closer air–ground coordination appeared, with US air power directly and consistently supporting United Front ground operations. Further, despite the success of a coordinated strategy in overthrowing the Taliban, relying on local allies had also produced problems. The United Front's rush to take Kabul had been against US wishes, and reflected the degree to which local interests may override those of the US. In the attack on Tora Bora, local Afghan forces had performed poorly, allowing al-Qaida fighters to escape, and appeared unwilling to risk their own lives for US interests. By Operation Anaconda the United States had learnt the lesson that there are limits on the extent to which local ground forces can be used in support of US operations. Their political agenda may be different and their combat motivation lacking. For Anaconda, the United States preferred to use its own troops despite the increased risk, suggesting that the strategy of using local ground forces in coordination with US air power may have only limited application.

By the end of 2001 over 3,000 US troops were on the ground in Afghanistan, mostly special forces, and their role was being hailed as a major element in the Coalition's success.[107] Moreover, as the guerrilla phase developed, major US combat formations were deployed on the ground in Afghanistan, including elements of the 10th Mountain Division and 101st Airborne Division, and combat operations involving a thousand or more troops began to occur. Nevertheless, the ground commitment was limited in comparison with both the Gulf War and, to take a guerrilla campaign from a previous age, Vietnam. The number of US service personnel placed in harm's way was comparatively small; US ground forces were 'not going to be an occupation army'; nor were they willing to play a role in the ISAF.[108]

Conclusion

The US conduct of operations in Afghanistan demonstrated many similarities with operations from the previous decade. Not least, the war was localised in Afghanistan; the enemy was identified as the Taliban regime and the al-Qaida terrorist organisation, with the Afghan people portrayed as suffering under an oppressive regime; there were significant efforts to minimise collateral damage; and US casualties were kept low. Although the United States did deploy ground forces in Afghanistan, running a heightened risk of casualties, this was only done in significant numbers when the Taliban had been beaten and when air power alone could not deal with the remaining enemy forces. Even then numbers involved were a few thousand and therefore on a similar scale to those deployed in the Balkans, not the tens of thousands in the Gulf War or Vietnam. An important qualification, however, concerns the localisation of the war. Although Operation Enduring Freedom was limited to Afghanistan, the 'war on terror' holds the possibility of spreading in two important respects. First, US officials have repeatedly made the point that Afghanistan was not the only state harbouring terrorists and that subsequent operations against other states are possible. Second, further terrorist attacks by al-Qaida within the United States in retaliation for US attacks in Afghanistan are possible – as the May 2002 arrest of Abdullah al-Mujahir on suspicion of planning a 'dirty bomb' attack, and the heightened security surrounding the first anniversary of the terrorist attacks suggest. This represents a very different form of asymmetric warfare from that seen in Kosovo or the Gulf War, and one that would clearly not be localised to the region.

Whereas the campaign in Afghanistan bore many similarities with Western military operations from the previous decade, September 11 initially appears to be very different. In particular the fact that the attacks were conducted in the United States itself and deliberately targeted against civilians made the attack different not only from the conflicts of the 1990s but from recent terrorist attacks as well (most notably the bombings of the East Africa embassies and the attack on the USS *Cole*). But in two important respects September 11 does demonstrate continuity with the new wars of the 1990s. First, September 11 constitutes an asymmetric attack that reflects a negative image of the type of war fought by the West. In other words, the pattern or character of war established by the West in the 1990s provides a basis for understanding the asymmetric attack of September 11. It is not that the pattern has been undermined; rather it has been reversed, much as the term 'asymmetry' might suggest. Second, September 11 was not the first terrorist attack to be attempted against large numbers of US civilians: the 1993 attack on the World Trade Center, the 1995 attempt to hijack passenger jets over the Pacific and the thwarted attack over the Millennium all predated September 11. The difference was that on September 11 the plan worked. The idea of the invulnerability of the United States in the post Cold War world had been a myth that was shattered on September 11. But the failure of previous attacks should not obscure the fact that US civilians were targets in the 1990s; and just as those attacks did not invalidate ideas concerning the transformation of war, neither does September 11.

Notes

* This chapter first appeared as Colin McInnes, 'A Different Kind of War: September 11 and the United States' Afghan War', *Review of International Studies*, 29, 2 (2003), pp. 165–84. © British International Studies Association, published by Cambridge University Press. Reprinted with permission.
† I would like to thank Martin Alexander, Nick Wheeler and Theo Farrell for their comments on earlier drafts of this chapter, and to the two anonymous referees [of *Review of International Studies*] for their comments.
1 'Washington File: President Bush's radio address Sept. [sic] 15 on terrorist attacks', p. 1. Available at: <http://www.usembassy.org.uk/bush76.html>, accessed on 19 September 2001.
2 See, for example Carl Connetta, *Strange Victory: A Critical Appraisal of Operation Enduring Freedom and the Afghanistan War*, Project on Defense Alternatives Research Monograph 6, 30 January 2002, p. 3 and fn. 2 p. 35. Available at: <http://www.comw.org/pda/0201strangevic.html>, accessed on 14 February 2002. For a dissenting view, see Lawrence Freedman, 'The Third World War?', *Survival*, 43, 4 (Winter 2001), pp. 66–7.
3 Martin van Creveld, *The Transformation of War*, New York: Free Press, 1991; Mary Kaldor, *New and Old Wars: Organized Violence in a Global Era*, London: Polity Press, 1999. Other examples of this literature include: Lawrence Freedman, *The Revolution in Strategic Affairs*, Adelphi Paper 318, Oxford: Oxford University Press for IISS, 1998; Michael Ignatieff, *Virtual War: Kosovo and*

Beyond, London: Chatto and Windus, 2000; Edward Luttwak, 'Towards Post-Heroic Warfare', *Foreign Affairs*, 74, 3 (1995), pp. 109–22; and 'A Post-Heroic Military Policy', *Foreign Affairs*, 75, 4 (1996), pp. 33–44; Colin McInnes, 'Spectator Sport Warfare', *Contemporary Security Policy*, 20, 3 (2000), pp. 142–65. It is important to distinguish between the 'transformation of war' debate and that concerning the revolution in military affairs. The latter focuses largely upon the impact of technology, especially information technology, upon military means. The transformation of war debate looks at broader changes in the international system and in society, as well as changes in technology and the character and experience of war.

4 For example, van Creveld, *Transformation of War*, Carl Kayser, 'Is War Obsolete?', *International Security*, 14, 4 (1990), pp. 42–64; Michael Mandelbaum, 'Is Major War Obsolete?', *Survival*, 40, 4 (1998/9), pp. 20–38; and John Mueller, *Retreat from Doomsday: The Obsolescence of Major War*, New York: Basic Books, 1989.

5 This analysis is taken from my *Spectator-Sport War: The West and Contemporary Conflict*, Boulder, CO: Lynne Rienner, 2002, especially pp. 51–78.

6 See for example Daniel Pick, *War Machine: The Rationalization of Slaughter in the Modern Age*, New Haven, CT: Yale University Press, 1993, p. 145, Samuel Hynes, *The Soldier's Tale: Bearing Witness to Modern War*, London: Pimlico, 1998, p. 225. There is some evidence questioning the extent to which this was always the case. That a people rather than a regime was identified as the enemy varied somewhat even in the two World Wars. John Dower for example has argued that in the Second World War the Americans viewed the Nazi regime as the enemy while ordinary Germans were not held to blame. At the same time Americans viewed the Japanese people as the enemy. John Dower, *War Without Mercy*, London: Faber, 1986.

7 President William S. Clinton, 'Address to Humanitarian Relief Organisations, Dearborn, Michigan, 16 April 1999', p. 1. Available at: <http://www.state.gov/www/policy_remarks/1999/990416_clinton_kosovo.html>, accessed on 12 June 1999.

8 Robin Cook, 'Message to the Serb people', FCO News, 1 April 1999. Available at: <http://195.166.119.98/servlet/Front?pagename=OpenMarket/Xcelerate/ShowPage&c=Page&cid=1007029391629&a=KArticle&aid=1013618396812>, accessed on 25 September 2002.

9 William S. Cohen, 'Department of Defense News Briefing, Office of the Assistant Secretary of Defense (Public Affairs), 19 December 1998', p. 1. Available at: <http://www.defenselink.mil/news/Dec1998/t12201998_t1219coh.html>, accessed on 12 June 2002.

10 'Prime minister reports on first night of Operation "Allied Force"'. Edited transcript of doorstep interview by the Prime Minister, Tony Blair, Berlin, 25 March 1999. Available at: <http://195.166.119.98/servlet/Front?pagename=OpenMarket/Xcelerate/ShowPage&c=Page&cid=1007029391629&a=KArticle&aid=1013618396569>, accessed on 25 September 2002.

11 This norm is also codified in international humanitarian law, as recently seen in the opinion given by the International Court of Justice on nuclear weapons. See Theo Farrell and Helene Lambert, 'Courting Controversy: International Law, National Norms and American Nuclear Use', *Review of International Studies*, 27, 1 (2000), pp. 309–26.

12 Martin Shaw, *Post-Military Society*, London: Polity, 1991; see also Christopher Coker, *Humane Warfare*, London: Routledge, 2001.

13 Although there were exceptions to this, most notably the 1990–1 Gulf War which saw some two million service personnel deployed by the Coalition. See Anthony

H. Cordesman and Abraham R. Wagner, *The Lessons of Modern War*, 4: *The Gulf War*, Boulder, CO: Westview, 1996, p. 114. Interestingly, the United Task Force deployment to Somalia at the end of 1992 is often portrayed as a major deployment, but the numbers involved – some 28,000 US troops – pale into insignificance with Desert Storm and were roughly half of the number of British casualties on the infamous first day of the Somme. Somalia may have been a major deployment in the context of the 1990s, but in the context of total war it was slight.

14 Cori Dauber, 'Implications of the Weinberger Doctrine for American Military Intervention in a Post-Desert Storm Age', *Contemporary Security Policy*, 22, 3 (2001), pp. 76–8. On casualty intolerance, see James Burk, 'Public Support for Peacekeeping in Lebanon and Somalia: Assessing the Casualties Hypothesis', *Political Science Quarterly*, 114, 1 (1999), pp. 53–78. Clearly casualty intolerance is a limitation rather than an absolute, and if interests and consensus are high, then states may be willing to accept high casualties (as the United States was in the Gulf War). But when either interests or consensus are missing, then this acceptance may be low and the loss of even a few service personnel will be sufficient to force a change in policy over military involvement. There is, however, some evidence to suggest that public tolerance for casualties is higher than nervous administrations give it credit for. Theo Farrell, for example, concludes that in Somalia 'The American public did not give up, its leaders did'. Theo Farrell, 'America's Misguided Mission', *International Affairs*, 76, 3 (2000), p. 591.

15 The events were widely reported in the broadsheets on the following day. The account here is taken from the CNN chronology, available at <http://cnn.com/2001/US/09/11/chronology.attack>, accessed on 28 May 2002, and from that given by the Prime Minister, Tony Blair, in his statement to the House of Commons on 14 September 2001. 'We need to mourn the dead; and then act to protect the living', Statement by the Prime Minister 14 September 2001, p. 2. Available at: <http://www.number-10.gov.uk/news>, accessed on 19 September 2001. It was speculated, not least by the US Administration itself, that the target for the third aircraft had not been the Pentagon but the White House. See 'Washington File: Powell calls for global coalition against terrorism', 12 September 2001, p. 5. Available at <http://www.usembassy.org.uk/terror141.html>, accessed on 19 September 2001.

16 For a discussion of this view, see Michael Cox, 'American Power Before and After 11 September: Dizzy with Success?', *International Affairs*, 78, 2 (2002), pp. 261–76. For dissenting views see John G. Ikenberry, 'American Grand Strategy in the Age of Terror', *Survival*, 43, 4 (Winter 2001), pp. 19–34; Steve Smith, 'The United States will emerge from this as a more dominant world power', *The Times*, 19 September 2001; and Stanley Hoffman, 'On the War', *The New York Review of Books*, 1 November 2001. Available at: <http://www.nybooks.com/articles/14660>, accessed on 9 January 2002.

17 'Washington File: Executive Summary, National Commission on Terrorism Report', 6 May 2000, p. 1. Available at: <http://www.usembassy.org.uk/terror112.html>, accessed on 19 September 2001.

18 US Department of State Office of the Co-ordinator for Counterterrorism, *Patterns of Global Terrorism 2000*, p. 1. Available at: <http://www.state.gov/s/ct/rls>, accessed on 19 September 2001.

19 *Patterns of Global Terrorism 2000*, p. 1; 'National Commission on Terrorism Report', p. 2.

20 'Press briefing by Ari Fleischer, 15 May 2002', p. 7. Available at <http://www.whitehouse.gov/news/releases/2002/05/20020515–7.html>, accessed on 16 May.

'Press briefing by Ari Fleischer, 16 May 2002', pp. 1–2. Available at: <http://www.whitehouse.gov/news/releases/2002/05/20020516–4.html>. See also Matthew Engel, 'Bush warned of hijacks before September 11', *Guardian*, 17 May 2002, p. 1.

21 Steven Simon and Daniel Benjamin, 'The Terror', *Survival*, 43, 4 (Winter 2001), p. 5; Freedman, 'The Third World War?', pp. 85–6.

22 'National Commission on Terrorism Report', p. 2.

23 'Washington File: Administration officials on terrorist attacks', 11 September 2001, p. 1. Available at: <http://www.usembassy.org.uk/terror139.html>, accessed on 19 September 2001.

24 'Washington File: Briefing by Rumsfeld, Shelton on Terrorist Attacks', 11 September 2001, p. 3. Available at: <http://www.usembassy.org.uk/terror 140.html>, accessed on 19 September 2001. One lawyer who had doubts over whether this was war was Marcel Berlins in his weekly column for the *Guardian*, 18 September 2001.

25 'Statement by the President in his Address to the Nation', 11 September 2001. Available at: <http://www.usembassy.org.uk/bush71.html>, accessed on 19 September 2001.

26 'Washington File: Bush remarks following meeting with his National Security Team', 12 September 2001, p. 1. Available at: <http://www.usembassy.org.uk/ bush73.html>, accessed on 19 September 2001.

27 'Text: Bush announces start of 'War on Terror': President addresses Joint Session of Congress Sept. 20', p. 2. Available at: <http://www.globalsecurity.org/military/ library/news/2001/09/mil-010920–usia01.htm>, accessed on 18 February 2002. See also 'Powell calls for global coalition against terrorism', p. 3.

28 Blair, 'We need to mourn the dead', p. 2. On 12 September the Prime Minister had also been reluctant, when asked, to state that this was war. 'US attack: Prime Minister's statement (Weds) including Q&A [sic]', 12 September 2001, pp. 5–6. Available at: <http://www.number-10.gov.uk/news>, accessed on 19 September 2001.

29 'Blair: "We are at war with terrorism"', interview on 16 September with CNN, pp. 1 and 6. Available at: <http://www.pm.gov.uk/news>, accessed on 19 September 2001.

30 'Bush announces start of "War on Terror"', p. 4.

31 See for example 'Text: President Bush announces military strikes in Afghanistan, 7 October 2001', p. 2. Available at: <http://www.globalsecurity.org/military/ library/news/2001/10/mil-011007–usia01.htm>, accessed on 18 February 2002. 'Transcript: Rumsfeld, Myers brief on military operations in Afghanistan, 7 October 2001', p. 9. Available at: <http://www.globalsecurity.org/military/ library/news/2001/10/mil-011007–usia04.htm>, accessed on 18 February 2002.

32 For a list of some of the more important measures, see 'The Global War on Terrorism: The First 100 Days', pp. 21–2. Available at: <http://www.whitehouse. gov/news/releases/2001/12/100dayreport.html>, accessed on 26 February 2002. September 11 also provided a boost for NMD. See for example Michael Sirak, 'USA weighs outlays for asymmetric threats', *Jane's Defence Weekly*, 3 October 2001, p. 3.

33 'The Global War on Terrorism', p. 3.

34 In his prepared statement on 12 September, for example, Tony Blair referred to the attacks as being 'not only on America but on the world'. He then referred to 'the full evil and capability of international terrorism which menaces the whole of the democratic world', before in questions stating that 'The United States has been singled out but there is no doubt that all these terrorists will regard us all as

targets . . . this is an attack on the free and democratic world as a whole'. 'US attack: Prime Minister's statement (Weds) including Q&A [sic]', 12 September 2001, pp. 2, 5. In his CNN interview on 16 September, the Prime Minister also stated 'What happened on Tuesday was an attack not just upon the United States but upon the free world'. 'Blair: "We are at war with terrorism"', p. 1.

35 Quoted in Simon and Benjamin, p. 8. Emphasis added. Bin Laden's *fatwa* was published in Al-Quds al-'Arabi on 23 February, 1998 and is available at: <http://www.ict.org.il/articles/fatwah.htm>, accessed on 25 February 2002.

36 According to Simon and Benjamin, although bin Laden's immediate concerns were with the oppressed state of Muslims, and the infidel occupation of Saudi Arabia and the al-Asqa mosque in Jerusalem, he also saw his battle as a war of civilisations, with the United States the principal malefactor. Simon and Benjamin, p. 8.

37 'Lobby briefing: 11 am, Tuesday 18 September 2001, US terror attacks', p. 2. Available at: <http://www.number-10.gov.uk/default.asp?pageid=4757>, accessed on 19 September 2001.

38 Nick Wheeler, 'Assigning responsibility for civilian casualties in Operation Enduring Freedom', draft manuscript February 2002, p. 1.

39 See McInnes, *Spectator-Sport War*, pp. 65–8.

40 According to data held by the Center for Defense Information, as of 21 August 2002 the figures for those killed on 11 September were 2,691 in the World Trade Center and an additional 147 in the two hijacked aircraft that crashed into the twin towers; 125 in the Pentagon and 59 in the hijacked aircraft; and 40 were killed in the hijacked aircraft that crashed in Pennsylvania south of Pittsburgh. See Center for Defense Information Terrorism Project, 'US and allied casualties: Sept [sic] 11, Operation Enduring Freedom and the anti-terrorist campaign', p. 1. Available at: <http://www.cdi.org/terrorism/casualties-pr.cfm>, accessed on 25 September 2002. The number of emergency workers (mainly firefighters but also paramedics) lost in the World Trade Center has been put at 343; a further 23 police officers and 37 Port Authority police officers were also killed. 'The Global War on Terrorism', p. 5.

41 'The Global War on Terrorism', p. 5.

42 Francois Heisbourg, 'Europe and the Transformation of World Order', *Survival*, 43, 4 (Winter 2001), p. 143.

43 Adam Roberts, 'Counter-Terrorism, Armed Force and the Laws of War', *Survival*, 44, 1 (Spring 2002), p. 8.

44 'Administration officials on terrorist attack', pp. 1–2.

45 'Statement by the President in his Address to the Nation', p. 1.

46 'Bush remarks following meeting with his National Security team', p. 1

47 'Bush announces the start of a "war on terror"', pp. 5–6. It is interesting in this context to examine the events surrounding the first anniversary of the attacks. In his televised address to the nation for example, President Bush couched his remarks very much in terms of a nation affected and challenged by the events of September 11. See 'President's remarks to the nation, Ellis Island, New York, 11 September 2002'. Available at: <http://www.whitehouse.gov/news/releases/2002/09/20020911-3.html>. See also Jonathan Freedland, 'What really changed?', *Guardian Weekly*, 12 September 2002. Available at: <http://www.guardian.co.uk/GWeekly/Story/0,3939,790679,00.html>, accessed on 24 September 2002.

48 In his study of the era of total war, for example, Brian Bond has argued that 'total war is just as much a myth as total victory or total peace'. Brian Bond, *War and Society in Europe, 1870–1970* London: Fontana, 1984, p. 168. See also Roger Chickering, 'Total War: The Use and Abuse of a Concept', in Manfred W.

Boemke, Roger Chickering and Stig Forster (eds), *Anticipating Total War: the German and American Experiences, 1871–1914*, New York: Cambridge University Press, 1999, pp. 13–28.

49 For example, Freedman, 'The Third World War?', pp. 64–76.

50 Ibid., p. 69.

51 See for example 'Bush announces start of War on Terror', p. 3.

52 Connetta, *Strange Victory*, pp. 7–8. For a list of campaign objectives, see for example 'Transcript: Rumsfeld, Myers brief on military operation [sic] in Afghanistan', 7 October 2001, p. 3. Available at: <http://www. globalsecurity.org/ military/library/news/2001/10/mil-011007–usia04.htm>, accessed on 18 February 2002. Wheeler, p. 1.

53 Franks' SASC Statement, p. 3.

54 Franks' SASC Statement, pp. 3–5; Senate Armed Services Committee, General Tommy Franks Witness Statement, 5 February 2002, p. 4. Available at: <http:// www.centcom.mil/news/transcripts>, accessed on 26 February 2002. Hereafter referred to as Franks' Witness Statement.

55 Anthony Davis, 'How the Afghan War was Won', *Jane's Intelligence Review*, February 2002, p. 6.

56 'Rumsfeld, Myers brief on military operations in Afghanistan', p. 4; Andrew Koch, 'USA's strategy takes shape', *Jane's Defence Weekly*, 17 October 2001, p. 2. Connetta, *Strange Victory*, pp. 8–11 and 30; Franks' SASC statement, pp. 5–6; Koch, pp. 2–3; Anthony Davis, 'UF Prepares Northern Offensive', *Jane's Defence Weekly*, 17 October 2001, p. 3. For a detailed chronology, see Emily Clark, 'Action Update', Center for Defense Information Terrorism Project. Available at: <http:// www.cdi.org/terrorism/actionupdate-pr.cfm>, accessed on various dates.

57 Connetta, *Strange Victory*, pp. 11 and 30; Lawrence Freedman, 'The Americans have left it too late to send in ground troops before winter', *The Independent*, 6 November 2001. Available at: <http://independent.co.uk>, accessed on 7 November 2001.

58 The distinction between coercion and brute force is Thomas Schelling's. See his *Arms and Influence*, New Haven, CT: Yale University Press, 1966, pp. 2–3.

59 Davis, 'How the Afghan War was Won', p. 9.

60 For example, in an article appearing on 14 November, but apparently written on at least 7 November, the otherwise well-informed Anthony Davis wrote from Afghanistan that 'Well-placed sources concede that that capture of Mazar[-e Sharif] will not be easy and despite the advance through Shulgareh and the intense air strikes, the city is unlikely to fall in the immediate future'. It fell on 9 November. Anthony Davis, 'US bombing boosts United Front's ground offensive', *Jane's Defence Weekly*, 14 November 2001, p. 3. See also Freedman, 'The Americans have left it too late'.

61 Connetta, *Strange Victory*, pp. 11–12 and 30–5; Davis, 'How the Afghan War was Won', pp. 6–11. A possible additional factor was the removal of support from the Pakistan Inter-Services Intelligence (ISI). On the relationship between the Taliban and the ISI, see Tim Judah, 'The Taliban papers', *Survival*, 44, 1 (Spring 2002), pp. 69–80.

62 Franks' SASC Statement, p. 5.

63 DoD [Department of Defense] News Briefing–General Tommy Franks, 4 January 2002, p. 1. Available at: <http://www.centcom.mil/news/press_briefings/Franks_ 4Jan.html>, accessed on 6 March 2002. Hereafter referred to as January 4 Briefing.

64 Connetta, *Strange Victory*, pp. 15–16.

65 January 4 Briefing, p. 2.

66 Defense Department Operational Briefing (Tampa, Florida), 14 December 2001, p. 1. Available at: <http://www.centcom.mil/news/press_briefings/FranksDec14. htm>, accessed on 6 March 2002. January 4 Briefing, p. 7.

67 USCENTCOM Press Briefing, 4 March 2002. Available at: <http://www. centcom.mil/news/transcripts/ Franks_mar04.htm>, accessed on 6 March 2002. Clark, updates for 4–10 March 2002 and 25 February–3 March 2002, accessed on 18 March 2002.

68 Clark, update for 4–10 March 2002, accessed on 18 March 2002.

69 Clark updates for 29 April–5 May, 8–12 May, 13–19 May and 20–26 May, accessed on 6 June 2002.

70 'The Global War on Terrorism', p. 3; Connetta, *Strange Victory*, pp. 3–4; Franks' Witness Statement, pp. 5 and 9; January 4 Briefing, p. 1.

71 Department of Defense, *Report to Congress: Kosovo/Operation Allied Force After-Action Report* (Washington, DC: Department of Defense, 2000), p. 31.

72 During military operations in Kosovo, NATO's commander General Wesley Clark had been based at NATO headquarters in Belgium.

73 Franks' SASC Statement, p. 7; Franks' Witness Statement, pp. 31 and 37. At the time of writing there is speculation that, should the US engage in military operations against Iraq, Franks' headquarters would be moved to the Gulf because of the size of the forces involved.

74 'President delivers state of the union address', 29 January 2002. Available at: <http://www.whitehouse.gov/news/releases/2002/01/20020129–11.html>, accessed on 6 June 2002.

75 Department of Defense News Briefing, Secretary Rumsfeld and General Myers, 16 January 2002. Excerpts available in Project on Defense Alternatives, 'Wider war watch: the war on terrorism and the impetus to widen it', entries for 16 January 2002. Available at: <http://wwwcomw.org/pda/widerwarwatch/index. html>, accessed on 14 February 2002. See this website more generally for an excellent review of the major statements and articles on the possible expansion of the war.

76 As reported by Julian Borger, 'Prepare for attack, Cheney tells US', *Guardian*, 20 May 2002, p. 1.

77 Julian Borger, 'US foils al-Qaida "dirty bomb" plot', *Guardian*, 11 June 2002, p. 1. The heightened security on the first anniversary of September 11 also revealed a fear of further attacks.

78 See for example *Kosovo After-Action Report*, p. 6.

79 Ibid., pp. 176–7.

80 See for example 'Prime Minister's statement in 10 Downing Street, 25 September 2001', available at: <http://www.number-10.gov.uk/news.asp?Newsld=2619>, accessed on 26 September 2001. 'Rumsfeld, Myers brief on military operation in Afghanistan', p. 3.

81 'President Bush announces military strikes in Afghanistan', p. 1.

82 Franks' Witness Statement, p. 1.

83 'The Global War on Terrorism', p. 6.

84 Nick Wheeler, 'Humanitarian intervention after September 11', draft March 2002.

85 Franks' Witness Statement, p. 22. See also January 4 Briefing, p. 6.

86 Embassy of the United States of America, Press Release 30 October 2001, 'Excerpt: Rumsfeld says Taliban to blame for casualties', p. 1. Available at: <http://www.usa.or.th/news/press/2001/nrot113.htm>, accessed on 23 January 2002. For a series of official statements on avoiding civilian deaths, see US Department of State, 'Fact sheet: US military efforts to avoid civilian casualties,

25 October 2001', p. 2. Available at: <http://usinfo.state.gov/topical/pol/terror/01102503.htm>, accessed on 1 January 2002.

87 Franks' Witness Statement, p. 25. See also Franks' SASC Statement, p. 8. The Chairman of the Joint Chiefs of Staff, General Richard Myers, told the Senate Armed Services Committee that, in early 2002, nearly 60 per cent of all munitions used had been precision-guided, compared to 10 per cent in the 1990/1 Gulf War. Franks' Witness Statement, p. 1.

88 Wheeler, 'Assigning responsibility', p. 9; Roberts, 'Counter-Terrorism', p. 19. Air Force misgivings over the emphasis being placed on avoiding civilian casualties were not new. During Kosovo a number had expressed similar concerns, most notably the commander of the air operation, USAF Lieutenant General Michael Short. See John A. Tirpak, 'Short's View of the Air Campaign', *Air Force Magazine*, 82, 9 (1999), p. 3. Available at: <http://www.afa.org/magazine/watch/0999watch.html>, accessed on 20 January 2000.

89 Connetta, *Strange Victory*, p. 20. See also Carl Connetta, *Operation Enduring Freedom: Why a Higher Rate of Civilian Bombing Casualties*, Project on Defense Alternatives Briefing Report no. 11, revised version 24 January 2002, p. 2 and Appendix 1. Available at: <http://www.comw.org/pda/0201oef.html>, accessed on 15 February 2002. Connetta's estimates of 1,000 to 1,300 civilian casualties by the end of 2001 is broadly in line with estimates from Human Rights Watch and by Reuters. Connetta, *Operation Enduring Freedom*, p. 2.

90 Connetta, *Strange Victory*, p. 22.

91 Connetta, *Operation Enduring Freedom*, p. 2.

92 Professor Marc W. Herold, 'A dossier on civilian victims of United States' aerial bombing of Afghanistan: a comprehensive accounting', December 2001, p. 9. Available at: <http://www.pubpages.unh.edu/~mwherold>, accessed on 2 January 2002.

93 Connetta, *Operation Enduring Freedom*, p. 2.

94 See Clark, 'Action update'. For Centcom's response, see 'Unclassified Executive Summary: Investigation of civilian casualties, Oruzgan province, Operation Full Throttle, 30 June 2002'. Available at: <http://www.centcom.mil/News/Reports/Investigation_Oruzgan_Province.htm>, accessed on 24 September 2002.

95 Connetta, *Strange Victory*, pp. 10 and 20; Peter Foster, 'US bombs "kill 107 villagers"', *Daily Telegraph*, 2 January 2002. Available at: <http://portal.telegraph.co.uk>, accessed on 21 January 2002; Edward Cody, 'Civilian deaths mustn't stall air campaign, US envoy argues', *International Herald Tribune*, 9 January 2002. Available at: <http://www.iht.com>, accessed on 21 January 2002.

96 January 4 Briefing, p. 6; 'The Global War on Terrorism', p. 7; Franks' Witness Statement, p. 22; 'US military efforts to avoid civilian casualties', pp. 1–2; Wheeler, 'Assigning responsibility', pp. 1–2 and 18; Connetta, *Strange Victory*, p. 10.

97 Connetta, *Operation Enduring Freedom*; Bearak, 'Uncertain Toll in the Fog of War', p. 1.

98 For example, neither Roberts, 'Counter-Terrorism', nor Wheeler in 'Assigning responsibility', appear wholly convinced that the United States had done all it could to have minimised civilian deaths, while Herold accuses the United States of a form of racism – the differential value of life – in preferring to save the lives of its own citizens over those in Afghanistan. Herold, 'Dossier on civilian victims', p. 6.

99 By mid 2002 however, the rhetoric from Washington over civilian casualties was less apologetic and somewhat more dismissive over civilian deaths, as seen in the

reaction to the 1 July killings. The extent and reasons behind this are unclear, but one possible reading of the reaction to 1 July is that, the United States having adopted a simple binary formulation of 'those not with us are against us', then there is somewhat less concern over killing or injuring villagers in regions thought to be hostile to the United States. In these instances, civilians are not innocent victims but of hostile intent. See for example 'Unclassified Executive Summary: Investigation of civilian casualties, Oruzgan province, Operation Full Throttle, 30 June 2002'. If correct, then this would of course indicate a departure from the framework identified above, but evidence for this is at present slight.

100 'Washington File: 15-09-01 Bush says US will do "whatever it takes" to defeat terrorists', pp. 2–3. Available at: <http://www.usembassy.org.uk/bush77.html>, accessed on 19 September 2001.

101 'Washington File: 17-09-01 Bush says US proud to lead fight against terrorism', pp. 1–2. Available at: <http://www.usembassy.org.uk/bush79.html>, accessed on 19 September 2001.

102 See for example comments by Senators Dayton and Sessions in Franks' Witness Statement, pp. 18 and 22.

103 January 4 Briefing, p. 2; Connetta, *Strange Victory*, p. 5. Connetta also claims (p. 5) 'at least' a dozen more accidental US deaths.

104 During the major combat involved in Operation Anaconda, for example, the number of US service personnel killed in action increased to nine, US CENTCOM Press Briefing, 4 March 2002, p. 1. For a detailed and up-to-date breakdown of casualties see the CDI database, 'US and allied casualties'.

105 For example, Connetta, *Strange Victory*, p. 18; Freedman, 'The Americans have left it too late'.

106 Although some have argued that in the final days of the campaign, NATO aircraft did support directly KLA operations. See for example Daniel A. Byman and Matthew C. Waxman, 'Kosovo and the Great Air Power Debate', *International Security*, 24, 4 (2000), pp. 28–9.

107 For example, Franks' Witness Statement, pp. 11 and 25. This stands in sharp contrast to a generation earlier when Franks' predecessor, General Norman Schwarzkopf, had been sceptical over the value of special forces in the Gulf War. See General Sir Peter de la Billiere, *Storm Command* (London: HarperCollins, 1993), pp. 191–2.

108 Franks' Witness Statement, pp. 3 and 7.

References

Billiere, Peter de la, *Storm Command*, London: HarperCollins, 1993.

Bond, Brian, *War and Society in Europe, 1870–1970*, London: Fontana, 1984.

Byman, Daniel A. and Matthew C. Waxman, 'Kosovo and the Great Air Power Debate', *International Security*, 24, 4 (2000), pp. 5–38.

Burk, James, 'Public Support for Peacekeeping in Lebanon and Somalia: Assessing the Casualties Hypothesis', *Political Science Quarterly*, 114, 1 (1999), pp. 53–78.

Chickering, Roger, 'Total War: The Use and Abuse of a Concept', in Manfred W. Boemke, Roger Chickering and Stig Forster (eds), *Anticipating Total War: The German and American Experiences, 1871–1914*, New York: Cambridge University Press, 1999, pp. 13–28.

Coker, Christopher, *Humane Warfare: The New Ethics of Postmodern War*, London: Routledge, 2001.

Cordesman, Anthony H. and Abraham R. Wagner, *The Lessons of Modern War*, Vol. 4: *The Gulf War*, Boulder, CO: Westview Press, 1996.

Cox, Michael, 'American Power Before and After 11 September: Dizzy with Success?', *International Affairs*, 78, 2 (2002), pp. 261–76.

Creveld, Martin van, *The Transformation of War*, New York: The Free Press, 1991.

Dauber, Cori, 'Implications of the Weinberger Doctrine for American Military Intervention in a Post-Desert Storm Age', *Contemporary Security Policy*, 22, 3 (2001), pp. 66–90.

Davis, Anthony, 'How the Afghan War was Won', *Jane's Intelligence Review*, February (2002).

—— 'US bombing boosts United Front's ground offensive', *Jane's Defence Weekly*, 14 November (2001).

—— 'UF Prepares Northern Offensive', *Jane's Defence Weekly*, 17 October 2001.

Dower, John, *War Without Mercy*, London: Faber, 1986.

Farrell, Theo, 'America's Misguided Mission', *International Affairs*, 76, 3 (2000), pp. 583–92.

—— and Helene Lambert, 'Courting Controversy: International Law, National Norms and American Nuclear Use', *Review of International Studies*, 27, 1 (2000), pp. 309–26.

Freedman, Lawrence, 'The Americans have left it too late to send in ground troops before winter', *The Independent*, 6 November 2001.

—— 'The Third World War?', *Survival*, 43, 4 (2001), pp. 61–88.

—— *The Revolution in Strategic Affairs*, Adelphi Paper 318, Oxford: Oxford University Press, 1998.

Heisbourg, Francois, 'The Day After: Europe and the Transformation of World Order', *Survival*, 43, 4 (2001), pp. 143–8.

Hoffman, Stanley, 'On the War', *The New York Review of Books*, 1 November 2001.

Hynes, Samuel, *The Soldier's Tale: Bearing Witness to Modern War*, London: Pimlico, 1998.

Ignatieff, Michael. 2000. *Virtual War: Kosovo and Beyond*, London: Chatto and Windus.

Ikenberry, John G., 'American Grand Strategy in the Age of Terror', *Survival*, 43, 4 (2001), pp. 19–34.

Judah, Tim, 'The Taliban Papers', *Survival*, 44, 1 (2002), pp. 69–80.

Kaldor, Mary, *New and Old Wars: Organized Violence in a Global Era*, Cambridge: Polity Press, 1999.

Kayser, Carl, 'Is War Obsolete?', *International Security*, 14, 4 (1990), pp. 42–64.

Koch, Andrew, 'USA's strategy takes shape', *Jane's Defence Weekly*, 17 October 2001.

Luttwak, Edward, 'A Post-Heroic Military Policy', *Foreign Affairs*, 75, 4 (1996), pp. 33–44.

—— 'Towards Post-Heroic Warfare', *Foreign Affairs*, 74, 3 (1995), pp. 109–22.

Mandelbaum, Michael, 'Is Major War Obsolete?', *Survival*, 40, 4 (1999), pp. 20–38.

McInnes, Colin, 'A Different Kind of War: September 11 and the United States' Afghan War', *Review of International Studies*, 29, 2 (2003), pp. 165–84.

—— *Spectator-Sport War: The West and Contemporary Conflict*, Boulder, CO: Lynne Rienner, 2002.

—— 'Spectator Sport Warfare', *Contemporary Security Policy*, 20, 3 (2000), pp. 142–65.

Mueller, John, *Retreat from Doomsday: The Obsolescence of Major War*, New York: Basic Books, 1989.

Pick, Daniel, *War Machine: The Rationalization of Slaughter in the Modern Age*, New Haven, CT: Yale University Press, 1993.

Roberts, Adam, 'Counter-Terrorism, Armed Force and the Laws of War', *Survival*, 44, 1 (2002), pp. 7–32.

Schelling, Thomas, *Arms and Influence*, New Haven, CT: Yale University Press, 1966.

Shaw, Martin, *Post-Military Society*, London: Polity Press, 1991.

Simon, Steven and Daniel Benjamin, 'The Terror', *Survival*, 43, 4 (2001), pp. 5–18.

Sirak, Michael, 'USA weighs outlays for asymmetric threats', *Jane's Defence Weekly*, 3 October 2001.

Smith, Steve, 'The United States will emerge from this as a more dominant world power', *The Times*, 19 September 2001.

Tirpak, John A., 'Short's View of the Air Campaign', *Air Force Magazine*, 82, 9 (1999), pp. 43–9.

US Department of Defense, *Report to Congress: Kosovo/Operation Allied Force After-Action Report*, Washington, DC: Department of Defense, 2000.

6

NEW WARS, OLD WARFARE?

Comparing US tactics in Vietnam
and Afghanistan

Kersti Larsdotter

The interaction between the air power and the special forces of the United States during Operation Enduring Freedom in Afghanistan has been heralded as an excellent example of an alleged change in war and warfare.[1] Some have been more cautious, stressing the continuities between the Afghanistan war and Western conduct of war during the 1990s.[2] Lawrence Freedman further criticises the hype of 'new war' based on the Afghanistan case and claims that 'the swift success' was the result of the war being 'fought as much in a tried and tested Afghan way of warfare as in a new Western way'.[3] Nevertheless, a pre-condition for the 'new' type of warfare, it is argued, is the technological developments over the last decades. The notion of a revolution in military affairs (RMA) has since the early 1990s seized the imagination of the American strategic community in particular. The RMA, it is claimed, is the result of the interaction between technological change, systems development, operational innovation, and organisational adaptation. These developments combine to fundamentally change the character and the execution of war.[4]

Among others, Grant T. Hammond argues that due to globalisation and the emergence of new weapon systems, the very essence of war is changing in a revolutionary way.[5] The technological transformation in areas such as sensors, communication and computers, space assets, missiles and precision-guided munitions (PGMs) is changing war and warfare. Both the arena where war is conducted – space and cyberspace – and the way it is conducted – its speed and weaponry – are being transformed. 'We are in the process of transforming space, time, energy, matter and information of war and warfare', Hammond argues; 'In short, what we might call the "physics of war" is changing'.[6] At the same time as the technological development, such as satellites and Unmanned Aerial Vehicles (UAVs) as well as other reconnaissance and surveillance sensors, have made it increasingly difficult to stay hidden, the spatial domain itself has been reduced through the increase in weapon range. This means that the enemy can be attacked from greater and greater distances. Due to the technological development, moreover, the concept of time has also been transformed in so far as there is less time between when a target is discovered and when one can strike. Data has become increasingly important. In intelligence, the actual processing of information has become more important than the collection of data, just as data in itself has become a more important target for attack, for example by overloading enemy sensor technology. It is also even more important nowadays to take into account a global opposition, since the information revolution has made it possible for nearly everyone to acquire information about what is happening at any given time or place.

Is this emphasis on technology valid in accounts of modern war? Have technological developments in munitions and communications altered the conduct of war in a dramatic way? Are the 'new' wars fought with methods of old warfare or has the conduct of wars changed? The aim of this chapter is to evaluate the impact of technology on recent warfare by comparing some features of US tactics in the wars in Afghanistan 2001–02 and Vietnam 1961–75, in particular with regard to the interaction between air power and special forces (SF).[7] What makes the most tangible level of war – the tactical level – interesting is that it is sometimes put forward as an indicator of change in warfare; it could also be argued that it is only when technological developments influence the tactical level that they have had an impact on warfare.[8] Moreover, as mentioned above, it has been the combined tactics of air power and special forces in Afghanistan that has attracted the most interest, since it has been considered a novelty and evidence of a fundamental change in warfare.

Since I am chiefly interested in whether technological development has led to a change in the conduct of war during the last decades, I have tried to eliminate the effect of other factors as far as possible. I have chosen to compare the American tactics used in the Vietnam War with the tactics used in Afghanistan during Operation Enduring Freedom, three decades later, because the campaigns in Vietnam and Afghanistan and their political military settings are to a great extent similar, while there has been a dramatic development in the area of technology. This argument will be further developed below. For now it will suffice to note that both of these conflicts have had a dramatic impact on American foreign policy and military strategy. In spite of achieving a kill ratio of between six and ten enemy soldiers for every American, releasing more bombs over Vietnam than during the entire Second World War, and using more than one hundred times as many helicopters as the French used in all of Indochina,[9] the US military was suddenly faced with failing support at home. The Vietnam War led to a major re-evaluation of the American military aims and organisation, and led *inter alia* to the evolution of new, radically different American doctrines.[10] Today, after the terrorist attacks of September 11 2001 on the United States, the

136

country faces a similar situation. George W. Bush has stated repeatedly that the United States is faced with a new type of war and once again there is feverish work under way to change the American military.

The objection that these conflicts are too close to one another in time for technological developments to be identifiable is unconvincing because many advocates of RMA argue that the Gulf War in 1991 signalled the beginning of the changes in the conduct of war.[11] The Vietnam War occurred well before this time period. Moreover, although some of the technologies, for example sensor technology, were used as early as in Vietnam (not least along the Ho Chi Minh Trail), it can be argued that this technology was somewhat experimental 30 years ago while it is well-established and regularly used today.

The next section will highlight some of the variables that influence the choice of tactics in war. Thereafter, the United States' tactics in both conflicts will be compared, followed by an assessment of the impact of technology on US tactics. In the final section, the results are considered in relation to the initial discussion of RMA.

The roots of tactics in war

There are many factors other than capability that influence the choice of tactics in a conflict. Many of these factors were similar in both Afghanistan and Vietnam, and should thus have had similar effects on the American choice of tactics. This section will elaborate on some of these factors. The impact of the one variable that differs significantly, technology, will be assessed later.

The character of the wars

The character of the conflicts had striking similarities. Both were mainly internal and the United States became involved only gradually. During Ho Chi Minh's and the Viet Minh's war against French colonial rule during the 1940s and 1950s, the United States supported France financially, paying 80 per cent of the French war expenses, and in 1954 it helped Ngo Dinh Diem obtain political power in South Vietnam. However, the dictatorial rule of Diem soon led to uprisings.[12] To keep the political unrest from spreading across the border to North Vietnam, the United States sent military advisors to South Vietnam and as early as 1957, American Special Forces began to assist the South Vietnamese military with the development of a Vietnamese Special Forces unit. Until 1961, the United States and South Vietnam focused primarily on developing a strong regular military force in South Vietnam to control the violence in the area.[13]

In 1965 the United States decided to use ground forces in South Vietnam as a response to the increase of Vietcong operations during 1961–5 and in 1966 United States forces launched their first prolonged offensive, which lasted for two years. After 1968 the so-called 'Vietnamisation' of the war took place, as the United States began to transfer responsibilities to the South Vietnamese forces in preparation for withdrawal.[14] The Americans suffered huge losses: of the nearly three million American soldiers that were active in Vietnam, approximately 60,000 died and more than 300,000 were injured in battle. The North Vietnamese and Vietcong lost approximately 1.1 million and six million were injured. Eventually, negotiations resumed between North and South Vietnam resulted in the last United States troops withdrawing from Vietnam in 1973. During the so-called Ho Chi Minh campaign in March 1975, the North Vietnamese achieved dominance and on 30 April the South Vietnamese government collapsed.[15]

As in Vietnam, the United States had been involved in war-ridden Afghanistan for a long time before becoming directly involved in the war. During the Soviet occupation (1979–89), the United States supported the Taliban struggle for autonomy in Afghanistan with finances and weapons.[16] After years of internal conflict that followed the Soviet withdrawal in the late 1980s, the Taliban eventually obtained political power in Afghanistan. This led to peace in most of the country. However, it also paved the way for various Islamic terrorist organisations, which established training camps in the country.[17] It was not until the attacks on the World Trade Center and the Pentagon on September 11 2001 that the US launched a military attack. The campaign started on 7 October 2001 and its objective, according to the United States, was to bring bin Laden and his al-Qaeda network to justice, to destroy al-Qaeda's infrastructure in Afghanistan, and to put an end to the harbouring of terrorists in Afghanistan – even if that meant the end of the incumbent regime.[18]

The US began its military involvement in Afghanistan with a massive bombing campaign, while small Special Operation Force ground teams were used as reconnaissance teams and as liaison for local opposition military forces. Later, US regular forces were deployed.[19] Al-Qaeda and the Taliban have been pushed to the sidelines of Afghan political life, but they are neither gone nor forgotten. There is an international peacekeeping force in the country, concentrated in the capital Kabul, but local warlords control most of the country's security resources.[20] Every day minor incidents occur and it seems that Taliban and al-Qaeda supporters are regrouping in the area.

The enemy's organisation and tactics

One of the most obvious factors influencing the choice of tactics is the opponent's organisation and tactics, as well as allied actors' organisation and tactics. The nature of the actors was similar in both conflicts. The Vietnam War was fought between the South Vietnamese government, the United States and other Coalition forces on the one side and the South Vietnamese guerrilla organisation, the Vietcong, together with North Vietnamese forces on the other. In Afghanistan, one party in the conflict consisted primarily of the United States, the local Afghan opposition (the so-called Northern Alliance) and other Coalition forces from, for example, Britain. The other party consisted mainly of the Afghan Taliban, supported by certain political factions in Afghanistan and surrounding countries, and the global terrorist network al-Qaeda. Hence, the American forces in both conflicts were supported by local forces and opposed by both regular and irregular enemy forces.

In Vietnam, the armed forces opposing the South Vietnamese government consisted primarily of three major groups: local and provincial Vietcong guerrillas; main-force Vietcong units; and regular North Vietnamese Army forces. The local Vietcong guerrillas usually operated as part-time soldiers, who blended in with the civilian population by day and became effective fighters by night. They operated in small units. The provincial Vietcong consisted of forces recruited from local villages and normally operated in their surrounding area. Main-force Vietcong units were better equipped and trained than the local and provisional Vietcong units and were fully capable of relatively large-scale and violent operations. Yet they could also break down into squads and platoons and operate in the same fashion as the local Vietcong. The North Vietnamese Army units were better equipped than the Vietcong units and possessed greater combat power. For example, in the latter phases of the war they used more conventional tactics and employed heavy artillery and tanks. They focused on mobility and kept the initiative in combat; if they ended up in a situation that was disadvantageous, they pulled back and spread out into smaller units. They often lay in ambush, trying to inflict casualties during the first few minutes of combat and then disappeared. They also used sniper fire, booby traps, mines, and mortars, and were exceptionally good at camouflage, deception and fighting under the cover of darkness. If their mobility was restricted they instantly developed elaborate networks of trenches, bunkers and tunnels that functioned as protection against American firepower.[21]

In Afghanistan, as in Vietnam, the United States fought against an opponent who was not a homogenous military organisation, but consisted principally of three major components: the indigenous Afghan Taliban, the predominantly foreign al-Qaeda; and other, non-al-Qaeda foreign allies of the Taliban. However, these three components differed in many important aspects, in the same way as did the Vietcong *cum suis* in Vietnam. Al-Qaeda fighters were much better trained and motivated than the Afghan Taliban. The Afghan Taliban, by contrast, often resembled a civilian militia rather than a professional army. Osama bin Laden's training camps throughout Afghanistan and neighbouring countries served primarily to prepare these troops for combat on Afghanistan's frontlines, and they were trained in several orthodox Western techniques as well as guerrilla techniques.[22] The Afghan Taliban, as well as al-Qaeda, were basically a light infantry force and did not have the heavy equipment necessary to defend cities and provide air defence; their major strength, manoeuvrability, was stifled in urban warfare.[23] The United States estimated that the Afghan Taliban and al-Qaeda units numbered somewhere around 50,000 troops, most of them equipped with AK assault rifles or mortars and rocket-propelled grenades. Before the US bombings started they also had about 650 tanks and armoured vehicles, some Soviet jet fighters and a few dozen transport planes.[24]

The Taliban forces began with positional, frontal warfare in which they tried to hold cities and defend fixed fronts and lines of supply. After the United States' intense bombing campaign at the beginning of the war, the enemy shifted tactics to traditional guerrilla warfare.[25] For example, they used hit-and-run attacks against American and Afghan soldiers. Their inferiority in troops and firepower led them to shoot the first rounds and then disappear. In this way, they used the same tactic as the Vietcong did three decades earlier.[26] Al-Qaeda and the Taliban quickly learned the tactics used by the United States, using for example communication security, dispersal, camouflage, use of cover and concealment, and exploitation of dummy fighting positions to draw fire and attention away from their real dispositions.[27]

Terrain and previous conflicts

There were also great similarities in terrain. Although the actual types of terrain differed considerably – low mountains, rainforest and swamps in Vietnam, arid high desert and high mountains in Afghanistan – it had a lot in common in offering a variety of alternative hiding places, and in both countries the terrain was quite inaccessible. The battle theatre of South Vietnam ranged from mountains to jungles to swamps and paddy fields. The mountainous area, which constituted two-thirds of South Vietnam, was rugged and covered with dense jungle.[28] The terrain in Afghanistan, by contrast, was dominated by high, snow-covered mountains (up to 3,500 metres) with deep, narrow, wooded, natural rock caves.[29]

In both cases, the irregular fighting forces of the US opponents had developed an extensive network of tunnels, caves, and in Vietnam also covered trails, to provide shelter and safe logistics for both soldiers and supplies. Some of these tunnels and trails were developed during earlier wars. The most important logistical lifeline between North Vietnam and the war in South Vietnam was the Ho Chi Minh Trail, which went through Laos. This was a network of 12,000 miles of well-camouflaged trails, footpaths and roads. The Viet Minh guerrillas deployed this network during their struggle against French colonial rule, 1946–54.[30] Underneath villages they constructed networks of tunnels from where they could conduct offensive operations, even if the village as such was overrun by the enemy.

In Afghanistan, the opportunities to develop and cover the same kind of trails did not exist, but the terrain still offered many natural hideouts and extended areas that were difficult to monitor. The Afghan Taliban made use of this and developed an extensive network of tunnels and entrenched caves during the Soviet war, two decades earlier. They used this for shelter and to hide ammunitions and other supplies. Since they had partly developed the network themselves, in the same way as the Vietcong had in South Vietnam, they were very experienced in the terrain, which they used to their advantage as often as possible in combating the US forces.[31]

Internal conflicts and support

At least at the strategic level, the United States ended up taking advantage of the demographic situation in both conflicts. In Vietnam there were many different minority groups. These lived separately from the rest of the population and had a strong desire for independence. In the 1950s, some of these minorities were involved in a conflict with the incumbent government, and during the Vietnam War, South and North Vietnam engaged in an intensive struggle to gain their support. North Vietnam covered the area with propaganda, which in turn led to extensive Psychological Operations (PSYOPS) and Civil Affairs actions (CA) by the South Vietnamese government and the United States, in order to regain the loyalty of the minorities.[32] A similar situation existed in Afghanistan, where the population was divided into several different ethnic groups, which were involved in protracted conflict with each other. Some of the groups supported the coalition while in other areas the Taliban received strong support.[33] When the Taliban spread propaganda on a large scale, especially during the first weeks of the conflict, aimed at getting the population of Afghanistan to turn against the American forces, the United States and the coalition tried to influence the various ethnic groups by way of PSYOPS and CA.[34]

Even outside each respective country there was a similar situation, where neighbouring countries lent support to one or the other parties. In Vietnam, the forces opposing the US received support from, among others, China, the Soviet Union, Cambodia's President Sihanouk, and Prince Souphanouvong in Laos, who with the assistance of Viet Minh had taken control of parts of Laos. In Afghanistan, sections of the Taliban forces had been built up and equipped by the Pakistani Intelligence Service (ISI).[35] Neighbouring states were also used by the Taliban and al-Qaeda fighters as a safe haven for recuperation and reorganisation.[36]

Comparing US tactics in Afghanistan and Vietnam

A very common American tactic in both the Vietnam War and in Operation Enduring Freedom was 'search and destroy' or 'find, fix, fight, finish'. This tactic is based on first searching for enemy groups in different ways, for example from the air, with ground troops or with different types of ground sensors. Once an enemy group has been located, forces are deployed to fix the enemy to prevent them from disappearing from the area. Finally, the area is subjected to massive fire, for example from air power and artillery. In short, the tactic is based on finding the enemy, fixing him with firearms or with mobile supporting troops, surrounding him with larger units, and destroying him through overwhelming artillery and air support.[37]

Since it is not the aim of this chapter to describe American tactics in general, I have chosen to focus on a few aspects of these tactics. I will discuss in more detail the use of SF as reconnaissance teams, mobility, the use of regular forces, Close Air Support (CAS), and Forward Air Controllers (FACs). In addition, I will briefly describe some of the developmental trends that are discernible in relation to technology, since in the debate on RMA, technology is often considered to embody the actual revolution in RMA.

Finding the enemy: SF as reconnaissance teams

To deter North Vietnam from continued aggression in the Vietnam War, the United States launched massive bombing campaigns on North Vietnam, using the most advanced technology available at the time.[38] One of the main objectives of the bombing campaigns was to reduce the enemy's mobility, and during 1965 air interdiction operations began against the Ho Chi Minh Trail in Laos. Due to the difficult terrain, poor weather and the enemy's excellent camouflage and deception techniques, relevant targets were extremely difficult to discover from the air. The American pilots realised that while speed was of utmost importance in dogfights (or to avoid enemy surface-to-air missiles, SAMs), it posed a problem in air-to-ground attacks since the speed allowed for only a split-second to decide about the target and whether to drop their load.[39]

Due to these problems, the Americans modified their tactics. In addition to continued strategic bombings, they used a combination of SF, attack planes and a network of ground sensors to locate their enemy. Since the major problem in Vietnam was to find the enemy, the American forces made use of pattern activity analysis, exotic technological devices like 'people sniffers', ground radar, side-looking airborne radar, active and passive night-vision devices, a variety of sensors, and imagery interpretation from photographic, infrared and electronic equipment. The difficult terrain and technological problems with the surveillance equipment led to the primary technique for finding the enemy becoming small ground-based SF reconnaissance teams. Such teams often had to search extensive areas in difficult terrain to find their well-hidden targets. These were very dangerous operations, since the enemy knew the terrain well, were skilled at hiding and used different types of mines, booby traps and ambush techniques. The SF teams used different types of semi-guerrilla tactics, such as a variety of ambush techniques, to locate the enemy. Both American and South Vietnamese SFs were used in long-range reconnaissance missions in South and North Vietnam, where they mainly located the enemy and gathered intelligence, but were also used to coordinate air attacks and conduct Battle Damage Assessment (BDA).[40]

As in Vietnam, the Americans began their operations in Afghanistan with a bombing campaign. Only a month after the attacks on the World Trade Center on September 11 2001, American forces were deployed in Afghanistan. The first military component was air power, including support from the US Marines and the US Navy. American air and missile attacks (of which several were aircraft carrier-based) were made on Taliban and al-Qaeda forces and bases. The ultimate aim of the bombing campaign was to destroy al-Qaeda's infrastructure and interrupt the support from their 'host nation'.[41] The American forces used a combination of air strikes from land-based B-1, B-2 and B-52 bombers, carrier-based F-14 and F/A-18 fighters as well as Tomahawk cruise missiles launched from ships and submarines.[42] However, the desired results of the bombings were not achieved here either. Air power alone could not locate and precision-bomb targets on the ground, and in spite of the rapid technological development of PGMs, ground forces were required to locate the enemy. The Taliban and al-Qaeda forces were very skilled at camouflage, deception and decoy techniques. When not in battle they also spread out across large areas, and on many occasions chose to fight in towns and populated areas, which made it even more difficult for American air power to strike without hitting the civilian population during attacks.[43]

Just as in Vietnam, the United States soon decided to involve a larger proportion of SF ground teams, which were supported by SF air support and domestic forces (mainly from the Northern Alliance). The SF teams were used mainly as intelligence teams and operated in small groups of three to four soldiers. They also conducted strikes and raids independently and jointly,[44] and they worked closely with Afghan SF teams, as advisers and coordinators of air strikes.[45]

Mobility: airborne troops

Once the enemy had been located, the most important factor became the close cooperation between ground and air forces. During the 1950s and 1960s, the US Army had further developed its own air fleet, and during the Vietnam War it was used on a large scale for the first time. Detailed operations and missions of the planes came under the exclusive control of the ground force commander, which generated very close cooperation between ground and air forces.[46] The helicopter, too, came to form a very important part of US forces and changed their tactics fundamentally. Its mobility and large carrying capacity made it an essential asset, and it proved to be a superior way of transporting matériel and soldiers. The helicopters enabled the Americans to transport entire units, and facilitated rapid manoeuvring together with rapid reinforcement, replacement or withdrawal of troops during battle. Once an

SF ground team or a small, light infantry force had located enemy forces, reinforcements were normally requested from nearby mobile units. These units were deployed around the enemy positions to fix him. Then, by flying in helicopter-based forces, units could quickly take up peripheral blocking or ambush positions in order to destroy escaping enemy forces.[47] One of the new methods was thus to use battalion-sized helicopter-based infantry forces in actual battle.[48] Helicopters were also used to transport other types of forces, such as SF.[49]

Since neither the North Vietnamese forces nor the Vietcong had proper air defences at the beginning of the war, they mainly attacked the helicopters at their landing zones. This made the Americans very vulnerable at landing. Therefore, they soon started to fly with two to four reconnaissance helicopters a few minutes ahead of each convoy of transport helicopters. In addition, attack helicopters began accompanying the transport helicopters. Standard convoys were soon developed, normally consisting of an armed Huey as command and control ship, seven unarmed transport helicopters for combat units, five armed helicopters for fire support and escort, and finally one helicopter for medical evacuation. To protect themselves further, they tried to make the actual disembarking of the soldiers as rapid as possible, to avoid attack. For a normal 12-ship formation, it took approximately two minutes for everyone to unload.[50]

In more recent American military operations, the use of helicopters for transport is something that is taken for granted, and many American forces, both SF and regular forces, are nowadays airborne or at least airmobile. This has clearly changed since the Vietnam War. In Afghanistan transport helicopters were used daily to move matériel and soldiers back and forth across the country, and SF teams were often deployed by parachute.[51] For example, Chinook helicopters were used to deploy SF reconnaissance teams to observation posts. Just as in Vietnam, they used reconnaissance helicopters that were deployed in advance, often Black Hawks, and Apache attack helicopters.[52] Most of the American and Allied forces were brought in with helicopters, partly due to the inhospitable terrain with high mountaintops. As in Vietnam, American and Afghan regular forces were flown in by helicopter and deployed as blocking forces around the enemy. However, one difference from the Vietnam War was that the helicopters were sometimes sent off without knowing their exact target areas. By being given detailed orders while on their way, it was possible to reduce the time between discovery and attack of enemy forces.

Blocking positions: regular forces

Another important component of the American tactics was the use of domestic regular forces. The increasing weight attached to public opinion at home during the Vietnam war, made it more and more important for the

American military to protect its own soldiers from attacks and to minimise casualties. This, in combination with other factors, led to the decision to increasingly rely on local South Vietnamese forces as the war progressed. At the start of the US engagement in Vietnam, as early as 1960, American SFs were sent to develop parts of the South Vietnamese Army. So-called Civilian Irregular Defence Groups were created, whereby different minority groups were trained to protect their own villages and to assist the South Vietnamese Army in various duties.[53] As the war evolved, it became evident to US policy-makers that this strategy was insufficient to effectively curb its opponents. In response, the United States began to deploy American regular forces in 1965. From that moment onwards, regular forces dominated the conduct of the war, even on the part of the North Vietnamese and Vietcong. For example, the US Marine Corps went to South Vietnam in March 1965 and the 173rd Airborne Brigade in May the same year. These regular forces were used, *inter alia*, to surround enemy positions and to push the enemy forces towards the blocking positions, the so-called 'hammer and anvil' tactics. The gradual escalation of US troops in Vietnam, however, ended in 1968, when US policy-makers, under domestic pressure to minimise casualties yet again, began to rely on South Vietnamese regular ground forces in their operations. This meant the start of the so-called 'Vietnamization' of the war.[55] Henceforth, with the exception of a relatively brief period in the middle of the war, the US strategy relied heavily upon domestic regular forces – rather than American – in the conduct of operations.

As in Vietnam, the Americans used domestic regular forces led by small SF teams during operations in Afghanistan.[55] However, the use of the domestic forces created a number of problems, and many enemy troops managed to escape during large operations.[56] Therefore, the United States soon deployed its own regular forces, such as the US Marines and Task Force 58, Army 101st Airborne Division (Task Force Rakkasan) and the 10th Mountain Division, to prevent the Taliban and al-Qaeda from moving freely in the country. The regular forces were used, for instance, in search-and-destroy operations, where they explored and destroyed large cave complexes and, if the enemy had dispersed into smaller groups, they were mostly used to find, fix and some-times finish the enemy.[57] For example, during Operation Anaconda in March 2001, regular forces were used as blocking forces and to drive the enemy ahead towards the blocking positions, while in August 2002, during Operation Mountain Sweep, soldiers from the Army's 82nd Airborne Division stormed Zormat and Shah-i-Kot in an attempt to remove the enemy from the Pakistani border.[58]

Overwhelming firepower: Close Air Support

During the Vietnam War, American air power came to be used as Close Air Support (CAS) in a way that had previously not been seen. Once the enemy had been encircled, they were attacked with massive firepower and destroyed. This was mainly carried out by requesting air support and rocket artillery. The ground forces became primarily finding and fixing forces, while artillery and air forces were used for fighting and finishing. When conducted in this way, it was thought, American casualties could be avoided.[59]

Consequently, in addition to supplying fire bases with artillery, armed helicopters and aerial rocket artillery provided important support for the ground forces. Helicopters with machineguns, rockets, and grenade launchers provided light-fire support, which was very effective against enemy forces operating out in the open. Aerial rocket-launcher units provided heavy-fire support, often in areas outside the requesting unit's direct artillery range. They could respond quickly to calls over great distances. When B-52 strategic bombers began to be used against tactical targets to 'prepare' them for ground attacks, the whole spectrum of air power was put at the disposal of the ground commander. The new 'smart bombs' made it even easier and with their help, one plane could carry out a mission, which in previous wars would have required many sorties.[60]

As the North Vietnamese and Vietcong forces lacked an effective air defence system at the beginning of the war, the US had the luxury of deploying planes without countermeasures for SAMs. However, at the end of the 1960s, the North Vietnamese and Vietcong began to acquire sufficient resources to combat air targets, so the United States introduced a number of new planes that could carry more weapons over longer distances. However, these planes had to drop their load from a higher altitude and at a higher speed, which reduced their accuracy. For CAS, the US developed the original solution of 'gunships'; for example, the more robust AC-147s and AC-130s were equipped with machineguns, thus enabling them to circle over a battle-field and provide support for ground forces with short notice. Eventually, helicopters too were equipped with robots and machineguns that the pilot could control.

In Afghanistan, the United States also used the combination of SFs, domestic and American regular forces, and CAS from all branches of the US armed forces. Once Taliban or al-Qaeda forces had been fixed, SF teams called for air strikes in the area. The air attacks were conducted by, for example, Marine Corps Cobra attack helicopters, Apache attack helicopters and A-10 attack planes, as well as B-52 and AC-130 Hercules bombers.[61] PGMs were used extensively, and their accuracy helped the ground offensive both by way of the strikes themselves and through the fact that their precision reduced the morale of the enemy.[62] CAS was also used for defensive purposes when, for example, reconnaissance SF teams were surprised by enemy fire. Normally the SF teams directly contacted F-15 or F-16 fighters that were in the area. These used machine guns and 500 lb bombs, which could be dropped as near as 50 metres from the position of the SF teams. Resources from other branches of the military, such as the Navy's F-14 fighter and AC-130 Hercules could also be called in. The Hercules normally circled high above the area and due to its long range, it could respond to calls from a wide area.

Coordination of air power: Forward Air Controllers

In Vietnam, the consequences of the close cooperation between ground and air forces in CAS operations quickly led to the discovery that liaison officers were required to facilitate coordination between air and ground components of an operation. Usually, these Forward Air Controllers (FACs) were stationed either on the ground or circled in the air, and they kept track of the positions of their own and the enemy's forces in order to direct helicopter and air attacks in detail.[63] Normally, FACs directed air strikes, assisted in exfiltrating teams that required it and provided radio relay. This tactic, which was developed jointly by the US Air Force and SF, resulted in one of the most important and productive applications of air power in Vietnam.[64] The developments in communication, together with the mobility of the helicopters, meant that large unit commanders could control their subordinates in a way that was previously unimaginable.[65]

In Vietnam, FACs served as the eyes of the ground commander while advising the ground commander in various situations. Ground commanders' requests for CAS went via the FACs before continuing up the communication chain to air force units available in the area. Then the air force units contacted the area FAC, who directed them to the target either by using radio to point out clearly visible ground marks or by using marking rockets, which emitted white smoke that could easily be seen by the plane circling above the battlefield. By continually orbiting above an area, FACs could request air power as soon as someone needed help. After a strike, the FACs also conducted BDA.[66] FACs coordinated the efforts of the ground commander, the attacking air forces, and command and control units by way of three different radios (FM for the ground troops, UHF for the air forces and VHF for command and control). At the same time, they had to maintain visual contact with their own ground and air forces, locate and mark ground targets, and avoid enemy ground fire.[67]

The role of FACs in Afghanistan was for the most part very similar to the role they had in the Vietnam War. Unlike in Vietnam, however, in Afghanistan they had access to new technology that facilitated the job considerably and they were stationed on the ground to a larger extent than in Vietnam. Air strikes were normally ordered by FACs, assisted by a variety of technically advanced equipment for pin-pointing targets. When using laser-guided bombs, a typical procedure was that FACs located enemy forces and, from quite a large distance, scanned in their positions using a laser range-finder, which gave them the exact coordinates of the target. Using encrypted radio transmissions, FACs sent the target information either to the theatre command centre, which relayed it to, for example, a high altitude bomber (such as a B-52) beyond enemy range (up to 38,000 feet) or directly to the bombers' crew, who fed them straight into the control systems of satellite-guided bombs. Some devices could transmit the coordinates direct to the bombardier while others went via the pilot or the commander; even photos or videos could be sent. After that, satellite-guided bombs were released with great precision.[68] From localisation of enemy forces to the bomb striking the target could, in the best cases, take only 19 minutes if the target was visible and the FAC close enough to give a positive identification. For fear of collateral damage, however, this time period could easily become considerably longer as pilots relied upon clearance from FACs and juridical personnel before releasing the bombs.[69]

The ground troops could also use lasers to point out a target, in order to set laser-guided bombs. The advantage of this technology was that it could follow a moving object, so the bombs received updated target data even after they had left their platform. The problem with these laser-guided bombs was that if something came between the target and the SF team after the bomb had been released, the laser lost contact with the target and the bomb received the wrong target information. A cloud of dust could be enough to break the laser.[70]

Assessing the impact of technology

As was mentioned earlier, air power as well as the close cooperation between ground and air forces played a very important part in the American tactics in both Vietnam and Afghanistan. The technological areas in which most changes have taken place are reconnaissance and surveillance, as well as in weaponry. This section will describe some of the developments in this area. Though helicopters played a significant role in both conflicts, the technology involved has not developed to any considerable extent.

In Vietnam, some of the reconnaissance and surveillance planes were equipped with visual and photographic reconnaissance equipment, and direct air-to-ground links made it possible for the ground forces to find out what the crews in the air were observing.[71] Some planes also had side-looking radar and infrared scanners, which allowed them to patrol at night.[72] One novelty that was used were the UAVs (then called Remotely-Piloted Vehicles, RPVs), which usually followed pre-programmed long-distance reconnaissance missions. They could gather photographic, infrared and electronic intelligence information, execute electronic countermeasures, and act as decoys. Their maximum altitude was 78,000 feet and the record for uninterrupted flight was 28 hours. They were approximately as big as modern-day Predator UAVs and were also used for leaflet dropping and surface-to-air missile (SAM) radar detection, location and identification. One model was even modified so that it could carry AGM-65 Maverick air-to-surface missiles.[73] However, perhaps the best reconnaissance came from light helicopter teams from the so-called 'air cavalry'. They were equipped with searchlight attachments (white and infrared) and image intensifiers. The light helicopter teams also used chemical 'people-sniffing' equipment, which could sense people through protective materials.[74]

US forces, while operating in Afghanistan, used a number of reconnaissance and surveillance techniques. One of the more mentioned and heralded features was the extensive use of UAVs, both the low-flying RQ-1 Predator with electro-optic/IR sensor equipment and Synthetic Aperture Radar (SAR) equipment, and the high-flying RQ-4 Global Hawk.[75] These were primarily used for reconnaissance, surveillance and communications. The Predator operated at 15,000 to 30,000 feet and could fly above a target for over 24 hours, record high-resolution images and send them to various command centres around the world in real time. They were also equipped with Hellfire missiles to attack targets.[76] They could mark targets with lasers for weapons from other platforms, or read off targets marked by other sources. The Global Hawk operated at approximately 60,000 feet and its sensors were similar to those on the U2 reconnaissance plane.[77] However, both the Global Hawk and the Predator had a tendency to crash in poor weather.[78] Hence, although UAVs were used in both conflicts, the number of sorties was significantly higher in the operations in Afghanistan and for the first time UAVs were used for strikes.

In Vietnam the US forces used several different helicopters and airplanes as fire support for ground forces, for example, different versions of UH-1 Huey and AC-1 Cobra helicopters as well as AC-130 Spectra gunships. The first genuine PGMs were used during the Vietnam War. Walleye, a television-guided glide bomb that was used extensively in Vietnam, was the first air-launched guided air-to-surface weapon to be used on a large scale in battle over a sustained period.[79] The GBU (Guided Bomb Unit) 8 and Homing Bomb System (HOBOS), a conventional Mk 84, 2,000 lb bomb, had a TV-like electro-optical guidance system in the nose as well as navigation fins to provide direction.[80]

In Afghanistan, the United States used B-52 and B-1 bombers, F-15 fighter planes and AC-130 Hercules (which saw action as early as in the Vietnam War, although in a less sophisticated version).[81] In the area of 'smart bombs', development has been rapid since the Vietnam War. Tomahawk cruise missiles were used, as were JDAMs, i.e. conventional bombs equipped with GPS satellite-guided system equipment and navigation fins, which meant that they could strike within yards of the target, as well as laser-guided bombs and Maverick missiles. Laser-guided bombs are normally released from 15,000 feet and JDAMs from 30,000 feet. JDAMs have the advantage of being cheaper than Tomahawk cruise missiles, can navigate better in poor weather, and can be carried on board B-2 and B-52 bombers. Moreover, Tomahawks have to be programmed before release, while air-launched ammunition can be controlled as required.[82] The US forces also used a new type of bomb, specifically designed for large cave complexes. This technique had been developed since 1996. Since it uses thermobaric rather than conventional explosives, it creates a pressure wave and an increase in temperature when it explodes, which is ideal for use in large cave complexes.[83]

Although US planes and helicopters in the Afghan war were still armed with 'dumb' weapons, the relative increase of the use of PGMs and their high technological standard when compared with those used during the Vietnam War clearly marks a significant development in the weapons area. Moreover, the targeting equipment that was used by FACs was far more advanced and far more accurate in Afghanistan than in Vietnam.

New wars, old warfare!

So, firepower became the predominant feature of American operations in the Vietnam War. Despite the mobility of the helicopter, manoeuvre was primarily used to find and fix the enemy. By concentrating on massive fire-power against the enemy, it was possible to minimise American losses but maximise the strength against the enemy. However, this tactic presupposed that the mobility of North Vietnamese forces and Vietcong was restricted, which, quite often, was not the case. They often managed to find escape routes and disappear before the US forces unleashed their firepower. As for operational mobility, the American forces were superior due to the transport helicopters, but as soon as they touched the ground they were slower than their enemies. So while American forces maximised their advantage with firepower, helicopters and mechanised forces, the enemy used surprise, mobility and short, intensive clashes to fight on their own terms. The development of communication, greater flexibility of command and control, the increased American mobility, and the nature of the enemy meant that tactical operations in South Vietnam bore little resemblance to previous operations. Parts of the war, however, showed typical signs of large-scale interstate conventional warfare, especially after 1970.[84]

Even though many analysts have argued that the United States' operations in the conflict in Afghanistan represent a completely new way of waging war, where the combination of small SF ground teams, the use of PGMs and domestic regular forces are the factors behind US success, the American forces still used a surprisingly orthodox air-to-ground theatre campaign, where heavy-fire support was a major factor of the force. The difference from the Vietnam War was that in Afghanistan the firepower came almost exclusively from platforms in the air and that the FACs played such an important role. The use of domestic regular forces and close cooperation between air and ground forces was clearly evident already in the Vietnam War.[85] As in Vietnam, the interaction between the air power and the ground forces was very important in the Afghan War. While air power was effective in manoeuvring ground forces and destroying the enemy's open resistance, it could not prevent the escape, reorganisation, or reinforcement of the enemy. Moreover, important enemy positions in cave complexes and urban areas could be searched thoroughly only by regular ground forces and SF ground teams.

SF reconnaissance teams were used in both conflicts in a similar fashion. Small teams were deployed, sometimes not larger than three or four people. They could be away for extended periods, and had to search through terrain and innumerable enemy caves and well-prepared paths and tracks. Here, the SF teams were very exposed, since the enemy had often prepared the paths and tracks with different types of mines and traps. The American decision to use SF so extensively in both conflicts was due, *inter alia*, to the difficult terrain, the opponents' well-developed paths and tracks, and previous experience of battle in the areas. In both cases SFs were also used as attack forces and for BDA.

The mobility provided by the helicopters was something that had not been experienced in the same way prior to Vietnam. Today it is a given. Even if airborne forces are currently used more extensively, the helicopters and the units were used in the same way in both conflicts. During the conflict in Vietnam a convoy system was developed that made it possible to transport large units in a very short time. The difference with the conflict in Afghanistan is that in Afghanistan the same mass transports were not used. However, it is more probable that this is caused by the difference between the total number of US troops in the conflicts, rather than by any significant change in tactics.

When it comes to the use of the regular forces, there are considerable similarities too. In Vietnam as in Afghanistan, the United States made use partly of local forces supported by American SFs and partly of American regular forces. The latter were used for blocking purposes in specific operations but also for search-and-destroy operations.

However, the greatest similarity between the two conflicts is probably the use of CAS. The US forces have used CAS to a large extent in both conflicts with great success, both in pre-planned situations as well as immediate support in situations where, for example, a US force had been ambushed. In both cases fighters, bombers and attack helicopters were frequently called upon. One of the greater differences is the extent to which PGMs were used. In Vietnam, the United States used television-guided Walleyes, GBU-8s and HOBOs, which were considered very accurate in their day. In Afghanistan, however, there were a number of PGMs with far greater accuracy. Nevertheless, PGMs were used in the same way in battle, even if safety distances allowed bombing even closer to one's own positions in Afghanistan. The increased use of PGMs also increased the need for FACs.

In its own way, the role of FACs has changed considerably, yet at the same time it has not changed at all since the Vietnam War. Both then and now, FACs were used in the air as well as on the ground. However, in Afghanistan it seems that an increasing number of FACs were on the ground, as opposed to Vietnam, when they were more often airborne. The largest difference seems to be the new technology. Instead of using three different radio frequencies and smoke bombs, FACs in Afghanistan used laser pointers and palmtops, on which correct coordinates were received via GPS. Sometimes FACs could also request CAS directly from the pilots instead of going via the command and control centre.

Conclusions

In this chapter, I have examined the impact of technology on recent warfare by comparing American tactics in the Vietnam War with those in the operation in Afghanistan. Have technological developments over the last few decades changed the conduct of warfare in – as the advocates of the RMA maintain – a revolutionary way? The aim has not been to provide a complete account of American tactics during these two conflicts. Instead, I have a focused on the much-heralded interaction of special forces and air power in Afghanistan. In particular this aspect has been presented as a new phenomenon and as evidence of the RMA. The study demonstrates, however, that the same tactics were used in the Vietnam War. Moreover, the search-and-destroy and the find, fix, fight, finish tactics have played an important role in both conflicts.

It is safe to say that American soldiers today have a number of new technological aids, when it comes to weaponry, reconnaissance, surveillance, and mobility, which appear to reduce the risk of friendly and civil casualties. This, however, does not mean that battle itself on the tactical level has changed to any large extent. The United States still uses a combination of large bombing campaigns, special forces, CAS, and air transportation of troops, as well as domestic and American regular forces. On a strategic level, they also use PSYOPS and CA in a similar way as during the Vietnam War.

In both wars, the United States used massive bombing campaigns to break the morale of the enemy forces, to reduce their mobility and to avoid large numbers of American casualties, but this was not successful in either of the cases. In both conflicts, the close cooperation between the air power and the ground forces, such as transport helicopters and CAS, was very important for the American success. Many of the tactics that are now taken for granted were developed in Vietnam, such as SFs as small, deep reconnaissance teams and FACs that search for and point out targets for air power circling high above the battlefield waiting for assignments. True, there has been considerable technological development. For instance, laser-guided bombs and JDAMs are now used with far greater accuracy than during the Vietnam War, but the tactics have not changed. Hence, the improved technology does not seem to have had any significant effects on US tactics.

As information superiority and initiative are considered important in contemporary warfare, it is natural to assume that current technology has reduced the time between the discovery of a target and its destruction. For instance, the links connecting FACs, laser range finders and UAVs with command centres, should facilitate this procedure. In some instances, in Afghanistan the time span was less than 20 minutes. However, in the Kosovo conflict three years earlier, the average time for clearance of stationary targets was 14 days(!).[86] Paradoxically, it seems that while technology has facilitated a faster decision-making process, it has also enabled more and more people to follow the war online (globalisation of information), which has resulted in the military becoming increasingly concerned about collateral damage, which in turn has increased the demands on identification and, consequently, extended the time for clearance, sometimes by several days. In conflicts where US forces face a highly mobile opponent, these factors can determine whether there is sufficient time to destroy a target or not.

Some RMA proponents argue that it takes time before change in military structures makes its presence felt. We will therefore not be able to see the consequences of the new systems for 10 or 20 years. Thus, a follow-up study may be required before one can falsify the notions of a revolution in military affairs.

For now, however, the question is rather whether it is other areas that are witnessing a revolution. Perhaps the enemy's tactics and technological level still largely determine the choice of tactics in battle. If so, it suggests that the RMA-inspired 'new war' only occurs if a highly developed state or organisation comes into conflict with another equally developed state or organisation. Is that where the true potential of technology could become apparent? Or, in the same way as air power introduced a new dimension to the battlefields of the past, are computers and the Internet – with their possible effects on civilian infrastructure – the new dimension where we will see an RMA? In that case, it would mean that the RMA of today is no longer about a revolution on the military battleground but a revolution that could possibly reduce the physical influence of war in the world.

Finally, this study casts doubt on the use of tactics as an indicator of forms of warfare. Despite the rapid development and implementation of new technology, the new wars are still fought with old methods of warfare.

Notes

1 Stephen Biddle, *Afghanistan and the Future of Warfare: Implications for Army and Defense Policy*, Carlisle, PA: Strategic Studies Institute, US Army War College, 2002, p. 1. See also Stephen Biddle, 'Afghanistan and the Future of Warfare', *Foreign Affairs*, 82, 2 (2003), pp. 31–46.

2 Colin McInnes, 'A Different Kind of War? September 11 and the United States' Afghan War', *Review of International Studies*, 29, 2 (2003), pp. 165–84. Reprinted in this volume.

3 Lawrence Freedman, 'A New Type of War', in Ken Booth and Tim Dunne (eds), *Worlds in Collision: Terror and the Future of World Order*, London: Palgrave, 2002,

p. 44. The quote reflects the notion that there is a link between a specific society and its way of conducting war. It is not my intention to pursue this idea further. It has been widely debated elsewhere whether the US has a specific way of conducting war. See for example Thomas G. Mahnken, 'The American Way of War in the Twenty-First Century', in Efraim Inbar (ed.), *Democracies and Small Wars*, London: Frank Cass, 2003, pp. 73–84 and Max Boot, *The Savage Wars of Peace: Small Wars and the Rise of American Power*, New York: Basic Books, 2002.

4 Douglas MacGregor, 'Future Battle: The Merging Levels of War', *Parameters*, 22, 4 (1992–3), p. 42 and Lawrence Freedman, *The Revolution in Strategic Affairs*, Adelphi Paper 318, New York: Oxford University Press, 1998, p. 11.

5 Grant T. Hammond, 'Globalization, Technology and the Transformation of the Security Environment: The Real Revolution in Military Affairs', paper presented at the meeting of the American Political Science Association in San Fransisco, August 2001.

6 Hammond, 'Globalization, Technology and the Transformation', p. 3.

7 I will use the acronym SF for Special Forces throughout the chapter for convenience rather than to shift between SF (as they were called during the Vietnam War) and SOF (Special Operations Forces, as they were called during the Afghan War). After all, despite organisational changes, they are the same units serving similar purposes.

8 Kaldor, for example, uses the methods of warfare, finances of war, and purposes of war to distinguish between 'new' and 'old' wars. Mary Kaldor, *New and Old Wars: Organised Violence in a Global Era*, Cambridge: Polity Press, 1999. For a criticism of using tactics as an indicator of types of war, see M. L. R. Smith, 'Strategy in the Age of "Low Intensity" Warfare: Why Clausewitz is Still More Relevant Than His Critics' (Chapter 2 in this volume). Moreover, the tactical level has hitherto been somewhat neglected in favour of the strategic level. For analyses of the Afghan war mostly focusing on the strategic level, see the contributions in Thomas R. Mockaitis and Paul B. Rich (eds), *Grand Strategy in the War Against Terrorism*, London: Frank Cass, 2003.

9 Paddy Griffith, *Forward into Battle: Fighting Tactics from Waterloo to Vietnam*, Chichester, UK: Anthony Bird, 1981, p. 110.

10 Robert A. Doughty, *The Evolution of US Army Tactical Doctrine, 1946–1976*, Fort Leavenworth, Kansas: Leavenworth Papers, Combat Studies Institute, US Command and General Staff College, 1979.

11 See for example Eliot Cohen, 'Technology and Warfare', in John Baylis *et al.* (eds), *Strategy in the Contemporary World: An Introduction to Strategic Studies*, Oxford: Oxford University Press, 2002, p. 243.

12 See for example Kevin Ruane, *The Vietnam Wars*, Manchester: Manchester University Press, 2000.

13 Department of the Army, *Vietnam Studies: US Army Special Forces, 1961–1971*, Washington DC: Department of the Army, CMH Publication, 1989, p. 5.

14 William Rosenau, *Special Operations Forces and Elusive Enemy Ground Targets: Lessons from Vietnam and the Persian Gulf War*, RAND Document No. MR-1408-AF, 2001, p. 6 and John J. Tolson, *Vietnam Studies: Airmobility, 1961–1971*, Washington DC: Department of the Army, 1973, p. 26.

15 Ruane, *The Vietnam Wars*, p. 127.

16 Kersti Håkansson, 'Taktik och stridsteknik i lågintensiva konflikter: En fallstudie av Operation Anaconda', in Arne Baudin *et al.* (eds), *En ny medeltid? En introduktion till militärteori i lågintensiva konflikter*, Stockholm: Försvarshögskolan, 2002, p. 71.

17 William J. Durch, *Afghanistan: Keeping the Peace Without Hardly Trying*, The Henry L. Stimson Center, 2002), p. 1 <www.stimson.org/fopo/pdf/Afghan_KeepingPeaceWithoutTryingrev112602.pdf> Last consulted 18 June 2003.
18 Center for Defense Information, *The US Military Campaign in Afghanistan: The Year in Review*, <http://www.cdi.org/terrorism/Afghanistan-one-year-later-pr.cfm> Last consulted on 17 February 2003.
19 Center for Defense Information, *The US Military Campaign in Afghanistan*.
20 Durch, *Afghanistan*, p. 1.
21 Doughty, *The Evolution of US Army Tactical Doctrine*.
22 Biddle, *Afghanistan and the Future of Warfare*, p. 14.
23 *Stratfor*, 14 November 2001.
24 *Associated Press*, 26 October 2001.
25 *Stratfor*, 14 November 2001.
26 *Christian Science Monitor*, 8 March 2002.
27 Biddle, *Afghanistan and the Future of Warfare*, p. 20.
28 Global Security, *Armor in Closed Terrain: US Army Experience in Vietnam*, <www.globalsecurity.org/military/library/report/1985/CTG.htm> Last consulted on 1 February 2003.
29 *Christian Science Monitor*, 8 March 2002.
30 Rosenau, *Special Operations Forces and Elusive Enemy Ground Targets*, p. 1.
31 Håkansson, 'Taktik och stridsteknik i lågintensiva konflikter', pp. 72–3.
32 Department of the Army, *Vietnam Studies: US Army Special Forces*, p. 20.
33 *Washington Post*, 11 March 2002.
34 Håkansson, 'Taktik och stridsteknik i lågintensiva konflikter', p. 86.
35 *Stratfor*, 26 December, 2002. Note, however, that only during parts of the US operation in Afghanistan did the ISI support the Taliban openly.
36 Rosenau, *Special Operations Forces and Elusive Enemy Ground Targets*, p. 5 and *Stratfor*, 14 November, 2001.
37 Doughty, *The Evolution of US Army Tactical Doctrine*, and Håkansson, 'Taktik och stridsteknik i lågintensiva konflikter'.
38 Jeffrey Jarkowsky, *'Boots on the Ground': Will US Landpower be Decisive in Future Conflicts?*, Carlisle, Penn.: US Army War College, 2002, p. 9.
39 Rosenau, *Special Operations Forces and Elusive Enemy Ground Targets*, p. 10.
40 Doughty, *The Evolution of US Army Tactical Doctrine* and Rosenau, *Special Operations Forces and Elusive Enemy Ground Targets*, p. 1.
41 Jarkowsky, *'Boots on the Ground'*, p. 15.
42 <www.globalsecurity.org> Last consulted on 10 January 2003.
43 Jarkowsky, *'Boots on the Ground'*, p. 15.
44 Ibid., p. 16.
45 Harold Kennedy, 'Will Special Ops Success "Change the Face of War?" ', *National Defense Magazine*, <www.nationaldefensemagazine.org/article.cfm?Id=721> Consulted on 20 December 2002.
46 Tolson, *Vietnam Studies: Airmobility*, p. 3.
47 Doughty, *The Evolution of US Army Tactical Doctrine*.
48 Griffith, *Forward into Battle*, p. 122.
49 Tolson, *Vietnam Studies: Airmobility*, p. 25.
50 Ibid., p. 36.
51 Kennedy, 'Will Special Ops Success "Change the Face of War?" '.
52 Doge Billingsley, 'Choppers in the Coils', *The Journal of Electronic Defense*, 25, 9 (2002), p. 38.
53 Department of the Army, *Vietnam Studies: US Army Special Forces*, p. 6.
54 Doughty, *The Evolution of US Army Tactical Doctrine*.

55 Jarkowsky, *'Boots on the Ground'*, p. 16.
56 Center for Defense Information, *The US Military Campaign in Afghanistan*.
57 <www.globalsecurity.org> Last consulted on 10 January 2003 and Jarkowsky, *'Boots on the Ground'*, p. 16.
58 Center for Defense Information, *The US Military Campaign in Afghanistan*.
59 Doughty, *The Evolution of US Army Tactical Doctrine*.
60 Ibid.
61 Håkansson, 'Taktik och stridsteknik i lågintensiva konflikter', p. 75.
62 Jarkowsky, *'Boots on the Ground'*, p. 16.
63 Griffith, *Forward into Battle*, p. 119.
64 Rosenau, *Special Operations Forces and Elusive Enemy Ground Targets*, p. 10.
65 Doughty, *The Evolution of US Army Tactical Doctrine*.
66 <www.wpafb.af.mil/museum/history/Vietnam/fac.htm> Site last consulted on 1 February 2003.
67 <www.cc.gatech.edu/fac/Thomas.Pilsch/AirOps/cas.html> Site last consulted on 1 February 2003.
68 Matt Kelley, 'US ground forces use lasers, satellites to guide air strikes', *The Associated Press*, <www. globalsecurity.org/org/news/2001/011206-attack01.htm> Last consulted on 22 February 2003, *Air Force News Archive, Secretary talks transformation*, <www.af.mil/news/Feb2002/n20020225_0304.shtml> Last consulted on 22 February 2003.
69 John T. Corell, 'From Sensor to Shooter', *Air Force Magazine Online: Journal of the Air Force Association*, 85, 2 (2002) and Milan Vego, 'What Can We Learn from Operation Enduring Freedom?', *US Naval Institute Proceedings*, 128, 7 (2002), pp. 28–33.
70 Kelley, 'US ground forces use lasers, satellites to guide air strikes'.
71 Tolson, *Vietnam Studies: Airmobility*, p. 41.
72 Griffith, *Forward into Battle*, p. 112.
73 Jim Garamone, *From the US Civil War to Afghanistan: A Short History of UAVs*, <www.Gordon.army.milAC/sumr02/uav2.htm> Last consulted on 19 February 2003.
74 Griffith, *Forward into Battle*, p. 113.
75 Terje Wahl, *Operasjon 'Enduring Freedom': Noen militaer-teknologiske beaktninger om kampene i Afghanistan hosten 2001*, FFI-Rapport 2002/00803 Oslo: Forsvarets Forskningsinstitutt, 2002, p. 9.
76 Center for Defense Information, *The US Military Campaign in Afghanistan*.
77 Garamone, *From the US Civil War to Afghanistan*.
78 Center for Defense Information, *Q & A on the Use of Predator in Operation Enduring Freedom*, <www.cdi.org/terrorism/predator-pr.cfm> Last consulted on 17 February 2003.
79 NAVAIR WD, *Walleye – first precision-guided air-to-surface weapon*, <www.nawcwpns.navy.mil/r2/mj/ar/WALLEYE2.htm> Last consulted on 19 February 2003.
80 Guided Bomb Unit-28 (GBU-28) BLU-113 Penetrator, <www.military.com/Data/EQG/GBU28.htm> Last consulted on 19 February 2003.
81 Michael Gordon, 'Military Analysis: War's Reality', *New York Times*, 3 March 2002.
82 Center of Defense Information, *The US Military Campaign in Afghanistan* and Erwin, 'Navy Aviation: Skills Surpass Smart Weapons'.
83 Andrew Koch and Kim Burger, 'USA Speeds Development of Thermobaric Weapons', *Jane's Defence Weekly*, 28 August 2002.
84 Doughty, *The Evolution of US Army Tactical Doctrine*.

85 Biddle, *Afghanistan and the Future of Warfare*, p. 1.
86 Corell, 'From Sensor to Shooter'.

References

Biddle, Stephen, 'Afghanistan and the Future of Warfare', *Foreign Affairs*, 82, 2 (2003), pp. 31–46.

—— *Afghanistan and the Future of Warfare: Implications for Army and Defense Policy*, Carlisle, PA: Strategic Studies Institute, US Army War College, 2002.

Billingsley, Doge, 'Choppers In the Coils', *The Journal of Electronic Defense*, 25, 9 (2002), pp. 38–47.

Boot, Max, *The Savage Wars of Peace: Small Wars and the Rise of American Power*, New York: Basic Books, 2002.

Cohen, Eliot, 'Technology and Warfare', in John Baylis *et al.* (eds), *Strategy in the Contemporary World: An introduction to Strategic Studies*, Oxford: Oxford University Press, 2002, pp. 235–53.

Corell, John T., 'From Sensor to Shooter', *Air Force Magazine Online: Journal of the Air Force Association*, 85, 2 (2002).

Doughty, Robert A., *The Evolution of US Army Tactical Doctrine, 1946–1976*, Fort Leavenworth, Kansas: Leavenworth Papers, Combat Studies Institute, US Command and General Staff College, 1979.

Freedman, Lawrence, 'A New Type of War', in Ken Booth and Tim Dunne (eds), *Worlds in Collision: Terror and the Future of World Order*, London: Palgrave, 2002, pp. 37–47.

—— *The Revolution in Strategic Affairs*, Adelphi Paper 318, Oxford: Oxford University Press, 1998.

Griffith, Paddy, *Forward into Battle: Fighting Tactics from Waterloo to Vietnam*, Chichester, UK: Anthony Bird, 1981.

Håkansson, Kersti, 'Taktik och stridsteknik i lågintensiva konflikter: En fallstudie av Operation Anaconda', in Arne Baudin *et al.* (eds), *En ny medeltid? En introduktion till militärteori i lågintensiva konflikter*. Stockholm: Försvarshögskolan, 2002, pp. 70–92.

Hammond, Grant T., 'Globalization, Technology and the Transformation of the Security Environment: The Real Revolution in Military Affairs', paper presented at the American Political Science Association in San Francisco. August 2001.

Jarkowsky, Jeffrey, *'Boots on the Ground' – Will US Landpower be Decisive in Future Conflicts?*, Carlisle, PA: Strategic Studies Institute, US Army War College, 2002.

Kaldor, Mary, *New and Old Wars: Organized Violence in a Global Era*, Cambridge: Polity Press, 1999.

Koch, Andrew and Kim Burger, 'USA Speeds Development of Thermobaric Weapons', *Jane's Defence Weekly*, 28 August 2002.

MacGregor, Douglas, 'Future Battle: The Merging Levels of War', *Parameters*, 22, 4 (1993), pp. 33–47.

McInnes, Colin, 'A Different Kind of War: September 11 and the United States' Afghan War', *Review of International Studies*, 29, 2 (2003), pp. 165–84.

Mahnken, Thomas G., 'The American Way of War in the Twenty-First Century', in Efraim Inbar (ed.), *Democracies and Small Wars*, London: Frank Cass, 2003, pp. 73–84.

Mockaitis, Thomas R. and Paul B. Rich (eds), *Grand Strategy in the War Against Terrorism*, London: Frank Cass, 2003.

Rosenau, William, *Special Operations Forces and Elusive Enemy Ground Targets: Lessons from Vietnam and the Persian Gulf* War, RAND Document No. MR-1408-AF, 2001.

Ruane, Kevin, *The Vietnam Wars*, Manchester: Manchester University Press, 2000.

Tolson, John J., *Vietnam Studies: Airmobility, 1961–1971*. Washington DC: Department of the Army, 1973.

US Department of the Army, *Vietnam Studies: U.S. Army Special Forces, 1961–1971*, Washington DC: Department of the Army, CMH Publication, 1989.

Wahl, Terje, *Operasjon 'Enduring Freedom': Noen militaer-teknologiske beaktninger om kampene i Afghanistan høsten 2001*, FFI-Rapport 2002/00803. Oslo: Forsvarets Forskningsinstitutt, 2002.

Vego, Milan, 'What can we Learn from Operation Enduring Freedom?', *US Naval Institute Proceedings*, 128, 7 (2002), pp. 28–33.

7

THE WARS IN FORMER YUGOSLAVIA IN THE 1990s

Bringing the state back in

Bob de Graaff

New wars

Mary Kaldor's view of the wars in Yugoslavia in the 1990s was in many ways refreshing. She rightly saw them as a contemporary phenomenon rather than, as many did at the time, a throwback to the Balkan past.[1] She ranked the wars in Former Yugoslavia together with other phenomena in post-communist Eastern Europe and wars taking place in Africa. According to her, these new wars involved:

> a blurring of distinctions between war (usually defined as violence between states or organized political groups for political motives), organized crime (violence undertaken by privately organized groups for private purposes, usually financial gain) and large-scale violations of human rights (violence undertaken by states or politically organized groups against individuals).[2]

The new wars, she thought, arose 'in the context of the erosion of the autonomy of the state and in some extreme cases the disintegration of the state',[3] which were in their turn caused by globalisation, 'a contradictory process involving both integration and fragmentation, homogenisation and diversification, globalization and localization'.[4]

Yugoslavia as victim of globalisation

So far, so good, as far as Former Yugoslavia is concerned. From the 1950s onward Yugoslavia's president Josip Broz Tito had relaxed political, social and economic tensions in his country by decentralising the power further and further at the level of the six republics and two autonomous provinces. This finally led to the 1974 constitution, which effectively turned the country into a confederation, each republic with its own economy, so much so that the extent of foreign loans was unknown at the federal level and in 1981 Yugoslavia's total foreign debt had to be established by foreign agencies. The Communist Party had already devolved to the republican level, so that one spoke of eight communist parties instead of one, nine if one counted the Communist Party membership of the federal army as a separate one.

Representatives of the republics and autonomous provinces formed the country's presidium. As long as Tito lived it did not matter that both the presidium and the so-called Federal Executive Council (the national cabinet) did not come to conclusions. Tito had been appointed president for life and as the ultimate referee he was able to draw his own conclusions all the more easily when others failed to do so. After Tito's death, however, the system went into disarray. Each year one of the eight representatives became president of the presidium in a pre-established order. All of them lacked the charisma of Tito, who, just like any other dictator, had failed to bequeath his power to a crown prince.

Shortly before Tito's death the ruined state of the economy had become apparent. Since the 1950s the country's economy had been dependent on foreign loans, which were extended freely at the time of the Cold War, when the US administrations tried to keep the Tito regime with its deviant course towards Moscow on its feet, as well as on the foreign currency that Yugoslav *Gastarbeiter* sent home from Western Europe. The latter flow of currency had been reduced in the 1970s in reaction to two consecutive oil crises. When the threat of the Cold War receded after Gorbachev had assumed power in the Soviet Union in 1985 and the Velvet Revolution took place in Eastern Europe in the late 1980s, the foreign aid from the US also dwindled rapidly. Countries like Hungary, Poland and Czechoslovakia, which took drastic measures to establish democracies and free market economies, became the chief beneficiaries of US aid instead of Yugoslavia, which was one of the last countries to do away with communism and, on top of that, did it in a half-hearted way, disguising communism as nomenklatura nationalism while so-called reforms to establish a free market were predominantly cosmetic.

International organisations such as the International Monetary Fund and the World Bank demanded that the Yugoslav political leaders re-establish a certain degree of central command in their country so as to be able to conduct a sound economic policy. As it was, the republics, greatly differing in economic wealth, had turned into fiefdoms, administered by incestuous elites of politicians and firm leaders. A republic such as Slovenia, whose leaders longed for entry into the European Community (EC), saw its wealth in relation to the EC countries diminish year after year. The heavy-handed Serbian policy towards Kosovo, aimed at taking away its autonomous status, further diminished the chances of a Yugoslav membership of the EC. Efforts from Belgrade authorities to re-establish a more unified decision-making system were thwarted by most republics, which saw them as barely disguised efforts by Serbs to regain their pre-war hegemony over the Yugoslav state.

The combined inaptitude of the Yugoslav system for necessary reform and the pressures from a changing outside world played the different parts of the country against each other in an irresoluble way. Once the Cold War was over and globalisation made itself felt in Eastern Europe, the complex state machinery of Yugoslavia, (un)guided by the most complex and incomprehensible constitution in the world, was a likely candidate for failure.

The resurgence of ethnic rivalries

In the West many remembered Tito as the magician who had managed to do away with ethnic rivalries in a country that had experienced the Second World War more as a civil war, based on ethnic differences, than as an occupation by fascist powers. However, Tito had not done away with ethnic rivalries at all. Rather, he had suppressed the memories of the Second World War, so that when after his death there was a certain liberalisation as to freedom of speech, this immediately gave rise to ethnic-nationalistic publications, which enlarged rather than subdued the memories of the Second World War that had been kept alive around family tables.

Furthermore, Tito sometimes could only use measures against one group if he did the same towards others. For instance, when he decided to move against the leaders of the so-called Croatian Spring in 1971, who had already by then set Croatia on a course towards independence, Tito felt the need to do the same with reformers among the Serbian Communist Party, a dreadful decision that in the end made possible the upward movement of a bureaucratic *apparatchik* as Slobodan Milosevic.

In areas where different ethnic groups lived together, Tito's regime had established the so-called ethnic clue to divide jobs, homes and other privileges. Meant to subdue ethnic tensions, this actually kept the sense of ethnic belonging alive. As Kaldor rightly remarks, the Tito regime 'institutionalised ethnic difference'.[5]

This caused no great problems as long as the economy kept functioning. Once the economy was on its downhill course, however, it started to matter whether one's boss was a Serb, a Croat or a Muslim. At least that was how many people perceived it and as the so-called Thomas theorem goes, 'If men define their situations as real, they are real in their consequences'.[6] In this case the consequences were a growing feeling of insecurity based on ethnic differences. In sight of free elections in 1990, more and more people turned towards political parties based on ethnic belonging, not so much out of ethnic pride as from insecurity and fear. According to Kaldor, this attitude is typical for the new wars. Ideological and/or territorial motives have been supplanted by 'an emerging political cleavage between what I call cosmopolitanism, based on inclusive, universalist, multicultural values, and the politics of particularist identities', based on nation, clan, religion, or language.[7]

Bringing the state back into the story

So far as Yugoslavia is concerned, there is nothing wrong with Kaldor's analysis. But when it comes to her description of the types of war that spring from these politics of particular identities we have to object. She thinks that the strategies of new wars are derived from counterinsurgency techniques, and that the units that fight these wars include 'a disparate range of different types of groups, such as paramilitary units, local warlords, criminal gangs, police forces, mercenary groups, and also regular armies, including breakaway units of regular armies'. She calls these units 'highly decentralized':[8] 'violence is increasingly privatised both as a result of growing organised crime and the emergence of paramilitary groups, and political legitimacy is disappearing'.[9] She even draws parallels with Western Europe and North America where, she thinks, violence in the inner cities can be typified as new wars and where, as far as the US is concerned, private security officers have come to outnumber police officers by 2 : 1.[10]

Not only does Kaldor miss the mark when she de-emphasises the role of emerging states in organising violence in favour of her idea of privatised violence, she is also wrong when she thinks that violence in the new wars, especially in Bosnia-Herzegovina, was used 'to control populations rather than to capture territory'.[11] The reason for misunderstanding the centrality of the state in the actions of warriors in Former Yugoslavia may be that the state has played a different role there than in the West. Therefore the building of an argument around the role of the state there and the way it uses violence should be based on both the events taking place and the way the West looked upon them.

In the case of the Former Yugoslavia the state should be brought back into the story of the wars of the 1990s at two moments. First, state authorities both condoned and instigated violence on purpose. Second, the conflict parties aspired to new forms of statehood. The centrality of the state was often overlooked in the West, because state actors in Former Yugoslavia tried to hide that they were behind the violence, as well how they aimed at creating new states. A third reason for misreading the centrality of the state in the conflict in Former Yugoslavia was the way violence was articulated there.

This will be shown by way of looking at the conflicts in Former Yugoslavia between 1991 and 1995, and especially by paying attention to the war in Bosnia-Herzegovina, which, in the view of Kaldor, has become 'the archetypal example, the paradigm of the new type of warfare'.[12]

Warlords?

Of course, the Yugoslav state crumbled in 1991 and 1992, but this does not mean that state authority disappeared from its territory. On the contrary, as has been described, even before 1991 the state of Yugoslavia had become very much decentralised. At the level of the republics, the state was strong before 1991 and tried to remain so thereafter. It was because the authorities at the republic level were the sole source of social, political and economic privilege that it mattered so much which ethnic group would win during free elections. It even mattered so much that people thought the only way to defend or gain these privileges was to make war, so that they would end up with as large a territory as possible in which they were sure their ethnic group would rule. The sense of insecurity – perceived or real, manipulated or authentic – made the conflicts in Former Yugoslavia people's wars right from the beginning. They became even more so after brothers and fathers had been killed and mothers and sisters raped. Then the wars gained their own momentum.

During the short war in Slovenia, the West still saw only the operations of the regular federal Yugoslav army. There was no talk yet of warlords. The reason for this was not only the short duration of the war itself. Serbia's president Milosevic considered Slovenia not worth the bones of a single Serb soldier, as he told the American ambassador in Belgrade.[13] There were hardly any Serbs living in that part of the country. Furthermore, with Slovenia leaving the federation, Milosevic's henchmen in the presidency, i.e. the representatives of Serbia, Montenegro, Kosovo, and Vojvodina, would outnumber those left after the departure of Slovenia, i.e. Croatia, Macedonia and Bosnia-Herzegovina. Of the latter only Macedonia was of minor importance to Milosevic.[14]

The republics that would be left at the mercy of Milosevic and his cronies decided each for themselves that they would leave the republic of Yugoslavia. Remaining at the will of Milosevic or even more nationalistic Serb leaders was obviously no option. Croatia declared its independence on the same day as Slovenia: 25 June 1991. Less than three months later Macedonia followed suit. The leadership of the SDA, the Bosnian Muslim party that had become the largest party in Bosnia during the 1990 elections, realised that declaring independence would be most difficult in their republic because of the presence of large groups of Serbs and Croats.

Nevertheless, two weeks before the declarations of independence of Croatia and Slovenia, on 9 June 1991 SDA leader and Bosnia's president Alija Izetbegovic, declared that 'the struggle for Bosnia has begun'.[15] The following day official Muslim representatives from all over Bosnia gathered at an SDA meeting in the Dom Milicije in Sarajevo to decide to prepare for the defence of the republic, as it was called. At this meeting the SDA leadership established a Council for the Defence of the Muslims, which would follow the dual policy of winning international recognition for Bosnia-Herzegovina and making preparations for the defence of Bosnia. In fact these preparations had already begun in March and April 1991 with the establishment of the *Patriotska Liga* (Patriotic League), the military branch of the SDA, and the private initiative of the *Zelene Beretke* (Green Berets), which counted 400 members at the time of the meeting in the Dom Milicije and was thereafter adopted by the SDA leadership.[16]

At about the same time that the Muslim Patriotic League was founded, the Bosnian Serb leaders got instructions from Belgrade that they should try to block any move in the Bosnian parliament that would obstruct the development of a Greater Serbia. The Bosnian Serb nationalist leaders hardly needed this exhortation. They would stand firm against any development that would make them an ethnic minority within an independent Bosnia.[17] In the following months the Bosnian Serbs were armed, mostly by the regular army or from the weapon stores of the Territorial Defence.

So, while on the one hand the state of Yugoslavia fell apart, new states that would spring from the remains were already in the making. As long as there were no major ethnic differences the transitions could even be smooth. If ethnic tensions loomed, political hopefuls with or without outside help began to organise precursors of state armies.

This was the case in Croatia, where about 12 per cent of the population consisted of Serbs. The leadership in Belgrade was determined that the territories where the Serbian presence was largest should not be included in an independent Croatia. A proportion of the Croatian Serbs followed this line, all the more eagerly when it turned out that president Tudjman, who had won the 1990 elections, took measures that were offensive to Serbs.

When the war broke out in Croatia in the summer of 1991, Western newspapers soon wrote about private warlords operating side by side with the regular federal army in the zones that the Serbs declared theirs.[18] They were either commanders of paramilitary groups or local militias. The most notorious of the paramilitary leaders were Zeljko Raznatovic, also known as Arkan, a former hired agent of the Yugoslav intelligence services; Vojislav Seselj, Milosevic's ideal opposition politician; Dragan Bokan, leader of the *Beli Orlovi* (White Eagles); and Captain Dragan, the so-called Rambo of Knin, leader of the *Knindjas*. Although not generally known at the time, it has since been convincingly established that they were under instructions from Milosevic with a licence to kill.[19] More widely known at the time was that the local militias had received their weapons from Belgrade. There could have been no Arkan, Seselj or Captain Dragan without the connivance, support and exhortation of the authorities in Belgrade. The paramilitary groups were organised by the so-called *vojna linija* (military line) within the Serbian Ministry of the Interior, consisting of close relations of Milosevic who guided these operations from within the State Security Service.[20] As Milosevic said to the leaders of the State Security Service in April 1993 – according to witness

C-48 at the Yugoslavia Tribunal in The Hague – when they told him that they had Arkan under control: 'Very well. Very well. You just keep him under control. We need people like this now but no-one should think that they are more powerful than the state.'[21]

These paramilitary leaders and militias had clear functions in bringing about a warlike situation. They attacked Croatian leaders to incite people to use more violence, as well as moderate Serb leaders who tried to mitigate the tensions. Attacking moderates of one's own ethnic group had the function not only of eliminating people who might think differently about the position of the Serbs in Croatia from the ethnic hardliners. By making it look like these moderates were the victims of Croats, the attacks contributed to the ethnic fear that led to the insecurity, which then made Serbs flock together under the protective wings of both the Serb-dominated regular army and the paramilitary groups.

Just as the paramilitary groups and militias had the role of inciting violence before the outbreak of war, they also sought to terrorise people from other ethnic groups during the process of ethnic cleansing. This started during the war in Croatia but reached its apex during the war in Bosnia in the course of the execution of the so-called RAM-plan, which revealed Milosevic and the Serbian military authorities as the masterminds behind the military operations.[22] In this process, the regular army would usually batter a community with artillery whereafter it gave free way to paramilitary groups to chase away the population, and then loot the place. To get the population on the run, a few people, mostly the local elite, would be killed, a certain number of women would be raped, often in public places, or some people would temporarily be held in camps. All this was meant to ensure that once the population as a whole could get away from their residences, they would do so. Often their houses were set on fire. This would seem to entail the destruction of capital assets, but it was the surest way to guarantee that the local people would not return.

Therefore, the paramilitary had little value as fighters.[23] They mostly undertook actions against defenceless civilians. Losses among the paramilitary were consequently small. Looting was their main occupation, which earned the Arkanovci the epithet of the 'trucking battalion'.[24] As a Western military observer remarked: 'The extensive weapon gear of the paramilitary, such as complete sets of knives, looked impressive, but was not very effective for military purposes'; 'such gear was for killing civilians, not enemy soldiers. If (. . .) the Serbs had believed that they were going to face people who could effectively shoot back, they would have carried more ammunition and fewer weapons.'[25]

In the initial stages of the wars in Croatia and Bosnia, paramilitary groups had been irregulars in the truest sense. In all cases, though, after a while the irregulars became regularised. Already on 3 October 1991 the irregular Serb forces in Croatia were declared part of the regular army.[26] In the autumn of

1993 the Bosnian government began to regularise its irregulars or, in case they refused, to arrest them. Occasionally, military gang leaders were even killed. More and more the Bosnian government army became a political army. Those officers who had SDA party membership were favoured. Political control of the army, which was disliked by officers who had not become SDA members and stood by their professional standards, increased. Similar developments took place on the side of the Bosnian Serbs.

All this attention for the paramilitary units, of which the largest counted no more than several thousand people, should not distract from the fact that they were heavily outnumbered by the regular armies. In Bosnia the government army numbered 200,000 men in early 1993 and 250,000 men a year later; the Bosnian Serb army between 60,000 and 86,000 military; and the Bosnian Croat army between 35,000 and 45,000 military, who had the support of some 15,000 soldiers of the regular Croat army.[27]

Although inroads could be made into the military hierarchy by calling on special units for special duties, the orders came from the politicians and therefore would only underline the state-like character of the war. In the case of the Bosnian-Serb Army, it has been established, by among others the International Criminal Tribunal for Yugoslavia, that the military lines of command were in place, for instance at the time of the massacres following the fall of Srebrenica. This was in spite of efforts by Bosnian Serb leaders to depict them as acts of revenge by the local population or as the behaviour of irregulars, who would not have been under the command of the regular commanders. Only on a very small scale, compared to the thousands who died in front of the execution squads in the aftermath of Srebrenica, did personal revenge play a role.

Realising state projects and territorial ambitions

The reason for the conflicts in Croatia and Bosnia was not the fact that individuals saw a chance to become local warlords and enrich themselves, or strove for other forms of aggrandisement. The reason was that political leaders in Serbia, Croatia and Bosnia had set their eyes upon state projects that were mutually exclusive.[28] Although Milosevic had probably embraced the cause of ethnic nationalism purely to retain his power status at a time that the Communist party of Yugoslavia had to give up its monopolistic control over the country, his rule endorsed the cause of a Greater Serbia in these years, as long as he thought it useful. The majority of the opposition in Serbia was no less and certainly more sincerely nationalistic and in favour of a Greater Serbia. Their parties, such as those of Seselj and Vuk Draskovic, had their own paramilitary branches. They fought in Croatia with the support of the Serbian Ministry of the Interior, as was the case with Seselj, or to be shot in the back, which happened to commanders who were loyal to Vuk Draskovic.

166

Using these groups seems to have had three functions that were central in the operations of Milosevic: one was that it directed the energy of the opposition away from threatening his own rule; the second was that the involvement of other groups enabled him plausibly to deny his own involvement, on which he was always very keen;[29] and the third was that he made accomplices.

Making accomplices was also one of the main reasons why Milosevic supported the occupation of part of Croatia's territory by Serb forces. He wanted Croatia's president Franjo Tudjman to participate in the carving up of Bosnia.[30] Not only had Tudjman a Greater Croatia as a long-term dream at the cost of the integrity of Bosnia-Herzegovina. He also needed some successes that would compensate for the loss of territory the Zagreb regime had endured during the war in Croatia.

The talks between Milosevic and Tudjman, both direct and indirect, about the partitioning of Bosnia-Herzegovina make it clear that the war in Bosnia was indeed about territory. Both Milosevic and the Bosnian Serb leaders claimed about two-thirds of Bosnia's territory before the war broke out.[31] Due to their superiority in arms the Bosnian Serbs got even more during the first few months of the war in Bosnia. After that the fronts stabilised, not through an intention to control populations instead of grabbing territory as Kaldor suggests, but because there was a stalemate, especially between the Bosnian Serb army and the Bosnian government army. The former had superiority in artillery, but was lacking in numbers. There were, for instance, so few artillerists around Sarajevo that they had to be moved from one artillery position to the other. The Bosnian government army had far greater numbers of military but they were unable to grab more territory, first because they lost out against artillery and second because their officers were rather inexperienced. The fact that after the first months of the war little territory changed hands occurred not on purpose but rather as the outcome of a stalemate, just as during the First World War little territory changed hands for years, but nevertheless millions died in efforts to grab a little more.

Least clear was the state project the Bosnian Muslim nationalist leaders had in mind. During the first 18 months of the war they were so much on the defensive that this lack of clarity was hardly a problem. When their army began to win victories, especially against the Croats, and the maps that international negotiators produced at the negotiating tables required definitive answers, the SDA leaders became divided.[32] Some of them held on to the officially proclaimed policy of a multi-ethnic Bosnia. The most radical of the fundamentalist leaders wanted a Muslim-dominated Bosnia; others a Muslim area that would combine parts of Bosnia with Muslim-dominated parts outside Bosnia, especially Sandzak. And still others chose for a small all-Muslim territory within Bosnia. In theory, only the latter could have made peace with the Serb and Croat nationalist leaders. These faction struggles within the SDA remained closed to most Western eyes. Such observers focused on Izetbegovic and regarded his indecisiveness as to the future of his country, which was wholly rational when understood against the background of the divisions in his own party, as a personal trait.[33]

Concealing the true aims

So here we had three different groups, each trying to realise their own state projects at the expense of the others. However, the plans were not always clear to the West, as the nationalist leaders in Former Yugoslavia did their best to conceal them from prying Western eyes. For a long time, Milosevic sought to present his case in Croatia to the West as if he was trying to maintain the integrity of Yugoslavia, albeit minus Slovenia. As long as he did so, he could 'sell' the operations of the Federal army (JNA), which became more and more a Serb army because of the withdrawal of military from other ethnic groups, as an internal Yugoslav affair, implying that the West should not meddle in this case. But there were additional reasons for Milosevic to do so. The top brass of the Federal army, among them its commander general Kadijevic, were not yet ready to give up Yugoslavia, as Milosevic had already done in the back of his mind in the summer of 1990 when he prepared for the adoption of a new Serb constitution, that had little relation to the federal constitution.[34] To Milosevic's irritation the leadership of the Federal army were undecided whether their military operations should include all of Croatia, with the objective of keeping Yugoslavia together, or whether they should concentrate on those parts of Croatia where many Serbs lived.[35] The result of this indecisiveness was that Federal troops in barracks outside the strongly Serb-inhabited areas could easily be surrounded by lightly armed Croatian troops. The ensuing surrenders were one of the main ways for the Croat troops to supply themselves with heavy weapons.

In spite of his annoyance with the JNA leadership, which at one time threatened to overthrow him, Milosevic still blocked the development of a purely Serb army because that would weaken his ploy to deceive the West into believing he was maintaining the Yugoslav state.[36] He even forced the Serb Minister of Defence Tomislav Simovic, who tried to realise a purely Serb army, to resign.[37] It was a major goal of Milosevic to make his rump-Yugoslav state the internationally recognised heir to the former federal Yugoslavia.[38]

Another reason for Milosevic not to unveil his true objectives too much was that the war in Croatia was rather unpopular with large numbers of the Serbs, both in Serbia and in Croatia. Many Serb youngsters dodged the draft or refused service while at the front. Croatian Serbs even left their areas and moved to Serbia to escape from being drawn into the conflict as military or militias. The Bosnian Serbs later did the same. There were immense morale problems among the military of the Federal army.[39] Partly for that reason, Milosevic always refrained from calling the military actions in Croatia a war. The obituaries in Serb newspapers, however, told a different story.

General Tudjman had his intentions set on incorporating Croatian-declared parts of Bosnia into Croatia. However, he could not do so openly, as he depended upon the goodwill of the West to realise the territorial integrity of the Croatian state. Meanwhile behind the scenes he and his representatives conferred with Milosevic about a deal on Bosnia, which they could thereafter force upon Izetbegovic. To a certain extent this approach was formalised after the failure of the Vance–Owen peace plan, and became known as the Owen–Stoltenberg or the *Invincible* plan. Not surprisingly the Bosnian Muslims did not go along. And in March 1994 the US administration pressed the Croatian authorities into accepting an agreement whereby the Croatian and Muslim parts of Bosnia would form a federation.

Perceptions of state violence

If the West had difficulties in seeing the state operators behind the acts of individual commanders in the field, the appearance of the violence in a haphazard way also gave the impression of spontaneous rather than state-organised or condoned violence. True, there was sometimes what the people in Bosnia call a *mali rat* (little war) within the war at large. If a Serb for instance had been coveting the car of his Muslim neighbour there was now a chance to get it by killing him; or if another thought he had a score to settle with a former teacher and heard that teacher was imprisoned, he might now see a chance to have his personal revenge by torturing him. The state monopoly of violence had given way to such indiscriminate acts.

To give a clearer understanding of the impact the role of the state could have, a story should be told about an event that took place near Srebrenica in 1971. A Muslim from the Muslim village of Konjevic Polje visited the fair in Bratunac. On his way home he entered, drunk as he was, a café in the Serbian stronghold of Kravica. He scolded at the Serbs raking up memories about the murderous role they had played against Muslims during the Second World War. He was stabbed in the back with a knife. Nevertheless, he jumped on the bar, took the knife out of his back and continued his harangue. The barman then grabbed his gun and shot him. Limping, the drunkard reached the door, where he died. The people from Kravica called those in Konjevic Polje to tell them that they could come and collect him. Those from Konjevic Polje duly arrived, guns in hand. The people of Kravica had expected nothing else. They were hidden in the cornfields, also with guns. A shootout started, but probably because of a general state of drunkenness, nobody got hurt. As soon as the authorities learned about this event, special police troops were sent into the area to calm the situation. They stayed there for several days to make sure that the trouble would not reoccur. Twenty years later the authorities in Belgrade armed the inhabitants in Kravica and policemen were involved in the first killing of Muslims that took place in the area in the fall of 1991, six months before the war in Bosnia broke out.[40]

This story shows several things. First, there was never a complete state monopoly of violence. There were guns scattered throughout the country before 1991 and martial prowess was thought to be one of the finer qualities of man. The omnipresence of weapons was augmented by the decision in 1968 to establish a Territorial Defence force. Actually, Tito and his comrades took this decision because they feared that the regular federal army would not be able to withstand a Warsaw Pact invasion, such as the one that took place in Czechoslovakia that year. The idea of territorial defence was meant to deter possible invaders; such a system of defence also served to enhance the myths surrounding the role of the partisan fighters during the Second World War, which had been used to legitimise the rule of Tito and his Communist Party.

Second, the difference between 1971 and 1991 was that in the earlier case the authorities repressed the violence while in the later one they condoned it. Indeed more so, they encouraged it by providing arms and guaranteed the perpetrators that they would get away with impunity. The very acts of delegation of the use of violence and the distribution of arms indicate that the use of violence originated at the state level. One of the policemen involved in the Kravica incident in 1991 played a major role in the ethnic cleansing operations around Bratunac in 1992. One day he would visit a Muslim village, telling the inhabitants that they were punishable if they did not hand in their weapons. The next day paramilitary gangs or militias would arrive to cleanse the villagers who had given up their ability to resist with arms.

From the viewpoint of the victims this cannot be called a lessening of the powers of the state. Indeed, the state threw its full weight behind criminal acts, even though its leaders tried to mask it. The same is true with the practice of ethnic cleansing in general.

The openness and gruesome character of the violence was difficult for people in the West to understand. It was even harder to understand that there were state authorities behind it. Karadzic played upon this unbelief and managed to get away with some of his actions by asking Western journalists how they thought he could be responsible for such cruelties. Or, worse, he managed to play upon Western doubts, by blaming Muslims and Croats for things his own troops had done.

Initially, the warring parties in both Croatia and Bosnia did not hinder journalists in reporting the violence, so that a Western audience was assured of a daily portion of 'prime-time horror'.[41] Not for the first time did the open character of the violence bewilder the West. As Allcock and Mazower have shown, attitudes in Western and Eastern Europe towards public and state-organised violence began to diverge in the nineteenth century.[42] The West started to hide acts of state violence, such as public executions, from the public eye. This process was helped by the fact that the state in Western Europe was stronger than that in Eastern Europe, where violence in border areas was more or less institutionalised and a complete state monopoly on violence was never achieved. This process of withdrawing the bloody side of state-organised violence in the West was enhanced shortly before the wars in Former Yugoslavia by the use of so-called smart bombs in the Gulf War. Wars seemed to have become as harmless as their virtual counterparts on computer screens.

But was the violence in Yugoslavia worse than that in Western wars? The British journalist Anthony Loyd asked his readers: 'Is dropping fire from aircraft onto civilians in Dresden more acceptable than cutting their throats with a knife in Bosnia? Apparently so.'[43] And his American colleague Peter Maass even indicated his clear preference for the low-tech war in Bosnia. According to Maass it had

> the cruel virtue of limiting the carnage each soldier could accomplish. Is a soldier who slits another person's throat more barbaric than a soldier who pushes a button that launches a missile that kills one thousand people? I suspect not. In the pecking order of barbarism, Bosnia's war could be topped.[44]

The wars in Former Yugoslavia were often fought not between soldiers but between soldiers and civilians who were branded as enemies. It was literally a war of slaughter; knives were important weapons. This retreat to such unsophisticated arms seemed to many in the West evidence that the state was not involved, but it surely was. Through its propaganda, it offered role models such as the *cetniks*, the *franc-tireurs* of earlier times. Again, the openness of the violence sometimes served an aim in the war. Arkan allowed the photographer Ron Haviv to accompany his troops to Bijeljina in early April 1992, when they committed their crimes there, probably to arouse the fear he thought people needed to have for his troops.[45]

Consequences

The part played by Milosevic and others at the state level during the wars in Slovenia, Croatia and Bosnia was no less central during the war in Kosovo. On the contrary, Milosevic appears to have taken an even greater role in 'micro-managing' the Kosovo war than in Bosnia and Croatia.[46] It is therefore understandable that the Prosecutor at the International Criminal Tribunal for Yugoslavia in The Hague began the proceedings against Milosevic with the war in Kosovo. As the process moved on to the war in Croatia, it was of great importance that the Prosecutor managed to produce witnesses who had been close observers of and even collaborators with Milosevic's policies. They could testify that Milosevic and his cronies had been deeply involved in the Serbian aggression in Croatia. Their oral testimonies make up for Milosevic's efforts to create no paper trails. Although he tried again,[47] it had become much more difficult for Milosevic to maintain his claim that the paramilitary forces had not operated within the ambit of his Interior ministry but had been purely local combat units.

Now that a permanent International Criminal Court has been established, it is to be expected that future politicians who violate human rights on a large scale will go to even greater lengths to destroy evidence of their wrongdoings. It is therefore not only a scholarly but also a moral duty of social scientists and historians to make every effort to find the connections between gross human rights violations at the local level and involvement at the state level, and thereby to unearth the efforts at state level to create plausible deniability.

Willingly or unwillingly, the wars in Former Yugoslavia produced strong ties between the authorities and criminals. On the one hand, criminals were used on purpose, for instance when in the summer of 1991 the Belgrade prisons opened their doors for inmates who were willing to join Arkan's troops, or when the Bosnian government needed them for the defence of Sarajevo. On the other hand, mobsters saw growth in their smuggling enterprises, which flourished under international sanctions regimes, along front lines and during sieges.

In the end, most states of Former Yugoslavia became weak states. This was not so much because of their size. Small countries like Luxembourg can be rather affluent. In the case of Former Yugoslavia Slovenia proves the case. Rather, the states became weak in particular because of the relations between the authorities and the mafia, bonds that had been forged during the war and were not untied once the war was over. Western administrators in post-Dayton Bosnia tried to conceal this fact for a long time, fearing that stories about corruption would endanger money flows to the region. However, the facts can no longer be hidden.

The process that began with Serbian efforts to strengthen the Yugoslav state, and was followed by efforts of other nationalities to create their own states that should protect them from ethnic threats, ended up with weak states dependent upon Western presence, a situation that comes close to neo-colonialism. Seven years after Dayton these states are still rather unstable; a Western presence is still required to prevent a relapse into violence, and several problems, such as the status of Kosovo and Montenegro, are still unsolved.

After Bosnia, new protectorates have been created at a rather high speed: East Timor, several African republics, Afghanistan, and new candidates for enduring Western presence are appearing on the horizon. This demand for military presences around the world is not only taxing for these protectorates themselves but is also endangering the hegemonic position of the West. After the era of de-colonisation the West profited from the fact that such demand was self-induced. Now the West has become overloaded with peace-keeping and peace-enforcing operations. Is this the new form that imperial overstretch will take, this time round in history?

Notes

1 Mary Kaldor, *New and Old Wars: Organized Violence in a Global Era*, Cambridge: Polity Press, 1999, p. 2. See also Mary Kaldor (ed.), *Global Insecurity: Restructuring the Global Military Sector*, London: Pinter, 2000, especially pp. 3–8.
2 Kaldor, *New and Old Wars*, p. 2.
3 Ibid., p. 4.
4 Ibid., p. 3.
5 Ibid., p. 35.
6 Robert K. Merton, *On Theoretical Sociology: Five Essays, Old and New*, New York: Free Press, 1967, p. 19.
7 Kaldor, *New and Old Wars*, p. 6.
8 Ibid., p. 8.
9 Ibid., p. 5.
10 Ibid., p. 12.
11 Ibid., p. 50.
12 Ibid., p. 31.
13 Warren Zimmermann, *Origins of a Catastrophe: Yugoslavia and its Destroyers*, rev. edn, New York: Times Books, 1999, p. 149.
14 J. C. H. Blom and P. Romijn, *Srebrenica: Een 'veilig' gebied. Reconstructie, achtergronden, gevolgen en analyses van de val van een Safe Area*, Amsterdam: the Netherlands Institute for War Documentation, 2002, p. 35. This is the so-called Srebrenica report. An English language version of this report can be found on the Internet: <www.screbrenica.nl.>.
15 Robert J. Donia and John V. A. Fine, *Bosnia and Hercegovina: A Tradition Betrayed*, 2nd edn, London: Hurst and Co., 1997, p. 228.
16 Blom and Romijn, *Srebrenica*, pp. 436–8.
17 Ibid., pp. 435–6.
18 See for example Duško Doder, 'Mysterious commander', *The San Francisco Chronicle*, 08–08–91. Cf. Stathis N. Kalyvas, ' "New" and "Old" Civil Wars: A Valid Distinction?', *World Politics*, 54, 1 (October 2001), p. 103, who notes that scholarly arguments about the 'new' wars often originate from incomplete or biased evidence derived from journalistic reports.
19 Jonathan S. Landay, 'Belgrade Regime Tied to Alleged War Crimes', *Christian Science Monitor*, 26 November 1993; George Rodrique, 'To divide and conquer: Serbian leader saved self by ruining nation', *Dallas Morning News*, 3 July 1994; 'Sarajevo could become "the Beirut of Europe", Karadzic warns', *Deutsche Presse-Agentur*, 27 November 1995; Jonathan McGeary, 'Face to face with evil', *Time Magazine*, 13 May 1996; Julian Borger, 'Milošević Case Hardens' and 'Inside Story: The President's Secret Henchmen', *Guardian* (London), 3 February 1997; Philip Smucker, 'International Criminals find a Home in Serbia', *Pittsburgh Post-Gazette*, 16 February 1997; Dušan Stojanovic, 'International News', *AP Worldstream*, 1 November 2000; Paul Williams and Norman Cigar, 'War Crimes and Individual Responsibility: A Prima Facie Case for the Indictment of Slobodan Milosevic', <wysiwyg://182/http://www.nesl.edu/center/balkan2.htm>, 1996 (consulted 19/12/00), I.5.c, IV.A, V.A.2, nVI.A.2, 21 and 173; Roger Cohen, *Hearts Grown Brutal: Sagas of Sarajevo*, New York: Random, 1998, p. 410; Duško Doder and Louise Branson, *Milosevic: Portrait of a Tyrant*, New York: Free Press, 1999, pp. 101–2; 'His Master's Voice: The Adventures of Hrvoje Šarinic in the Land of the Serb Aggressor', *Bosnia Report*, New Series no. 8 (January–March 1999); and Lenard J. Cohen, *Serpent in the Bosom. The Rise and Fall of Slobodan Milosevic*, Boulder, CO: Westview Press, 2001, p. 135.

20 Blom and Romijn, *Srebrenica*, pp. 267–75 and Adam LeBor, *Milosevic: A Biography*, London: Simon & Schuster, 2002, pp. 176, 189, 191.
21 Chris Stephen and Emir Suljagic, 'Milosevic linked directly to war crimes', *Tribunal Update*, No. 310, 2 May 2003.
22 Cf. LeBor, *Milosevic*, p. 175.
23 See for example Norman Cigar, 'The Serbo–Croatian War, 1991', in Stjepan G. Mestrovic (ed.), *Genocide After Emotion: The Postemotional Balkan War*, New York: Routledge, 1996, pp. 68–9 and Norman Cigar, 'Serb War Effort and Termination of the War', in Branka Magas and Ivo Zanic (eds), *The War in Croatia and Bosnia-Herzegovina, 1991–1995*, London: Frank Cass, 2001, p. 212.
24 Nenad Pejic, 'Medien und Krieg in Jugoslawien', *Europaeische Rundschau*, 4 (Herbst 1992), pp. 57–65, p. 60.
25 David Rieff, *Slaughterhouse: Bosnia and the Failure of the West*, London: Vintage, 1995, p. 157.
26 Florence Hartmann, *Milosevic: La diagonale du fou*, Paris: Denoël, 1999, p. 199.
27 Blom and Romijn, *Srebrenica*, pp. 533, 535 and 550.
28 Kalyvas, '"New" and "Old" Civil Wars', p. 105 notes that warlords are state-builders.
29 'His Master's Voice', *Bosnia Report*, January–March 1999.
30 Hartmann, *Miloševic*, p. 175; Javier Perez de Cuellar, *Pilgrimage for Peace: A Secretary-General's Memoir*, Basingstoke: Macmillan, 1997, p. 483.
31 Hartmann, *Miloševic*, p. 126. Steven L. Burg and Paul Shoup, *The War in Bosnia-Herzegovina: Ethnic Conflict and International Intervention*, Armonk, NY: M. E. Sharpe, 1999, p. 82; Erich Rathfelder, *Sarajevo und danach: Sechs Jahre Reporter im ehemaligen Jugoslawien*, München: 1998, p. 26; Norman Cigar, *Genocide in Bosnia: The Policy of 'Ethnic Cleansing'*, College Station: Texas A & M University Press, 1995, pp. 39– 40, W. Zimmerman, *Origins*, p. 179; and Davor Butkovic, 'Mesic: I drugi su hrvatski politièari svjedoèili pred istra_iteljima Suda u Haagu!', *Globus*, 16 May 1997, pp. 15–16.
32 Blom and Romijn, *Srebrenica*, pp. 1016–21.
33 Examples in Blom and Romijn, *Srebrenica*, p. 418.
34 Ibid., pp. 123–4.
35 Jovic, *Dani, passim*; Kadijevic, *View*, p. 145; and Norman Cigar, 'Serb War Effort and Termination of the War', pp. 201–2.
36 Borisav Jovic, *Poslednji dani SFRJ*, Beograd: Politika, 1996, pp. 349 and 389; and Dobrila Gajic Glisic, *Srpska Vojska: Iz Kabineta Ministra Vojnog*, pp. l. s.a., 28, 41, 80, 84, 85, 90 and 92.
37 Blom and Romijn, *Srebrenica*, pp. 274–5.
38 Ibid., p. 380.
39 Ibid., pp. 260–4.
40 Ibid., *Srebrenica*, p. 908.
41 *Wall Street Journal*, 28 May 1992, p. A10, quoted in Thomas Cushman and Stjepan G. Meštrovic, 'Introduction', in Thomas Cushman and Stjepan G. Mestrovic (eds), *This Time We Knew: Western Responses to Genocide in Bosnia*, New York: New York University Press, 1996, p. 9.
42 John Allcock, *Explaining Yugoslavia*, London: Hurst and Co., 2000, pp. 381–4 and Mark Mazower, *The Balkans: A Short History*, New York: Modern Library, 2000, pp. 148–9.
43 Anthony Loyd, *My War Gone By: I Miss It So*, London: Anchor, 2000, p. 141.
44 Peter Maass, *Love Thy Neighbor: A Story of War*, New York: Alfred Knopf, 1997, p. 150.
45 Blom and Romijn, *Srebrenica*, p. 612.

46 LeBor, *Milosevic*, p. 282.
47 Mirko Klarin, 'Comment: Milosevic and the Red Berets' and Chris Stephen, 'Courtside: Milosevic's trial', *IWPR's Tribunal Update*, No. 295 (6–10 January 2003).

References

Allcock, John, *Explaining Yugoslavia*, London: Hurst, 2000.

Blom, J. C. H. and P. Romijn, *Srebrenica. Een 'veilig' gebied. Reconstructie, achtergronden, gevolgen en analyses van de val van een Safe Area*, Amsterdam: The Netherlands Institute for War Documentation, 2002.

Burg, Steven L. and Paul Shoup, *The War in Bosnia-Herzegovina: Ethnic Conflict and International Intervention*, Armonk, New York: M. E. Sharpe, 1999.

Cigar, Norman, 'Serb War Effort and Termination of the War', in Branka Magas and Ivo Zanic (eds), *The War in Croatia and Bosnia-Herzegovina, 1991–1995*, London: Frank Cass, 2001.

——'The Serbo–Croatian War, 1991', in Stjepan G. Mestrovic (ed.), *Genocide After Emotion: The Postemotional Balkan War*, New York: Routledge, 1996.

——*Genocide in Bosnia: The Policy of 'Ethnic Cleansing'*, College Station: Texas A & M University Press, 1996.

Cohen, Lenard J., *Serpent in the Bosom: The Rise and Fall of Slobodan Milosevic*, Boulder, Colorado: Westview, 2001.

Cohen, Roger, *Hearts Grown Brutal: Sagas of Sarajevo*, New York: Random, 1998.

Cushman, Thomas and Stjepan G. Mestrovic (eds), *This Time We Knew: Western Responses to Genocide in Bosnia*, New York: New York University Press, 1996.

Doder, Duško and Louise Branson, *Milosevic: Portrait of a Tyrant*, New York: Free Press, 1996.

Donia, Robert J. and John V. A. Fine, *Bosnia and Hercegovina: A Tradition Betrayed*, 2nd edn, London: Hurst, 1997.

Glisic, Dobrila Gajic, *Srpska Vojska: Iz Kabineta Ministra Vojnog*.

Hartmann, Florence, *Milosevic: La diagonale du fou*, Paris: Denoël, 1999.

Jovic, Borisav, *Poslednji dani SFRJ*, Beograd: Politika, 1996.

Kaldor, Mary (ed.), *Global Insecurity. Restructuring the Global Military Sector, Volume III*, London: Pinter, 2000.

——*New and Old Wars: Organized Violence in a Global Era*, Cambridge: Polity Press, 2000.

Kalyvas, Stathis N., '"New" and "Old" Civil Wars. A Valid Distinction?', *World Politics*, 54, 1 (2001), pp. 99–118.

Klarin, Mirko, 'Comment: Milosevic and the Red Berets', *IWPR's Tribunal Update*, No. 295 (6–10 January 2003).

LeBor, Adam, *Milosevic: A Biography*, London: Simon & Schuster, 2002.

Loyd, Anthony, *My War Gone By: I Miss It So*. London: Anchor, 2000.

Maass, Peter, *Love Thy Neighbor: A Story of War*, New York: Alfred Knopf, 1997.

Mazower, Mark, *The Balkans: A Short History*, New York: Modern Library, 2000.

Merton, Robert K., *On Theoretical Sociology: Five Essays, Old and New*, New York: Free Press, 1967.

Pejic, Nenad, 'Medien und Krieg in Jugoslawien', *Europaeische Rundschau*, No. 4 (1992), pp. 57–65.

Perez de Cuellar, Javier, *Pilgrimage for Peace: A Secretary-General's Memoir*, Basingstoke: Macmillan, 1997.

Rathfelder, Erich, *Sarajevo und danach: Sechs Jahre Reporter im ehemaligen Jugoslawien*, Munich, Germany: C. H. Beck, 1998.

Rieff, David, *Slaughterhouse: Bosnia and the Failure of the West*, London: Vintage, 1995.

Stephen, Chris and Emir Suljagic, 'Milosevic linked directly to war crimes', *IWPR's Tribunal Update*, No. 310 (2 May 2003).

Stephen, Chris, 'Courtside: Milosevic's trial', *IWPR's Tribunal Update*, No. 295 (6–10 January 2003).

Zimmermann, Warren, *Origins of a Catastrophe: Yugoslavia and its Destroyers*, rev. edn, New York: Times Books, 1999.

8

INTERNATIONAL OPERATIONS TO CONTAIN VIOLENCE IN A COMPLEX EMERGENCY

John Mackinlay*

Western armed forces spent much of the 1990s disengaging themselves from the mental strait-jacket of peace-keeping doctrine and the thrall of writers who insisted on its rigid separation from other military operations.[1] Despite resistance to change, both the military contributors and the humanitarian organisations have gradually adapted themselves to a new strategic era. International responses have developed under pressure from a young field executive at the front lines of an altered conflict environment. By the end of the 1990s, Kosovo could be regarded as a benchmark in this development. Although the intervention in Kosovo was not a trouble-free operation, it demonstrated a degree of acceptance of the use of military force that would have been unimaginable at the beginning of the decade. It also represented a way of coping with stabilisation and a tacit framework for civil–military cooperation.[2]

Collectively, the international response had achieved containment. An operational structure began to emerge; the comparatively short stabilisation phase was followed by the scaling down of the campaign-capable elements of the military force, and the arrival of burden-sharing international structures began to create a long-term bureaucracy, which could last for several decades in the manner of a traditional peace-keeping garrison. But before military doctrine writers could institutionalise the lessons of the Kosovo campaign, Osama bin Laden's attacks on the United States pushed them across the threshold of another chapter of events. By demonstrating that an internationally organised insurgent force could reach out from a distant place and strike at the heart of the richest and most powerfully protected cities, bin Laden also torpedoed containment as a universally acceptable response. It was no longer enough to contain the problems of a conflict zone that sheltered a globally organised insurgent force; there was now an imperative to defeat and dismantle an adversarial structure that could survive and foster anarchy in weakened states. This turn of events was set to cause operational change and to move institutional thinking much more swiftly than the 10 years it took, doctrinally speaking, to get from Cambodia to Kosovo.[3] This chapter suggests that September 11 has compelled us to notice and react to developments that had been gradually altering our security for some time.

Defining the adversary

In the early 1990s, British doctrine formulaters were conspicuously vague about the nature of the adversary. In *Wider Peacekeeping*,[4] the authors suggested that there could be 'local armed opposition' and that this could be organised as 'numerous parties' who thrived in a general 'absence of law and order'.[5] However, in case these vague descriptions were used as a basis for training, the reader was also warned that 'guarding consent' was the key to success and that a force that took sides or acted in a confrontational manner was likely to find itself on the wrong side of the 'consent divide',[6] from where recovery would be impossible. Until 1996, commentators on military doctrine and academics continued to insist on the importance of separating peace-keeping from other military operations.[7] This frequently rehearsed discussion prevented international forces on the ground from seeing that they now had a much more active role to play.[8] In the circumstances of a complex emergency, they could not succeed if they continued to regard themselves as placatory umpires acting at the benign interface between disciplined military forces.[9] Their role required them to stabilise a violent area and restore a monopoly of power, placing it into the hands of an approved or elected government. In carrying out this task they faced an adversary. The failure to recognise this situation led to an imprecise definition of their real tasks, which was reinforced by the continued use of 'peace-doing' labels to describe a military activity that had less and less to do with traditional peace-keeping. Post Cold War contingencies were explained as peace-enforcement, peace-building, peace-making, and so forth, but in reality the military task of restoring a monopoly of violence in the crisis zone had more in common with the deeply unfashionable principles of counterinsurgency.[10] The military community was looking in the wrong direction for its sources of past experience.

This problem was additionally complicated by confusions of definition. In 1995 the UK Ministry of Defence defined insurgency as the

> actions of a minority group within a state who are intent on forcing political change by means of a mixture of subversion, propaganda and military pressure, aiming to persuade or intimidate the broad mass of people to accept such a change.[11]

This recognised the systemic nature of an insurgent movement, which required a similarly systemic counter-strategy. But in some failing states, this definition was already blurred by elements of the host government, which acted in the manner of insurgents, pillaging state resources and terrorising particular communities within the population. A greater problem arose from the confusion with terrorism; in the media the word 'terrorism' was being used synonymously with insurgency. However, in UK doctrine there was an important distinction; terrorism was the military tactic of the insurgent. 'Terrorism' therefore referred to the 'use of indiscriminate violence to intimidate the general majority of people in a state to accept the political changes advocated by the insurgents'.[12] Terrorism was merely the weapon or the tool of the insurgent; it was not a viable *modus operandi* on its own. Behind a successful terrorist there had to be an intelligence-gathering system, funding, a logistic organisation, and above all, political cells that were derived from a much wider supporting constituency within a population. Isolated extremist groups without a genuine political manifesto usually did not survive for long, but terrorist cells that could move and operate from within a larger insurgent organisation generally could, and therefore were extremely dangerous. By the mid 1990s, the effect of global change in the conflict areas was putting the existing definition of terrorism and insurgency under pressure. Although the world did not suddenly change on September 11, bin Laden forced us to see that the definitions had been widening for some time.

The globalisation of insurgency

In rich and safe countries, transport, communications, commercial trans-actions, and the flow of ideas and information had been proliferating for more than a hundred years.[13] But in poorer states these facilities were sparsely developed, and since the preceding colonial regimes, this condition had allowed governments to exercise control through monopoly. Only large and powerful organisations, usually authorised by the government, could reach the heart of the wilderness areas, move bulk cargoes, communicate internationally, and transfer large sums of money, allowing governments, which were otherwise weak and undemocratic, to control the population.

Global change upset this monopoly. Dispersed rural populations were concentrating in the urban areas.[14] Improvements in transport technology had produced cheaper 4 × 4 vehicles, which began to arrive through the retail market in the developing regions. Aid programmes reinforced their impact as instruments of change by building new road systems. A similar proliferation of options in communications,[15] the transfer of information, ideas and comercial activities effectively removed a weak government's controlling monopoly.

The concept of 'portable wealth' expanded from its narrower definition as gold, gemstones and drugs to include large cargoes. The small entrepreneur could now reach the wilderness areas with the same facility as the government,[16] remove these resources and trade them illegally on markets that avoided international trading regulations.[17]

The small entrepreneur was in many cases acting for the local war leader who held the territory that contained these vulnerable resources. Global change had altered the balance between weak governments and local forces that sought to overthrow them; weak governments became weaker and local insurgents stronger. In richer and more developed states, different kinds of techniques and tactics emerged by which the insurgent could take advantage of a new proliferation of communications; the image of a movement and the visibility of its actions became almost more important than its military impact. The propaganda value of the deed had become more significant than the deed itself. Millions of potential supporters could now recognise an insurgent leader and listen to his speeches without actually meeting him. Simultaneously, migration had spread poor and displaced communities into rich, safe states where employment and living conditions were more favourable. Using a proliferation of global systems, it was now possible to harness the insurgent energy of a population that was dispersed across several states. Within migrant communities, their frustrations, their sense of exclusion and feelings of outrage could be exploited, using the same communications that the host state enjoyed.

Different categories of insurgency

These developments expanded the definition of insurgency; it was no longer possible to see the widening variety of insurgent movements as variations on the same theme. There were now several kinds of insurgent forces. The distinctions between them were not so much a matter of their apparent intent as anarchists, egalitarians, traditionalists, pluralists, separatists, and preservationists but in their practical manifestation.[18] Their declared intentions were easily altered by day-to-day political expedient but their command structures, political organs, recruiting systems, and logistic infrastructure had taken years to develop and were a much surer measure of their real purpose.

Several distinct categories of insurgent forces had emerged.[19] *Lumpen forces*, which were a response to a weak-state environment, were horizontally organised and the command linkages between fighting units were fragile, encouraging disloyalty and opportunism among junior commanders. In a *Lumpen* force, individual fighters tended to be selfishly motivated and the units were militarily weak with a local operating range. *Clan forces* were in some respects similar to *Lumpen* forces, with the important distinction that their organisation was based on family groups that were related to a particular clan or tribe. This gave them a significant long-term survivability that dictated a different counter-strategy approach. *Popular* forces were a response to a stronger state in which the insurgent had less freedom of movement and required to be better organised. Popular forces had vertical structures and more developed international elements as well as an effective organ for mobilising political support. Individual followers were comparatively educated, motivated and formally trained as fighters.

A fourth category, the *global* force was supported by a very narrow sample of one case, the al-Qaeda. However, their significance was that the social conditions and prevailing sense of exclusion exploited by al-Qaeda could also be aroused and, using similar techniques, copied by other internationally dispersed communities. The global force was a virus that could flourish in a very modern culture. Although in some respects it was similar to the popular force, its revolutionary objectives were much wider than the overthrow of the regime of a particular state. Global insurgents were organised to survive in an international environment using supporting cells and communities in different countries. Militarily, the global insurgent had demonstrated an international reach and was emphasising a different tactic of insurgency that relied on the visibility of a deed rather than its practical consequences.

The manifestation of several distinct forms of insurgency was significant for the international peace interventions during the 1990s. In their efforts to protect themselves and promote a peace process, international forces had developed different operational approaches, which corresponded to the different type of insurgent force they encountered in the Balkans, sub-Saharan Africa, and Asia. By the end of the 1990s, the emergence of more potent forms of insurgency was set to challenge our acceptance of the *ad hoc* nature of containment operations.

Defining the containment strategy

By the time Kosovo had been stabilised, an increasingly familiar operational process (described below) drew together the principal actors of an emerging culture of military intervention, based largely on the NATO experience in the Balkans. This process could be identified as having two or three operational phases that occurred between the arrival of a military intervention force and its reaching a plateau of activity that indicated the start of a garrison phase. The following events or conditions distinguished each phase, although by no means all were manifested in every one of the contingencies that arose in the 1990s.

Phase 1: Intervention

Prior to the deployment of ground forces:

- Steering group or contact group of nations puts pressure on warring parties in a potential or active conflict zone by sanctions and threatening action.

- International forces achieve military superiority in the conflict area by use of conventional forces, including warships and combat aircraft.
- Warring parties make outward show of accepting the concept of a peace process at a signing ceremony.

On deployment of ground forces:

- International military forces move tactically into the conflict area. Immediate tasks: establish security, restore law and order, assist humanitarian survival, and restore basic civil amenities.
- Operational area at this stage is under military control.

Phase 2: Stabilisation

- Initially there is not an effective nucleus or presence of humanitarian agencies, or a viable level of development funding.
- The international military force makes efforts to restore shelter and amenities for the civil community, using short-term funds supplied directly by individual governments to their respective national contingents.[20]
- The international forces move to suppress overt armed resistance to the peace process; consequently armed resistance re-organises to a covert structure.
- Results of consolidated appeal by humanitarian agencies and bilateral funds begin to reach the conflict area.
- Effective humanitarian presence increases.
- The military scales back presence from the humanitarian sphere of responsibility.
- The international military forces reduce their campaign-capable element.

Phase 3: Garrisoning the conflict zone

- Arrival and establishment of UN and regional organisations, which organise and supervise trustee governance, law and order, development, economic recovery, etc.
- Military commander relinquishes all previous influence over and control of non-military activities.
- Establishment of the High Representative of the authorising power.
- Civil agencies carry out peace-building and nation-building programmes.
- Some military units focus on what amount to counter-insurgency tasks.

This approximate model does not seek to depict the circumstances of a particular operation. Instead, it merely serves as a basis from which to illustrate the nature of the containment strategy that emerged from that period.

After September 11

The attacks on the United States on September 11 2001 diminished the significance of Kosovo as a milestone in our doctrinal development. In its response, the US efforts went beyond containment and moved the intervention community, if such a thing existed, across the threshold of a new chapter of operations. The September 11 attack served to reduce, or remove altogether, the comfort of distance and the perception of a safety curtain around the rich, safe countries, which habitually responded to complex emergencies and the hostile forces at their epicentre. The emerging operational model that represented the success of the Kosovo genre was jeopardised by the demonstrated capability of an insurgent force based outside the United States, to mount a devastating attack on its most protected cities. Western nations, their financial centres, travel facilities, culture, and institutions were directly threatened. This increased their resolve to contribute armed forces in a more committed and interventionist way towards a collective solution.

To be fair, it was unlikely that, faced with the suddenly altered template represented by Afghanistan, the allied leaders and their forces would immediately arrive at the correct long-term solution. Understandably, the intervention developed in an *ad hoc* manner. Initially, the sequence of events followed the familiar routines of a containment approach: political pressure, bombing campaign and a tactical build-up that led to military efforts to dominate the area. A large and apparently inexperienced international media contingent enthusiastically reported the bombing and then the tactical arrival in Kabul. Nevertheless, the Taliban and al-Qaeda were not effectively crushed and the list of wanted figures was not significantly reduced.

However, in the first few months after the arrival of the military forces, several events and characteristics distinguished what has happened in Afghanistan from the 1990s or Kosovo model of containment. Two differently constituted military forces, with separate tactical missions, co-existed in the same space: the International Security Assistance Force maintaining security in the Kabul urban areas, and under a separate commanding authority and as a separate entity, the mainly US/UK troops campaigning to destroy the Taliban and al-Qaeda in a wider area of interest that extended over the north-west frontier provinces of Pakistan and northward into Kashmir. The major element of the latter force was directed at a higher level from a national HQ in the United States. In the stabilising phase, its main aim was not just to contain the opposing forces but to destroy them and dismantle their organisation. To achieve this, the campaigning element comprised a greater proportion of combat troops and special forces, who were more powerfully supported by combat aircraft, mortars and artillery. There were also developed structures for gathering intelligence, including the uninhibited but not always effective use of human intelligence, deep patrolling, and elaborate arrangements for prisoner screening and long-term interrogation.

After the initial euphoria evaporated, there were operational disappointments arising from a lack of awareness by both the press and defence public relations officials on the real nature of the military task.[21] The constant references to 'terrorism' and the 'war on terrorism' had focused public expectations on an unlikely outcome. 'Terrorism' implied a narrowly military counter-activity, but al-Qaeda was more than a terrorist organisation.

Conceptual failure

By continually using the wrong definition, both the military and their commentators had failed to see or acknowledge bin Laden's real strengths and the nature of his organisation. Since the late 1980s, he had created an insurgent movement and a cellular structure that extended to over 63 different countries.[22] The cells were supported by an array of dispersed, dispossessed, displaced, and migrant populations that numbered in millions. The visible al-Qaeda units in Afghanistan were the lesser part of the problem; it was the invisible cells across the world that immediately threatened Western lifestyles. Al-Qaeda was more than a superficial network of terrorist squads; it was a globally dispersed insurgent movement with well-developed commercial, logistic, intelligence gathering, public relations, and political as well as ideological elements.[23] It could not be removed by a military expedition or the narrowly forceful techniques implied by talk of counter-terrorism or a 'war on terrorism'.

Stamping out al-Qaeda required a more systemic approach that would have to be politically led and driven by something more sophisticated than a desire for military retribution. In the rush to claim, explain and re-label the al-Qaeda phenomenon, commentators and even the military staff itself had abandoned some hard-won lessons. Nevertheless, despite the novelty of al-Qaeda's international dimension, Western tenets of counter-insurgency were still valid.

Contrary to the expectation of the public-relations machinery, a counter-insurgency campaign would be a very slow moving affair, which might require many thousands of man-hours of patrolling and intelligence gathering for one short contact with the enemy. But more than that it required a sophisticated political policy at the highest level that could separate the insurgents from their supporting constituency. It was useless just to offer vast financial rewards for information leading to the capture or death of wanted al-Qaeda men if the populations that sheltered them were resolutely opposed to the culture that stood for a 'war on terrorism'. The main effort could not be invested in a military manhunt across the Afghanistan foothills; it had to be a bigger political campaign to secure the support, the hearts and minds, of the al-Qaeda diaspora. Bin Laden's supporters could only be reached and possibly subverted by a coordinated campaign that drew together all the elements of the international response; politically, they might respond to better living conditions and having the self-esteem that arose from possessing a place in the world. If this was also part of bin Laden's manifesto, the political counter-strategy would be to wrest these banners from the insurgent and adopt them in a different form.

Beyond the Afghan crisis zone, the United States led the effort to track down and destroy the wider, global dimension of al-Qaeda's organisation. The scrutiny of illegal traffic in weapons, drugs and human beings intensified. Military assistance missions were despatched to several states that were potential refuges for al-Qaeda including Sudan, Yemen, the Philippines and Indonesia. Around the world the movement of shipping and private aircraft was monitored more closely and satellite-imagery was remonopolised for a while by the United States.[24] Electronic communications were screened and intercepted, and where possible, transfers of money tracked and audited. Migration was more carefully watched and the unregulated or unlawful movement of individuals, communities and populations across borders became a higher priority for intelligence units. The organisation and deployment of these efforts have given the United States, as the framework-providing nation, an unusually powerful influence over the management of the intervention into Afghanistan.

Although September 11 had energised the speed and military intensity of the United States/Western response to this particular contingency, no distinguishable pattern has yet emerged that could become a model for future operations. The international dimension of the Western response had an incremental, *ad hoc* character; it was a reactive array of isolated activities, not a coherent political offensive. There was nevertheless an irresistible motive for making every effort to defeat al-Qaeda.

Improving the intervention model

The success of international reactions to al-Qaeda has been patchy. This is a reasonable expectation, given the suddenness of the need to find a new approach and the previously low level of international cooperation from which a response had to be developed. But the imperative to remedy the lack of international cooperation in emergencies is now stronger and will be further strengthened, not diminished, by each new outrage against the West. Therefore, in the event that September 11 proves to be a significant milestone in the improvement of the international response, what important elements of success may emerge in a new regime of intensive commitment?

The response to a complex emergency, in which the crisis area is threatened by a popular or global insurgency, will need to have three defined elements: the military intervention forces; the civil agencies in the crisis zone; and the civil and military elements acting against the insurgent movement's international dimension. A successful campaign to restore the crisis area and completely disarm and dismantle the insurgent units, which lie at the heart of the problem, will require the following steps.

First, one must have a better definition of the adversary. A complex emergency arises from several different strands of degeneration that coalesce over a long period to transform a state or sub-region into a humanitarian disaster area. The insurgent movement, which may be established at the epicentre of the crisis zone, is just one of these destructive strands but it is also likely to be a key to the long-term solution. For without first of all achieving a degree of personal security, the local population may not benefit from development or governmental reform. The process of defining the security problem and in particular the nature of the opposition to the peace process or restoration of a monopoly of violence to the government, also defines the nature of the response. It may be necessary to confront and even to destroy the opposing insurgent movement; conversely, the insurgents may become the nucleus of a future government after the election. In both cases it is important to identify the constituents of the insurgent movement, the degree of their popularity and the extent to which they are internationally established. The clear identification of these factors will precede and shape a successful international response.

Second, a politically driven counter-strategy needs to be developed. No insurgent movement has ever been defeated solely by the military techniques that are implied by 'counter-terrorist' operations. A military counter-strategy must be preceded and led by a coherent political campaign plan. One of its key objectives is to isolate the active cells of the insurgent movement from their supporting constituency.

Third, the number of independent actors in the operational area should be reduced. The international response to a complex emergency has been inherently unmanageable because it has too many independently moving parts that are controlled from beyond the crisis area by different interests. After September 11, it should be in the hands of a single nation or small group of nations, to control and reduce the number of individual participants.

Fourth, a strategic directorate needs to be created. At the highest coordinating level, possibly in a single location beyond region of the crisis, a strategic directorate is required to integrate the efforts of the three elements of the response.

Fifth, a director of operations needs to be established. The director of operations in the operational area will control both the international military force and the civil agencies. With greater authority vested in this post, it will at last be possible to overcome the distant influence of the UN 'barons' in Geneva and New York, as well as the nationally motivated defence ministry officials, and create a unity of purpose that is the pre-requisite for success.

Sixth, the international dimension of operations needs to be integrated with the operational level. Where the opposing insurgent forces have a developed international supporting structure, the responding nations will require a commensurately organised international dimension to their operations. This will include the control, monitoring and sharing of: domestic intelligence; migration of communities; movement of cargoes, personnel, ships and private aircraft; currency, commercial transactions and banking information; electronic communications as well as the ongoing countermeasures for drugs, weapons, etc. These diverse activities need to be integrated at every level and centrally controlled by a single strategic directorate.

In the current climate of poor international and interagency cooperation, these suggestions will seem optimistic, overly centralised and over-controlling. But it is worth pointing out that they contain very little that is essentially new. The concept of a director of operations to control the military, the police and the civil elements in a campaign to restore internal security was developed and successfully used in the 1950s. Embryonic versions of strategic and operational level directorates, and the desire to have fewer actors in the operational area, are already in the public domain. In the past, what has been lacking is the international commitment to put it all together. For better or for worse, September 11 may now provide the missing ingredient.

Notes

* This paper is derived from two larger studies by the same author: *Globalisation and Insurgency*, Adelphi Paper No. 352, New York: International Institute of Strategic Studies, 2002 and 'Opposing Insurgents During Peace Operations' *International Peacekeeping*, Special Issue, Thierry Tardy (ed.), *Peace Operations in World Politics after September 11th* (forthcoming).

1 For example: Alan James, 'Internal Peacekeeping' in David Charters (ed.), *Peace-keeping and the Challenges of Civil Conflict Resolution*, Federicton, New Brunswick: Centre for Conflict Studies, University of New Brunswick, 1994; Charles Dobbie, 'A Concept for Post-Cold War Peacekeeping', *Survival*, 36, 3 (1996), p. 123; and Allen Mallinson, 'No Middle Ground for United Nations', *Jane's Defence Weekly*, 21 (14 May 1994). Colonel Mallinson was, at the time, a British staff officer closely involved in the development of a doctrinal response to the post Cold War contingencies.

2 This growing sense of a community is well represented in the record of the 2000 Copenhagen CIMIC Conference: Peter Viggo Jakobsen (ed.), *CIMIC: Civil–Military Co-operation* and the DUPI Report, No. 9 *Lessons Learned and Models for the Future*, Copenhagen: Danish Institute of International Affairs, 2000.

3 Referring to the structures of the UN Transitional Authority in Cambodia UNTAC. See United Nations, *Blue Helmets: A Review of UN Peacekeeping*, 3rd edn, New York: UN Department of Public Information, 1996.

4 UK MoD, *Wider Peacekeeping*, London: HMSO, 1994.

5 Ibid., page 1-7 under 'Characteristics'.

6 Ibid., page 2-12 under 'The Consequences of Crossing the Consent Divide'.

7 After 1996, the publication of 'Peace Support Operations' (see note 5) began to acknowledge a more flexible response to 'grey area' operations.

8 A clash of views took place between authors who represented the Wider Peace-keeping version of doctrine development (see note 1 above and Charles Dobbie,

the principal writer of Wider Peace-keeping) and authors such as Richard Connaughton, 'Time to Clear the Doctrinal Dilemma', *Jane's Defence Weekly*, 21 (9 April 1994), pp. 19–20. For a contemporary account, see also Christopher Bellamy, *Knights in White Armour*, London: Pimlico, 1996, pp. 150–70, especially the section 'A Clash of Doctrines'.

9 The image of the peace-keeper as a referee was reinforced in official doctrine, see UK MoD, *Wider Peacekeeping*, pp. 2–8, paragraph 15: 'The Importance of Impartiality'.

10 UK MoD, Chief of General Staff, 'Counter Insurgency Operations', in Army Field Manual Vol. 5: *Operations Other than War*, Army Code 71596 London: MoD, 1995, Chapter 3 'Principles'.

11 UK MoD, Army Field Manual Vol. 5: *Operations Other than War*, p. 1-1.

12 Ibid., p. 3-4.

13 David Harvey shows that improving the speed of ships and land transport had been compressing the world since 1850. David Harvey, *Conditions of Post Modernity*, Oxford: Blackwell, 1989, cited in Ed Hoogvelt, *Globalisation and the Post Colonial World*, 2nd edn, London: Palgrave, 2001.

14 For example, see an account in UNDP East Africa, *Somalia: Human Development Report 2001*, New York: UNDP, 2001, p. 58.

15 Frances Cairncross, *The Death of Distance 2.0: How the Communications Revolution will Change our Lives*, London: TEXERE Publishing, 2001.

16 In a Maoist insurgency, the wilderness areas referred to an extensive refuge where an insurgent could survive in a space so wild that the technical and numerical advantages of the government forces were greatly reduced and combat would therefore be on the insurgent's terms.

17 The genre of literature that explains this process is represented by David Keen, *The Economic Functions of Civil Wars*, Adelphi Paper No. 320, New York: International Institute of Strategic Studies, 1998, and the contributions in Mats Berdal and David Malone (eds), *Greed and Grievance: Economic Agendas in Civil Wars*, Boulder, CO: Lynne Rienner, 2000.

18 Christopher Clapham, 'Analysing African Insurgencies', in Christopher Clapham (ed.), *African Guerrillas*, Oxford: James Currey, 1998, pp. 6–7 and UK MoD, Army Field Manual Vol. 5: *Operations Other than War*, p. 1-4 and p. 1-5.

19 The discussion and analysis of the four categories of insurgent forces is derived from Mackinlay, *Globalisation and Insurgency*.

20 In an unpublished study by the Centre for Defence Studies, King's College, London (for UK MoD in 2000), it was found that government funds were used to finance the initial restoring efforts of their incoming military contingents on their arrival in Bosnia and Kosovo (US, UK and the Netherlands, for example).

21 UK Royal Marines' initial 'search and destroy' operations in May 2002 failed to make any significant finds, as might have been anticipated by an elementary knowledge of counter-insurgency operations. However, an inexperienced and impatient press corps was wrongly led to expect more exciting results by equally inept Whitehall briefers. The result: a rancorous denunciation of the operational plan and the Royal Marine ethos.

22 When the Afghan campaign ended, al-Qaeda's recruiting and manpower-organising machinery went into reverse cycle to disperse up to 22,000 surviving mujahidin veterans back to their countries of origin. The destinations of the majority of the fighters were: Saudi Arabia – 5000; Yemen – 3000; Egypt – 2000; Algeria – 2800; Tunisia – 400; Iraq – 370; Libya – 200; and a balance dispersed to Jordan, United Arab Emirates, Sudan, Lebanon, Syria, and to Western countries. The estimated total is between 15,000–22,000. See Adam Robinson, *Bin Laden:*

Behind the Mask of the Terrorist, Edinburgh: Mainstream Publishing, 2001, pp. 113–14.

23 Until 2001, Bin Laden controlled his forces in the manner of a corporate chief executive. His command system worked best when it was concentrated in one safe base. His management technique was to delegate into functional areas. These operated individually and could also be separated in space, but their most successful manifestations have been in Jeddah, Sudan and Afghanistan, when he could locate them together and move easily between them in a coordinating role. His chief functional areas were financial operations, military operations, media and information policy, legal/religious policy, and political policy. He also had a highly effective travel and movements department. See *Oxford Analytica*, 16 January 2002, pp. 1–3 and Robinson, *Bin Laden: Behind the Mask*, p. 203.

24 Bhupendra Jasani, 'Orbiting Spies: Opportunities and Challenges', *Space Policy*, 18 (2002), pp. 9–13.

References

Bellamy, Christopher, *Knights in White Armour*, London: Pimlico, 1996.

Berdal, Mats and David Malone (eds), *Greed and Grievance: Economic Agendas in Civil Wars*. Boulder, CO: Lynne Rienner, 2000.

Cairncross, Frances, *The Death of Distance 2.0: How the Communications Revolution Will Change Our Lives*, London: TEXERE Publishing, 2001.

Clapham, Christopher, 'Introduction: Analysing African Insurgencies', in Christopher Clapham (ed.), *African Guerrillas*, Oxford: James Currey, 1998, pp. 1–18.

Connaughton, Richard, 'Time to Clear the Doctrinal Dilemma', *Jane's Defence Weekly*, 9 April 1994.

Dobbie, Charles, 'A Concept for Post-Cold War Peacekeeping', *Survival*, 36, 3 (1996), pp. 121–48.

DUPI, *Lessons Learned and Models for the Future*, DUPI Report, No. 9, Copenhagen: Danish Institute of International Affairs, 2000.

Hoogvelt, Ed, *Globalisation and the Post Colonial World*, 2nd edn, London: Palgrave, 2001.

James, Alan, 'Internal Peacekeeping', in David Charters (ed.), *Peacekeeping and the Challenges of Civil Conflict Resolution*, Federicton, New Brunswick: Centre for Conflict Studies, University of New Brunswick, 1994, pp. 3–24.

Jasani, Bhupendra, 'Orbiting Spies: Opportunities and Challenges', *Space Policy*, 18, 1 (2002), pp. 9–13.

Keen, David, *The Economic Functions of Civil Wars*, Adelphi Paper No. 320, New York: International Institute of Strategic Studies, 1998.

Mackinlay, John, 'Opposing Insurgents during Peace Operations', *International Peacekeeping 2003*, Special Issue, Thierry Tardy (ed.), *Peace Operations in World Politics after September 11th*.

—— *Globalisation and Insurgency*, Adelphi Paper No. 352, New York: International Institute of Strategic Studies, 2002.

Mallinson, Allen, 'No Middle Ground for United Nations', *Jane's Defence Weekly*, 14 May 1994.

Robinson, Adam, *Bin Laden: Behind the Mask of the Terrorist*, Edinburgh: Mainstream Publishing, 2001.

UNDP East Africa, *Somalia: Human Development Report 2001*, New York: UNDP, 2001.

United Kingdom MoD, *Wider Peacekeeping*, London: HMSO, 1994.

——Chief of General Staff, *Army Field Manual Vol. 5: Operations Other than War*, Army Code 71596. London: MoD, 1995.

United Nations, *Blue Helmets: A Review of UN Peacekeeping*, 3rd edn, New York: UN Department of Public Information, 1996.

9

THEORIES OF
GLOBALISATION AND
SUB-STATE CONFLICT

Paul B. Rich

In this chapter I will be examining the extensive debate on globalisation in International Relations (IR) and its relevance to analysis of conflicts beneath the level of the state, including state breakdown and 'state failure'. In the first part I shall address some of the main features of the globalisation debate and the degree to which globalisation appears to be eclipsing both the state and state sovereignty in the international system. I shall then proceed in the second part to discuss the nature of sub-state conflict explanations for the intensification of ethnic, religious and insurgent conflict in the period since the end of the Cold War. This is then followed by a discussion of the new and distinct form of military challenge presented by the international terrorist movement al-Qaeda, while in the final part I shall attempt to show that the theory of globalisation provides only a weak level of explanation for conflict at the sub-state level, and that a far more robust theoretical explanation lies in the concept of 'non-trinitarian warfare' and its detailed application to the terrains of state fragmentation and breakdown.

The debate over globalisation

Globalisation, which can be defined after Charles Oman as 'the growth, or more precisely the accelerated growth, of economic activity that spans politically defined national and regional boundaries'[1] has been used to explain a variety of processes at work in the international system, though for some critics its all-encompassing nature suggests that its level of explanatory power may be rather limited. As both a term and a pattern of intellectual discourse, globalisation increasingly entered the arena of debate in IR in the course of the 1990s. For some IR theorists, the term promised a new series of analytical avenues, marked by a strong sense of an emergent triumphalism of Western liberal democratic values at the end of the Cold War. In some respects this echoed wider public discussion over the 'end of history' in the early 1990s, for the post Cold War order appeared to be defined by a declining level of ideological conflict as Western liberalism emerged without any serious ideological challenge following the demise of Marxism.[2]

For some IR theorists globalisation also promised to offer a new theory of historical progress away from the nation state towards various forms of supranational modes of governance. By the early 1990s the narrow theory debate within IR between neorealists and neoliberals appeared tired and overwhelmingly dominated by US strategic concerns and interests. 'Interdependence' as an analytical concept appeared to have run its course and to offer few fresh analytical insights. By contrast, 'globalisation' appeared to offer a new discursive terrain for debating both power relations and ideological conflicts in an international arena in which socialist critiques of capitalism appeared to have run out of steam.[3]

The globalisation concept also came at a time when there was an analytical impasse as far as studies of developing societies were concerned. The 1970s debate on development versus underdevelopment and hopes of a New International Economic Order had failed to come to fruition. Development Theory had always had only a slender intellectual impact on IR as a discipline, especially during the Cold War period when the dominant conception of security was anchored in state-centric realist theories of self-interest and power projection. The 1980s proved to be a decade of the triumph of market-led economics and attention tended to turn towards more political avenues as the 'third wave' of democratisation opened up a number of formerly authoritarian regimes to varying processes of democratic rule.

Some critics on the left have begun to doubt the basic democratic credentials of the globalisation concept. Andreas Novy, for instance, has argued in the context of Brazilian economic and political transformation in the 1990s that globalisation is a 'discursive strategy' that limits the number of winners and facilitates the establishment of an anti-democratic elitist social order, as it separates power from the state and offers no political arena for resistance to the impact of market-led economics.[4] 'Globalisation' has become for many activists a term of political opprobrium, signifying a narrow Western domination of the global economy and free reign for multinational companies to exploit.

Nevertheless, the debate over globalisation has been important for the way it has opened up one of the central concepts of realism in IR – the state – to closer scrutiny in the international context. The mainstream of IR was initially rather resistant to the concept and built walls around the functioning of the internal structures of the state. The domestic realm remained a separate sphere for neorealist conceptions of the state as this had been defined by Kenneth Waltz in the late 1970s, although it was these internal dynamics that were eventually to lead to the demise of the Soviet Union and the ending of the Cold War – a process which most neorealist scholars in IR were embarrassingly unable to predict.[5]

The theory of globalisation thus seriously exposed what Ian Clark has termed the 'Great Divide' in IR, based on the belief that 'for analytical purposes, we can pretend that there are two separate spheres of political action, the domestic and the international'.[6] For Clark, this divide may not be unbridgeable when globalisation theory conceptualises the state as having some degree of political autonomy. If the state is seen as entirely defined by the external forces of globalisation, then this effectively ends up with an alternative structuralism to that of the neorealists, with the difference being that the defining dynamic is now economic rather than one based on anarchy and power. Clark challenged the rather simplistic economic liberalism at the core of the globalisation thesis of the early 1990s with a rather more sophisticated conception of a positive-sum relationship between the state and globalisation. Instead of a zero-sum relationship, whereby the advance of globalisation ensures a progressive retreat of the state, a positive-sum relationship means that globalisation and the reconstitution of the state occur in tandem.

Such an approach, argues Clark, avoids a 'mechanistic, timeless and depoliticised account of globalization'.[7] It means that, in contrast to the arguments of Novy and others, a developing state need not be entirely at the mercy of external globalising forces, but rather can act as:

> the broker of globalization, a key player in determining whether the costs of international disciplines should be borne domestically (e.g. nineteenth-century free trade and the gold standard) or the costs of domestic disturbance should be borne by the overthrow of international regulation (e.g. in the 1930s).[8]

This argument in relation to globalisation echoes work of scholars such as Linda Weiss, who has argued that economic liberalism, along with Marxist critics of globalisation, have done much to create a myth of state powerlessness, though outside the Anglo-Saxon world models of capitalist industrialisation such as those of Japan and the Asian Tigers suggest that the state can perform a critical strategic role and indeed act as the 'midwife' of globalisation.[9]

This re-centring of globalisation in relation to the state separates out what might be termed a mainstream globalisation theory that incorporates the state from what James Mayall has called the 'hyper globalisers', whose faith in advancing global capitalism (like that of Marx in communism) ensures the eventual withering away of the state.[10] This approach also opens up globalisation to a wider debate on international political transformation and the progressive emergence of an 'international civil society'. For some theorists, this process has the capacity over time to drive states in an increasingly democratic direction, as well as equipping them with the mechanisms to constrain the unhampered economic forces unleashed by global capitalism. In part this argument stems from the political transformation in Eastern Europe at the end of the Cold War. Even if the democratic revolutions in Eastern Europe had overthrown systems of state socialism and moved towards various forms of private enterprise, they had at least been revolutions of a kind that might in time spread on a global basis.

For what might be termed the radical school of globalisation theorists, therefore, globalisation contains at least the potential to advance forces of democratisation, which in turn, can strengthen – not weaken – the state. Martin Shaw, for example, has suggested that the post Cold War pattern of democratisation is likely to be different to previous patterns after 1945, where superpower conflict and ideological rivalry intervened to destabilise nascent democratic structures. Popular democratic movements lead to a regrouping of political elites and appeal less to nationalist identities than to universal standards of democracy that have become increasingly understood at the popular level. Moreover, this sort of democratic revolution can lead to the enhancement of the state, as it secures a new base of political legitimacy. Small states, though, will still need continuing international support if they are to remain viable.[11]

However, this body of theory has little to say on the increasing numbers of developing states that in the course of the 1990s underwent severe internal political crisis and, in some cases, actual collapse. The spectacle of state collapse in Somalia following the flight of the former dictator Siad Barre and the intervention of a UN force dramatically exemplified this process and brought it to global attention in 1993 as US special forces engaged in a bloody firefight with the followers of the warlord Mohammed Aidid in Mogadishu – a spectacle now brought to the big screen with the film *Black Hawk Down*.[12] State collapse as a result of severe ethnic or religious tension has been a major feature of international politics in the period since 1991, leading to various forms of low-level military conflict, which have been extremely costly in terms of lives lost and property destroyed.

This was not part of the original globalisation thesis, which was premised upon the advancing integration of states into a single global economy. Instead, it appears to represent a variety of forms of resistance to globalisation, as resort is made to military methods to sustain local interests in a manner that the original globalisers had not thought possible.

The reasons for the inability of globalisation theory to explain violent sub-state conflict are in part a reflection of the intellectual roots of globalisation. As a theory it is really a modern restatement of older forms of liberal discourse. From its very roots in the nineteenth century, European liberalism has had only a poor understanding of warfare and its origins, seeing it largely within a paradigm of militarism. In the Anglo-Saxon world at least, this stood for the decisive influence of the military on civilian government and the negative image of all that nineteenth-century liberals held dear in terms of the progressive expansion of representative government.[13] As we have already seen, liberal internationalists shared with Marxists a disdain for the state and looked to the market as a means for the release of human entrepreneurial and inventive capacities. States might have a role to play in securing order in societies and channelling potentially aggressive nationalist energies into more stable channels, but ultimately they represented a break on human progress since they were liable to be captured by backward-looking military and aristocratic elites, which could lead them into war with their rivals.

The international model that liberals would later look back to in the twentieth century was only really established in the latter half of the nineteenth century and was underpinned by force, especially in the colonial context. Ultimately this international order owed much to the hegemonic power and authority of Britain, the one 'superpower' of the epoch. Nevertheless, this order was buttressed by nascent international institutions, such as the Gold Standard regulated by the Bank of England, and liberals came increasingly to see this whole order as a natural phenomenon rather than one that was rooted in state power.[14]

The liberal era of globalisation in the second half of the nineteenth century was one pivoted around Cobdenite concepts of free trade as well as Clausewitzean ideas of rival sovereign states willing, on occasions, to project military force and go to war in order to pursue their political interests. It was only with the breakdown of this order in 1914, as two armed alliances resorted to four years of total industrialised warfare, that it became necessary to rethink the basis of international order.

After 1919, liberalism became anchored in Wilsonian ideas of internationalism as a means of transcending older balance of power ideas and moving the axis of international theory towards the idea of a nascent international society that would increasingly limit the power and authority of the sovereign nation state. This internationalism led to newer forms of international organisation (first the League of Nations and later, in a more qualified way, the United Nations) at the supra-state level to secure a new era of world peace. As the power vacuum in Central Europe in the 1930s exacerbated the drift towards war, many liberals abandoned the faith that their nineteenth-century forbears had had in the rights of small nation states. These came to be seen (in the late 1930s and 1940s at any rate) as troublesome entities, which could enhance nationalist passions and again foment war or intervention by larger and more aggressive states. It seemed far more significant to start trying to build larger political entities, if only at the regional level, to prevent the recurrence of inter-state war.[15]

The post 1945 era progressively undermined the utopianism of this inter-war liberal internationalism as the advancing rhetoric of colonial nationalism and the rights of colonised people to be free of European colonial rule once more ensured a drift towards the rights of small nations. It was in this climate that a huge number of new states gained entry into the UN from the 1950s to 1980s. Many gained little more than 'juridical' rather than 'empirical' statehood, as they secured independence through the impact of international political opinion rather than by force of arms. This in many cases left them weak and with little internal political legitimacy, in turn raising serious questions about whether it is actually possible in every instance to revive states that have collapsed.[16]

These are in essence the intellectual roots of the contemporary rhetoric of globalisation and it is not particularly surprising that it fails to understand or provide any really satisfactory means of explaining contemporary state breakdown and sub-state conflict in IR. In the next section we will look at theories of sub-state conflict and whether they can be in any way integrated into the mainstream globalisation theory, or whether they point towards an alternative body of theory to explain political behaviour at the international level.

Sub-state conflict and the decline of trinitarian war

Conflict beneath the state has significantly intensified in the period since the end of the Cold War. While this has only actually destroyed a handful of the world's 191 states, such as Angola, Somalia, Afghanistan, Zaire, and Sierra Leone, it has exposed a major weakness at the heart of the Westphalian model of the nation state. Numbers of states in the developing world lack anything more than 'juridical' sovereignty and can only sporadically impress their authority outside the capital and major towns. Many are threatened with a variety of ethnic and religiously-based secessionist movements, ensuring a basic disharmony between communities.

This outbreak of violent conflict at the sub-state level has prompted a number of analysts – who we shall term military revisionists – to rethink the nature of war in the contemporary world, since mainstream globalisation theory presumed (in a manner befitting its nineteenth-century liberal ancestors) a progressive decline in warfare as developing states became progressively integrated into the global market economy. For Martin van Creveld, in particular, this new type of conflict represents a shift from what he has termed 'trinitarian war' between states to various forms of 'non-trinitarian war'. 'Trinitarian war' is a term borrowed from Clausewitz and refers to the dominant mode of warfare in international history from the period of the French Revolution. It refers to the division of labour that occurs in wars, between governments that direct them, the professional militaries that fight them, and the people who suffer the consequences and generally pay the cost of them.[17] This kind of warfare reached its culmination in the period of industrialised 'total war' in the first half of the twentieth century, and thereafter has come under progressive challenge from a variety of insurgent movements and low-intensity conflicts in the period since 1945.

'Non-trinitarian war' resembles what Mary Kaldor has called 'new war' in that it marks a collapse of the former distinctions between professional militaries, states and civilian populations.[18] States themselves have in many cases either imploded or collapsed, or else declined in influence to a point where they are little more than one of the militarised social formations that now participate in the vicious terrain of warlord politics. Non-trinitarian or new wars are usually characterised by ethnic cleansing, privatised militaries sustained by the trafficking in drugs or precious commodities like diamonds or hard woods, and a parasitic economy that may be indebted to a number of external Western companies (or in the case of some West African diamond producers even al-Qaeda).

The arguments of the military revisionists have been questioned by some IR scholars, particularly for overstating their case. Martin Shaw has argued that 'new war' still has a number of continuities with the old in that it is often sustained by state actors in the international system: Bosnian state breakdown and the resulting rival warlord politics was partly a proxy war between Serbia and Croatia, while the same could be argued for Afghanistan, where rival warlord factions were sustained by neighbouring states such as Pakistan, Iran and Russia as well as Saudi Arabia and Western states.[19] A similar view is developed by Bob de Graaff in his chapter in this book, where he argues that the origin of the civil war in the former Yugoslavia was at the state level.[20] It is thus by no means clear that the internal dynamic of sub-state conflicts needs to be explained by a totally new body of theory to that of the dominant paradigm of globalisation.

However, on another level, the mainstream theory of globalisation is under challenge from a rather different quarter when it comes to trying to explain the failure of the state in whole areas of the developing world, especially Sub-Saharan Africa. While warfare in these regions was largely seen as peripheral to that of developed states, the US journalist Robert Kaplan rather stood this on its head in his influential article 'The Coming Anarchy', published in the *Atlantic Monthly* in February 1994. Kaplan argued that the warfare now being waged in West African countries such as Liberia and Sierra Leone was a harbinger of much wider sorts of conflicts in the coming century. This new warfare was being waged by deracinated young men, leaving the countryside as a result of overpopulation and environmental degradation. The emergence of this militant and highly armed youth was now a new dynamic behind the warfare breaking up the weak states of West Africa, and was one that would not be easily contained by Western interventions as had occurred in the former Yugoslavia.[21]

Kaplan's somewhat notorious article effectively reinforced the arguments of the military revisionists, though it suggested that the military transformation from trinitarian war was being initiated *within* the developing world rather than being imposed *on* it. For Africanist critics, Kaplan's thesis was really a statement in a new form of older notions of African culture being essentially barbaric. Paul Richards, in a study of war and youth in Sierra Leone, has argued that there was no environmental crisis on the lines suggested by Kaplan and the real dynamic behind the war in the early 1990s was political. The war that was being waged by the youth from the rainforest needed actually to be seen as a form of performance. This was reflected, for instance, in the way they dressed themselves up in bizarre garb including body parts, tried wherever possible to hold press conferences with the international press, and championed the image of *Rambo*, the lone warrior in the forest and outsider from American society, the film of which they watched on copious videos available even in the bush.[22]

A similar criticism of Kaplan has been developed by Stephen Ellis in a penetrating study of the Liberian civil war in the late 1980s and early 1990s, *The Mask of Anarchy*. Ellis also attacks what he sees as a 'new barbarism' thesis at the heart of Kaplan's article and points to the way that all wars develop their own codes and rituals. The view that some wars are more 'barbaric' than others principally relates to the rules by which they are fought, whether written or otherwise. To this extent the apparent barbarism of the Liberian civil war needs to be understood as stemming from the religious basis behind many of the rituals of its protagonists. The apparent 'anarchy' in Liberia was really only a 'mask' behind which deeply held religious values were being expressed.[23]

The emergence of various forms of 'warlords' in the developing world thus presents an interesting challenge to both international theorists and theorists of 'postmodern' forms of warfare. The central imperative of warlordism is really the generation of new sets of cultural and ethical values when these are seen to have broken down in the society at large. Strictly speaking, warlords and warlord activities are extremely old; some analysts have found their origins in ancient China or Europe after the collapse of the Roman Empire.[24] However, in their modern form warlords are in many respects the products of contemporary globalisation as they search for new identities in a globalised mass culture. Contemporary warlord formations are far less parochial and insular phenomena than those of previous eras, and need to be seen as responses by marginalised youth in societies with weak or collapsed states where orthodox notions of familial authority and social order bequeathed from the colonial era have effectively collapsed. In some instances, a warlord formation can exert a regional influence – as in the case of Joseph Kony's Lords Resistance Army (LRA) in Uganda, which has developed a regional network across the Uganda/Sudan border and has become an important player not only in Uganda itself but also in the regional war in southern Sudan between the Sudanese government and Sudanese Peoples Liberation Army (SPLA).[25]

Warlords, moreover, effectively act as gangs writ large and their activities in turn exacerbate further organisation by other social groups who emerge as rivals for control of territory, resources, markets, or access to women. Warlord and warrior armies collapse older distinctions between soldier and civilian, and at the same time act as primitive forms of governance when wider structures of state power and authority have collapsed. Warrior leaders construct an alternative model of ethical allegiance rooted in identity formation and order through a strict, usually genderised, hierarchy of male domination and the charismatic authority of the warlord leader. In some cases this kind of warrior formation may form the nucleus of a reconstructed state, as in the case of the National Patriotic Front of Liberia (NPFL) of Charles Taylor that managed to some degree to re-invent the state in Liberia in a more patrimonial form. The resulting patrimonial state was one where the political leadership exerted more or less direct control over processes of economic accumulation without the intervention of a state bureaucracy, which had been effectively dismantled.[26]

For military analysts, the emergence of warlordism in the post Cold War era underlines a basic difference in the mode of warfare between developed states with professional militaries and warlord-dominated societies where central government has broken down. In the former the soldier is taken out of civilian life and trained to be a disciplined professional answering to a clear chain of command. War is generally pursued by such militaries to fulfil the strategic aims of states. The logical outcome of this mode of warfare is Clausewitzean strategic doctrine, whereby the army of one state seeks to attack another state's centre of gravity and has a logical end state for its military operations.

In the latter, by contrast, warlord and militarised formations may seek to observe some of the features of conventional militaries by having a chain of command and strategic goals. In all essentials, though, they are ethnic or clan-based militias with a strong leaning towards a warrior code and culture of warfare. Warriors are to be distinguished from military professionals by the fact that they are not taken out of society and placed in an isolated military structure. Like guerrillas, partisans and popular militias, they train and operate within their own society. However, unlike guerrillas, partisans and popular militias, warriors have a far less sophisticated conception of warfare. The skills acquired in waging war are largely derived from within the society concerned, possibly with the help of a few former military professionals if any are to hand. Warriors live a far more hand-to-mouth existence and often develop out of teenage gangs who have acquired a lot of weapons and cash from activities such as plundering, looting, smuggling, and drug dealing. What warrior gangs lack in formal military training they make up for in extensive local combat experience, usually defending a well-defined territory in the countryside or zone within a city. Warrior bands are bound together by strict codes of combat, understanding each other's strengths and weaknesses, and for the most part they stick to small light weaponry to sustain a high level of mobility – in pick-up trucks in the case of the Taliban warriors in Afghanistan, or 'technicals' with a mounted machine gun in the case of the clan-based warlords in Somalia.[27]

Warriors lack any developed strategic doctrine and are usually under the control and direction of local warlord or strong man, who will usually be wary of devolving too much control to a local field commander for fear of being upstaged. This is a mode of warfare that is inherently limited in its range and intensity and it is hard to see how it can possibly spread onto a global scale as Kaplan has suggested. Such a mode of warfare can on occasions outmanoeuvre Western military forces, as was dramatically demonstrated in Mogadishu in 1993, particularly when the Western media is itself to hand to report events in graphic detail.

However, on a longer-term trajectory, this form of warrior warfare may well be contained by well-planned peace support operations (PSOs). Well-armed militias often prove in the event to be weak opponents for Western forces, even when the latter are nervous at the possibility of politically damaging levels of casualties. The rapid collapse of the Taliban regime in Afghanistan pinpoints the inherent limitations of lightly armed and mobile militia formations that were unable to resort to guerrilla insurgency when faced with the prospect of sustained bombing followed by a US-led military incursion.[28]

The challenge from al-Qaeda

What Kaplan could not predict in 1994, however, was the attempt to mobilise a global network of Islamic revolutionaries behind al-Qaeda's terrorist campaign against the West. Unlike the previous patterns of military conflict in the developing world this chapter has discussed, this represented a full-scale strategic attack on the West and a dramatic demonstration of how the networks secured by globalisation could be used to strike at the visible symbols of Western economic and military supremacy in the form of the Twin Towers and the Pentagon.

As John Mackinlay has pointed out, there was a widespread conceptual failure in the West to understand Bin Laden's strengths and weaknesses. Mackinlay also suggests that al-Qaeda is really a globalised form of insurgency, a rather novel formation, which may possibly be a portent of many more such movements in the coming century with the general advance of globalisation.[29] However, this thesis rather over-simplifies the complex multi-layered nature of the al-Qaeda network, which is at heart a terrorist organisation with cadres of nomadic global terrorists of the kind that launched the September 11 attacks. At the same time, the organisation also consists of a series of networks and linkages with local insurgent groups in various parts of the Islamic world, especially in Kashmir, Chechnya, and South East Asia, including the Philippines and Indonesia.

In some cases, the efforts to mobilise local insurgent groups behind al-Qaeda have been rebuffed. The career of one of his operatives, Emad Abdel wahid Ahmed Alwan, otherwise known as Abu Mohammed, illustrates this particularly well. Abu Mohammed went to Africa from Afghanistan in June 2001 with the objective of uniting Islamic groups in Egypt, Algeria, and Sudan as well as Sub-Saharan Africa under the overall aegis of al-Qaeda. In early 2002, Mohammed reached Algeria, where he tried to contact Hassan Hattab, leader of the radical Islamist *Groupe Salafiste Pour Prediction et Combat* (GSPC), with the aim of getting him to attack targets with international rather than local significance in return for al-Qaeda funds. Hattab appears not to have been interested. Abu Mohammed then went on to contact a number of other movements in Sub-Saharan Africa before finally being killed by Algerian security forces in November 2002.[30]

The al-Qaeda network is loosely organised and resembles in some respects modern business organisations with its decentralised structure of authority and reliance upon local level initiative for the formulation of new 'projects'.[31] This flexibility has enabled it to regroup following the reversal it suffered resulting from the US-led invasion of Afghanistan in late 2001 following the September 11 attacks.

Bin Laden has been fairly crucial to the al-Qaeda network's success since he has provided it with a degree of ideological coherence and charismatic leadership as he has appealed to a global Islamic jihad against the West and a revival of the medieval caliphate. To this extent the organisation is not the best example of what some analysts have termed 'new terrorism' in the post Cold War period marked by a general disdain for ideology and strategic goals, what Mark Juergensmeyer has termed 'the anti order of the new world order of the twenty-first century'.[32] It does, though, share some of the public-performance features of the warlord formations we have examined in places like West Africa, though on a far grander scale with a series of dramatic attacks in frequently unexpected places.

The religious terrorism that drives much of al-Qaeda's followers is really part of a quest for what Juergensmeyer has termed 'cosmic war', which employs images of warfare on a grand scale as part of a process of collective psychological empowerment of followers who believe they are ordained by God to wage war against evil. War thus becomes not only 'the context for violence but also the excuse for it'.[33] In this sense the movement can be seen as seeking some form of renegotiation of the terms of contemporary international globalisation as al-Qaeda seeks to mobilise a global Islamic withdrawal from the 'McWorld' of the West and the revolutionary overthrow of corrupt Middle East regimes that are seen to be conniving with its continued domination over the Islamic world.[34]

There is little chance of engaging in serious diplomatic dialogue with such an organisation, though this may by no means be the case with some parts of its insurgent base. Throughout the Middle East a number of Islamist movements in Algeria, Egypt, Turkey, and Morocco have engaged in extensive dialogue with the state. In some instances the movements have resorted to terrorism, since they see no other way of prosecuting their goals. However, they may draw back from terrorism activities if opportunities are opened up for dialogue with their respective national governments.

Al-Qaeda seeks to internationalise a multiple series of sub-state conflicts throughout the developing world. Its calls for a revolutionary Islamic internationalism come in the wake of previous secular internationalism movements, most notably that of the Third Communist International after the Bolshevik Revolution in Russia in 1917. This fell prey to the cynical promotion of Soviet state interests under Stalin from the late 1920s onwards. There is a strongly internationalist quality to the al-Qaeda organisation, which has managed to recruit among the disaffected *umma* right across the Islamic world, though in some ways it parallels the former internationalism of the Communist International, which was controlled by the most cruel and authoritarian of men in the Soviet NKVD and its successor, the KGB. This ended up hardening into a basically authoritarian pattern of politics and it is possible to see a similar pattern in the intelligence-obsessed terrorist organisers at the heart of al-Qaeda.[35]

Al-Qaeda has managed to penetrate most societies in the world where there are sizeable Muslim communities, and in the process established 'the most complex, robust and resilient money-generating and money-moving network yet seen'.[36] It has creamed off profits from providing goods and service to many Muslim communities around the world as well as engaging in a variety of activities including money laundering, drug trafficking, and black marketeering. It has even engaged in illegal trading in precious stones such as diamonds from West Africa, striking deals that were reputed to be worth $20 million in the months before September 11.[37] Al-Qaeda has also established bank accounts around the world as a means of disguising its funds, which in many cases it has received from private individuals or Islamic welfare organisations. Tracking these links down will in many cases take years and will depend upon heightened international cooperation.[38]

So has al-Qaeda finally secured a radical transformation in the nature of warfare in the modern globalised international system, or is it still ultimately beholden to a series of localised sub-state conflicts? In some respects it is still too early to reach a definitive conclusion on this as the organisation's resilience is currently being tested as it seeks to re-establish itself following its removal from Afghanistan. Even if Bin Laden is captured or killed it seems highly likely that the movement will be able to continue for a long while yet.

Al-Qaeda can be seen in a number of respects as the most important military response to date from the developing world to the Western-dominated globalised international order that was established in the aftermath of the Cold War: as one US analyst, Paul J. Smith, has noted, 'Al Qaeda represents the worst that globalization has to offer'.[39]

Looking at the worst possible outcome of the present US-led 'war on terror', the long-term strategic threat posed by al-Qaeda to the West is ultimately one of 'civilisational war'. Such a war would involve the mobilisation of at least a significant part of the Islamic world and some form of attempted disengagement from the global economy. This presumes a series of revolutionary overthrows of a number of key Islamic states such as Pakistan, Saudi Arabia and Indonesia, and the loss in these states of any sort of effective Western political influence. This might not seem an immediate prospect but it needs to be seen within a longer-term process of progressive economic marginalisation of large parts of the Islamic world as a result of the impact of economic globalisation hitting countries with rapidly expanding populations. In 1980, for instance, Muslims constituted 18 per cent of the world's population while by 2025 this is projected to rise to 30 per cent. At the same time, in the Middle East, North Africa and Pakistan large numbers of Muslims are effectively disengaging from the global economy. Middle East countries are growing at two-thirds the rate of developing countries, leading to the dismal prospect of huge numbers of young unemployed Muslims coming of age over the next 20 years with little hope of buying into the lifestyles of the developed West.[40]

It is possible to conceptualise civilisational war in a number of different forms.[41] The more 'moderate' form just outlined might lead to a revival of a Cold War-type stand-off between the West and an Islamic-led global alliance, with terrorist and insurgent movements being financed and supported by both sides in a series of proxy wars in peripheral states. A more revolutionary or crusader form, on the other hand, would be one driven by radical Islamists eager to wage a full-scale *jihad* against the West involving spectacular terrorist attacks and large-scale Western military responses. This though would be a form of crusading warfare beyond the bounds of contemporary nationalism, in which the goals would be predominantly religious and linked to the ideal of a revival of the Islamic caliphate.[42] While extremely unlikely, this latter model would clearly be a grim prospect, with warfare and military action taking place with large casualties and considerable savagery on both sides.

Whatever the case, the infusion of the military and strategic conceptions into globalisation requires that we develop a rather more robust concept of it. As this chapter has sought to show, the intellectual roots of globalisation were largely liberal ones, which took little or no account of warfare and armed conflict. This has left the concept rather impoverished. By linking it to some of the new military revisionism it emerges considerably strengthened and capable of providing potentially better levels of explanation for international crises.

The limits of globalisation theory

In 1996, it was still possible for one IR analyst, John A. Hall, to conclude that 'what happens outside the North is of less and less importance to international order'.[43] Globalisation appeared to have ensured the progressive

marginalisation of the developing world, which was now increasingly fragmented and lacked even the tenuous identity of the 'third world', popular in
the 1960s and 1970s. The military conflicts of the developing world also
appeared generally peripheral to Western strategic interests as most attention
focused on the missile capabilities of a small number of 'rogue states' such as
North Korea, Iran and Iraq. Collapsed states were perceived as either terrains
that were out of bounds or else the arenas for Peace Support Operations with
the long-term aim of state reconstruction and nation 'building, as in the cases
of Sierra Leone and East Timor.

The crisis of September 11 has begun a reshaping of this post Cold War
international order and raised the prospect of a return to interstate conflict in
the twenty-first century. Contrary to the theory of new warfare developed by
Mary Kaldor, it is by no means possible to conclude that globalisation has
ushered in a new age of cosmopolitanism and the accompanying prospect of
global democracy.[44] This mode of argument to some degree repeats one of the
fallacies of the earlier school of interwar liberal idealists, who confused what
they *wished* to see happen (growing international rule of law under the aegis
of institutions such as the League of Nations) with what they asserted *was*
happening in international politics.

Moreover, it is wise not to make too much of the range and intensity of
globalisation for all the amount of rhetoric that has accompanied the
development and popularisation of the theory in recent year. Sceptics such as
Paul Hirst have pointed to the limits of internationalisation in the current
global economy. There are, he argues, very few real multinational companies
that are not located in one major host nation, usually one of the major
developed states. Similarly, there is little evidence of a significant transfer of
output, employment, and trade from developed to underdeveloped states,
thus severely limiting the scale of the 'globalisation' that has occurred in
recent decades.

States, too, remain significant actors in the international realm, though
with varying degrees of power and influence. The one really coherent
Westphalian state remains the United States and it is thus possible to argue
that since the end of the Cold War what has really been occurring internationally is the reverse of real globalisation, in the form of the spread of
American power, ideas and institutions on a global scale.[45] This 'Anglo-
Saxon' economic and ideological hegemony is unlikely to continue without
growing international political and ideological resistance, and indeed one
major form that this has begun to take is that of international terrorism led by
the al-Qaeda network.

It is of course possible to see the current phase of US unipolar domination
of the international system as a transitional one and that ultimately some new
international balance of power will reassert itself. However, the overwhelming
military superiority of the United States over its international rivals makes
this an unlikely prospect in the near future. Real and 'authentic' globalisation,

it can therefore be argued, has yet to develop out of its United States and Anglo-Saxon dominated form, certainly on lines that can lead to the entrenchment of democracy at the international level.

Some theorists such as Martin Albrow and Martin Shaw point to the concept of 'globality' as a new form of global society in contrast to that of 'globalisation', which really refers to the *process* of growing multiple interconnectedness at the global level.[46] 'Globality' is the condition at the international level where a major breaking-down of spatial limits has occurred and where international institutions have acquired a global reach. It is thus to be contrasted to the more market-orientated form of 'globalisation' that has occurred largely under the aegis of major Western multinational companies. The 'globality' concept certainly sets up a new form of Weberian ideal type at the international level and provides a useful guide to further research. Theories of 'globalisation', as this chapter has sought to show, have been rather weak on defining the sort of end state towards which current trends are moving.

However, we should not assume from the Albrow and Shaw argument that there is some sort of teleological process involved in the 'globality' concept. While acknowledging the centrality of warfare in the formation of the current global order, Shaw is reluctant to acknowledge its possible continuation in future forms of 'globality':

> The pre-global world of the late nineteenth century was a divided world of competing nation states–empires; the *emergent global world* of the twenty-first century is a world in which political unification has occurred so that territorial boundaries between state jurisdictions are no longer, in many cases, borders of violence. Instead of the violent competition of empires or blocs we have an *emergent global authority structure in which nation statehood, while more universal, is also largely delinked from its historical context of war.*[47]

This is prophetic rather than analytical language and again tends to repeat the idealist fallacy of confusing what the author would like to occur with what may actually occur. There is no hard and fast rule in international relations that ensures these processes must by definition occur, and Shaw is largely repeating the sort of unification rhetoric rampant in EU bureaucratic circles on a wider plane.

The future may well be rather more fluid, with a continuing centrality of inter-state warfare. The breakdown of weak states has not ensured the domination of a completely 'new' form of war, since the warlord factions are both supported in many cases by states and themselves seek the control of states as an ultimate political goal. We may thus be living in more of a transitional period, in which a number of weak states that were supported by large-scale patrons during the Cold War are now having to struggle to survive in a rather more insecure international political order. While some may ultimately fail, the net result may well, in the longer term, be an increase rather than a decrease in the number of sovereign states in the international political system. In this process, interstate warfare could be a major defining characteristic in the emerging global order of the twenty-first century.

Notes

1 Charles Oman, 'Globalization, Regionalization, and Inequality', in Andrew Hurrell and Ngaire Woods (eds), *Inequality, Globalization, and World Politics*, Oxford: Oxford University Press, 1999, p. 37.
2 Francis Fukuyama, *The End of History and the Last Man*, New York: The Free Press, 1992.
3 Gert Schmidt, 'Globalisation: Capitalism on Trial Again', *Cambridge Review of International Affairs*, 14, 2 (2001), pp. 309–10.
4 Andreas Novy, 'From Rhetoric to Political Economy: The Case of Brazil', *Cambridge Review of International Affairs*, 14, 2 (2001), p. 304.
5 Kenneth Waltz, *Theory of International Politics*, Reading, Mass.: Addison-Wesley, 1979.
6 Ian Clark, 'Beyond the Great Divide: Globalization and the Theory of International Relations', *Review of International Studies*, 24, 4 (1998), p. 478. See also Ian Clark, *Globalization and International Relations Theory*, Oxford: Oxford University Press, 1999.
7 Clark, 'Beyond the Great Divide', p. 491.
8 Ibid., p. 497.
9 Linda Weiss, *The Myth of the Powerless State*, Cambridge: Polity Press, 1998.
10 James Mayall, 'Globalization and International Relations', *Review of International Studies*, 24, 2 (1998), pp. 248–9.
11 Martin Shaw, 'War and Globality: The Role and Character of War in the Global Transition', in Howon Jeong (ed.), *The New Agenda for Peace Research*, Ashgate: Aldershot, 1999, pp. 61–80.
12 For an examination of the political context of this film, see Susan L. Carruthers, 'Bringing it all back home: Hollywood returns to war', in Paul B. Rich and Tom Mockaitis (eds), *Terrorism and Grand Strategy*, London: Frank Cass, 2003.
13 For a discussion of this concept, see in particular, Volker R. Berghahn, *Militarism: The History of an International Debate*, Leamington Spa: Berghahn Press, 1981.
14 Paul Hirst, *War and Power in the 21st Century*, Cambridge: Polity Press, 2001, p. 66.
15 In IR this liberalism was exemplified by the functionalist model of inter-state integration developed by the Rumanian Anglophile David Mitrany at the LSE.
16 See, in particular, Robert H. Jackson, *Quasi-States: Sovereignty, International Relations, and the Third World*, Cambridge: Cambridge University Press, 1990.
17 Martin van Creveld, *The Transformation of War*, New York: The Free Press, 1991.
18 Mary Kaldor, *New and Old Wars: Organized Violence in a Global Era*, Cambridge: Polity Press, 1999.
19 Shaw, 'War and Globality', p. 285.
20 Bob de Graaff, 'The Wars in Former Yugoslavia in the 1990s: Bringing the State Back In' (see Chapter 7 in this book).
21 Robert Kaplan, 'The Coming Anarchy', *Atlantic Monthly*, 273 (1994), pp. 44–76.

22 Paul Richards, *Fighting for the Rain Forest: War, Youth and Resources in Sierra Leone*, Oxford: James Currey, 1996.

23 Stephen Ellis, *The Mask of Anarchy: The Destruction of Liberia and the Religious Dimension of an African Civil War*, London: Hurst, 1999, p. 22.

24 Paul Jackson, 'Warlords as Alternative Forms of Governance System', *Small Wars and Insurgencies*, 14, 2 (2003).

25 Paul Jackson, 'The March of the Lords Resistance Army: Greed or Grievance in Northern Uganda', *Small Wars and Insurgencies*, 13, 3 (2002), p. 45.

26 William Reno, 'Reinvention of an African Patrimonial State: Charles Taylor's Liberia', *Third World Quarterly*, 16, 1 (1995), pp. 109–19.

27 I am indebted to some of the ideas expressed in Jeffrey B. White, 'A Different Kind of Threat: Some Thoughts on Irregular Warfare', *Studies in Intelligence*, 39, 5 (1996), <www.cia.gov/csi/studies/96 unclass/iregular.htm>.

28 Warren Chin, 'Operation Enduring Freedom: A Victory for A Conventional Force Fighting an Unconventional War?', in Rich and Mockaitis (eds), *Terrorism and Grand Strategy*.

29 John Mackinlay, *The World Today*, 51, 11 (2001).

30 Jason Burke *et al.*, 'Terror that Haunts Africa', *Observer*, 1 December 2002.

31 Peter L. Bergen, *Holy War: Inside the Secret World of Osama bin Laden*, London: Phoenix Paperbacks, 2002, p. 32 and Yael Shamar, 'Osama bin Laden: Marketing Terrorism', 22 August 1998, <www.ict.org.il/articles>.

32 Mark Juergensmeyer, 'Understanding the New Terrorism', *Current History*, 99, 636 (2000), pp. 158–63 and Bruce Hoffman, *Inside Terrorism*, New York: Columbia University Press, 1998.

33 Mark Juergensmeyer, *Terror in the Mind of God*, Berkeley: University of California Press, 2001, p. 149.

34 Roland Jacquard, *In the Name of Osama Bin Laden*, Durham: Duke University Press, 2002, p. 111.

35 For details of this see Fred Halliday, *Revolution and World Politics*, Houndmills: Macmillan, 1999, p. 130.

36 Rohan Gunaratna, *Inside Al Qaeda: Global Network of Terror*, London: Hurst, 2002, p. 61.

37 Amelia Hill, 'Bin Laden's $20m African "Blood Money" Deals', *Observer*, 20 October 2002.

38 Yael Shahar, 'Tracing Bin Laden's Money' <www.ict.org.il>.

39 Paul J. Smith, 'Transnational Terrorism and the al Qaeda Model: Confronting New Realities', *Parameters*, 32, 2 (2002), p. 45.

40 Steven Simon and Benjamin Daniel, 'The Terror', *Survival*, 43, 4 (2001), p. 13.

41 On civilisational conflicts, see for example, Samuel P. Huntington, *The Clash of Civilisations and the Remaking of World Order*, New York: Simon & Schuster, 1996.

42 'In modern terms holy war is most likely to be invoked when religious fervour and radical nationalism converge', Peter Partner, *God of Battles: Holy Wars of Christianity and Islam*, London: HarperCollins, 1997, p. 310.

43 John A. Hall, *International Orders*, Cambridge: Polity Press, 1996, p. 141.

44 Kaldor, *New and Old Wars*, and Mary Kaldor, 'Cosmopolitanism and Organised Violence', paper prepared for the Conference on 'Conceiving Cosmopolitanism', University of Warwick, 27–29 April 2000, see <http://www.theglobalsite.ac.uk/press/010kaldor.pdf>.

45 Hirst, *War and Power in the 21st Century*, p. 137.

46 Shaw, 'War and Globality', pp. 61–80.

47 Ibid. (emphasis added).

References

Bergen, Peter L., *Holy War: Inside the Secret World of Osama bin Laden*, London: Phoenix Paperbacks, 2002.

Berghahn, Volker R., *Militarism: The History of an International Debate*, Leamington Spa: Berghahn Press, 1981.

Carruthers, Susan L., 'Bringing it all back home: Hollywood returns to war', in Paul B. Rich and Tom Mockaitis (eds), *Terrorism and Grand Strategy*, London: Frank Cass, 2003.

Chin, Warren, 'Operation Enduring Freedom: A Victory for A Conventional Force Fighting an Unconventional War?', in Rich and Mockaitis (eds), *Terrorism and Grand Strategy*. London: Frank Cass, 2003.

Clark, Ian, *Globalization and International Relations Theory*, Oxford: Oxford University Press, 1999.

——'Beyond the Great Divide: Globalization and the Theory of International Relations', *Review of International Studies*, 24, 4 (1998), pp. 479–98.

Creveld, Martin van, *The Transformation of War*, New York: The Free Press, 1991.

Ellis, Stephen, *The Mask of Anarchy: The Destruction of Liberia and the Religious Dimension of an African Civil War*, London: Hurst, 1999.

Fukuyama, Francis, *The End of History and the Last Man*, New York: The Free Press, 1992.

Gunaratna, Rohan, *Inside Al Qaeda: Global Network of Terror*, London: Hurst, 1992.

Hall, John A., *International Orders*, Cambridge: Polity Press, 1996.

Halliday, Fred, *Revolution and World Politics*, Houndmills: Macmillan, 1999.

Hirst, Paul, *War and Power in the 21st Century*, Cambridge: Polity Press, 2001.

Hoffman, Bruce, *Inside Terrorism*, New York: Columbia University Press, 1998.

Huntington, Samuel, *The Clash of Civilizations and the Remaking of World Order*, New York: Simon & Schuster, 1996.

Jackson, Paul, 'Warlords as Alternative Forms of Governance System', *Small Wars and Insurgencies*, 14, 2 (2003).

——'The March of the Lords Resistance Army: Greed or Grievance in Northern Uganda', *Small Wars and Insurgencies*, 13, 3 (2002).

Jackson, Robert H., *Quasi-States: Sovereignty, International Relations, and the Third World*, Cambridge: Cambridge University Press, 1990.

Jacquard, Roland, *In the Name of Osama Bin Laden*, Durham: Duke University Press, 2002.

Juergensmeyer, Mark, *Terror in the Mind of God*, Berkeley: University of California Press, 2001.

——'Understanding the New Terrorism', *Current History*, 99, 636 (2000), pp. 158–63.

Kaldor, Mary, 'Cosmopolitanism and Organised Violence', paper prepared for the Conference on 'Conceiving Cosmopolitanism', University of Warwick, 27–29 April 2000.

——*New and Old Wars: Organized Violence in a Global Era*, Cambridge: Polity Press, 1999.

Kaplan, Robert D., 'The Coming Anarchy', *Atlantic Monthly*, 273 (1994), pp. 44–76.

Mackinlay, John, *The World Today*, 51, 11 (2001).

Mayall, James, 'Globalization and International Relations', *Review of International Studies*, 24, 2 (1998), pp. 239–50.

Novy, Andreas, 'From Rhetoric to Political Economy: The Case of Brazil', *Cambridge Review of International Affairs*, 14, 2 (2001), pp. 290–307.

Oman, Charles, 'Globalization, Regionalization, and Inequality', in Andrew Hurrell and Ngaire Woods (eds), *Inequality, Globalization, and World Politics*, Oxford: Oxford University Press, 1999, pp. 36–65.

Partner, Peter, *God of Battles: Holy Wars of Christianity and Islam*, London: HarperCollins, 1997.

Reno, William, 'Reinvention of an African Patrimonial State: Charles Taylor's Liberia', *Third World Quarterly*, 16, 1 (1995), pp. 109–19.

Richards, Paul, *Fighting for the Rainforest: War, Youth and Resources in Sierra Leone*, Oxford: James Currey, 1996.

Schmidt, Gert, 'Globalisation: Capitalism on Trial Again', *Cambridge Review of International Affairs*, 14, 2 (2001).

Shaw, Martin, 'War and Globality: The Role and Character of War in the Global Transition', in Ho-won Jeong (ed.), *The New Agenda for Peace Research*. Ashgate: Aldershot, 1999, pp. 61–80.

——*Post-Military Society*, London: Polity Press, 1991.

Simon, Steven and Daniel Benjamin, 'The Terror', *Survival*, 43, 4 (2001), pp. 5–18.

Smith, Paul J., 'Transnational Terrorism and the al Qaeda Model: Confronting New Realities', *Parameters*, 32, 2 (2002), pp. 33–46.

Weiss, Linda, *The Myth of the Powerless State*, Cambridge: Polity Press, 1998.

Waltz, Kenneth, *Theory of International Politics*, Reading: Addison-Wesley, 1979.

White, Jeffrey B., 'A Different Kind of Threat: Some Thoughts on Irregular Warfare', *Studies in Intelligence*, 39, 5 (1996).

10

ELABORATING THE 'NEW WAR' THESIS

Mary Kaldor

What many of the critics of the 'new wars' thesis miss is the policy implication of the argument. By describing the conflicts of the 1990s as 'new', I wanted to change the way policy-makers and policy-shapers perceived these conflicts. In particular, I wanted to emphasise the growing illegitimacy of war and the need for what I called a cosmopolitan policy response – one that put individual rights and the rule of law as the centrepiece of any international intervention (political, military or civil).

Dominant understandings of these conflicts among Western policy-makers were of two kinds. On the one hand, there was a tendency to impose a stereo-typed version of war, drawn from the experience of the last two centuries in Europe, in which war consisted of a conflict between two symmetrical warring parties, generally states or proto-states with legitimate interests, what I called 'Old Wars'.[1] In such wars, the solution is either negotiation or victory by one side, and outside intervention takes the form either of traditional peace-keeping, in which the peace-keepers are supposed to guarantee a negotiated agreement and the ruling principles are consent, neutrality and impartiality, or of traditional war-fighting on one side or the other, as in Korea or the Gulf War. On the other hand, where policy-makers recognised the shortcomings of the stereotyped understanding, there was a tendency to treat these wars as anarchy, barbarism, or ancient rivalries, where the best policy response was containment, i.e. protecting the borders of the West from this malady. I wanted to demonstrate that neither of these approaches was appropriate, that these were wars with their own logic, but a logic that was different from 'old wars' and which, therefore, dictated a very different policy response.

Of course, my analysis was not just about new ways of seeing war. I agree with the critics who say that many of the features of new wars can be found in earlier wars, and also that the dominance of Cold War thinking clouded our ability to analyse 'small wars' or 'low-intensity conflicts'. Nevertheless, I do think that the 'new wars' argument does reflect a new reality – a reality that was emerging before the end of the Cold War. Globalisation is a convenient catch-all concept to describe the various changes that characterise the contemporary period. I would like to stress three interrelated developments that have deeply affected the character of contemporary conflict.

First of all, the increase in the destructiveness and accuracy of all forms of military technology, as a consequence of the Clausewitzean logic of extremes, has made symmetrical war, war between similarly armed opponents, increasingly difficult. The first Gulf war between Iraq and Iran was perhaps the most recent example of symmetrical war – a war much like the First World War, that lasted for years and killed millions of young men, for almost no political result.

Second, global communications (information technology, cheap air travel) has greatly increased the visibility of war as well as the sense of solidarity with strangers. Kant's point that the world community had shrunk to the point that a right violated anywhere is felt everywhere has become a reality only in recent decades. The media have become part of the 'game of war' and transnational communities, for example diasporas, profoundly influence the funding, techniques and politics of wars.

Third, I agree with those globalisation theorists who argue that globalisation has not led to the demise of the state but rather its transformation.[2] But I consider that the state is changing in different ways and that, perhaps, the most important aspect of that transformation is the changing role of the state in relation to organised violence. 'New wars', as I have always argued, are associated with state disintegration under the impact of globalisation. But there are other types of state transformation associated with other forms of organised violence. I accept the criticism made by Martin Shaw and others that 'new wars' are only one type of conventional conflict. Spectacle wars, humanitarian intervention or failed counter-insurgencies can all be understood as contemporary political/military experiments reflecting different ways in which states have evolved in the context of globalisation.

In this chapter, I will start by responding to the debate about 'new wars'. I will then discuss the other main type of contemporary war, what I call 'spectacle war' and try to show how both types of war are ways of adapting to the three developments summarised above. In the final section, I will discuss briefly what this means for Clausewitzean thinking and for policy.

'New wars' revisited

I have used the word 'war' because I think it is important to emphasise the political character of these conflicts and the fact that these are wars fought in a rational way for political ends. Despite the assertions of de Graaff and Kalyvas, I have never suggested that the wars are fought only by non-state actors, nor that the motivation is purely economic. On the contrary, my point is rather that in a context of state disintegration, it is increasingly hard to distinguish between state and non-state actors, political and economic motives, or what is domestic and civil as opposed to international or inter-state. Henderson and Singer suggest that the term 'new wars' is a 'typological hodge podge'. I agree. My problem is that I find it hard to fit most contemporary conflicts into earlier typologies because they depend on a clear definition of the state. Thus was the war in Bosnia an extra-state war between the Serbian and Croatian states and Bosnian people, an intercommunal war between Serbs, Croats and Muslims, an inter-state war between Serbia, Croatia and Bosnia-Herzegovina, or an intra-state war within Yugoslavia? Nor do I find what Henderson and Singer call the aetiologies associated with each type of war convincing as an explanation for the Bosnian war. And I would have the same problem when thinking about Israel/Palestine, Kashmir or the current conflict in the Congo.

One of the difficulties with the traditional categorisations of war is that the state is taken as a given, an entity or a thing. States are actually organisations or sets of relationships that continually have to be reproduced. They are processes that are always changing. 'Old Wars' were wars of state-building: that is to say, through wars, taxes were raised, borrowing was regularised, administrative efficiency was increased, domestic security was improved, and above all, the idea of the nation was constructed.[3] New Wars are wars of state unbuilding, that is to say they speed up a process that has often begun under the impact of economic and cultural liberalisation, especially in formerly authoritarian states, where tax revenue falls, corruption increases, domestic security deteriorates, and integrative national ideas are undermined.

In what follows, I shall focus on the war in Bosnia-Herzegovina not only because I used the example of that war as the paradigmatic case of a 'new war' but also as a way of replying to Bob de Graaff, who uses the same example. De Graaff argues that I underestimate the role of the state and points out that the warring parties in that war all had state projects. This is, of course, true, but they were projects for dismantling the Yugoslav state and for controlling bits of the state apparatus to further the interests of particular groups and networks rather than the citizens as a whole. (In that sense, one can perhaps talk of private rather than public interest.) I will elaborate this point in relation to the goals, methods and forms of finance of 'new wars', as I did in my book.

The goals of 'new wars' can be defined in terms of identity politics, that is to say, the claim to control the state or bits of the state in the name of an exclusive group identified in terms of ethnicity, religion or tribe. This type of exclusive politics, whether based on ethnicity, religion or clan, can be contrasted with universalistic ideologies like earlier liberal nationalism or socialism, which proposed a state-building project for the entire population. There is plenty of evidence to show that the vast majority of contemporary conflicts are identity conflicts, in contrast to the conflicts of two decades ago.[4] It is true that earlier left/right struggles in the so-called third world often masked particularistic struggles, but I do believe that the legitimising discourse is important in the way that it influences how wars are fought. It is also true that exclusive nationalists or religious fundamentalists often favour democracy or social welfare, but only for the exclusive group. Such ideologies are state-fragmenting, not state-building ideologies.

I take the view that identity politics are constructed, not legacies of the past, and that the construction of nationalist or religious ideologies is a form of political mobilisation in the context of the failure of earlier ideologies, and that both the new media and war itself are forms of political mobilisation. Of course, such ideologies must resonate with people to be successful; political mobilisation has to build on memories of past injustices, as well as on ethnic interpretations of popular grievances that may be associated with the impact of structural change. Both Milosevic and Tudjman were popular when the wars began and they both used the media and (especially Tudjman) diaspora influence to spread their brand of exclusive nationalism. The totalitarian legacy should not be neglected; Yugoslavs, as in other authoritarian societies, were in the habit of accepting their leaders' ideologies; voting was understood as a symbol of loyalty as much as a form of choice.[5] In the absence of communist leaders, religious and nationalist leaders were able to mobilise votes, although in the case of Bosnia, it should be stressed that they argued in the pre-war elections that this was the way to live together. But violence and the idea of struggle was a crucial way to sustain and reproduce nationalist fervour in a situation where the conditions of everyday life were rapidly deteriorating. Moreover, the expulsion of people of a different ethnicity was critical in retaining political control, especially through the ballot box – not only because the nationalist parties relied on the votes of people of their own nationality but also because population expulsion left a legacy of bitterness and complicity that shored up support for the extreme nationalist parties.

In support of his argument that the wars in Yugoslavia must be understood in state terms, de Graaff points out correctly that, on the Serbian side in the Bosnian war, Milosevic played a leading role, that the various para-military groups operated under his command and that it was the same on the Croatian side. On both the Serb and the Croat side, the armies consisted largely of former regular forces – the territorial defence force in the Croat case and the ex-Yugoslav army in the Serbian case. The Bosnian side was much more decentralised, with separate commands in Sarajevo, Tuzla, Bihac, and Zenica organised in very different ways, although all except Bihac came together by the end of the war even though there were always tensions between, for example, the more multi-cultural units created in Tuzla and the more Muslim-dominated overall command.[6] De Graaff is also right to say that the para-military groups are not the same as warlords, who control territory. There were warlords, however. These were the political representatives who controlled local municipalities and came together in, for example, the Bosnian Serb Assembly. Fikret Abdic in Bihac was a typical warlord, recruiting the local trade unions into the army.

Because the warring parties described themselves as 'states' and because they made use of bits of the former state apparatus and had the appearance of statehood, we should not be deluded into thinking these were state-building projects. The para-military groups may have followed Milosevic's orders but it is not clear whether they were actually paid by the state; the 'right to be first to loot' was reported to be their main form of payment. This was not a command system in the way that we understand a traditional military command or political control. It was much more of a network combining bits of the state apparatus, para-military groups, warlords, and organised crime groups, who came together for mutual support within the framework of a legitimising narrative based on an ideology of ethnic exclusion.

De Graaff tells the story of how communal violence in a village in Bosnia-Herzegovina was repressed by the authorities in 1971 but condoned and even encouraged in 1991. He uses the example to show that violence originated at state level. But the point is rather that a state, or bits of the state, that encourages violence cannot be described as being engaged in state-building. He also says that the story shows that there was no monopoly of violence in 1971 because the villagers had guns. This is rather like saying that Switzerland has no monopoly of violence because citizens keep their guns at home or that the United States has no monopoly of violence because guns can be privately owned. Under the system of territorial defence, citizens did have guns in the former Yugoslavia and this undoubtedly facilitated the wars of the 1990s. But the point is surely that unauthorised use of guns was forbidden, and in 1971 the authorities quite properly reacted against the unauthorised use of violence.[7]

In defining the character of 'new wars', I think the operational level is key. Contrary to what some critics claim, no one has ever argued that there has been an increase in the number of wars nor in the overall level of casualties.[8] My own data suggest that both the numbers of wars and overall casualties have remained roughly constant every decade since the end of the Second World War. What has increased is the ratio of civilian to military casualties and the numbers of displaced persons per conflict.[9] Henderson and Singer claim that civilian casualties were always high outside Europe and they cite as an example the Second Philippines War.[10] It is, of course, true that what I call 'old wars' are the stylised wars of Europe in the eighteenth, nineteenth and early twentieth centuries, and that wars outside Europe always displayed a different pattern and often involved much brutality against civilians. Nevertheless, in the five decades since 1945, when all wars did take place outside Europe, there has been a steady increase in the ratio of civilian to military casualties in war as well as in the numbers of displaced persons per conflict, suggesting a change in the way that war is fought.

Perhaps the most characteristic feature of new wars is that violence is directed against civilians not as a side effect of war but as a deliberate strategy. The warring parties avoid battle and even cooperate. The aim is to control territory through political rather than military means. In the case of the Bosnian war, the aim was to create ethnically pure territories so as to ensure political control by the nationalist parties, paradoxically through elections. Genocide, massacres, ethnic cleansing, or rape as a weapon of war all have to be understood as forms of political mobilisation, ways in which warring parties construct ethnicity as a political instrument. De Graaff is right to say that the warring parties in Bosnia-Herzegovina were interested in grabbing territory but the way they did so was not through military battles but through population expulsion. The reason for the long-lasting stalemate was precisely because the various parties avoided battle.

De Graaff says the paramilitaries were not much use as fighters. If by that he means that they were not much use in military combat, the same argument can be made about the regular troops. The typical tactic for ethnic cleansing on the Serbian side involved cooperation between regular forces, who killed at a distance, and para-military groups, who entered localities once people had been terrorised by artillery bombardment and inflicted atrocities on Muslims and intellectuals. This was a tactic used in Croatia, Bosnia and Kosovo, and has been observed in other regions, East Timor for example, where regular forces retain the fiction of operating within the laws of war. Both para-military forces and regular forces were used against civilians rather than in fighting against each other, or at least, only to a very limited degree.

I agree with Isabelle Duyvesteyn that this type of warfare is not guerrilla warfare. There are still combatant groups, which do fight in ways that could be described as guerrilla warfare, that is to say violence is directed against strategic targets, like policemen or communications centre. The KLA in Kosovo and the NLA in Macedonia both tried to minimise civilian casualties and to direct their violence against agents of the state as a way of provoking overreactions by the Serb and Macedonian states respectively and winning international sympathy. In Colombia, the FLN and the FARC adopt guerrilla-type tactics, while the right-wing para-militaries use the tactics of 'new wars' although, over time, the approaches tend to become more similar.

But nor do I think the 'new wars' have much in common with conventional warfare, despite the presence of men in uniform or para-military groups in distinctive dress. 'New wars' may involve more fighters than classic guerrilla wars but, in comparison with 'old wars', participation in war is very low. Although Duyvesteyn emphasises battles in cities, most violence even in the cities is directed against civilians and not against opposing combatants. The combatant groups carve up cities into differently controlled areas and may often cooperate. The new warfare borrows from guerrilla warfare the idea of controlling territory in a political rather than military way and makes use of regular forces. But its mode of operation is distinct from both.

The third new characteristic of 'new wars' is the method of financing. Of course, loot and plunder is nothing new. But loot and plunder, together with various criminal activities, support from the diaspora and 'taxation' of humanitarian assistance are the main forms of finance in new wars. Both taxation and state sponsorship from abroad have declined. If the centralised command economy was modelled on 'old wars', then the new criminalised informal underside of the global economy could be said to reach its most extreme expression in 'new wars'. This new type of informal economy is, moreover, no longer marginal to the formal economy; it is directly sponsored by the ruling elites. Max Weber made the point that organisations are shaped by their methods of finance. The states that are involved in 'new wars' face declining tax revenue and instead increasingly depend on various illegal forms of revenue. Towards the end of the war in Bosnia when the Bosnian Serb side was becoming exhausted, there were attempts to centralise the command system and create a war economy financed by taxation, but the Bosnian Serb Assembly resisted because it would have reduced their individual freedom of manoeuvre to engage in, for example, cigarette smuggling, which was a big source of income.[11]

In other words, the fissiparous ideology, the attacks on civilians and the growing reliance on semi-legal or criminal sources of income accelerate the process of state weakening and, at the same time, strengthen the political positions of exclusivist political factions. Far from resolving conflicts, the factors that led to war are accentuated in the aftermath of war. The war leaves a legacy of grass-roots nationalism as a result of massacres and atrocities actually experienced. The various political parties have an interest in keeping those experiences fresh as a way of sustaining their positions. As criminal activities spread, so the warring parties also develop a vested interest in the conditions under which such activities thrive. This is why, as I have stressed elsewhere, these wars are difficult to end and difficult to contain. These are illegitimate wars both because the operational level directly involves violations of the laws of war and human rights law not as a side effect but as deliberate tactics and because the financing of wars involve breaking economic laws.

De Graaff says that the West failed to see that the warring parties were states. I think the West made the opposite error, treating the various warring parties as if they were states with legitimate interests, as in an 'old war'. Had the West from the start insisted on the illegitimacy of ethnically pure states and of the use of violence, the various negotiators would not have been so easily exploited by the various warring parties as an instrument to confirm the 'facts' they created on the ground, namely ethnically pure territories.

The analysis of new wars, however, also suggests weak points that could be exploited in a more appropriate policy response. It is very difficult to sustain long-term rule based on insecurity and violence. It is also difficult to sustain a criminalised economy. Like NGOs on 'soft money', the warring parties are always on the edge of exhaustion and there is always a temptation to prefer low-paid jobs or education to the risks associated with criminal sources of income that depend on violence. This is why temporary ceasefires provide an opportunity for setting in motion alternative strategies.

What Hoffman calls the 'new terrorism' should be considered a subset of the new wars. The 'new terrorism' is characterised by exclusive ideologies in place of left/right ideologies, networks as forms of organisation instead of centralised command systems, indiscriminate violence against civilians instead of strategic targets, and criminal financing instead of state sponsorship.[12] One difference is that the attacks on civilians are not a way of controlling territory. But they are a form of political mobilisation, a way of making real the sense of struggle. As Bin Laden put it in 1999: 'We seek to instigate the [Islamic] nation to get up and liberate its land'.[13] The attack on the World Trade Center succeeded, probably beyond the wildest dreams of the perpetrators, in publicising the global Islamic idea. In December 2001, in a videotaped message to Al Jazeera, he said: 'Regardless if Osama is killed or survives, the awakening has started, praise be to God'.[14]

Spectacle war

The other type of contemporary conflict that I failed to discuss in my book on 'new wars' is what I call 'spectacle war'.[15] 'Spectacle war' is sometimes called 'spectator-sport war',[16] 'virtual war'[17] or 'virtuous war'.[18] 'Spectacle wars' are fought by the United States using superior technology, primarily air-borne technology and advanced information and communications technology. The term 'spectacle' refers to the fact that although the wars are fought by American regular forces, the American people are only required to be spectators – they do not have to participate in any meaningful way by, for example, paying additional taxes or risking their lives. James Der Derian uses the term 'virtuous war' in order to combine both the virtual character of the war and the notion of virtue, the idea that the war is being fought in a noble cause. 'Virtuous war relies on virtual simulation, media manipulation, global surveillance and networked warfare to deter and if need be to destroy potential enemies. It draws on just war doctrine (when possible) and holy war doctrine (when necessary).'[19]

The United States is the only state large enough and rich enough to be able to act unilaterally in a global era; Javier Solana uses the term 'global unilateralist' to describe American policy. 'Spectacle war' has to be understood not as something totally new but as an evolution from 'old war' under the impact of the interrelated developments that are described in the introduction to this chapter.

In terms of goals, 'spectacle wars' are about a moral crusade, about spreading the American model of democracy. They reproduce a narrative based on the American victory in World War II, in which the United States came to the aid of the Europeans, using superior technology, to defeat evil and construct democracy. This narrative plays a critical role in the American conception of patriotism; it is a non-ethnic nationalism. The origins of 'spectacle war' lie in the imaginary war between East and West during the Cold War period, when this narrative was institutionalised through the military influence on US governmental structures. Appeal to this narrative through, for example, pictures of Bush landing on an aircraft carrier at the supposed moment of victory in Iraq, is very important for domestic political mobilisation, for shoring up support for the President. In old wars, the mobilisation of people around a nationalist narrative was also important but it can be argued that, at least in the idealised version of old wars, this was consequence rather than cause. In old wars, governments pursued their geo-political interests and needed popular mobilisation in order to gain support in the form of taxes or soldiers.

At the operational level the aim is not to occupy territory, although this is what the Americans found themselves trying to do in Iraq; it is to topple regimes. As McInnes points out, these are counter-regime wars rather than counter-state wars. To achieve this, the Americans aim to combine destruction of key strategic targets, 'shock and awe' to impress the enemy (and people watching back home), and to minimise civilian casualties – although not at the expense of American casualties. As a matter of fact, the methods have not changed much since World War II, as Kersti Larsdotter points out in her masterly comparison of Afghanistan and Vietnam. They involve a combination of aerial bombardment at long distance and rapid offensive manoeuvres, despite the changed names every decade – AirLand Battle, Revolution in Military Affairs, and now Defence Transformation. What has changed is that the readiness to risk lives is even less than earlier and, of course, the advent of new technologies. In effect information and com-munications technologies have been grafted onto existing structures and ways of thinking. What has greatly improved is precision and destructiveness.

Before the war in Iraq, 'spectacle wars' were air wars and it was argued that the unwillingness to commit ground troops reduced the effectiveness of 'spectacle war'. In Yugoslavia, for example, the air attacks could not prevent the acceleration of ethnic cleansing in Kosovo; as Wesley Clark, then SACEUR, put it at the time, 'you cannot stop para-military murder from the air'. In the case of Afghanistan, in particular, it is argued that had more American troops been committed to the battle for Tora Bora (December 2002) or later to Operation Anaconda (an operation in March 2002 in the Shah e Kot valley where al-Qaeda operatives were hiding) Osama Bin Laden would not have got away, even though many more Americans might have died.[20] But the Iraqi example shows that ground superiority is much more difficult to achieve than air superiority. And this is also the experience of, say, the Russians in Chechnya. Although the Americans were able to destroy the government rapidly, they have great difficulties in establishing security.

In terms of financing, 'spectacle wars' are also more like old wars in that they are financed out of taxation. But unlike old wars, they do not require additional taxation. Indeed the war in Iraq has been accompanied by tax cuts and nobody, except to a limited degree professional soldiers and even they are surprised, is expected to risk their lives. In a way, these are also state-unbuilding because the wars divert attention from the dismantling or erosion of public services.

What 'spectacle war' and 'new wars' have in common are three characteristics that differ from 'old wars' and are the consequence of global developments. First, they are both asymmetric: different ways of adjusting to the increased destructiveness of all types of military technology and the difficulty of fighting symmetric wars. 'Spectacle war' involves advanced technological military forces arrayed against much weaker enemies. In 'new wars', violence is directed against civilians. Second, both types of war are about political mobilisation through violence rather than about achieving specific military objectives. In 'new wars' political mobilisation is achieved directly through violence. In 'spectacle wars' violence is symbolic, at least from the point of view of the Americans. But 'new wars' always have a spectacle element – blowing up historic buildings, for example, or the Twin Towers of the World Trade Center, perhaps the most spectacular act of violence of all times. And, of course, spectacle wars do involve real violence. Third, both types of violence speed up processes of state disintegration, erosion or transformation that are taking place under the impact of globalisation. Typically, new wars are a form of transition between authoritarian states and failed states. 'Spectacle wars' mask deregulation and 'reform' of public services.

'Spectacle war' and 'new wars' tend to reinforce each other. First of all, by reproducing the narratives of World War II or the Cold War, 'spectacle wars' elevate third-world tyrants/criminals into powerful 'enemies'. Saddam Hussein or Osama Bin Laden mutate into Hitler or Stalin, who were powerful as well as evil. Second, 'spectacle wars' involve the construction of a sort of hierarchy of lives, which contributes to the sense of exclusion. American lives are the most privileged, followed by foreign journalists and international officials, then come local civilians and, finally, at the bottom, local combatants who, if they can be lured into the open, are often killed en masse from the air. In Iraq, the Coalition forces put great effort into minimising civilian casualties, although not at the cost of risking the lives of Coalition soldiers. In war, however, it is not possible to avoid civilian casualties. War implies legitimate killing by agents of the state whereas terrorism, for example, is viewed as criminal violence by non-state actors. But there is a fine line between heroes, who kill in war, and murderers. The problem is that terrorists and new warriors themselves define what they are doing as war. Thus, the language of war and, above all, the destructiveness of war can perversely end up legitimising the actions of the terrorists.

Civilian casualties in both Afghanistan and Iraq were very low by the standard of 'old war' but very high if viewed as human rights violations. In both cases, civilian casualties were higher than the numbers who died in the World Trade Center attacks.[21] At the same time, of course, the massive violence inflicted against civilians by terrorists and 'new warriors' provides a humanitarian justification for 'spectacle wars'. 'New wars' reinforce the narrative of 'spectacle war'.

Third, 'spectacle wars' (and also economic sanctions) contribute to the destruction of the formal economy and the spread of criminalisation – something we observed in Serbia and, most dramatically, in a few days, in Iraq.

Of course, these two types of war are ideal types. Not every conflict fits neatly. For example, Russia's war in Chechnya and India's role in Kashmir might be better described as neo-modern warfare, since both Russia and India use their military forces to try to control territory in rather traditional ways. But what these examples show is how difficult it is nowadays to occupy territory militarily. Grozny has been reduced to rubble – Fred Cuny, the celebrated humanitarian worker who was executed in Chechnya, said Grozny made Sarajevo seem like a picnic. But despite the destructiveness, Russian forces cannot impose security and the war drags on, fed by trading in boot-legged oil between Russian forces and Chechen rebels, and involving massive casualties, especially civilian, and population displacement; in other words, many of the hallmarks of a 'new wars'.

And what about the Israel/Palestine war? The Palestinians fit the 'new war' category – they are 'new terrorists' aiming to inflict high numbers of civilian casualties. But how should we describe the Israelis? Are they neo-modern forces trying to occupy territory? Or are they using high-tech military capabilities as a sort of 'spectacle', with forays into Palestinian territory in which civilian deaths are treated as collateral damage, in order to show the Israeli public that something is being done as well to mobilise support in the diaspora in the United States and Europe? Or are these 'new war' tactics aiming to perpetuate insecurity so as to shore up the position of the right in Israeli politics?

Conclusion

Mike Smith argues that Clausewitzean strategic thought still applies to 'new wars' and criticises van Creveld and others, including myself, for describing the new conflicts as post-Clausewitzean. He is right, of course, that these wars are rational, in the Anglo-Saxon meaning of instrumental rationality; the tactics serve the goals of the warring parties. But Clausewitz was writing in the early nineteenth century and was deeply influenced by Hegel.[22] For him, reason applied to the legitimate interests of the state, which acts in the universal interest, that is to say, on behalf of the whole nation. The idea that what private groups acting in their own selfish interests do could be counted as reason was quite contrary to the thinking of the Enlightenment.

There is also another important reason why both 'spectacle war' and 'new wars' depart from the Clausewitzean paradigm. This has to do with the decline of what Thomas Schelling called 'compellance'.[23] Clausewitz defined war as 'an act of violence designed to compel an opponent to fulfil our will'.[24] What he meant by that was the use of military means to defeat another state; for him battle was the decisive encounter, which he compared to cash transactions in the market place. My point is that 'compellance' in this sense is extremely difficult nowadays. Both 'new wars' and 'spectacle wars' are primarily about political mobilisation. In 'new wars', the combatants avoid fighting against each other; rather violence is directed towards civilians. 'Spectacle wars' do, of course, use violence against weakly armed opponents but domestic political mobilisation is what matters.

What does this argument imply about policy responses? Henderson and Singer say there is nothing new about the kind of proposals I put forward for restoring political legitimacy and extending the international rule of law; these were Woodrow Wilson's ideas, for example. What is new, I think, is that these ideas have gained substance and the hard-nosed so-called realist approach is become increasingly unrealistic. This is partly because of the decline of 'compellance' and the limits to the utility of military power. It is also because cosmopolitan perspectives, even if they do not call themselves cosmopolitan, are more widespread. Memories of the Holocaust and Hiroshima are becoming part of a global narrative that underpins the growing acceptance of human equality.[25] The deliberate killing of people of a different nationality, even as 'collateral damage', is no longer acceptable especially if it can be observed on television. World-wide opposition to the war in Iraq, when 15 million people demonstrated on the same day, illustrates the growing illegitimacy of all types of war. In addition, often as a consequence of global public pressure, the last few years have seen a considerable strengthening of international law, culminating in the establishment of the ICC, as well as growing practical experience of humanitarian agencies, peace-keepers, civil society groups in developing strategies to counter 'new wars'.

I am not against the use of force. On the contrary, I favour humanitarian intervention to prevent crimes of humanity, crimes of war, massive violations of human rights, or genocide. I favoured the Kosovo intervention although I was critical of the 'spectacular' means. But humanitarian intervention means thinking about the use of force in a new way – a point I have made elsewhere. What military force can achieve is extremely limited. Given the character of 'new wars', military force can be used effectively to protect civilians, through safe havens, for example, and to freeze fighting. They can also arrest individuals responsible for criminal acts. Peace-keepers need to be more 'robust' than they were in Bosnia, and to make use of advanced technology and some military techniques; but at the same time, they need to act on the principles of policing where the aim is to minimise all casualties, not merely your own. Military forces can be used as 'containment' not as 'compellance'. Moreover, to be legitimate, which is essential for the restoration of the legitimate control of violence, military forces have to be authorised through appropriate procedures and their behaviour has to conform to internationally agreed rules.

The way I propose to use military force is perhaps new. But importantly what is new is my emphasis on civil society in underpinning political legitimacy both at local and global levels. Woodrow Wilson still had a Clausewitzean faith in the integrity of states; nowadays there is much less trust in formal political institutions, and civil society has the job of monitoring, pressing for, and underpinning international interventions designed to help individual human beings.

Notes

1 When I use the term 'old wars', I am referring to this stylised form of war, not merely to earlier wars.
2 David Held *et al.*, *Global Transformations*, Cambridge: Polity Press, 1999. Ian Clark, *Globalisation and International Relations Theory*, Oxford: Oxford University Press, 1999. Anthony Giddens, *The Runaway World: How Globalisation is Reshaping Our Lives*, London: Profile Books, 1999.
3 Charles Tilly, *Coercion, Capital and European States AD 990–1992*, Oxford: Blackwell, 1992. Michael Mann, 'The Roots and Contradictions of Modern Militarism', *States, War and Capitalism*, Oxford: Blackwell, 1988.
4 Mary Kaldor and Diego Muro, *Religious and Nationalist Militant Networks*, in M. Kaldor, H. Anheier, M. Glasius (eds), *Global Civil Society 2003*, Oxford: Oxford University Press, 2003.
5 Two anecdotes illustrate this point. Draskovic, the nationalist leader who opposed Milosevic, tells how when he was campaigning, he met a peasant who told him he was a monarchist and a nationalist. 'Then you must vote for me', Draskovic said. 'No', said the peasant, 'I will vote for Milosevic. When you are leader, I will vote for you.' I found a similar attitude when I visited Srebrenica. A so-called domestic Serb, one of those who had lived in Srebrenica before the massacre, told me that he did not like his new Serb neighbours from Sarajevo and that he missed his former Muslim neighbours; indeed he sometimes goes and meets them secretly. When I asked him how he votes, he told me that he voted for the Serb radical party, perhaps the most extreme nationalist party.
6 De Graaff's description of the founding of the Bosnian army in 1991 through the establishment of the Muslim Patriotic League and the Green Berets is exaggerated. These were volunteer groups, largely based in Sarajevo. When the war began Bosnia had no army. Izetbegovic relied on notorious criminal groups to defend Sarajevo at the beginning of the war. Other regions created their own self-defence. In Tuzla, for example, the local Social Democrat Mayor organised a defence based on the police and volunteers, which successfully kept the Serbs out of Tuzla for the whole war. In Zenica and Bihac, the local trades unions were recruited.
7 I am reminded of a funny British television show in which the heroes are two gay Dutch policemen; they have nothing to do because the Dutch government has legalised burglary. Essentially de Graaff is saying that the Serbian state legalised

communal violence. In a formal sense this is true but what does it imply about the very meaning of a state and law?

8 See for example: Christopher Coker, 'Globalisation and Insecurity in the Twenty-first Century: NATO and the Management of Risk', *Adelphi Paper 345*, London: International Institute of Strategic Studies, 2002.

9 Mary Kaldor and Basker Vashee (eds), *Restructuring the Global Military Sector: Vol. I New Wars*, London: Pinter Press, 1997. Mary Kaldor, *New and Old Wars: Organised Violence in a Global Era*, Cambridge: Polity Press, 1999.

10 Errol A. Henderson and David Singer, '"New Wars" and Rumours of "New Wars"', *International Interactions*, 28, No. 2 (2002).

11 Xavier Bougarel, *Anatomie d'un Conflit*, Paris: Decouverts, 1996.

12 Bruce Hoffman, 'Change and Continuity in Terrorism', *Studies in Conflict & Terrorism*, 24 (2001), pp. 417–28.

13 Jason Burke, *Al Qaeda: Casting a Shadow of Terror*, London: IB Taurus, 2003, p. 35.

14 Ibid., p. 238.

15 Mary Kaldor, 'American Power: From Compellance to Cosmopolitanism?', *International Affairs*, January (2003). See also Mann, 'The Roots and Contradictions of Modern Militarism'.

16 See contribution of Colin McInnes in this volume.

17 Michael Ignatieff, *Virtual War: Kosovo and Beyond*, London: Chatto and Windus, 2000.

18 James Der Derian, *Virtuous War: Mapping the Military–Industrial–Entertainment Complex*, Boulder, CO: Westview Press, 2001.

19 James Der Derian, '9/11: Before, After and Between', in Craig Calhoun, Paul Price, and Ashley Timmer (eds), *Understanding September 11*, New York: New Press, 2002, p 180.

20 Michael O'Hanlon, 'A Flawed Masterpiece', *Foreign Affairs*, May/June (2002).

21 In the war in Afghanistan there were around a thousand to 1,300 civilian casualties from 'collateral damage', but thousands more died as a consequence of the worsening humanitarian crisis and some 500,000 people fled from their homes; in addition some thousands of Taliban and al-Qaeda troops were killed. (Carl Connetta, 'Strange Victory: A Critical Appraisal of Operation and Enduring Freedom and the Afghanistan War', *Project on Defense Alternatives, Research Monograph No. 6*, 30 January 2002). The best figures we have for Iraqi civilian casualties, drawn from individual press reports, are a minimum of 5,500 and a maximum of 7,200 (Iraqbodycount.net). An NGO called CIVIC (Campaign for Innocent Victims in Conflict) is currently conducting an inquiry into civilian casualties through house-to-house interviews and the initial results suggest much higher numbers. For comparison, the total number of deaths in terrorist incidents in 2002 was 725 and the total number of dead in the World Trade Center attacks was 2,440 people.

22 They both died in the same cholera epidemic in 1831.

23 Thomas C. Schelling, *Arms and Influence*, New Haven, CT: Yale University Press, 1996.

24 Carl von Clausewitz, *On War*, ed. and transl. Michael Howard and Peter Paret, London: David Campbell, 1993.

25 Roland Robertson, *Globalisation: Social Theory and Global Culture*, London: Sage Publications, 1992. Daniel Levy and Natan Sznaider, 'Memory Unbound: The Holocaust and the Formation of Cosmopolitan Memory', *European Journal of Social Theory*, 5, 1 (2002), pp. 87–106.

References

Bougarel, Xavier, *Anatomie d'un Conflit*, Paris: Decouverts, 1996.

Burke, Jason, *Al Qaeda: Casting a Shadow of Terror*, London: IB Taurus, 2003.

Clark, Ian, *Globalisation and International Relations Theory*, Oxford: Oxford University Press, 1999.

Clausewitz, Carl von, *On War*, ed. and transl. Michael Howard and Peter Paret, London: David Campbell, 1993.

Coker, Christopher, 'Globalisation and Insecurity in the Twenty-first Century: NATO and the Management of Risk', *Adelphi Paper 345*, London: International Institute of Strategic Studies, 2002.

Connetta, Carl, 'Strange Victory: A Critical Appraisal of Operation and Enduring Freedom and the Afghanistan War', *Project on Defense Alternatives, Research Monograph No. 6*, 30 January 2002.

Der Derian, James, '9/11: Before, After and Between', in Craig Calhoun, Paul Price, and Ashley Timmer (eds), *Understanding September 11*, New York: New Press, 2002.

—— *Virtuous War: Mapping the Military–Industrial–Entertainment Complex*, Boulder, CO: Westview Press, 2001.

Giddens, Anthony, *The Runaway World. How Globalisation is Reshaping Our Lives*, London: Profile Books, 1999.

Held, David *et al.*, *Global Transformations*, Cambridge: Polity Press, 1999.

Henderson, Errol A. and David Singer, '"New Wars" and Rumours of "New Wars"', *International Interactions*, 28, No. 2, 2002.

Hoffman, Bruce, 'Change and Continuity in Terrorism', *Studies in Conflict & Terrorism*, 24 (2001), pp. 417–28.

Ignatieff, Michael, *Virtual War: Kosovo and Beyond*, London: Chatto and Windus, 2000.

Kaldor, Mary and Diego Muro, *Religious and Nationalist Militant Networks*, in M. Kaldor, H. Anheier and M. Glasius (eds), *Global Civil Society 2003*, Oxford: Oxford University Press, 2003.

—— 'American Power: From Compellance to Cosmopolitanism?', *International Affairs*, January (2003).

—— *New and Old Wars: Organised Violence in a Global Era*, Cambridge: Polity Press, 1999.

—— and Basker Vashee (eds), *Restructuring the Global Military Sector: Vol. I New Wars*, London: Pinter Press, 1997.

Levy, Daniel and Natan Sznaider, 'Memory Unbound: The Holocaust and the Formation of Cosmopolitan Memory', *European Journal of Social Theory*, 5, 1 (2002), pp. 87–106.

Mann, Michael, 'The Roots and Contradictions of Modern Militarism', *States, War and Capitalism*, Oxford: Blackwell, 1988.

O'Hanlon, Michael, 'A Flawed Masterpiece', *Foreign Affairs*, May/June (2002).

Robertson, Roland, *Globalisation: Social Theory and Global Culture*, London: Sage Publications, 1992.

Schelling, Thomas C., *Arms and Influence*, New Haven, CT: Yale University Press, 1996.

Tilly, Charles, *Coercion, Capital and European States AD 990–1992*, Oxford: Blackwell, 1992.

11

RETHINKING THE NATURE OF WAR

Some conclusions

Isabelle Duyvesteyn

The aim of this volume, reflected in the different contributions, has been to explore the nature of modern war and warfare, mainly in the developing world. The premise, as outlined in the introductory chapter, was that in the existing debate about the nature of war, attention to strategy, with a few exceptions, has been found wanting. It has not only been the strategy of the belligerent parties, often non-state organisations, that has received insufficient attention but also the strategies pursued by the powers that intervene in these armed conflicts that deserve further investigation. Regarding the strategies of the belligerents, this volume has presented several important interpretations. Not only can these strategies be analysed as either insurgency or conventional war; suggestions have been made to view them as a completely new type of war. The warring organisations, such as those in the Balkans and in Africa, have been analysed with special attention to aspects such as the role of the (former) state and local practices of war. The operations of the intervening states have also been discussed. Here the different routes to mediation and the use of military instruments have been presented. The question has been asked whether counter-insurgency techniques are the best way to deal with these wars or whether a completely new approach is necessary.

The aim of this chapter is to bring together the different conclusions of the authors and to compare and contrast them to highlight their contributions to existing debates and to outline issues yet to be solved. The different terminology that the individual authors have used will not be the subject of further analysis. What is clear is that all of the authors have focused on armed conflict in the developing world, i.e. the former Second and Third World, in which non-state warring organisations have played an important role. Since the authors' conclusions are diverse, a synthesis is not what the chapter will work towards. Indeed, it may be presumptuous and analytically misleading to assume that a synthesis on such a diverse phenomenon is possible. Still, the

225

contributions of this volume are in need of further exploration in order to make clear what is the original contribution of this work to the existing debate and to place these arguments into their context.

The arrangement of this chapter is thematic. The different contributions will be compared in order to assess their conclusions regarding four important themes that are essential to understand the strategic landscape of today's wars. First, the actors will be discussed; what suggestions are the contributions making regarding the actors involved in these wars? Needless to say, the types of actors and their capability and motivations are important factors determining the strategy that is chosen in fighting. Second, what methods do these actors use in pursuit of their aims? Do they follow Clausewitz or is there another logic at work? Is the strategy used as means to an end, or is war symbolic? Third, the outcomes of the actions of the actors; if the actors use symbolic means, do they strive for real outcomes or vice versa? What is the objective of the struggle? Fourth, the countermeasures; what can outside forces do to mitigate the effects of these wars or to mediate between the belligerents? This chapter will seek to provide a coherent presentation of the wide-ranging conclusions in these four areas.

Debating the nature of modern war: the analytical framework

The actors and institutions of war

Actors and institutions of war serve as a useful starting point for this discussion since they partly influence the conduct of war. In short, actors, instead of tactics, deserve separate investigation in order to understand contemporary war. Almost parallel to the withering of the Cold War, arguments about the end of the state have gained popularity. Is the state still the most important organising unit in international affairs? Experts arguing that the end of the state is in sight saw confirmation in several striking cases of state collapse during the 1990s. State collapse, however, was not a new phenomenon. Even before the end of the Cold War states had ceased to function and had created problems in, for example, Uganda in the early 1980s. Moreover, and perhaps less recognised, state birth (or state re-creation) was more common than state collapse. This indicates that the state, as an organisational form, is far from threatened by extinction. Nevertheless, not only units larger than the state such as supranational institutions and multi-national corporations seemed to gain in importance or at least to gain in the attention that was devoted to their functioning. Ideas about globalisation, which have repeatedly been referred to in several contributions, form part of this argument. Also, non-state units, such as groups of diverse ethnicity, clan, tribe and religion, received more attention as their role in armed conflicts in the developing world was deemed large. In particular the arguments about 'warlordism', banditry and religious terrorism form part of this stream of thinking. Links between all these non-state actors have also been recognised, such as those between warlords and global trading networks.

Determining what is the role of these different actors is crucial for a proper understanding of the nature of war and the strategies that are used in warfare. Several suggestions have been made in the contributions in this volume. Mike Smith argues that in fact the actors in war are almost of secondary importance to the overarching concept of war in which they are incorporated. The essence of the concept of war as developed by Clausewitz and discussed in the introductory chapter remains, according to Smith, essentially the same. Even when the actor and the objective have become more complex and unusual in recent years compared to Clausewitz's time, there is essentially nothing new under the sun. Smith sees the term political violence as a truism; following Clausewitz, politics and military are intimately linked: 'All violence will be carried out with a goal or rationale in mind. It may not be ideologically inspired in a traditional sense but there will always be a reason.' This point of view equates reason and rationality with politics. It is, however, by no means certain that rationality is exclusively connected to politics – or for that matter, that politics is rational. On top of that Mary Kaldor points out that the way in which Smith approaches rationality is not the same as the Enlightenment conception of reason: 'The idea that what private groups acting in their own selfish interest do could be counted as reason was quite contrary to the thinking of the Enlightenment', of which Clausewitz was an exponent. Reason, in this perspective, should be linked to universal interests instead of selfish ones. However, Kaldor does not deny that even what she calls 'new wars' are rational and political undertakings.

As the other contributions show, this rational approach to war might do an injustice to the rich and varied reality of actors and their motivations in contemporary wars. Smith's arguments do not seem to clearly deal with the irrational, symbolic and post-modern views of violence. This is important since Smith incorporates the al-Qaeda network in his political argument. He seems to equate al-Qaeda's apparent rationale and mostly religious logic with politics. In his contribution, Paul Rich, by contrast, seems to recognise some 'public performance' or symbolic aspects in al-Qaeda operations. Hence, there seems to be disagreement about the nature of politics, which needs to be clarified in further research.

When looking at war in the past decades, Smith points out, we have compared wars mostly on the basis of the ways in which they were fought, their tactics or '*modus operandi*' as he calls it, while the actors involved have been heaped together under the rubric of 'irregular'. He questions this approach to war: 'focusing on tactical modality as the principal defining element of low-intensity conflict, can lead, and has in the past led, to an obsessive concern for developing counter-measures, sometimes to the detriment of comprehending the long-term drivers of a conflict'. Kersti

Larsdotter agrees with this point of view. She points out that the tactical level of war does not provide the correct focus for understanding war. However, this criticism leaves an important question unanswered: when you cannot compare cases even on the basis of methods, it will be difficult to generate and refine theories on the conduct of war. Hence, although helpful in some respects, the criticism – if followed – may inhibit research into other military theory issues in modern war.

The role of global actors has been addressed in several contributions. Whereas globally operating non-state actors have not themselves engaged in armed conflict, with the striking exception of al-Qaeda, as Colin McInnes has described, globalisation is an important concept in the study of contemporary wars. The underlying logic of the globalisation argument can be seen as building on Adam Smith's theorem that free trade prevents wars, i.e. economic integration as it has been refined by generations of integration theorists between international actors prevents armed conflict breaking out. Rich has questioned the applicability of the globalisation concept in understanding these wars. He points out that many of these wars are sustained by states, while the state in the perspective of globalisation is reduced to irrelevance. Ethnicity, demography and environmental pressures have led to the use of military force, whereas these sub-state issues have also been declared unimportant. Furthermore, warlords and their fighters, which he sees as most important actors, have a limited strategic doctrine; how are they supposed to operate globally? These are the reasons why globalisation, as he sees it, is not a viable explanation for modern war.

However, the globalisation concept might be short-changed by Rich when he argues that it falls short of offering an explanation for both the outbreak and the conduct of war. State breakdown can occur because the state has indeed become irrelevant and is replaced by other ways of organising power relationships in a certain territory, such as in the case of Somalia. Furthermore, it is precisely the connections between the warlord organisations, global trading networks and international business, also stressed by Kaldor and exemplified again by the Somali case but also by the Liberian one, that sustain the rebel organisations and thereby the wars.[1] Rich does signal that it is economic hardship, as a by-product of uneven global economic development, that may lead to armed conflict, in which locally active warlords can play an important role.

When questions remain about the role of global actors, does the state offer a better perspective for understanding the actors? Smith's political view of war seems to find confirmation in the case studies of Bosnia and Somalia. Often the political logic of these wars is linked to state (re-)building projects. The state, according to Bob de Graaff in his discussion of the war in the former Yugoslavia, is an under-investigated issue in this armed conflict. The links the warring groups had to the Yugoslav state, on whose orders they were in fact operating, have not been properly recognised. Instead we have been blinded by the nationalist and ethnic sentiments that were personified in Slobodan Milosevic. The separate political projects of the warring factions in Yugoslavia were in fact nation-building exercises, which were mutually exclusive and went against the preferences of the main mediating and intervening powers. Rich has called attention to the warlord argument. This will be dealt with below, but here we should note his conclusion that even these sub-state undertakings can be part of a state-building process from which the state can emerge stronger and more viable than before the armed conflict. He is even tempted to predict that an ensuing state-strengthening process will lead to an increase in interstate warfare in the twenty-first century.

Kaldor holds the diametrically opposite point of view. She argues that instead of seeing the warring factions in Bosnia as potential states in the making, we should realise that they have been attributed too much state-building potential. Precisely this treatment has compounded the problems in Bosnia. As opposed to Rich, who is critical of the globalisation arguments, Kaldor finds the concept of globalisation a useful tool for understanding not only the transformation but also the disintegration of states. Globalisation is one development that, together with technological advances and international communications, has contributed to the unique character of the wars.

These new wars are in fact wars of state-unmaking. They lead to the break-up of the state based on exclusive identities, such as ethnicity and tribe. Warring factions using these labels claim distinct pieces of the former state's territory. However, Kaldor does leave an important question unanswered in her contribution: what happens after the war is over? Will the fragmentation of the state lead to new state-like creations or, since she stresses that the warring factions were accorded too much state-building potential, will this lead to other unviable states?

Those who see the demise of the state as a given locate the phenomenon of contemporary war either in the context of new wars, as does Kaldor, or construe it as a sub-state continuation of familiar forms of war. John Mackinlay sees the present-day actors in armed conflicts as 'global insurgents'. His account finds room both for the globalisation argument and for the fundamentally new-war interpretation of non-state actors who have not been seen operating before. In his contribution, he first described the emergence of globalisation and its links to insurgency organisations, which recently have started to differ from previous insurgent groups mostly 'in their manifestations'. He then identified four types of insurgents: lumpen, clan, popular, and global.

The lumpen insurgents have gelled together because of short-term, predominantly selfish interests, and their action radius is decidedly local given their limited military power. Clan insurgents operate together based on family relationships, which guarantees a longer lifespan for these forces, while their military operations also remain limited. Popular insurgents operate based on antipathy towards a strong state, with their military potential supported by outside powers. Global insurgents, as a single-case category, are exemplified by al-Qaeda and its operations. Global insurgents, Mackinlay notes, place emphasis on the 'visibility of a deed rather than the practical consequences'.

Although useful, Mackinlay's categorisation neglects possible overlaps. Global insurgents, it can be argued, have links to both clan and popular forces – as with the al-Qaeda fighters in Afghanistan, where both clan forces have operated and a popular resistance to Soviet occupation formed fertile soil for the organisation of insurgency operations. Again, in Somalia clan forces overlapped with lumpen forces based on economic dissatisfaction. In the wars in West Africa, the lumpen forces often overlapped with ethnic categories. In the more distant past, the communist insurgents in Malaya, a popular insurgent force according to Mackinlay's definition, came almost exclusively from the ethnic Chinese community. Here a variation on the clan/family aspect overlaps with the popular aspect.

Rich argues that the most viable way of understanding war in the developing world is provided by the warlord perspective. Even though he suggests we might not need a new theory to explain warlord behaviour, these individuals and the role they play are a new phenomenon. They have entered the stage as a product of globalisation, as part of a search for a new identity, while their ways of operating are based on methods that were already present in antiquity. The warlord is a local strong man, with a limited military capacity and strategic doctrine. Rich doubts whether these individuals can ever exert influence on a global scale. Al-Qaeda, he argues, does not equate with the warlord model and constitutes a separate category. However, Rich's argument does not seem to recognise not only the warlord and clan politics of Afghanistan, which have links with the al-Qaeda network, but also the connection between global trade and warlords, which allows the latter to strengthen and extend their power.

These suggestions about how we should view the actors in armed conflict in the developing world also raise the problem of the presence of multiple actors, who pursue different objectives at different times over the course of a war. This was an issue in the conflict in Somalia, as Isabelle Duyvesteyn suggested. The actors in this armed conflict cooperated when it was to their advantage but also went their separate ways as circumstances demanded. Even different sections of the same movements could adopt different postures. The unitary actor model is thus difficult to sustain in these wars, which can render analysis somewhat problematic.[2]

It has become clear that a focus on group behaviour is important, either on a global level beyond the reach of the state, or below the level of the state with armed groups operating very locally, with or without links to the global level. It is precisely to the operation of groups that we should look for answers about how these actors work.[3] This focus on group action might pose problems for the Clausewitzian model, in which there is always political direction to a war. Depending again on the definition of politics, it deserves further investigation whether politics is present in *every* social organisation conducting war.[4]

To understand war it is not only necessary to look at the actors involved. Actors and institutions of war vary over time and space, and although there is undoubtedly a connection between actor and conduct of war – the type and strength of the actors, it can be argued, determine to a large extent the type and intensity of the combat they are able to wage – an account of the actors is not tantamount to an account of the conduct of war.

The methods and conduct of war

It has been argued that the methods of fighting war have changed recently. Colin McInnes put forward the case that since the early 1990s there has been a transformation of the Western conduct of war. He listed four important aspects that characterise this transformation, which has continued since the September 11 attacks. First, as opposed to the Cold War period when escalation was always a risk, wars since the early 1990s tend to be very localised. Second, Western states engaging in armed conflict take great pains to stress that they are fighting against an opposing regime and not against the population of that state. This is closely connected to the third characteristic, the ambition to limit collateral damage, to decrease the suffering of the population and to strike only specific military targets. Fourth, military engagements are carried out by small numbers of military professionals instead of large conscript armies.

Despite these striking characteristics it can be questioned whether these features have substantially altered the nature of war and its conduct. When, for the sake of argument, ranged alongside the views of Clausewitz and Smith, these features do not exclude the political nature of war. As a matter of fact, all the examples McInnes uses show military force to be an instrument of the state, in particular of the United States. Rather, the political nature is reinforced by the stress on the conflict being against a regime instead of its population. Though the military professionals may have a 'business relation-ship' with the state, they still fight on behalf of this state. Furthermore, the conduct of war, which will be discussed further below, is characterised by both direct and indirect fighting methods, is not affected by the changes McInnes suggests. Both guerrilla/insurgency and conventional wars can be fought under the conditions McInnes has identified. He recognises this himself in his description of the war in Afghanistan. In short, as he clearly points out, circumstances have changed but the nature and conduct of war seem to have remained the same.

When looking at methods of war in particular, some scholars have pointed out that in recent wars there has been no method in the fighting, which has therefore lost all rationality. Others have argued that methods of war have not changed. In this latter line of thinking, some have followed the existing insurgency warfare school. Several writers in this school of thought, but by no means all, distance themselves from the revolutionary insurgency model à la Mao. The aim of the insurgents is to attack state power, which they aim to take over. The way to achieve this is through indirect fighting techniques, for example avoiding main confrontations with the enemy and striking with lightning speed at the weak points of the opponent. Another line of thinking has pursued the perspective of contemporary wars in the developing world as regular warfare. When looking at warfare on the European continent, it can be observed that prominent features of today's wars in the developing world, such as famine as an instrument of war, plundering, living off the land, and avoiding direct confrontations, were also present in Europe, most notably during the early modern period.

The contributions in this volume show considerable divergence in how they see the role of rationality in war. The Kaplan *cum suis* argument, that the wars in West Africa he described in his article 'The Coming Anarchy' involved irrational brutes driven by blood thirst and barbarity, was perhaps too extreme.[5] However, several authors in this volume have adjudged the wars under investigation, or some of their aspects, to be irrational. Mackinlay, for instance, points in this direction. Others, such as Smith, de Graaff, Duyvesteyn, and Kaldor, emphasise the rational aspects of war.

Regarding the exact methods that have been used, there is also little agreement. Several authors stress that insurgency and irregular combat is the most important prism through which we should view these wars. Mackinlay, for instance, argues the case for seeing the struggle between the al-Qaeda terrorist network and Western states as a contest that is being fought according to familiar insurgency patterns, this time played out on a global stage. A qualitative change has occurred, which has enabled insurgent movements to act globally. Still, their operations have familiar characteristics. Larsdotter, comparing the cases of Vietnam and Afghanistan, follows to a large extent the insurgency perspective but importantly points out that in both cases conventional operations also found a place. The organisation, tactics, and the use of terrain in both cases led to a similar type of war, in which indirect fighting methods dominated for long periods of time.

Both Smith and Duyvesteyn present arguments that seriously question the validity and applicability of the insurgency or guerrilla war concept. While Smith argues that it should be viewed as a tactic of war, Duyvesteyn notes that even as a tactic of war, the concept remains problematic given the definitions of terrorism. Furthermore, both see the distinction between guerrilla and manoeuvre warfare as problematic. Avoiding the strength and concentrating on the weakness of the opponent is the essence of both. Stathis Kalyvas aims to rescue the concept of guerrilla war and views it as a valuable category in understanding the different wars we are confronted with. Despite the criticism, it should not be forgotten that for many practitioners of war, these distinctions between guerrilla war, terrorism and manoeuvre warfare have been a given, for example they have been taught by the military doctrines of Western armed forces.

Duyvesteyn seeks to pave the way for an interpretation of sub-state wars as conventional. In the debate, there is a strong bias towards regarding conventional war as a kind of war that should involve state actors. Duyvesteyn argues that this is not necessarily the case. Furthermore, there is a bias against regarding conventional war as the method of war mainly used in international conflict, which is also unmasked as a fallacy by Kalyvas and Larsdotter. For de Graaff, the conventional idea of war as involving openly operating forces engaged in large-scale operations is to an important degree applicable. In the case of the former Yugoslavia, conventional armed force was used with assistance from or complemented by irregular forces, which were controlled by state power. This played on Western fears, in particular of becoming involved in a partisan war, which largely explains their refusal to engage in large-scale operations with ground-forces.

These interpretations of guerrilla and conventional warfare methods must contend with the very local practices of combat in the developing world. One only has to think of the use of disguises and extreme acts of cruelty that have been a notable feature of recent wars in West Africa, as noted in Rich's contribution. De Graaff argues that cruelty had been practised more openly in Eastern Europe compared to the West. Public executions, for example, were performed by the state in the open and this practice endured there much longer. This might provide an explanation for the cruelty witnessed in the wars there. Duyvesteyn argues that these phenomena are not necessarily in contradiction with war regarded from an instrumental perspective: cruelty has accompanied war throughout the ages.

The view Smith has presented would encompass both the guerrilla and the conventional warfare perspectives. The development during the Cold War of the ideas of the revolutionary guerrilla has led, as he contends, to an unnatural and almost unjustifiable distinction within the category of war. Following Clausewitz's logic, this distinction is not necessary. War should be seen as a contest of will, and coercion can be just as important as a means as destruction. This view is supported by the examples of the former Yugoslavia and Somalia: there, both direct and indirect fighting techniques or methods were employed. It seems likely that both can occur during the course of any conflict. Even in the case of al-Qaeda, as discussed by Larsdotter and McInnes, it can be seen in the confrontations in Afghanistan that both forms of warfare have been used in tandem.

Mary Kaldor finds little value in the above arguments when presenting the case for new wars. The conduct and methods of these new wars, which she contrasts with old wars based broadly on the European model derived from World War I, are fundamentally different. The logic of the use of force in new wars is that force is directed against the civilian population. She points to the increase in civilian casualties in war since 1945 and the increase in refugees as a result of armed conflict in the same period. She argues that targeting the population is a deliberate strategy aimed at controlling territory. Violence is concentrated in rural areas. In this respect she challenges the argument presented by Duyvesteyn that the capital city and urban areas generally are the main focus of armed interaction. This kind of new war, Kaldor argues, overlaps to a large extent with criminalised violence. This violence is geared towards financing the war effort. She seems to bypass the fact that in many of the old wars criminal activity also flourished because of the lack of state control. Even the state itself can be guilty of this practice, as she notes in the case of Bosnia. Part of the new war concept is the new terrorism, which exhibits the same features of indiscriminate violence against civilians and criminal sources of finance. This terrorism, however, is not geared towards the control of territory but aimed at politically mobilising an audience.

While this new war is the dominant form of war today, according to Kaldor, at the same time the old form of war has transformed itself into so-called spectacle war. These spectacle wars seem to be the reverse side of new wars because they are largely fought by the United States, relying on high technology, financed by the regular American tax system. The American people are just spectators here. The aim in spectacle war is either a 'moral crusade' to spread American democracy around the globe or to remove unwanted regimes. Both new and spectacle wars have in common that they are linked to the process of state-unmaking.

Stathis Kalyvas sees all the categories of war identified so far as representing phenomena in the real world. He sets out to distinguish warfare from types of war. Regardless of the conduct of war, it should not be forgotten that the methods used do not necessarily say a lot about the type of war that is being fought; just because one is fighting in a particular kind of conflict, it does not mean that one has to conduct a certain type of warfare. This is something that is consistently confused in many military doctrines. It also means that methods of warfare – like the actors in war – are problematic when used as criteria to categorise war.

Kalyvas points to a new and interesting research agenda that identifies the different kinds of warfare that could be used in fighting civil wars. He distinguishes three ideal types of warfare: conventional civil warfare; irregular civil warfare; and symmetric non-conventional warfare. This last category comes closest to the new wars identified by Kaldor. Symmetry or asymmetry is mainly found in the means at the disposal of the warring parties. However, this leaves open to question whether (a)symmetry can be found in other areas, such as the finances, control and conviction, which can make the difference between success and failure in war. Other valuable distinctions could then be made: is asymmetric conventional war not possible?

Based on these three types Kalyvas offers three hypotheses. Conventional civil war is the result of a *coup d'état* that was unsuccessful. Irregular war is the result of insurgency in the countryside. Symmetric non-conventional war is the result of a break-down of the state. The second and third hypotheses in particular can easily be confused. While these three conjectures still await empirical testing, Kalyvas already offers some theoretical propositions. These again relate to his typology. The polarisation thesis – the more polarised a society the more violence can be expected – should be placed in the conventional civil war category. The military thesis – if a military faction suffers military vulnerability violence can be expected to be great – relates to the irregular model. The Hobbesian thesis – the more independent military actors that are present the more violence can take place – matches the symmetric non-conventional model. The novelty of Kalyvas' contribution is that he theorises about how violence causes violence. It is not only war itself that needs explanation; so too do the causes of variation in war and how this evolves as war continues. A suggestion for further research here would be the inclusion of other explanatory theories, such as relative deprivation, greed versus grievance theories or the security dilemma, in order to more clearly understand these armed conflicts.

The purposes of war

If the strategies of the warring parties are a means to an end, what aims do they seek to achieve? When the actors are driven by rational-choice considerations and use force in an instrumental way, what can be said about the attainment of the objectives or the outcomes of these wars? Existing interpretations, as discussed in the introductory chapter, have focused on political objectives, economic and resource considerations, ethnic, clan, and tribal driving forces, and religious desires that could be translated into an outcome in these wars.

At least two problems present themselves here. First, by asking the question about the purposes of war, it precludes answers from irrationalist and post-modern interpretations of war. These perspectives reject an instrumental view on war. However, as Smith has noted, in psychology there is little evidence of purposeless actions. The 'visibility of the deed', as Mackinlay put it, as an example of symbolic violence, does nevertheless imply a certain instrumentality. The use of force is intended to make a statement. The force and the violence are thus not the end; an effect does enter into the calculation.

Second, can we always believe the actor when he states his preferences and aims? Even if warring organisations make public statements about their purposes, it can be difficult to distinguish true military and political aims from propaganda and information that will make it easier to 'sell' the aims to an international or domestic audience. This was particularly apparent in the wars in the former Yugoslavia, as De Graaff points out. This poses a major problem for those who suggest that classifications of war can be made according to the purposes of war. Looking at the activities and deeds of the actors can be one step in deducing their real aims. If so, however, we are back to using conduct of war as a criterion. Without necessarily resorting to Smith's argument that there is only one category of war, the discussion suggests that classifications of war are infested with problems.

Disagreement exists among the contributors over what the desired outcomes for the fighters would be. Duyvesteyn puts forward the argument that in their strategies African fighters, such as in Somalia, had their eyes set on urban centres, in particular the capital. This translates to the political centre of the former state. De Graaff in his discussion of the former Yugoslavia and Rich argue in a similar vein that state projects are important aims or objects in the struggles. Kaldor presents a political case as well pointing to the projects for homogenous ethnic, religious or tribal territories. Even the new terrorism is based on exclusive ideologies. She claims that these wars of identity are based on exclusivity in different ways than are nationalism, socialism or decolonisation wars of the old war type. However, it should not be overlooked that nationalism, socialism and decolonisation have extremely strong links to identity as well, and on top of that they are also exclusive. Other nationalities, the bourgeoisie and elite, and the colonisers were most certainly excluded. What is the difference between Serbian nationalism and earlier forms of nationalism, such as German or Irish, if not identity and exclusivity?

Not only control of the state but also wider aims have been ascribed to warring organisations. Islamic rule, addresses to a global audience and symbolic messages are some of the suggestions that have been presented in the various contributions. This should be included in assessments of the actors' motivations. As Smith has suggested, more awareness of the social and political context of a conflict is needed fully to appreciate the outcomes the fighters strive for.

The issue of desired outcomes is intimately bound up with the question of what constitutes victory in these wars. What is the definition of victory in modern war? Has the definition of the centre of gravity changed or is it still largely defined in the same way, as Duyvesteyn has attempted to show. Furthermore, in light of the RMA debate, is killing still the essential element in warfare, as the practice of recent wars has shown, or can the same raising of the cost of war for the protagonists be realised in non-lethal warfare? At least on first inspection, killing seems to be a vital part of the logic of al-Qaeda, supposedly the best example of a global post-modern actor. These questions deserve further investigation in order to appreciate the purposes of belligerents. In any event, the issue of desired outcomes is closely connected to the possible countermeasures that could be taken.

The countermeasures

Several countermeasures that intervening states can take to mediate in these armed conflicts have been suggested in the literature. Counterinsurgency, conventional measures, and policing tasks have all been put forward as ways of responding to the actions of the warring parties or to their effects. These suggestions seem to circulate independently of the assessments of the types of war that are being waged in the battle theatres. One example is the discussion about peace-keeping and peace-enforcement measures, which have not always been clearly linked to discussions about the type and nature of war. What are the suggestions raised by the authors in this volume? What can be done against the warring organisations that have been the focus of this book?

In his contribution Smith describes the development of counter-insurgency doctrine out of British colonial policing experience. At the same time he criticises the development of this doctrine for having produced a distortion in strategic thinking. He argues that it is not so much Clausewitz as the nuclear deterrence theories that blinded experts from investigating other aspects of strategic studies during the many decades of the Cold War. The development of nuclear deterrence theories and the unpopularity of Clausewitz have antecedents in this period. Clausewitz seemed obsolete in relation to the madness of mutual assured destruction, in which the political logic of war flew out the window because it would lead to suicide. The nuclear deterrence theories had set the stage for a misrepresentation of Clausewitz's ideas. Correct assessments of war fighting then became difficult, hampering the development of proper countermeasures.

Mackinlay has very clear suggestions about what can be done. He argues that NATO's experience during the wars in the Balkans has been formative in the development of military intervention culture and practice. He outlines a detailed set of operational phases of military interventions, stretching from deterrence through to deployment and stabilisation, ending with a 'garrison phase'. Despite the development of this detailed process of intervention, the containment that it represented no longer proved feasible after the September 11 attacks in the United States. A new strategic landscape had emerged. Mackinlay argues that counter-insurgency principles are still valid, even in the case of al-Qaeda. In particular, the development of a political answer to diminish the appeal of that organisation deserves a large effort through intelligence gathering and 'hearts and minds' campaigns. Overall, he argues there are several keys to success in intervention operations. Among them he counts the institution of a strategic directorate and a director of operations to facilitate operations and make them more effective. Rich shares Mackinlay's opinion that peace support operations can play a role in the modern strategic landscape.

Duyvesteyn, even though she presents an argument for a conventional perspective on wars, suggests in her conclusion that counter-insurgency measures should not be excluded. Furthermore, all the aspects and elements that fuel the conflict should be considered in devising countermeasures against the fighters. Mackinlay seems to agree with Duyvesteyn that solutions to these conflicts should first and foremost be found on the political level.

Kaldor is extremely sceptical about the opportunities military force offers to mitigate new wars. She suggests that the use of military force should be limited to the protection of civilians, the arresting of individuals who are accused of war crimes and the overall containment of the violence. These seem to be the most salient features of the military operations in Bosnia, which cannot really be called successful in the respects she stresses, such as in the case of Srebrenica.

Despite developments in technology and the so-called 'revolution in military affairs', Larsdotter argues that the US tactics of war have remained essentially the same since Vietnam. The American preference for the use of airpower continues to mark the strategic domain. Air to ground campaigns, special forces, local allies, and close air support are but a few of the most significant similarities between the Vietnam and Afghanistan campaigns. Larsdotter concludes that 'improved technology does not seem to have had any significant effect on US tactics'.

Another problematic aspect of the RMA debate is that the technological developments may invite asymmetric responses, as others have pointed out. Superiority in armaments could provoke the opponent to pursue asymmetric responses, in particular seek high casualty rates in order to attain its goals. This is exactly what happened on September 11 according to McInnes: 'The pattern of war developed by the West set the agenda for asymmetric attacks against the West'. The increasing reliance on technology comes, furthermore, with an increased vulnerability. If everything is linked to everything in a system of systems, one strike might prove lucky. Countermeasures, as the contributions have shown, can be envisaged on every level of strategy. The different authors offered suggestions ranging from political solutions to psychological operations and search-and-destroy actions in order to gain the upper hand in the wars under scrutiny.

Rethinking the nature of modern war

In the introductory chapter to this study, three debates that have presented ideas about the nature of modern war were discussed. The first was about the applicability of Clausewitz's thought to modern predominantly internal wars in the developing world. The second focused on the RMA, while the third concerned post-modern interpretations of war. In regard to the first debate, several of the contributions in this volume, in particular those by Smith, Duyvesteyn and de Graaff, should be seen as further attempts to swing the pendulum of the debate back in the direction of Clausewitz. Since the debate about the nature of war gained momentum in the early 1990s attention has moved consistently away from the views of this nineteenth-century scholar. Instead, non-trinitarian explanations, non-instrumental and non-political aspects have moved to the forefront. A structured re-evaluation and re-appreciation of Clausewitz has long been overdue, and this book has offered some suggestions in that direction.

Rational and instrumental interpretations of armed conflicts have dominated the thinking about war presented in this volume. Rich, placing the globalisation arguments squarely within the liberal project, shows that their explanations for internal war can and should be seriously questioned. However, he does not pursue the globalisation argument to its ironic conclusion: when the state erodes as a result of further globalisation forces, the liberal agenda must lead to an illiberal future. A complete lack of democratic control over economic and global processes goes directly against the foundations of liberalism. While globalisation arguments can be questioned, the last word has not yet been said about the value of their explanations of the outbreak and conduct of war.

The discussion about the future of the state is perhaps unjustifiably but nevertheless intimately bound up with the discussion about the relevance of Clausewitz, and seems only to be in its first stages. Clausewitz has been read, mistakenly according to some, from a state-centred perspective. State-building projects have been placed firmly on the map by several contributions in this book. Non-state warfare can have state- and nation-building aims and effects. Furthermore, the state also forms the main focus in dealing with terrorist threats such as from al-Qaeda. Not only Clausewitz but also the state should be placed firmly on the map again.

Warlords, terrorists and other enterprising individuals involved in armed combat have also received attention. Their activities, as has been argued, should not always be seen as in contradiction to state-centred warfare. War in all its manifestations and war as a state-building exercise have been offered as perspectives in this volume. Here as well, Clausewitz could be applicable, although not all the authors agree that he is. The Clausewitzian under-standing of war, it can be argued, is neither linked exclusively to state actors nor to conventional war-fighting methods. The type of war and the strategies used to wage it should not be confused. The contribution this volume has made is that it has demonstrated and stressed that internal war is not by definition fought with the methods of low-intensity or unconventional warfare.

Concerning the second debate on the RMA, the divide that exists between the Western discourse on the nature of war, the RMA discussion and the practices of war in the developing world is striking. This divide is more than an open invitation for asymmetrical warfare. The asymmetrical attack of September 11 is thus widely expected to be only the beginning of more asymmetric warfare in the future. Importantly, Larsdotter has pointed out that despite technological advances the tactics of the American forces have not fundamentally changed. This raises a fundamental question of whether technological developments do indeed influence tactics.

The third debate about post-modernism has not been dealt with at length in this volume. None of the contributors have presented arguments about post-modern war as a game with only symbolic value, even though Kaldor's spectacle war goes slightly in this direction. This should not be seen as invalidating the post-modern claim. What several authors did stress, in particular Duyvesteyn and Rich, were the local rules and practices of warfare, which did involve symbolism. Rich and McInnes noted a symbolic aspect to the al-Qaeda terrorism, which could be placed in this school of thought. The cultural perspective and the study of the context of war forms one of the avenues that can be pursued in further research.

Conclusions: where do we go from here?

Has the nature of war fundamentally changed? Arguments in this book have gone both ways. There is a clear call for more attention to strategy in its widest conception in the discussion about the nature of warfare. Divergence of opinion remains apparent on many issues. The use of terminology to describe modern war has shown a wide range of sometimes overlapping terms and concepts. The debate about whether there are indeed any new aspects to modern war has been far from resolved. Essential in the course of this debate would be a clear understanding of what is new and how it could be made operational. The perspectives held on the methods of modern wars showed a wide divergence of opinion. This is closely linked to the terminology debate. All these aspects are important in arriving at answers and devising counter-measures from outside forces for modern wars. Understanding what these wars are all about is the first step towards developing strategies for their resolution.

What avenues can be identified to further pursue the debate about the nature of war? The discussion about the relevance and accuracy of the analytical concepts used is of paramount importance. Smith's discussion of the origins of the distortion in the debate about warfare and the subdivision of typologies, in effect, asks for a careful investigation of conceptual clarity, which he contends has been lacking even in many authoritative studies of war. Thinking through the tools for analysis is crucial. While agreement about the terms and concepts will be difficult to reach – not least because some of the terms have been 'politicised' – the use of the concepts for analytical purposes is important with respect to answers and conclusions that are reached.

The stress on local and cultural practices of warfare could, as noted already, present another viable avenue for further investigation of the nature of war. Rituals and local expressions of power and military prowess were present in many African battle theatres and in the Balkans. These expressions carried symbolic weight. More attention to the role of culture in warfare seems appropriate in this respect. The strategic culture of the warring parties deserves more attention. Anthropology and cultural studies seem logical fields to incorporate more strongly in the study of war.

Concepts, culture and context are but a few suggestions for further research. Understanding war was, according to Clausewitz, a primary task for a soldier when engaging in battle. The concepts that are used have far-reaching consequences for our understanding of war. Culture and context are important not only in understanding the opponent but might also point to avenues for mitigation and mediation. The task of correctly understanding the nature of war is nevertheless still paramount, and will remain so as militarised crises continue to unfold in the emerging twenty-first century world order.

Notes

1 William Reno, *Warlord Politics and African States*, Boulder, CO: Lynne Rienner, 1998.
2 See also Jan Angstrom and Isabelle Duyvesteyn, 'Evaluating Realist Explanations of Internal Conflict: The Case of Liberia', *Security Studies*, 10, 3 (2001), pp. 187–222.
3 Jan Geert Siccama, 'Clausewitz, van Creveld and the Lack of a Balanced Theory of War', in Gert de Nooy (ed.), *The Clausewitzean Dictum and the Future of Western Military Strategy*, The Hague: Kluwer Law International, 1997, pp. 25–42, p. 34.
4 Isabelle Duyvesteyn, *Clausewitz and African War; Politics and Strategy in Liberia and Somalia*, London: Frank Cass, 2005.
5 Robert D. Kaplan, 'The Coming Anarchy: How Scarcity, Crime, Overpopulation, and Disease are Rapidly Destroying the Social Fabric of our Planet', *Atlantic Monthly* (February 1994), pp. 44–76.

References

Angstrom, Jan and Isabelle Duyvesteyn, 'Evaluating Realist Explanations of Internal Conflict: The Case of Liberia', *Security Studies*, 10, 3 (2001), pp. 187–222.
Duyvesteyn, Isabelle, *Clausewitz and African War; Politics and Strategy in Liberia and Somalia*, London: Frank Cass, 2005.
Kaplan, Robert D., 'The Coming Anarchy: How Scarcity, Crime, Overpopulation, and Disease are Rapidly Destroying the Social Fabric of our Planet', *Atlantic Monthly*, (February 1994), pp. 44–76.
Reno, William, *Warlord Politics and African States*, Boulder, CO: Lynne Rienner, 1998.
Siccama, Jan Geert, 'Clausewitz, van Creveld and the Lack of a Balanced Theory of War', in Gert de Nooy (ed.), *The Clausewitzean Dictum and the Future of Western Military Strategy*, The Hague: Kluwer Law International, 1997, pp. 25–42, p. 34.

INDEX